THE MAN WHO CAPTURED WASHINGTON

CAMPAIGNS & COMMANDERS

GREGORY J. W. URWIN, SERIES EDITOR

CAMPAIGNS AND COMMANDERS

GENERAL EDITOR
Gregory J. W. Urwin, *Temple University, Philadelphia, Pennsylvania*

ADVISORY BOARD
Lawrence E. Babits, *Greenville, North Carolina*
James C. Bradford, *Texas A&M University, College Station*
Robert M. Epstein, *U.S. Army School of Advanced Military Studies, Fort Leavenworth, Kansas (retired)*
David M. Glantz, *Carlisle, Pennsylvania*
Jerome A. Greene, *Denver, Colorado*
Victor Davis Hanson, *Hoover Institution of Stanford University, Stanford*
Herman Hattaway, *Leawood, Kansas*
J. A. Houlding, *Rückersdorf, Germany*
Eugenia C. Kiesling, *U.S. Military Academy, West Point, New York*
Timothy K. Nenninger, *National Archives, Washington, D.C.*
Bruce Vandervort, *Virginia Military Institute, Lexington*

THE MAN WHO CAPTURED WASHINGTON

Major General Robert Ross
and the War of 1812

John McCavitt and Christopher T. George

University of Oklahoma Press | Norman

Library of Congress Cataloging-in-Publication Data

McCavitt, John.
　The man who captured Washington : Major General Robert Ross and the War of 1812 / John McCavitt and Christopher T. George.
　　pages cm. — (Campaigns and commanders ; volume 53)
　Includes bibliographical references and index.
　ISBN 978-0-8061-5164-9 (hardcover : alk. paper)
　1. Ross, Robert, 1766–1814. 2. United States—History—War of 1812—Biography. 3. United States—History—War of 1812—Campaigns. 4. Generals—Great Britain—Biography. I. George, Christopher T. II. Title.
　E353.1.R75M35 2016
　355.0092—dc23
　[B]
　　　　　　　　　　　　2015024751

The Man Who Captured Washington: Major General Robert Ross and the War of 1812 is Volume 53 in the Campaigns and Commanders series.

The paper in this book meets the guidelines for permanence and durability of the Committee on Production Guidelines for Book Longevity of the Council on Library Resources, Inc. ∞

Copyright © 2016 by the University of Oklahoma Press, Norman, Publishing Division of the University. Manufactured in the U.S.A.

All rights reserved. No part of this publication may be reproduced, stored in a retrieval system, or transmitted, in any form or by any means, electronic, mechanical, photocopying, recording, or otherwise—except as permitted under Section 107 or 108 of the United States Copyright Act—without the prior written permission of the University of Oklahoma Press. To request permission to reproduce selections from this book, write to Permissions, University of Oklahoma Press, 2800 Venture Drive, Norman, Okla. 73069, or e-mail rights.oupress@ou.edu.

1 2 3 4 5 6 7 8 9 10

Interior layout and composition: Alcorn Publication Design

*Dedicated to our wives,
Donna George and Siobhann McCavitt,
for all that you are to us.*

Contents

List of Illustrations	ix
Acknowledgments	xi
Introduction	3
1. "Young Bob" Ross	7
2. "The Most Comfortable Warrior a Man Could Wish to Serve With"	23
3. "Secret" Orders	40
4. "Too Late" for the Chesapeake	55
5. "Up Hill, Down Dale"	67
6. "They Are Not in a Condition to Strike at Washington"	79
7. High Noon at Bladensburg	116
8. "Hero of Bladensburg"	127
9. To Burn or Not to Burn	139
10. Courteous Conflagrator	150
11. "Feelings of Most Acute Misery"	166
12. "We Have Lost Our Good General"	179
13. Ramifications	193
Epilogue	208
Notes	221
Bibliography	269
Index	293

Illustrations

Figures

Major General Robert Ross	92
Mrs. Elizabeth Ross	93
Lieutenant General Sir George De Lacy Evans	94
Rear Admiral Sir George Cockburn	95
President James Madison	96
Brigadier General William Henry Winder	97
Commodore Joshua Barney	97
Dolley Madison	98
John Sioussat	99
George Washington	100
The Fall of Washington . . . or Maddy in Full Flight, ca. 1814	101
Captain Henry Shaw	102
The President's House, ca. 1814	103
A View of the Capitol after the Conflagration of the 24th August 1814	104
Waterfront fire, probably the burning of the Washington Navy Yard, 1814	105
The Taking of the City of Washington in America, 1814	106
Capture of the City of Washington, 1815	107
Washington, ca. 1815	108
Johnny Bull and the Alexandrians, 1814	109
Francis Scott Key	110
Death of General Ross at Baltimore, ca. 1859	111
The Death of General Ross, near Baltimore, ca. 1816	112

John Bull and the Baltimoreans, ca. 1814 — 113
Ross of Bladensburg coat of arms — 114
Ross Monument, Rostrevor, Northern Ireland — 115

Maps

British Advance on Washington, D.C., August 1814 — 80
Battle of Bladensburg, August 24, 1814 — 128
British Operations around Baltimore,
 September 12–15, 1814 — 180

Table

3.1 Adjutant General's Office, Toulouse, 16 May 1814,
 General Orders — 46

Acknowledgments

When historians from different countries combine to work on a joint project, the task is challenging at the best of times. Moreover, when they live on opposite sides of the Atlantic, it raises the bar that much more. Since agreeing to coauthor this book on Major General Robert Ross in 2008, Christopher George and I have not only cemented our working relationship but become great friends too. The assistance of the people and institutions we wish to acknowledge reflects the transnational nature of this project from its inception.

In September 1992 Christopher George visited Rostrevor, Northern Ireland, the hometown of General Ross, where he profited from meeting local historians Gerald Fay and Robert Linden. Coming to an interest in General Ross much later, John McCavitt also benefited from the research of Fay and Linden, along with John Joe Parr. Indeed, Linden, besides being a font of knowledge, is a great family friend. Francis De Courcy Hamilton, a Ross descendant, has provided invaluable assistance to us both. The authors were also very fortunate to be welcomed into the home of the general's remaining descendants in Rostrevor, the Campbell family, Stephen, Jackie, and their adorable daughter, Vicky, a talented equestrian like her famous ancestor, Robert Ross.

Spreading his wings to undertake research in the United States in 2009, John was warmly welcomed at both the White House and Capitol, famously or infamously burnt by Ross's forces. Bill Allman, curator of the White House, provided prompt and enthusiastic assistance. Dr. Richard Baker, historian of the Senate, was equally welcoming, as was his successor, Dr. Donald Ritchie, on a later occasion. John and his family will never forget the insights provided by William C. Allen, architectural historian of the Capitol, during a private tour. At the invitation of Dr. Donald Kennon of the U.S. Capitol Historical Society, John had the honor to address the society on two occasions. Dr. William Bushong afforded him a memorable opportunity to deliver a lecture on General Ross and the burning of the White House at the White House Historical

Association (WHHA). Alexandra Lane of the WHHA provided prompt and courteous assistance in facilitating the use of a number of images. Exchanges with Dr. Sidney Hart and Rachael Penman at the National Portrait Gallery of the Smithsonian Institution were nothing if not always fascinating—and great fun.

Visiting the Patuxent and Baltimore areas associated with General Ross's campaign, Chris George introduced John to some of his circle of War of 1812 researchers and enthusiasts during one memorable fieldtrip: Robert Reyes, Larry Leone, Ross Kimmel, and Bill Pencek, a key Maryland official charged with organizing Maryland's bicentennial commemorations. Scott S. Sheads at Fort McHenry, Baltimore, generously shared the fruits of many years of research. John's initial trip to the Washington area was greatly facilitated by Norman Houston at the Northern Ireland Bureau in Washington, D.C., the first, though certainly not the last, time that he afforded generous hospitality to John; his wife, Siobhann; and his sons, Mark and Niall—fellow travelers, researchers, and copyeditors. Winfield Lane in Georgetown has become a home away from home thanks to Norman.

A note of thanks is owed to the Ministerial Advisory Group Ulster Scots Academy for funding a vital research trip. Newry and Mourne Council offered practical assistance on various occasions, with Gerard McGivern, whose family were the last occupants of the caretaker's cottage at the Ross monument in Rostrevor, playing a leading role. Others who afforded assistance in one form or another include Lord and Lady Ballyedmond, Lord Laird, Professor Kevin Whelan, the late Dowager Lady Rosemary Brookeborough, Dr. Edward Furgol, Dr. Jim Gardner, Dr. Charles Brodine, Dr. Charles Neimeyer, Christine Hughes, Dr. Donald Kennon, Dr. Patrick Fitzgerald, Don Shomette, Nicholas Dunne Lynch, Nancy Cox, Tinker McKay, Vince Vaise, and Charles Markell.

The following institutions must also be acknowledged. In Northern Ireland: Public Record Office of Northern Ireland, Belfast, County Antrim; Ulster-American Folk Park, Omagh, County Tyrone; and The Inniskillings Museum, Enniskillen Castle, County Fermanagh. In England: The Fusiliers Museum, Bury, Greater Manchester; National Archives in Kew, Richmond, Surrey; Shropshire Regimental Museum, Shrewsbury Castle, Shrewsbury, Shropshire; National Army Museum, London; National Maritime Museum, Greenwich; and The British Library, London. In the Republic of

Ireland: The National Library of Ireland and Trinity College, both in Dublin. In Scotland, The National Library of Scotland, Edinburgh. In Baltimore, Maryland: Manuscripts Department, Maryland Historical Society; Fort McHenry National Historic Site and Shrine; The Star-Spangled Banner Flag House; and Special Collections, Sheridan Libraries, Johns Hopkins University. In Washington, D.C.: Manuscripts Division, Library of Congress; National Archives; Naval History and Heritage Command, U.S. Navy; Special Collections, Georgetown University; Special Collections Research Center, Estelle and Melvin Gelman Library, George Washington University; Office of the Curator, White House; and White House Historical Association.

In scholarly terms Donald E. Graves offered many insights and recommendations over a number of years. Dr. Ralph E. Eshelman and Major John R. Grodzinski read proofs of the manuscript and provided a wealth of invaluable advice. Remaining factual and interpretive errors are the responsibility of the authors. An immense debt of gratitude is also owed to Kevin Chambers, an oracle of information on different aspects of Ross's career and on the American campaign of 1814 in particular.

One of the great joys of this research project was the opportunity to engage with fellow researchers and authors. Throughout there has been a willingness to pool our research in a spirit of camaraderie and friendship, reserving the right to disagree in our interpretations. And there have been many social occasions to treasure, not least when John and his wife were hosted by Peter Snow and his wife, Ann, in London when his book *When Britain Burned the White House* was launched. Steve Vogel, author of *Through the Perilous Fight*, and his wife, Tiffany, also made the McCavitts welcome a number of times in Barnesville, Maryland. And there were some fine occasions when Chris and his wife, Donna, and later Peter Snow, Steve Vogel, and Don Hickey came to Rostrevor. All appreciate just why Major General Robert Ross hoped to retire to his idyllic home village.

The Man Who Captured Washington

INTRODUCTION

In the sweltering heat of August 1814, a "little army" of British soldiers, sailors, and marines made a "dash" on Washington, D.C., more than fifty miles from their landing site, without cavalry or artillery support, bar a handful of small-caliber cannon and Congreve rockets. When Ross's troops made landfall, John Armstrong, the U.S. secretary of war, was justifiably skeptical about the likelihood of a British attack on the infant American capital. Realistically he asked: "Have they artillery? No. Have they cavalry? No. Then don't tell an old soldier that any regular army will or can come."[1] But come they did, even though greatly outnumbered and outgunned and eventually out of range of the safety of their naval support. The astonishingly audacious attack was led by Major General Robert Ross—the man who captured Washington.

Having disembarked his small invasion force by August 20 almost immediately after a protracted 4,000-mile voyage from Bordeaux, France, Ross fought the Battle of Bladensburg, occupied Washington, burned most of its public buildings, and returned his men to their landing place on the banks of the Patuxent River by August 29, in the process marching over 100 miles in suffocating heat.[2] A writer to the *Morning Chronicle* in London characterized it "A Nine Days Wonder." Without the tone of triumphalism, the sense of amazement at what had transpired was shared by *Poulson's American Daily Advertiser*, which exclaimed: "Six months ago, no one could have thought such an event could have possibly taken place. But this is the age of wonders!" To military theorist Baron De Jomini, Ross's operation was "unparalleled in history. . . . [T]he world was astonished to see a handful" of British troops seize the U.S. capital.[3]

Despite leading what Peter Snow recently described as "one of the most daring and successful military enterprises" in British military history, Robert Ross has never been the subject of a major study.[4] Besides his campaign in America, his highly distinguished military career fighting the French from 1799 until 1814 is worthy of exploration in its own right. In battles from his first action in the Helder in Holland (1799), to near the Pyramids in Egypt (1801), to the plains of Calabria in southern Italy (1806), to the lofty heights of the Pyrenees (1813) during the Peninsular War, Ross developed a reputation as a brave and intrepid soldier. In large measure, however, he has become a forgotten general. So much so, indeed, that the impressive one-hundred-foot obelisk erected to his memory in his native village of Rostrevor in Ireland has lain derelict until recent years. In part, of course, his obscurity is attributable to the fact that one of the wars in which he made his name, the War of 1812, has been itself "forgotten."[5] And Ross is by no means the only successful and enterprising British commander of his generation who has suffered this fate. The life stories of a number of other generals whose careers spanned the continents of Europe and North America at that period have also languished with the passage of time, including Major General James Kempt. The paths of Ross and Kempt crossed in famous battles in southern Italy, Portugal, and Spain. And then there is Major General Ned Pakenham, a Peninsular War hero too and brother-in-law of the Duke of Wellington, who was killed at the Battle of New Orleans in January 1815.

What makes Ross different from other British generals serving in the Napoleonic Wars and the War of 1812, whose careers have receded from the limelight with time, is the fact that his short-lived campaign in North America elevated him to the status of a national hero in Britain. His prominence in the United States endured for longer. Ross, it will be shown, cast a shadow on the presidencies of James Madison, James Monroe, and John Quincy Adams. Paradoxical though it now seems, while the capture of Washington demoralized Americans at the time, many U.S. citizens regarded Ross then, and for years afterward, as a dashingly brave and yet humane officer. Modern military officers have much to learn from him. In both Britain and America, however, his star in the historical firmament has long since faded.

There are many reasons, therefore, for rekindling interest in Major General Ross, a courageous, charming, and charismatic figure. Shedding new light on his military service before his expedition to the United States is warranted since he had already earned widespread acclaim in Britain for his military exploits in Europe and North Africa. Besides, a study of his prior career offers insights into the capability and character of the man who captured Washington, the values that made him tick, and the pressures he was under, including his personal life and the trying circumstances involving his wife's serious illness.

This study is primarily concerned with Ross's highly eventful three weeks of campaigning in America, owing to its military and political significance at the time. Ross exploited Royal Navy capabilities to pursue a river-based approach to attacking key targets in the Chesapeake Bay region, including Washington and Baltimore. British operations focused on the rivers Patuxent, Potomac, and Patapsco. In detailing his campaign in Maryland, a number of glaring misconceptions must be addressed. While it is often popularly thought that the burning of Washington's public buildings materialized as a result of a preconceived plan, in truth what transpired resulted from the circumstances that Ross encountered in theater. To his advantage of being able to dictate the initiative owing to his amphibious capability may be added American mistakes and inadequate preparations that the general exploited. It is not possible to understand the achievements and limitations of his campaign without examining the actions of his adversaries. The conventional notion that Ross's strike on Washington backfired by uniting a hitherto bitterly divided American nation behind the war needs to be revisited. In a similar vein, contemporary British reaction to his raid is best understood in the context of appreciating party politics of the period.

While a number of books have covered the capture of Washington and the subsequent British attempt to seize Baltimore, Ross remains in the shadow of Rear Admiral George Cockburn during these operations. This relationship needs to be recalibrated. It is vitally important to bear in mind that there was a bitter dispute between the British army and Royal Navy at the time about who should take primary credit for the raid on Washington. Naval officers were particularly keen to promote the role of Cockburn, of course. In large measure their accounts have dominated the historical narrative. This has resulted in Ross being depicted as a "soft" and "somewhat anonymous" commander, even a "weak" leader, wholly pliable in the hands of his Royal Navy colleague who was essentially directing the land-based operations.[6] It will be argued that this greatly exaggerates the role of Cockburn at the expense of Ross.

To sustain this reassessment, we draw on a raft of fresh evidence, not least from British War Office and Admiralty records. Much new information is gleaned from documentation written by key army and naval officers involved in the American campaign. This includes a fascinating contemporaneous account written by Lieutenant George De Lacy Evans, military secretary to Ross, entitled "Memorandum of Operations on the Shores of the Chesapeake in 1814." Additional insights are afforded by senior Royal Navy officers who served with him: Rear Admiral Cockburn's "Memoir of Services," original manuscript versions of Rear Admiral Edward Codrington's letters, and Rear Admiral Pulteney Malcolm's private letters to his wife. The result is a much more nuanced understanding of British operations at the time, not least in revealing the personality conflicts, rivalries, and tensions over military strategy that pervaded the leadership.

In compiling this narrative, period newspapers, British and American, have been pored through. Donald Hickey has observed that the digital age not only has made it much easier to search these databases but also that doing so is helping revolutionize our understanding of the War of 1812. While there are both opportunities and pitfalls in using contemporary prints from either side of the Atlantic, their value to this study is enormous, for they include a wealth of additional eyewitness accounts or pertinent contemporary commentary. And it is more than the fact that governments and commanders on both sides regularly relied on newspapers as sources of information about events occurring thousands of miles away, at times getting initial reports of important developments from them.[7] In vital respects it will be shown that newspapers played an important role at times in shaping events during Ross's campaign in the United States.

While the burning of the White House (known during the nineteenth century as the President's House or the Executive Mansion) is Ross's major claim to fame or infamy, most Americans, Britons, and Irishmen do not know the name of the general presiding over the act. It is time to resurrect Ross's military career, one that spanned from the Pyramids, to the Pyrenees, and to the banks of the Patuxent, Patapsco, and Potomac, revealing him to be an extraordinary soldier. In representing Ross as a figure in world history and in reevaluating his American campaign in particular, this book seeks to make a significant contribution to military history.

CHAPTER I

"Young Bob" Ross

Robert Ross, the man who captured Washington, D.C., on August 24, 1814, was a younger son of a minor gentry family with estates in County Down in present-day Northern Ireland. The Ross family lands largely encompassed the village of Rostrevor and its environs, or *Ross*trevor as it was once known due to its ties to the Ross family.[1] Overlooking Carlingford Lough from the foot of the Mourne Mountains, this area inspired what C. S. Lewis later called his "idea of Narnia."[2] Paradoxically, Ross and many of his fellow Irishmen would forsake their lovely island to spend much of their lives on foreign shores. The Emerald Isle is widely known as the "Land of Saints and Scholars," but in Ross's time it could have justly been called the "Land of Soldiers."

Ross's paternal ancestors lived in Ayrshire, Scotland, before emigrating to Ireland, taking part in the Protestant settlement of large parts of Ulster in the early seventeenth century. They were tenants on Hamilton lands in Portavo on the Ards Peninsula in County Down. Robert's great-great-grandfather George Ross married the daughter of Captain Hans Hamilton. The Rostrevor estate was bought as a wedding gift for his great-grandfather Robert, member of Parliament for Killyleagh, "originally" a Presbyterian. His grandfather was lord mayor of Dublin in 1748–49. By the time Robert Ross was born in 1766, his family on his father's side had converted to the Church of Ireland.[3] His religion had an important bearing on his life's journey. It explains in no small measure why he ended up serving in the British army, whereas many of the Scots Presbyterians in the north of Ireland who suffered from religious discrimination had either emigrated to the United States or fought for the United Irishmen against the British Crown in 1798.

In terms of Robert's maternal bloodline, his mother, Elizabeth Adderly, was originally from Inishannon, County Cork, but latterly from the Circus, Bath. She was the half-sister to the first Earl of Charlemont, the leader of the Irish Volunteers and a passionate believer in the legislative independence of Ireland. She inherited

7

£36,000, which her husband used in 1786 to buy various properties in County Down from his brother, including the family's principal ancestral seat of Rostrevor. According to the *Gentleman's Magazine,* published in London in 1815, among other "near relatives" of Robert Ross were the "ennobled families" of Ludlow, Riversdale, Bandon, and Doneraile. Of a Scots-Irish bloodline on his father's side and Anglo-Irish on his mother's, the educational, social, and political circles the future general moved in qualify him to a degree to be considered Anglo-Irish. A product of a multilayered society in terms of identity, it may be more accurate to describe him as "Anglo-Scots-Irish."[4]

In terms of Robert's more immediate family background, his forebears were steeped in a military tradition. His uncle, also called Robert, rose to the rank of colonel and fought in the French and Indian War (1754–63). He was wounded at the Battle of Monongahela in 1755, serving in the Crown forces with none other than George Washington.[5] Ross's father, who became a major in the army, fought in the same war, a conflict most famously remembered from a British point of view for the "heroic death" of Major General James Wolfe on the Plains of Abraham as the British seized control of Quebec in 1759. Major Ross also distinguished himself that year at the Battle of Minden (in modern-day Germany).[6]

Trinity College Dublin records suggest that Robert Ross, the future general, was born in Dublin, where his father was stationed in 1766 and where the family had political connections. Other accounts indicate that Rostrevor was his birthplace.[7] Whatever the truth of the matter, there is no doubt that he retained a profound affection for his home village. Owing to ill health in his family circle, he spent time in southern France as a child, picking up there fluency in French and "a little Spanish."[8]

As the second son of a gentry family, military service beckoned for Robert. Like his contemporary Arthur Wesley (later Wellesley), the future Duke of Wellington, and so many of their fellow countrymen, they were to be "food for powder," as Wesley's mother once said of her own son.[9] No doubt many in the officer corps were inspired by tales of chivalry and motivated by the quest for military glory.[10] The youthful Wesley and Ross had other things in common. Both enjoyed playing the violin. They moved in the same social circles. Of the few snippets known about them when they were young, the Iron Duke's nephew later recounted an amusing incident at a dinner party in Dublin that Ross, then a "college boy," attended. "In the middle of dinner, a little aide de camp, a playfellow of Ross's came in. They amused each other at dinner with running pins into each other, and made such a noise" that Ross's uncle could stand no more. "G–d d—n it, boys, if you cannot be quiet, go out into the yard and play ball, but don't disturb the dinner." Robert's companion was Arthur Wesley.[11] Unlike Ross, Wesley never went to university, although he went to Eton and later attended the famous military riding school at Angers in France, where he was registered as a "gentilhomme Irlandaise."[12] Ross managed to complete his degree at Trinity College Dublin, but only just, it appears.

At age seventeen, Robert matriculated at Trinity College Dublin on October 11, 1784, the same day as his older brother, Thomas. Before entering university, they both had the same "private tutor," a Mr. Young. They were known in college records as "Mr Ross Junior" and "Mr Ross Senior." An anecdote circulating in Britain in 1820 recounted that Robert got into trouble with the provost of the college, John Hely-Hutchinson, and a tutor named Adair who "shared the unpopularity of his employer." After a quarrel with Adair, "the future general revenged himself on his antagonist, by caricaturing him (for which art he had a peculiar talent) in the act of bestowing a salutation on a very unseemly part of the prevost's [sic] person.... He posted it on the College gate, and it nearly procured him the honours of an expulsion." Extant college records at Trinity do not shed any light on this affair. There is one intriguing reference in the board register from July 1788 that indicates that Ross may have had disciplinary issues. Along with his brother and a number of other students, he is recorded as signing a declaration that stated, "we the under named do hereby promise that we will attend at some future commencement to take the oath required by Law to be admitted to the Degree for which the Grace of the House has been granted to us."[13]

Ross had a keen, sometimes wicked, sense of humor, although in the reported prank targeting the college hierarchy he appears to have gone over the top. Whether the incident was connected to his membership in the Old Historical Society at Trinity, which the college authorities endeavored to suppress, is not clear. Reportedly, to belong to the society, "one needed wit, conviviality and above all the approval of one's peers to enter." Ross fitted this bill perfectly. He is listed among those members of the society delivering addresses at the opening or closing of sessions or obtaining medals. With time, he not only chaired meetings but also was elected treasurer. Among his contemporaries in the society was Wolfe Tone, who later became famous as the leader of the United Irishmen, revolutionaries who wanted to establish an Irish republic independent from the British Crown.[14]

After he received his degree at Trinity in early 1789, Ross began his military career as an ensign in the 25th Regiment of Foot. He joined his unit in November at Gibraltar, where it was doing garrison duty. That he did not enlist until he was nearly twenty-three years old suggests that Ross had been considering other career options. Morale in the British army was low when he enlisted, not least due to the aftermath of losing the American colonies. According to Henry Bunbury at the time, when war broke out on the Continent in 1793, the British army was "lax in discipline, entirely without system, and very weak in numbers." There was a public outrage against the Duke of York for the failures of an expedition to Flanders in 1794, leading to the ill-deserved nursery rhyme that will be forever associated with his name, "The Grand Old Duke of York." The duke had his limitations as a field commander, but he had a knack for organization and was known at the time as the "soldier's friend."[15]

The system whereby commissions and promotions up to the rank of lieutenant colonel could be purchased often meant that wealth trumped talent and that some officers achieved relatively high rank at a young age. That is not to deny that those advanced included a clutch of highly talented officers. Lowry Cole (lieutenant colonel by the time he was twenty-one), Edward Pakenham (major by the time he was seventeen), Arthur Wellesley (lieutenant colonel at twenty-four), and to a lesser extent Robert Ross were the beneficiaries of this system. Ross, though, apparently was unable to afford to purchase the rank of lieutenant colonel, the key to unlocking the door to further promotion to the rank of general. While promotions were still affected by purchase, a new breed of officers was to transform the British army into a seemingly invincible fighting machine.[16]

Apart from playing the purchase system, Ross's professional prospects benefited from the relationship that he struck up with a member of the British royal family, Prince Edward Augustus (Prince Edward), the fourth son of George III and Queen Charlotte and father of the future Queen Victoria. Having begun his military service with the 25th Regiment at the start of August 1789, Ross's connection with Prince Edward, colonel of the 7th Regiment, the Royal Fusiliers, developed while they were both stationed in Gibraltar during 1790–91. With the British colony reportedly "drowning in alcohol," Edward's attempts to restore discipline included "closing many of the pubs and wine houses." Hardly surprisingly, he was soon despised by many of his men.[17]

According to a popular school of thought, Prince Edward only survived a short time in Gibraltar before he was exiled to Canada owing to the "poor treatment" of his troops. Nathan Tidridge, his biographer, maintains that the issue was more health related as the prince suffered from the Mediterranean heat. While many others evidently considered him a good riddance from Gibraltar, Ross, by contrast, obtained six months' leave of absence from his regiment at the end of May 1791 and accompanied Prince Edward on board HMS *Resistance* when the Royal Fusiliers sailed to British North America. Describing Ensign Ross as "a young man of very excellent conduct and very promising parts," the prince requested that he should be given the next vacancy arising for a lieutenant in the Royal Fusiliers without purchase. This duly occurred in July of that year.[18] Ross's maturity and intelligence were perhaps key factors that caught the eye of Prince Edward.

Ross arrived in Quebec in August 1791. During his time in Canada, a mutiny occurred in the Royal Fusiliers resulting from Prince Edward's overbearing, sometimes tyrannical, personality. As a result, the unpopular royal was targeted in an assassination plot. It has been memorably remarked of this blue blood that "mutiny seemed to follow" him "as night does the day."[19] By contrast to his patron, Ross was to forge a reputation as a strict disciplinarian who still managed to enjoy the great affection of his men.

The young officer was based at Quebec until September 1794, when he moved to Halifax. In April 1795 Prince Edward granted Ross five months' leave, more than likely connected with the death of his father. With Britain on a war footing with revolutionary France, his patron selected him for promotion without purchase to captain in a newly created second battalion of the Royal Fusiliers. Ross was pleased to "reflect, that his conduct was such as he thinks merited his Royal Highness's approbation." While steadily progressing through the ranks in his military career, on a domestic level trouble brewed. His mother successfully challenged the decision of his deceased father to leave all his wealth to his eldest son, Thomas.

In 1796 Robert Ross thus inherited a share of his father's estate, which remained "undivided." Having become a captain in the Royal Fusiliers, he transferred to the 90th Regiment at the end of 1795 after securing a promotion to major by purchase, paying "no more than" £2,600 as the rules stated at the time.[20] His investment did not turn out to be as lucrative as he intended, for his battalion was disbanded soon after and he was eventually put on half pay. His military career was revived in May 1798, when the *London Gazette* recorded his appointment as "Major of Brigade to the Forces in South Britain," including in the London area.[21]

While Ross was serving in Canada and later in England, the United Irishmen were planning a rebellion at home. Rostrevor was to be bitterly divided between support for the Crown or the rebel cause. Visiting the village twice in 1792, Wolfe Tone, the leader of the United Irishmen, struggled to stir sedition. Tone recalled of his first visit, when he rode along the shoreline there: "Beautiful! Mourne, the sea etc. Sit up very late and talk treason." On a return journey later that year, he had dinner with thirty people, including Catholics and Protestants. When the United Irishmen were mentioned once more, there was "universal approbation. . . . [W]onderful to see how rapidly the Catholic mind is rising, even in this tory town . . . , one of the worst spots in Ireland."[22] By 1797 the village was swarming with rebels. The upsurge in membership in the area resulted not just from Tone's persuasiveness but also from alienation caused by the excesses of British forces in the South Down area, where a "notorious" fencibles regiment, the Ancient Britons, was stationed.[23] Tom Dunn, the Catholic village "hedge school" master in Rostrevor and a United Irishman, would become a victim of brutally repressive measures. He was flogged to death in August 1798.

Having been appointed major of brigade in South Britain in May 1798, Robert Ross was not in Rostrevor at the time schoolmaster Dunn was killed.[24] Indeed, there is no evidence that he was involved in military operations of any kind in Ireland during the 1798 rebellion. Be that as it may, opinion was to be deeply divided in Ross's home village about his service in the British army, and it is distinctly possible that there was much lingering bitterness over the events of that year. During his lifetime, Ross was revered and reviled in his locality. And this occurred despite the fact that his family had a liberal view in religious matters. Not only did they grant land for a new Anglican church during Robert's time on the church vestry, but permission was also granted for a Catholic church and a Presbyterian meeting house to be erected in the village where the family were landlords.[25] The Catholic inhabitants of the parish of Kilbroney passed formal votes of thanks to Ross's brother, Thomas, the local vicar, for making the land available in 1809 for the Catholic church and for contributing, along with other local Protestants, handsomely to it.[26]

The year 1799 proved to be pivotal in the life of Robert Ross. At the time he was lodging in Maddox Street, Mayfair, London. With the death of his Uncle Robert, known to some as "Bob Ross," a client of Lord Downshire and the long-serving and influential MP for Newry in the Irish parliament, the prospect of a political career opened up.[27] Writing from London, Robert Johnson suggested that Lord Downshire should consider setting up "young Bob Ross" as a candidate to replace his uncle, believing that he would get elected easily owing to the high esteem his uncle had enjoyed locally.[28] Instead, "young Bob" opted to continue with his army life.

Ross exchanged to the 20th Regiment in August 1799. Hitherto known as the "Old and the Bold," the unit's most famous battle honor by that time had been the Battle of Minden (1759). Before the year was out, the major was to see his first action in the Helder region of Holland, fighting against Franco-Dutch forces. According to Charles Fedorak, there were "sound strategic reasons" for this major amphibious offensive. Commanders hoped that the opening of a second front in the west would not only succeed in diverting French troops from operations in Central Europe but also perhaps open the way for a successful advance on Paris. Prior to embarkation for the Helder Campaign, the 20th was joined by 1,800 militia volunteers. Two battalions were formed. Serving in the 1st Battalion (1/20th), Ross played a crucial role in helping mold the militia into an effective fighting force. This was a far from easy task, which became clear when hostilities commenced. "A militia officer named Musket, a very fierce-looking man, his face covered with black whiskers, &c., took fright almost at the first shot, set spurs to his horse, galloped for his life to the Helder, embarked for England, and was never afterwards heard of."[29]

Part of a "second wave" of troops in the campaign, Lieutenant John Colborne of the 1/20th recalled landing "without our baggage on a cold, rainy night, and were on the bare sands with no food and no wood." Ross played a conspicuous part during the action that followed. On September 10 he found himself inland and in command of four companies in Krabbendam, a small but important village in advance of the main British line. At daybreak Ross observed a large enemy column advancing toward him. Heavily outnumbered, he was soon outflanked. Running out of ammunition, Ross withdrew to the main line.[30]

The British army commander, Lieutenant General Sir Ralph Abercromby, ordered a counterattack. He spurred the 20th into charging the French and Dutch. Realizing that many in its ranks were militia, "scarcely more than civilians in uniform," the general exhorted them with typical British understatement: "Come along! You are as safe here as if you were in Norfolk!" Resupplied with ammunition, Ross fearlessly led his men in the attack to retake the village. Under ferocious assault, the enemy were forced to withdraw, the ground left littered with their dead and wounded, believed to number 1,000 all tolled. When the fighting ended, there were heavy casualties in the 1/20th as well, including seven officers. Among the latter was Ross, shot in the thigh and "severely wounded." Very badly hurt too on this campaign was a friend in the 2nd Battalion, Captain Henry Torrens, later military secretary at Horse Guards in London.[31]

Torrens testified that Ross's conduct during the Helder operation displayed "the strongest traits of gallantry and good judgement," characteristics that were to define his military service. Abercromby "witnessed the conduct of Major Ross, which was particularly marked by gallantry and intrepid daring," according to a leading British politician at the time, Nicholas Vansittart. Large numbers of militia having swelled the ranks of the regular battalions for the campaign, the British units proved no match for the enemy, with the exception of the 20th and 40th Regiments, which greatly distinguished themselves in spite of this drawback.[32]

Early in 1800, both battalions of the 20th were posted to Cork in Ireland, reaching Bantry Bay on the third day of their voyage. Due to foul weather, it would be twenty-one days before the troops disembarked. These were the same type of gales that had prevented a 15,000-strong French invasion force landing there in December 1796 to assist the United Irishmen. That Ireland remained a major strategic concern for the British was equally apparent on the very first Sunday the 20th spent in the country, when troops attended the local Protestant church. Private James Downing recalled going to the service fully armed owing to fears about rebel activity. He was also struck by the "heads hung up" in the streets of those who had been "slain, as great examples for the rest."[33] For the British government, there was a lingering worry about the prospects of another Irish revolt.[34]

In June 1800 the 20th was detailed to take part in an expedition to Belle Isle, an island off the French coast. The attack was abandoned and Minorca ended up being the destination instead. Meantime, for his services in the Helder, Ross was promoted to the rank of brevet lieutenant colonel in the army on New Year's Day, 1801—though his regimental rank remained major. News of Ross's promotion reached him when he was serving in Minorca where he was chosen to command a light-infantry battalion.[35]

It was not long before Ross would see further action. An army led by General Abercromby had landed at Aboukir Bay in March, seeking to drive the French out of Egypt, where their presence menaced trade routes as well as potentially threatening British control of India. The British victory at the Battle of Alexandria on March 21 marked the turning point in the campaign, despite the mortal wounding of Abercromby. French forces that had retreated to Alexandria and Cairo, however, still remained. It was against this background that Ross gave up command of his light-infantry battalion in June 1801 for the opportunity to serve with the 20th in the final stages of operations in Egypt. There was tremendous excitement in the regiment at the prospect of fighting the French again. But the two battalions of the 20th also comprised substantial numbers of militia who had volunteered for a period of five years' service—in Europe only. Both battalions participated in the Egyptian campaign following a successful resolution of this limited-service problem. Lieutenant Colonels George Smyth and Ross were instrumental in persuading the militia to volunteer for Egypt, where they served close to the pyramids. On a personal level, during the same month, Ross passed up an opportunity to purchase a lieutenant colonelcy in the regiment at the cost of £3,500.[36]

With great anticipation then, the 20th embarked on transports at Port Mahon, Minorca, on June 22. They formed part of a convoy of thirty-one transports carrying a reinforcement of nearly 3,000 troops, provisions, and stores. They were destined for an army based near Alexandria commanded by Abercromby's successor, Major General

Sir John Hely-Hutchinson, son of John Hely-Hutchinson, provost of Trinity College Dublin and Ross's onetime adversary. It was during this campaign that Ross and George Cockburn acted in concert for the first time. Cockburn, captain of HMS *La Minerve,* was the convoy commander. The voyage took about twenty-four days. A passenger on Cockburn's ship recalled the rousing attempts to boost morale during the passage. When the transports came close, Smyth and Ross ordered their band to play "Rule Britannia" and to hail their naval colleagues with three cheers. Cockburn's men returned the compliment, playing "The British Grenadiers," manned the rigging, and reciprocated with three cheers.[37]

While serving with the 1/20th in Egypt, Ross participated in an audacious nighttime attack on a French outpost close to Fort des Bains, near Alexandria, on August 25. Bayonets fixed, the troops sallied silently forth with their muskets unloaded. One hundred enemy soldiers were captured or killed. The French counterattacked with 1,000 men in a blaze of artillery and musket fire. In response, British onshore and gunboat batteries opened fire as the 1/20th and a small detachment of the 26th Dragoons held firm. For distinguishing itself once again in action, the 20th secured "Egypt" as a battle honor and a sphinx as a regimental emblem.[38]

During these operations, the ranks of the regiment were not to be decimated by enemy action, but by sand. Opthalmia afflicted the "majority" of the officers and men. At one stage there were 240 "blind" men in the 1/20th alone. Private Downing, one of the 80 men who lost their sight permanently, later recorded his exploits in his "easy Verse," recalling, "A blast of wind blew in my eyes, / Which seem'd like burning coals." British success in the expedition to Egypt boosted morale. Abercromby's achievement in leading his men to stirring victories against the French boosted confidence.[39] According to Donald E. Graves, not only had "victory been gained over the veterans of Bonaparte's famous Army of Italy" but also "the Egyptian campaign [had] provided excellent training for a generation of young officers."[40]

After the cessation of hostilities in Egypt, the 20th was transferred to Malta, arriving on December 9. With the Peace of Amiens in March 1802, the regiment was reduced from two battalions to one. During this period of reorganization, John Colborne spent several months on leave with some fellow officers in Sicily and Calabria. Among his companions was Ross, still a bachelor at thirty-six years of age, although soon to wed. While the officers enjoyed themselves thoroughly, their adventures met with a mixed response. On one occasion local people fired at them through the windows of an inn. Colborne knew no reason, "unless it was that one of his companions had given some offence in the town during their visit." A more friendly encounter occurred when the high-spirited travel companions lost their way late at night, perhaps inebriated, and ended up in a river. Directed afterward to the home of a local gentleman, their kind-hearted host looked after them for several days. The trip lasted some three months, during which time they scaled Mount Etna and Mount Vesuvius. They also immersed themselves in Italian culture to such a degree that Colborne later claimed that he became a "perfect master of Italian." Ross, likewise a talented linguist, self-deprecatingly claimed to have become "acquainted... slightly with Italian."[41]

Soon after his Italian escapades, Ross traveled to London. On December 9, 1802, he married Elizabeth Catherine Glascock, from Dublin, in St George's Church, Hanover Square. Like himself, Elizabeth, was a keen musician. A bachelor for so long, Ross readily took to family life. After the renewed declaration of war on France by Britain on May 18, 1803, he returned to his regiment at Malta. The officer was accompanied by his wife, who began her "campaigning" that September. On assuming command, Ross presented the 20th with a new set of colors.[42]

As far as John Colborne, later Field Marshal Seaton, was concerned, during its time in Malta, the regiment was in the "highest order. I really think there is no regiment in the service that has so much *esprit de corps* as the 20th." There was a healthy mix of duties and recreation on the island. Officers enjoyed frequent dinners with the station's commanding officer, Major General William Anne Villettes. Parties, masquerades, and balls alleviated the tedium of garrison life. At one such masquerade, Colborne and his fellow actors borrowed Ross's donkey without permission only to bump into their commander. Examining the animal carefully, Ross exclaimed, "Why, I do believe that is my donkey!" His indulgent response to the prank made the occasion all the more memorable for those involved. Highly regarded for his amiable personality, through force of character and personal example on the battlefield, the officer forged a strong bond with his troops that evidently inspired them to great achievements and to endure great sacrifices.[43] Added to that was a hard edge from a man who insisted on the highest standards of discipline and physical fitness.

By 1804 Ross had earned a reputation as an outstanding officer, and the 20th was regarded as one of the best regiments in the British army. Not surprisingly, General Villettes rated him highly. But this hard-won status was jeopardized following a series of incidents involving members of the regiment and the local Maltese population that culminated in a battle of wills between Ross and the island's civilian commissioner, Sir Alexander Ball. Captain Edmund Byron of the 20th was arrested by order of General Villettes for assaulting a local resident called Dalton, whose "officiousness, obstinacy and ill language," it was conceded, had caused considerable provocation. The general was concerned about the growing number of similar complaints about the conduct of British troops. Ross was ordered to apprise Byron of the verdict of a court of inquiry at an assembly of his fellow officers in the regiment. The officers were to be well warned that such behavior could incur the disapproval of the king. Having delivered the salutary message, Byron was to be released. Concluding his correspondence to Ross, Villettes emphasized that "it gives me the greatest concern to be reduced to the disagreeable necessity of censuring any officer of the 20th Regiment, whose general conduct under your good management has met with my entire approbation."[44]

Before long, a further altercation took place involving officers of the 20th, for which Captain Charles Steevens landed himself in trouble with the local judiciary. When the matter became the subject of a court hearing, Steevens was alleged to have "threatened in open Court to take vengeance himself" against his accuser. On this occasion Ross sprang to the defense of his subordinate. Describing the captain as "a man of remarkably pacific and quiet disposition" who had himself been struck on the head by a stone in the incident, he maintained that the judge had been swayed by the complainant's exaggeration.[45]

A pattern of incidents emerged at this time in which officers and men of the 20th Regiment were to be at the receiving end of harsh justice, in Ross's view, at the hands of the local civilian authorities. At the heart of the matter was the role played by Commissioner Ball, who was regarded "as too partial to the natives." Exasperated, Ross evidently had had enough when an incident involving a pig escalated into a major controversy. According to Ross, the prevalence of swine running wild in the streets provided the background.

A fracas ensued when one pig "nearly ran between the legs" of one of his soldiers, who then kicked it to prevent his trousers being soiled. The soldiers, "of unquestionably good character," according to Ross, were promptly attacked by Maltese onlookers.[46]

After making a personal visit to the scene of the incident in company with a police officer, Ross had one of the suspected attackers seized by his troops and handed over to a civil magistrate. He also appealed to Ball to have the Maltese mob prosecuted. "Should it appear that the soldier has been the aggressor you may depend upon it," the officer wrote, that "he shall be punished in the most exemplary manner." The subsequent judgement reached by the Maltese authorities infuriated him. One of his soldiers, the court declared, far from being innocent, was judged to have been the guilty party.[47]

Faced now with having to live up to his promise of making an example of the soldier who had been adjudged the offender, Ross challenged the validity of the evidence and judgment. In a highly sarcastic letter to Ball, he averred that the "act of villainy" perpetrated on one of his soldiers had been "totally passed over and unnoticed" in the judgment. And Ross reminded the commissioner of the serious nature of the offense involved. "You well know sir what a British soldier would have suffered had he been capable of acting such a part."[48] Without specifically stating the nature of the penalty, it is clear that this would have resulted in a flogging. While an absolute stickler for discipline in his ranks, Ross was not about to punish an innocent man.

Enraged by this response, Ball referred his behavior to Villettes. On being informed of the verdict, he claimed that the commanding officer of the 20th directed a tirade of abuse at the six Maltese witnesses who had testified against his soldiers. For a time it seemed as if the matter was going to be referred to London. Undaunted by this potential escalation, Ross wrote, "with me it could never be a wish to push matters to such an extremity, but, if pushed I shall not shrink from the trial." Widely regarded as an affable man with whom it was almost impossible to quarrel, his dispute with Ball was evidently one of the few exceptions to this rule.[49] If pushed, Ross was not afraid to fight his corner. While evidently slow to anger, this normally mild-mannered man bridled at injustice or impropriety. The dispute eventually fizzled out.

During this prolonged stint of garrison duty, Ross put his men through their paces in rigorous exercises. Like his famous predecessor in command of the 20th, James Wolfe, Ross believed in the importance of stamina. He was following in the footsteps too of Lieutenant General Sir John Moore, who insisted on arduous physical training for the troops under his command. Essentially, Ross was training his men as if they were light infantry. Captain Steevens, one of Ross's officers, later recalled that his commander took "drilling" extremely seriously. On a regular basis the regiment was taken into the countryside at five o'clock in the morning and did not return until one o'clock in the afternoon. "I have seen the men of my company with their white trousers quite wet, as if just washed, entirely from excessive perspiration." Cross-country training sessions frequently lasted eight hours. Steevens was not pleased: "the *best* of the *joke was, that no other corps in the island was similarly indulged.*" He pulled no punches in his criticism of his commanding officer's training regimen, which was discontinued, he claimed, following representations by the regimental surgeon.[50] These punishing exercises, however, may have been in part just that, punishment of officers and men for bringing the regiment into disrepute.

While Ross expressed a hope that he might be able to purchase the lieutenant colonelcy of the regiment during his time in Malta, he was unable to do so. By the time the 20th left the island, Elizabeth Ross had given birth to two children. A boy, David, was born on September 27, 1804, while a daughter, Laetitia, who died young, was born on September 19, 1805. Barely a couple of months after his daughter's birth, Ross and the 20th were posted to mainland Italy as part of an army that was initially under the command of Lieutenant General Sir James Craig. The British were soon forced by superior French forces to withdraw to Sicily. The following year Ross rose to national fame when the 20th played a crucial role in the memorable battle of Maida, fought on July 4, 1806, in Calabria. A relatively small-scale affair by comparison to some of the grand set-piece battles of the Napoleonic Wars, its psychological effect proved to be very significant; its importance in British military history is testified to this day in the naming of the Maida Vale District of London. Lieutenant General Sir John Stuart, the new army commander charged with defending Sicily, opted for attack as the best means of defense. And so originated the "Descent on Calabria," a British seaborne operation to the southern coast of Italy.[51]

In evaluating the role of the 20th during the battle, it is worth emphasizing that it had been sent aboard transports on a diversion to draw attention from the landing of Stuart's army on the Calabrian coast. Having completed this maneuver, Ross was ordered to "follow the fleet as soon as he might consider these purposes accomplished." Disembarking from its vessels, the 20th arrived at Maida as the battle was raging, the landing craft having taken on board so much "surf" that fresh cartridges had to be secured. "Without waiting for orders," Ross deployed his regiment.[52]

Lieutenant Colonel Sir Henry Bunbury, quartermaster general of the army, is regarded as the "principal chronicler" of the Battle of Maida. It appears that it is just as well that Ross used his initiative as Stuart is portrayed wandering through the battlefield, oblivious to danger but giving orders to no one. The 20th coming across the countryside at the double, Bunbury immediately rode over to them. Explaining how the battle was unfolding, he was impressed by the manner in which Ross "caught the spirit of the affair in an instant." Pressing onward, his battalion drove off French sharpshooters before encountering enemy cavalry. Completely unfazed, Ross's composure had a reassuring influence on his men: "You have the advantage, soldiers, the sun is in their eyes. Steady!" Then the infantry unleashed a withering volley that "sent them [the cavalry] off in confusion to the rear." Passing to the left of Brigadier General Lowry Cole's brigade, Ross then wheeled his regiment to the right and opened up a devastating and decisive fire on the enemy. According to Henry Torrens at the time, a general view prevailed among fellow officers that Ross's intervention instigated the rout of the French, a view shared by a recent historian of the battle. His skill in reading battlefield situations and making instant decisions was to be a feature of his career. It was also to be defined once again by an intrepid spirit that Lieutenant General Stuart warmly acknowledged in his official dispatch.[53]

British losses in the battle were minimal, with just forty-five killed. The only officer to die was Captain Murdock Maclaine, son of Gillean Maclaine of Seal-castle, the Island of Mull, Scotland, commanding the light-infantry company of the 20th. Ross wrote to a friend of Captain Maclaine's in Edinburgh, describing how he died courageously leading his men. In an insight into his military mindset, Ross referred to the "general grief prevalent among his friends and acquaintances at his loss. . . . His brave company, who led the charge of the bayonet in battle, and by whom he was much beloved, had ample vengeance for his death in the havoc which they made among the enemy."[54]

While Ross accrued well-earned laurels for his actions, the brunt of the fighting had been borne by other units. Cole's brigade was reckoned to have been engaged in the heaviest fighting. Lieutenant Colonel James Kempt's light battalion also played a crucial role in the victory. For Bunbury, however, the "most brilliant parts on this little stage were acted by Colonels Kempt and Ross: to them the glory of the fight at Maida is chiefly due." Along with sixteen other officers, several years later Ross received the "Maida" medal struck by order of George III.[55] It was the first, but by no means the last, of the medals he was to earn during his distinguished military career.

William Windham, former secretary of war, speaking in Parliament following the victory, argued that Maida had "broken the charm" of French claims of military superiority over the British. Meanwhile, Captain Colborne, writing to a relative, boasted, "I now begin to think, as our ancestors did, that one Englishman is equal to two Frenchmen." The "astonished [French] invincible" had been "mowed down by a well directed fire."[56] The immediate legacy of the battle was even more important. Building on the success of the British operation in Egypt in 1801, Maida ensured that the cult of the French "invincibles" had been exploded as a myth. The cult of Wellington's "invincibles" was soon to begin—and Ross was at the heart of it.

CHAPTER 2

"THE MOST COMFORTABLE WARRIOR A MAN COULD WISH TO SERVE WITH"

As reports of the victory at Maida on July 4, 1806, circulated in Britain and Ireland, Ross attracted his first national attention. Before long he petitioned for promotion on behalf of himself and several of his officers. Lieutenant General Henry Fox, endorsing this request, vouched that Ross was "a most active, intelligent and gallant officer—and I can safely affirm that there is not a better officer at the head of any regiment in His Majesty's service." It was not until early 1808, however, that his regimental promotion to lieutenant colonel was confirmed. In the meantime, after its battle exploits the 20th returned to Sicily, where it stayed until the latter part of 1807.[1]

John Colborne later recalled a light-hearted moment of messroom high jinks from this period that reveals once more that Ross was a highly popular, good-humored commander who was a master at cultivating camaraderie. The officers of the 20th invited their counterparts in the 52nd Regiment to dinner, including a young officer named Diggle. Two young officers from the 20th told Diggle that it was their regimental custom to propose a toast, "Confusion to all General Officers." With Ross seated at the head of the table, Diggle duly fell for the prank and proposed a toast: "D—n all General Officers!" Appalled, his brother officers in the 52nd later held a meeting at which his future with the regiment was discussed. Understanding completely what had transpired, Ross interceded with his counterpart in the 52nd and told him "not to take any notice of it, as it was all a joke."[2]

Not all senior officers would have made light of Diggle's indiscretion. Ross was the exception, not the rule—at least according to Robert Blakeney, who knew him well. In his memoir he singled him out as a role model for regimental commanders, "at once . . . the father and brother of every officer in his corps." That being the case, through the respect he cultivated, no one would ever dare to take a liberty with him. And in dealing with the occasional indiscretions of young officers, Ross responded indulgently and in a good-humored fashion.[3] After all, he had been a livewire himself in his youth.

Ross evidently succeeded in fostering a spirit of comradeship, even a family atmosphere, among his officers. In his mid-thirties by the time he married, his concern for his wife and young children was to be equally manifest.[4] In the autumn of 1807, Napoleon sent a large army under General Jean-Andoche Junot to take possession of Lisbon. Lieutenant General Sir John Moore received orders to sail from Sicily with the 20th and other regiments to support the Portuguese. John Colborne, military secretary to Moore at the time, later recalled receiving orders for embarkation. The army had not been informed of the destination when Colborne was approached by Ross. "Can you tell me where we are going, or give me the least hint, whether east or west? It is of the greatest consequence to me, for if we go east, I shall leave Mrs Ross here, but if west, we may be off anywhere, and in that case I should see her off for England directly." Considering Ross an honorable man, Moore granted Colborne permission to tell him.[5]

The intention to land in Portugal was later aborted, and the 20th ended up returning to England. Owing to quarantine regulations, the troops were not disembarked for three days. Arriving at Portsmouth on January 7, 1808, after serving two campaigns abroad, the soldiers conformed to the conventional norm on such occasions, soon frequenting the ale houses throughout the local district. At parade the following morning, there was hardly a sober man in the ranks. Ross was furious. Ever alert to maintaining good discipline, considerable evidence reveals that the lieutenant colonel tried to restrain his troops from drinking to excess, particularly when they were on active service. This was to pay dividends when the regiment was posted abroad once again. In the meantime, Ross's mother died that April.[6] It was not long afterward before he and his siblings became embroiled in a major dispute over family assets.

The 20th Regiment next saw combat in Portugal in 1808, when the British became involved in the Peninsular War after the French seized control of Spain and Portugal. During two spells of service in Iberia, Ross greatly enhanced his reputation as a regimental officer and later proved his mettle as a general officer commanding a brigade. His initial involvement resulted from a British decision to send an expeditionary force to Portugal. Lead elements under Arthur Wellesley landed at Mondego Bay, one hundred miles north of Lisbon, in August 1808. Later that month some of Ross's men arrived in time to participate in the Battle of Vimeiro on August 21, Wellesley's second engagement of the Peninsular War. Only part of the 20th saw action, however, due to a shortage of landing craft. Ross missed the battle and, eager for the fray as always, was hugely disappointed.[7] Before the year ended he was to see more than his fair share of fighting, culminating in the hardships of the retreat to Corunna in northern Spain, when the British army was forced to withdraw from the peninsula. The 20th, under Ross's leadership, earned laurels as part of the rearguard during the harrowing retreat and the final battle. The initial experiences in Portugal, however, were much more pleasant.

Keen to sustain the momentum with his victory at Vimeiro, Wellesley wanted to pursue the retreating French. He was to be overruled by a more senior officer, Sir Harry Burrard, second in command of the British expeditionary force. This cautious approach was endorsed in turn when Sir Hew Dalrymple, the overall commanding officer, arrived. Negotiations with the French followed, the upshot of which was the controversial Convention of Cintra, allowing the French to withdraw from Portugal after their defeat at Vimeiro. While Wellesley did not agree with this decision, which had been taken by Dalrymple, he was caught up in the furor that followed and along with Dalrymple and Burrard faced an official inquiry in London. As a result of the convention, Dalrymple assigned Ross the command of a corps that took possession of the Portuguese frontier town of Elvas and nearby Fort La Lippe, close to the border with Spain.[8] The local inhabitants were very friendly. It was their first time encountering British troops. Ross's ability to speak some Spanish, some considered, was a key factor in establishing good relations.[9]

It was not long before things soon turned sour for the British army, by now led by Sir John Moore. After a series of exhausting marches over a distance of some four hundred miles from Lisbon to the Salamanca area of Spain, the army found itself outnumbered almost two to one by a renewed French onslaught led by Marshal Nicholas Soult, one of Napoleon's most capable generals, forcing Moore to withdraw to Corunna. British troops and their camp followers suffered grievously en route in bitter winter weather. The retreat, with the 20th serving as part of the rearguard, was in full swing by Christmas Day, 1808. In freezing conditions the troops were instructed to wade through a stream rather than risk a delay crossing a narrow nearby bridge. From time to time the 20th and other rearguard elements had to halt to fight off the pursuing French. On one such occasion Thomas Plunkett, an "officer-hunter" serving with the 95th Rifles, killed the commander of a French force, a General Colbert. Witnessing what had transpired, the chivalrous Ross was sorry to see such a gallant opponent meet his end.[10]

During the withdrawal, the British became ever more desperate. Discipline in the ranks deteriorated amid drunken disorder. At Calcavelos, Ross paraded a straggler from another regiment who had been badly mutilated by the French, an horrendous spectacle. To prevent drinking to excess, whenever his regiment reached a town, Ross ordered the officers to stay with their men rather than billet separately. Less-disciplined troops paid a heavy price, not least in Bembibre on New Year's Day, 1809. As an officer of the 28th Regiment recorded, that town appeared as if it had been stormed and sacked. "Rivers of wine ran through the houses and into the streets, where lay fantastic groups of soldiers . . . , women, children, runaway Spaniards and muleteers, all apparently inanimate, except when here and there a leg or arm was seen to move, while the wine oozing from their lips and nostrils seemed the effect of gunshot wounds." General Moore, fearing that the French might cut across the British line of march, abandoned the wayward soldiers and their camp followers after the 28th's men had spent most of the day trying to get their drunken compatriots to their feet. Pursuing French cavalry took no notice that the staggering stragglers left to their own devices were intoxicated and had thrown down their weapons; the dragoons hacked men, women, and children indiscriminately.[11]

The 20th coped remarkably well with the trials of the retreat due to the men's high levels of physical fitness insisted upon by Ross. Sir Edward Paget, commander of the rearguard, described the lieutenant colonel as "the most comfortable warrior a man could wish to serve with." Through intoxication or exhaustion, increasing numbers of troops in other regiments, by contrast, lagged behind as the British retreated through mountainous terrain. A number of soldiers and camp followers had no shoes or stockings, "and their legs were as red as the coats of fallen soldiers which they had buttoned over their heads." Ross picked up a little boy whose parents were believed to have perished and mounted him on the front of his saddle.[12]

Among the horrific and heartrending scenes experienced by Ross and his men at the time was the decision to destroy the majority of the horses prior to embarkation at Corunna, only the mounts of the generals and staff officers surviving. Some were thrown off cliffs or stabbed, others were shot or finished off with hammers. Besides losing baggage and equipment worth £90, Ross also had two horses and a mule shot at Corunna. One of them was reported to be a "beautiful chestnut Arab" that he had purchased in Egypt and for which he had once been offered 150 guineas.[13] Originally, it was Moore's intention that the rearguard regiments, which had endured the hardships as well as the dangers of the withdrawal, would be the first to be evacuated; he attempted to ensure that the 20th got away safely. Unable to get a proper crack at the French during the retreat, though, the 20th was listed as one of several regiments spoiling for a fight. Allocated a role in the reserve when the battle commenced, the "Old and the Bold" saw further action in repelling a French attack before boarding ship.[14]

A famous fighting withdrawal in the annals of the British army, it was nevertheless a retreat and marked yet another occasion when British military intervention on the Continent had ended in failure. On its return to England, the 20th was reputed to have lost the fewest men of any regiment, having only fifty-eight missing and one hundred sick.[15] For his role in this campaign, Ross received the second of his gold medals. Among the first troops to reach English shores, the 20th brought news that although the French had not captured the entire army as many believed, the British commander, Sir John Moore, had been killed. After surviving the perils and hardships of sustained military action, the regiment now was to be thinned by fever in England.[16]

Ross returned from action to encounter protracted legal troubles in the wake of his mother's death in April 1808. A long-running saga ensued concerning the division of family lands and property, mainly in County Down, Ireland. At the core of the dispute about splitting the assets into three equitable proportions was his brother Thomas's "very particular desire that he shall have the Rostrevor division."[17] Revealing a profound attachment to his native village, Robert Ross was determined to hold on to property there. In order to attend to family affairs, he requested leave of absence from the army on a number of occasions.[18] In the end, his bequest included a share in the Rostrevor estate and an annual income of £1,000. This did not include the family mansion there, a substantial property known as the Lodge, an "enchanting spot" that was his "usual retirement" in the village, as a correspondent at the time described it, which was inherited by his brother. Perhaps this is when Robert built "a very neat and elegant cottage" in Rostrevor called the Ghann on the bank of a small river of that name. For some years after his mother's death, Ross had extensive periods of leave, perhaps connected with domestic considerations, including arranging his new home. A correspondent later wrote to him while he was serving in Spain that on his return, "it would be pleasant to stretch ones limbs upon the Gan [sic]."[19]

Before the 20th departed on its next expedition to the Walcheren (a series of islands in the Scheldt delta, Holland) in August 1809, more than 500 officers and men, many of them recruits from the militia, boosted its ranks to 900 men. Once more Ross was charged with the task of transforming militiamen into effective fighting troops as his regiment took its place in what was referred to as a "Grand Expedition," comprising an army of some 40,000 men and requiring six hundred vessels. The strategic objectives included opening a second front to relieve pressure on the Austrians. What is more, French fleets based in the Scheldt delta threatened British shores and supplies and could be used to mount an invasion of England. In the Walcheren, apart from one isolated occasion, not a single shot was fired in action by the 20th. The sole exception involved Ross, ever alert and to the fore. Pursuing some spies with a small number of his men, shots were fired at their French adversaries, who managed to escape. Overall, though, a stalemate had developed. In the pestilent conditions of the region, large numbers of men on both sides succumbed to death as a result of the "Walcheren fever," a form of malaria. While almost 4,000 British troops died from the disease, just 106 were killed in action during the entire expedition.[20]

When the 20th returned to Colchester, England, from the Walcheren operation, not many more than 200 men were fit to march into the barracks, with some 600 others sick. That the regiment was entitled to almost £1,000 of prize money awarded in consequence of service in the Walcheren was little comfort for the trials the soldiers had endured there. It is also clear that the harrowing experience had a lingering effect on the health of the troops. A field return of the regiment in May 1810 reported that the unit was "unfit for immediate use." Of a hardy disposition, there is no evidence that

Ross suffered ill health at this time. Evidently considered a rising star, later the same year he was appointed as an aide-de-camp to the king and promoted to the rank of colonel. To mark these distinctions, he was among the guests at a "private Levee" and was presented to the king.[21]

After the devastating effects of the Walcheren expedition, it was to be 1812 before the 20th was posted back to the Continent. In the meantime the unit was based for the most part in Ireland, primarily in Mallow, County Cork. Mrs. Ross gave birth to another child there, Elizabeth, in May 1811. Over a period of time, her husband fashioned a battle-ready regiment once more. The men were frequently drilled, instructed in field duties, and rehearsed for all warfare contingencies. Benjamin Smyth, in his history of the 20th, intriguingly refers to an operation in which the regiment marched through "disaffected districts" of County Cork when "many illegal assemblies were suppressed." As late as 1811 an officer from Napoleon's Irish Legion visited Dublin to assess potential support for a French invasion. Ireland, a huge manpower resource to the British army, was believed by London authorities to remain a melting pot of discontent. The tense relations between Roman Catholics and Protestants in Rostrevor at the time reflects the volatile mood in the country. William Todd Jones, a liberal Protestant, reported from there in January 1811 "that there are Nocturnal Meetings of the Peasantry, in this County: and that we Protestants are to be killed, and salted up for export, by the express polite invitation of his Holiness to the Irish Catholiks [sic] under the good natured suggestion of Buonaparte [sic] himself."[22]

While stationed in County Cork, Ross often visited Rostrevor. During prolonged periods of leave there, he continued to deal with regimental affairs. His nephew later fondly recalled that in "his youth I knew most of the officers of that distinguished corps. Never was a body of men animated by a more chivalrous spirit!" Among those officers who visited Rostrevor, it seems likely, was Thomas Falls, a native of the nearby garrison town of Newry.[23] He served as aide-de-camp to Ross in various campaigns. The vestry records of Kilbroney Parish Church in Rostrevor, where Thomas Ross was vicar, mention the colonel being present when the Barrack Green was granted as the site for a new church in March 1811.[24] Traveling home in January 1812, he drew out £100 and made arrangements for various payments, including a subscription to the *Patriot* newspaper.

Mrs. Ross not only gave birth in Rostrevor to a second son, Robert, in May 1812, but the couple also made plans to build a "country residence" on the outskirts of the scenic village.[25]

Having spent much time attending to his domestic affairs, Ross was becoming increasingly frustrated with his military career. During the summer of 1812, he petitioned for command of a brigade but was informed by his old friend and former "brother officer" in the 20th, Henry Torrens, military secretary at Horse Guards in London, that he was too far down the list of colonels, which went by seniority at that rank, for his request to be granted. Torrens held out the prospect that the best chance for his ambition was at the battle front, where the casualty rate among high-ranking officers was very high but the promotion prospects were good.[26] Such battlefield advancement beckoned with the imminent departure of the 20th from Ireland to the Iberian Peninsula. The return of this "distinguished regiment" to the thick of the action was noted in British newspapers in October 1812, not least because his "present Majesty has already awarded them three badges for their honourable conduct in the field." Bound for Lisbon, the troops stopped off for a day in Corunna. Some officers had hoped to visit the battlefield where they had fought in January 1809, but they only had time to pay their respects at the grave of Sir John Moore.[27]

The "campaigning" of Mrs. Ross was to enter a new phase when she followed her husband to the Continent with her young family.[28] As Dianne Graves has remarked, army wives of the period offered "strength and support, beauty and brains, courage and determination, they demonstrated their worth and often proved to be assets to their husbands." At this period Mrs. Ross certainly measured up to that billing. The 20th was stationed at Pesquira during the winter of 1812–13. The regiment was assigned to the fusilier brigade commanded at the time by Sir Edward Pakenham, the brother-in-law of Arthur Wellesley, now Earl of Wellington. Having not seen action on the Continent for three years, and despite its past glories, the 20th had to prove itself once again to its more recently battle-hardened brother regiments in the brigade.[29]

In late April 1813, Ross petitioned yet again for command of a brigade. Wellington replied that he would be more than happy to oblige when he was in a position to do so, though he went on to observe that there were several officers "senior to you without brigades."[30] Ross's disappointed ambition at this stage of his career, however, should not be attributed to the military conventions of the period alone. His prolonged and repeated periods of leave, which he appears to have used to attend to private affairs in Rostrevor over several years, may in part have resulted in his regiment remaining in Ireland rather than being transferred back to the battle front.

Ross's frustration was soon to be resolved by a radical decision made at Horse Guards in London to relax the rigid rules governing army promotions. It departed from established practice with a view to overhauling the command of the army due to a shortage of officers at the rank of major general. Robert Ross was promoted to major general in the army by brevet on June 4, one of a number of officers with ranks as colonels in the army dating from 1810 who were advanced in this manner. Not all the newly promoted generals could be given field commands, however. Torrens acknowledged some "embarrassment" might result as "no Brevet has occurred for many years which includes the promotion of so many useful officers to the rank of Major General." Four positions were left vacant on the Home Staff to accommodate newly promoted officers who could not be given commands in Wellington's army. Ross was among three officers named by Torrens, however, as among the "best officers in the service."[31] Not surprisingly, Wellington soon decided to utilize his abilities in the field and was to be richly rewarded for doing so.

Launching a new offensive in Spain, Wellington's army engaged the French at the Battle of Vitoria, a one-sided affair fought on June 21, 1813. The manner in which the French fled the battlefield was remarkable. They left behind baggage worth five million francs, 151 cannon, and what was described as a "mobile brothel." Ross's role in the battle is not clear, although army records show that he was awarded a medal as a major general in command of a brigade. At Vitoria, according to the remarks of the British chancellor of the exchequer some years later, Ross "exhibited such proofs of innate talent, that he was selected to take the separate command of a brigade."[32]

Shortly after Vitoria, Ross was appointed to command the fusilier brigade, consisting of the 1st Battalion, 7th Regiment (1/7th); 20th Regiment, and 1st Battalion, 23rd Regiment (1/23rd). He had, of course, previously served with the 1/7th. This brigade was part of the 4th Division, commanded by his fellow countryman Lieutenant General Lowry Cole, with whom he had fought at the Battle of Maida. The division shot to national fame as a result of the so-called

Battle of the Pyrenees, a series of bloody engagements during a nine-day period beginning July 25. Casualties were numerous on both sides. Shamed by the disaster of Vitoria and with the borders of France itself now threatened, Marshal Soult, the newly appointed and highly rated French commander who had distinguished himself in driving the British to Corunna some years earlier, vowed to expel the "enemy from those lofty heights which enable him proudly to survey our fertile valleys."[33]

Soult attempted to pour large numbers of men through the relatively weakly guarded passes at Roncesvalles and Maya. The initial action involving Ross's brigade occurred at the former pass, a key strategic point high in the Pyrenees that had been the scene of famous battles stretching back to the days of Charlemagne. Ross, good soldier and historian that he was, noted that Roncesvalles was "famous for feats in the days of chivalry."[34] Before long the valor of Ross's men made their mark on the annals of its history. The fighting occurred on July 25 after Wellington, in a rare mistake, divided his forces as he sought to break the resistance of the French garrisons at San Sebastian and at Pamplona simultaneously. Cole recalled that late at night on July 24, he was informed by Major General John Byng that he was expecting to be attacked the next morning. Ross's brigade was ordered to march at first light to strengthen Byng's left flank.[35]

According to an officer in the 20th Regiment, Ross was told by a spy that a French attack was imminent and decided to begin the ascent into the pass immediately with the 1/7th and the 20th to counteract it. The 1/23rd was to wait for the signal of a white tablecloth being hoisted on a sergeant's pike before proceeding with the baggage. Ross moved out with the 1/7th and 20th, reaching Roncesvalles by daybreak, then signaled the 1/23rd to follow at dawn. He attempted to seize the initiative by being prepared to engage the enemy with all available forces rather than wait for his full complement of men to deploy. During the difficult nighttime ascent, the troops resorted to dragging themselves forward by the roots of trees or even crawling on their hands and knees.[36] Had Ross not used his initiative and reached the crest of the Linduz Ridge in the nick of time, the French would have poured through the pass. As it was, his fusilier brigade was about to bear the brunt of an attack by numerically superior enemy forces.

What happened next was the stuff of legend. Captain George Tovey of the 20th led a famous bayonet charge against the French.

He later recalled that when enemy light troops opened fire, Ross, "who was on the spot," shouted an order for a company to immediately advance. Tovey volunteered, soon clearing away the French skirmishers only to then encounter the leading elements of the main enemy column, which had just reached the summit. Called upon to surrender, instead Tovey shouted to his men, "bayonet away, bayonet away." Shocked by the impetuous attack, the French fled from the brow of the hill. This desperate fight has been described as "one of the rarest things in the Peninsular War, a real hand-to-hand" battle with the bayonet.[37] What lent the British advance added drama was the fact that a "dense cloud" hugged the ridge where the fighting took place, concealing the approaching French. The leading detachment, with Ross at its head, had hardly disappeared into the mist before they were attacked by overwhelming numbers. For his courage the general publicly thanked Tovey "on the spot" and ensured that his act of bravery and leadership was mentioned in the official dispatch penned by their divisional commander.[38]

Military historian Donald E. Graves records that Ross was pushing elements of the 20th and a German rifle company up the Linduz Ridge when they suddenly came upon the advance forces of no less than three divisions, nineteen battalions in all, although owing to the terrain only five French battalions were involved in the fight. Following Tovey's gallant bayonet attack, Ross retreated with his men to a line taken up by troops in the 20th, their colors flying. When the French attempted to charge through the narrow pass, they were mown down by sustained volleys.[39]

The line was held against repeated attacks, the French frustrated time and again as first the 1/23rd and then the 1/7th succeeded the 20th in repelling them. Casualties were heavy on both sides. When the firing had ceased, Sergeant John Cooper recalled the haunting sights and sounds of suffering. Close by, an injured or dying Frenchman piteously cried out, "A mon Dieu! A mon Dieu!" Near Cooper's feet lay two of his comrades, one dead, one dying. "The brains of the latter were protruding above his eyes. I knew him and thought he looked up at me: but there was no utterance or sound, sobs excepted."[40]

Faced by a heavy concentration of French troops trying to force their way through the passes of Roncesvalles and Maya, some 30,000 to the 11,000 British, the senior commanders at the scene, Cole and Lieutenant General Thomas Picton, decided that there was no choice but to retreat, disobeying the orders of Wellington, who was livid with what had transpired. A participant in the fierce fighting at Roncesvalles, Lieutenant John Hankey Bainbrigge, firmly believed that but for Ross's initiative in preventing a surprise attack, the British army would have suffered "a terrible disaster."[41]

The retreat from Roncesvalles took place during the night. An officer in the 20th noted that campfires were lit and kept burning to give the impression that the British remained in position. How the French did not hear the "swearing, grumbling, stumbling and tumbling" of the retreating forces is another matter. The troops, it appears, were particularly disgruntled, believing that they had stolen away in the dark and left their wounded to the mercies of their enemies and mountain wolves. Those too badly wounded to be removed were gathered together near the fires. "Small cards were then pinned on their jackets, having a few words written on each in French, consigning them to the mercy of our gallant enemy." The French duly attended to the injured men.[42]

The retreating troops, slowed up by baggage and perhaps by camp followers, were vulnerable to attack. Alert to the danger, Wellington arrived on the scene at the bridge at Sorauren. Dismounting his horse, he casually began writing an order. Despite repeated warnings that the French were rapidly approaching, he coolly finished his dispatch before remounting his horse and exiting from one end of the village at a gallop as enemy cavalry entered the other. It was a near-run thing. Besides having had two horses shot from under him while campaigning in India, during the Peninsular War, as Peter Snow has noted, Wellington was "lucky in that he escaped death so often when many of his senior colleagues and aides were killed or wounded around him." His fearless forays also nearly led to his capture at Talavera, Salamanca, and Echelar. Wellington later reflected that the key to his success was that "I was always on the spot—I saw everything and did everything for myself," even if it was risky.[43] He and Ross, childhood friends, were cut from the same cloth in this respect.

Wellington's presence at Sorauren not surprisingly boosted flagging spirits. The scene was soon to be set for another vicious battle in which Ross's brigade would again be found where the fighting was fiercest. On the night before the engagement began, a thunderstorm burst out, considered to be a lucky omen by the British on so many occasions. The heavy rain this time, many believed, delayed the French onslaught. But when it finally commenced, the main thrust was directed against a ridge occupied by the 4th Division. The French encountered ferocious resistance from Ross's fusilier brigade. At the height of the battle, with his line threatened on the flank, Ross sent an aide-de-camp, Lieutenant William O'Donnell, to keep Wellington informed of enemy movements. Despite being substantially outnumbered, the brigade repulsed a series of attacks—with all three battalions bayonet charging the French. When the right wing of his brigade was exposed by a Portuguese regiment having retreated following an irresistible enemy onslaught, Ross had no choice but to fall back too. The battle now hung in the balance. At this critical point Wellington ordered the 3/27th and 1/48th Foot, also from the 4th Division and having been held in reserve, to charge the French with the bayonet. The counterattack swept them from the ridge that they had gained at such cost.[44]

The French attack having been thwarted, the battleground at Sorauren became known as "Cole's Ridge." Previously nicknamed the "Supporting Division," Cole's command was now called the "Enthusiastics." It was a measure of the acceptance of the 20th into the fusilier brigade that these "hardy old veterans" of campaigns stretching back to the Helder in 1799 were called the "Young Fusiliers." The rising reputation of the 4th Division, it was no coincidence, occurred while Major General Ross led that brigade to such effect. It should also be recognized, however, how highly General Cole also valued the services of Lieutenant Colonel Ellis of the 1/23rd, who commanded the brigade on a number of occasions.[45]

After the battle, Ross's brigade waited for news of Wellington's official dispatch, which was featured in a *London Gazette Extraordinary* of August 16. The "gallant 4th Division" was singled out for having "surpassed their former good conduct." Every regiment charged with the bayonet, and the 1/40th, 1/7th, 20th, and 1/23rd did so four different times. Their officers set them the example, with General Ross having two horses shot from under him. That Ross was extremely fortunate to have escaped serious injury or death was indicated by the fact that he was struck in the stomach by a ball that bruised him without penetrating. He was among those officers who received a vote of thanks in the House of Commons.[46] Events at Sorauren reinforced his growing reputation as a courageous and inspiring commander who led by example. But they also showed that amid heavy fighting, Ross remained aware of the big picture.

He was not prepared to throw caution to the wind when his position became untenable, a strength indicated by his tactical retreat.

The 4th Division, and the fusilier brigade in particular, made their mark by their actions at Roncesvalles and Sorauren but at a terrible price—with 627 fusilier casualties. Wellington, not a man given to exaggeration, described Sorauren as "fair bludgeon work." Lieutenant Colonel Ellis of the 1/23rd, among the wounded, reported that his battalion was reduced to 160 effectives, taking into consideration the casualties, sick, and those attending the wounded.[47] Not a single captain of the 1/7th led his company from the battlefield, while there were nearly 200 casualties. As for the 20th, the two actions resulted in some fifteen officers and 240 men being "put *hors de combat.*" Among the officers wounded was Lieutenant Thomas Falls, Ross's aide-de-camp. Clearly, being close to the general was a dangerous occupation for man or beast. Lieutenant Bainbrigge, who lost an arm during the heavy fighting at the time, later recorded that Ross, whom he described as adored by all the men who ever served under his command, visited him as he was recovering. Generous as ever, the major general offered Bainbrigge whatever money he required from his own purse.[48]

Ross described the momentous events to his brother-in-law, Ned Glascock. "Since my last, I have neither eaten the bread of idleness, nor has the grass grown much under my feet." Without going into detail about his own actions, he described the recent engagements as even more glorious and brilliant than the Battle of Vitoria. Glascock, who knew many of the officers of the 20th, can have been under no illusions about the ferocity of the fight when Ross described the heavy casualties the regiment had incurred. Not mentioning that he had been bruised by a ball, the general described himself as "perfectly well." Ross's exploits in the Pyrenees were followed closely in Ireland. William Waggett, a friend from Cork with whom he shared a passion for music, wrote to signify his delight in reading the *London Gazette,* which heralded Ross's exploits in the "Pyrenean Fights." Meanwhile, at an assembly in Cork in September 1813, it was agreed to present him with the freedom of the city in honor of his military achievements.[49]

As for Lieutenant Colonel Andrew Wauchope, who succeeded to the command of the 20th on Ross's promotion a few months previously, he would not survive the Peninsular War. Among the possessions of the major general remaining in the hands of his descendants is a sword that was dedicated to him on August 2, 1813, on the heights of Echelar by his regimental successor.⁵⁰ It was a memorable day in more ways than one, for by its close, Wauchope was mortally wounded. That same day too at Echelar, Wellington only narrowly avoided injury, death, or capture once again when he was fired upon during a reconnaissance mission. At the end of ten days of almost incessant fighting, both armies remained where they had begun—at the passes of Roncesvalles and Maya. The physical demands on the troops during these engagements in the Pyrenees were extraordinary. Lieutenant O'Donnell recollected that "after days of hard fighting and indescribable fatigue, he would be often glad to snatch a short repose on the cold ground, with his head pillowed on the flinty rock."⁵¹

After the momentous events at Roncesvalles and Sorauren, the fusilier brigade was largely held in reserve. The men then settled down to winter quarters near Bayonne, France. For some, this was the first time that they "kept" Christmas since they had begun serving on the peninsula. Meanwhile, Sunday services were held in a field near the sea. Considered a "Christian Hero" by an officer who served with him, it is likely Ross attended these services. Pies and puddings were baked, and many "warmed their toes by dancing jigs and reels." The respite for the brigade in terms of heavy fighting came to an end when campaigning resumed in February 1814.⁵² The troops once again became embroiled in close-quarter fighting that resulted in heavy casualties—and Ross in the thick of the fighting as usual.

It was on yet another Sabbath day that the Battle of Orthes was fought, February 27, 1814. Cole's 4th Division was ordered to take the village of Saint-Boes, defended by General Eloi Taupin and the French 4th Division. The attack was led by Ross's brigade. At first the British managed to secure a position in the church and graveyard, "all ready for its victims," on the outskirts of the village. The brigade soon came under a heavy onslaught, the air darkening with enemy shells, however, and was forced to retreat. Taupin's men then charged only to be driven back in turn. Ross then led a second assault on Saint-Boes, this time falling dangerously wounded to a musket ball that hit him in the jowls. For a time it was believed that the wound would prove fatal.⁵³

Four times Cole's division charged, one bloody frontal assault after another, only to be repulsed. Heavy firing continued in the village. Sergeant Cooper of the 1/7th recalled that his company ended up "firing in rapid bopeep fashion" after some of his comrades discovered a large quantity of wine. The "game" became "Drink and fire, fire and drink." The battle had become so intense that "the combatants were completely enshrouded in smoke."[54] Cole's 4th Division was forced to retire when a decisive intervention by the 1/52nd, led by Ross's close friend Lieutenant Colonel Colborne, was crucial in swinging the battle. Besides the serious injuries to Ross and a minor wound suffered by Wellington, a French general, Jean-Pierre Bechaud, was killed.[55]

The British suffered 2,200 casualties in the battle, with Ross's brigade, numbering barely 1,000 men in action, losing 304. No wonder one fusilier called it a "murderous action." At times Wellington deemed a bludgeoning, frontal assault necessary. Ross's brigade, and the 4th Division in general, had softened up the French in Saint-Boes, even if it fell to other units to carry the day. The valor of the enemy troops impressed their British counterparts. A surgeon operating on a French veteran remarked, "I hope you don't feel much pain," to which the wounded man replied, "cut deeper, sir, and you will find the Emperor: he's buried in my heart!" Another old soldier, who was having his arm amputated, cried out "Vive l'Empereur! Vive Napoleon!"[56]

Ross was again among a number of officers voted the thanks of Parliament for the Battle of Orthes, of which the action at Saint-Boes was a part. Recovering from his wounds afterward, he wrote to Glascock making light of the seriousness of his condition. "You will be happy to hear that the hit I got in the chops [jowls] is likely to prove a mere temporary inconvenience. I am doing remarkably well, and trust in two or three weeks to be equal to the fight." Such bullishness from a man who was reluctant to lie down, whether from his own injuries or having horse after horse shot from under him, is unlikely to have pleased his wife. "She is now at my elbow." On hearing news of his wounding, Elizabeth Ross set out on a nearly ninety-mile, five-day journey across snow-clad mountains to be by her husband's side. As the general acknowledged, "her anxiety and spirit carried her through, enabling her to bear the fatigue without suffering from cold or bad weather."[57] As it turned out, she may well have reached the limits of her fortitude in the face of such adversity. This may explain why she became so ill by the time Ross was subsequently posted to America.

It was a measure of this man of action that Ross's principal regret about Orthes was not his actual wound, but having received it early in the battle. Wellington shared his disappointment. In his dispatch after the battle, the British commander expressed "his warm approbation of the exertions of the gallant general (Ross), whose services I was unfortunately deprived of early in the battle." Not one to praise lightly, never mind enthusiastically, Wellington's remarks were occasioned by professional admiration and had nothing to do with childhood friendship.[58] Equally clear, while only a junior in terms of military experience as a general officer, Ross had cut a dash for himself as a hard-hitting commander who was rapidly rising in estimation.

By the time his career fighting the French was over, Ross had accumulated a unique set of medals. Having been seriously wounded in the Helder region of Holland in 1799 and now at Orthes, Ross had seen service in the deserts of Egypt, the parched climes of Malta, and southern Italy and had led his troops in bayonet charges against the armies of Napoleon high in the Pyrenees in sweltering midsummer heat. "No doubt Major-General Ross, in his lonelier moments in the heat of such exotic places, must have thought of the cool winding Lough, the cool green fields, and the tree-covered hills of his Irish home in Rostrevor, County Down."[59]

Even though Robert Ross spent most of his adult life serving abroad with the British army, it is clear that his home village remained close to his heart. It was remarked of him at the time that "like every great and good man he loved the scenes of his youthful days." And it was to his Irish family seat that he planned to return when his military career ended. Ross had settled on a location for a new country mansion on the outskirts of Rostrevor and even personally saw to the planting of trees and the laying out of an approach.[60] But his fighting days were not yet over.

CHAPTER 3

"Secret" Orders

It was some months before General Ross could resume his duties after he incurred such a serious wound during the Battles of Orthes. But with it, his days of fighting the French were over. Napoleon's abdication in April 1814 signaled the imminent conclusion of the war. For the British government, this afforded the opportunity to scale back military spending as well as redirect resources to the war declared against the British by the U.S. Congress on June 18, 1812. Instead of making his eagerly awaited return to Ireland, Ross was designated to participate in operations in the United States, departing with "secret orders."[1] Explaining how he came to have a semi-independent command charged with undertaking an "enterprize" in North America instead of only a brigade in a larger amphibious army is vital to understanding what transpired when he landed in the United States.

The din of battle in Europe had not subsided when the British government considered where to strike with at least part of its "invincible" army in the concurrent war against the United States. By early January 1814, in anticipation of Napoleon's defeat, Lord Bathurst, secretary for war and the colonies, was consulting Wellington about a proposal to send 20,000 men to America. This was to be the military dimension to a "grand expedition" that would mount seaborne offensives against targets on the eastern and southern coasts of the United States.[2] The Royal Navy commanded these waters, after all, so the seizure of New Orleans and pursuit of additional strategic interests in Louisiana became the expedition's ultimate goal.[3] It is not without significance in this regard that War Office documentation dealing with these matters is entitled "Expedition to the Southern Coasts."[4] A focus on this southern strategy coincided with the appointment of Vice Admiral Sir Alexander Cochrane to the command of the North American station in December 1813. According to Roger Morriss, these issues had been "fully discussed" with him in London prior to his appointment. Governor of Guadaloupe since 1810, Cochrane had ample time to assess the strategic situation in the Gulf of Mexico. He was also keenly aware of the lucrative prize pot that could be secured by the capture of New Orleans. In terms of army command, it was originally intended that a much more senior officer than Major General Ross would take charge of these amphibious operations.[5]

In assessing Ross's role in the war with the United States, it is important not only to understand the issues that gave rise to hostilities but also to have an appreciation of the military situation by the time he became involved. Known today as the War of 1812, at the time Federalists, bitter political enemies of President James Madison, called it "Mr. Madison's War," while the administration's supporters labeled it the "Second War of Independence." In Britain it was called "the American war."[6] Longstanding American grievances included British restrictions on U.S. trade, the infamous "Orders in Council," which forced neutral ships to call into British ports and pay a duty. The Royal Navy's impressment of American seamen also rankled—the British navy was desperate for manpower in the war against Napoleon. Meanwhile, "War Hawks" in Congress eyed a land grab in British North America—Britain's difficulty with France was America's opportunity.

The consequent American invasion of the Canadas made little progress. British forces under the governor general, Lieutenant General Sir George Prevost, the "Savior of British North America," fought a successful holding operation.[7] With the focus on the grand stage in Europe, the conflict with the United States was a sideshow for the British. It was quipped at the time that "half the people of England do not know there is war with America, and those who did have forgotten it."[8] But this was about to change. With Napoleon defeated, Wellington's troops, with which he had once famously stated he could "go anywhere and do anything," faced the prospect of being demobilized or redeployed to other theaters.[9] Troops in other commands as well as in garrison were also under consideration for service in North America. The U.S. declaration of war was viewed as a stab in the back when Britain was engaged in a costly war with France. It was not going to be forgiven lightly. For many, there was a score to settle. In the case of Cochrane, his grudge against the Americans dated back to the War of Independence, during which his brother was killed. The prevalence of a vengeful spirit being acknowledged, it is also important to stress that others, like Ross, regretted that hostilities had broken out between two nations so allied by kindred. It was his ardent hope that peace would soon be concluded.[10]

James Bayard, one of the American peace commissioners in London at the time, noted in the late spring of 1814 that the British resented the growing wealth and maritime capability of the United States and that they were determined "to crush us altogether and if that be impracticable to inflict such wounds as will put a stop to our growth or at least retard it."[11] In June, fellow peace commissioner Albert Gallatin signified that the British desire to teach America a lesson was a widely held viewpoint. The American negotiators were meant to be feeling the heat. British military preparations at this time had a fourfold purpose: securing the borders of British North America, undertaking amphibious operations with the ultimate objective of targeting New Orleans and Louisiana, cranking up pressure on the American negotiators to agree to favorable terms for the British, and if that failed, bringing force to bear so the Americans would heel "like spaniels," as Vice Admiral Cochrane put it.[12]

In Britain President Madison replaced Napoleon as a figure to despise. Radical newspaper editor William Cobbett claimed that war fever was stoked up by *The Times* as well as vested interests that had profited from conflict.[13] The public anticipated that Madison would be deposed, sharing Cochrane's aspiration in this respect. Surveying British newspapers of the time, Troy Bickham notes how victory against France "inflated the British national ego" and that there was a "supporting chorus throughout the British Isles" to reduce the United States to a "client state." Whatever about the popular clamor at the time, even though the British government was determined to cow the United States to some extent, this was not an attempt to "quash" American independence.[14]

Between January and May, military correspondence indicates that a decided shift in British strategy in North America was being seriously considered, defense giving way to offense. British ministers shared the popular appetite to punish the Americans. In mid-April 1814 Colonel Henry Torrens, military secretary at Horse Guards in London, wrote that "the government have determined to give Jonathan [a British nickname for the 'wayward' United States] a good drubbing." This corresponded with the view of the new senior Royal Navy officer operating on the American station.[15]

When hostilities with France ended in April 1814, Wellington's invincibles started to assemble in the Bordeaux area, waiting to find out where the next posting would be—whether back home to Britain and Ireland or to America—or indeed if their units were to be disbanded or their periods of service terminated. And while there was tough-talking rhetoric in the British press and among senior military officers in relation to the American war, the reality was that the government was not only war weary but also faced competing demands when it came to redeploying forces. Discontent was said to be brewing in Ireland once again. Before the year was out, the Insurrection Act was renewed, following a lapse of several years. Torrens was astounded to learn that the "Irish government require 40,000 men!" Whether for garrison purposes or to bolster security in the country, twenty-four of Wellington's regiments were reassigned there at the conclusion of the war with France.[16]

Ross, his wife, Elizabeth, and their young family were caught up in the suspense of what was going to happen next—would he receive another posting or would he retire to Rostrevor? Meanwhile, back in London decisions had already been made about the redeployment of troops and the coalescing plans for the American expedition. On the same day that Bathurst wrote to Wellington to begin assembling regiments for service in America, he also wrote to Prevost to assure him that he could expect reinforcements at the earliest opportunity. In rapid succession the 29th, 97th, 1/6th, and 1/82nd—the latter two Wellington units—were selected for service in Canada. The 4/1st Battalion (Royal Scots) and the 1/62nd joined them.[17]

The main focus of British military preparations at this time centered on what Torrens described as the "expedition of magnitude" against the coast of the United States. Bathurst emphasized that it was to be "independent and that this corps d'armée is not intended to fall under the command of Sir George Prevost or of Sir John Sherbrooke [lieutenant governor of Nova Scotia]."[18] The use of the term "corps d'armée" was no accident. A concept honed by Napoleon, it was meant to be a self-sufficient military unit. This substantial seaborne strike force was to link up with the fleet under Cochrane's command. The admiral had been appointed with a specific brief to implement a more robust offensive policy on targets along the Atlantic coast of the United States with a view to pressuring the American government into conceding to terms to end the war promptly. Fire and sword was to be the order of the day. In January 1814 Cochrane requested "a quantity of combustible material . . . calculated for burning ships, wharfs, Block Houses, etc."[19]

For the new commander, separating the northern and southern states was also a cherished goal. Even more, New Orleans was the plum prize to him, for strategic as well as personal reasons. As he wrote even before the American war broke out, "whoever has possession of the mouth of the River [Mississippi] must have the inhabitants of the interior more or less under his control." There was also the tempting prospect of a share in a vast pot of prize money that the capture of New Orleans offered, one estimated to be 20 million dollars.[20]

Examining British trans-Atlantic troop movements in 1814, historian Donald E. Graves has documented that army regulars in North America were to "more than double—from 19,477 to 48,163 officers and men." In general terms, while the redcoats were indeed coming, they were not comprised mainly of Wellington veterans. Of the reinforcements sent, the Peninsular army contributed twenty-one units. A further twenty-three units were drawn from other commands.[21] More specifically, in relation to the planned amphibious army that was being assembled in the late spring, correspondence sent to the Commissariat Department in the Peninsular army indicates that it was to comprise 17,000–18,000 men, including cavalry and artillery units. A total of 13,000–14,000 men were to come from Wellington's army, with others drawn from commands in the Mediterranean.[22]

The ultimate strategic objective was to be an attack on New Orleans, weather permitting, in December 1814. Having discussed potential intervening targets while in London with Bathurst at the War Office and with Robert Dundas, Lord Melville, first lord of the Admiralty, Cochrane recapped these deliberations in a detailed letter to Melville based on the premise that a very substantial amphibious force was going to be placed at his disposal. He weighed whether and how to attack New York, Boston, or Philadelphia. Should Baltimore be targeted, its capture should be followed up by marching on Alexandria, Georgetown, and Washington. Annapolis, Richmond, and Norfolk were all considered assailable too.[23]

Under the original plan, generals were *invited* to take part in the operation. Because these senior officers were not *ordered*, it made it easier for them to demur. Command of the expedition was to be offered to Sir John Hope, with Sir Rowland Hill (soon to be ennobled Lord Hill) as second choice. Other generals being considered to command the two divisions included Sir Lowry Cole, Major General Charles Colville, Major General James Kempt, Sir George Murray,

Sir Edward Pakenham, and Sir Henry Clinton. In an effort to flatter Clinton into agreeing to become involved, he was informed that only the best troops and officers had been selected for the expedition. This was not entirely true, however, as Wellington endeavored to ensure that his famous Light Division remained in Europe.[24]

Yet hoping for Hope to lead the American expedition proved forlorn. In the middle of April, during a sortie near Toulouse, he was wounded and taken prisoner by the French. Due to his wound, Hope informed Bathurst on May 2 that it was not possible for him to command the American expedition. Wounded or not, though, he made it very clear that he did not wish to participate. With just over a month before the first troops were to embark, therefore, Bathurst was faced with the prospect of having to scramble for a replacement commanding officer. Lord Hill, Wellington's "favourite subordinate" and known affectionately to his troops as "Daddy," was the preferred choice. But Hill did not want to go to America either. Writing to his sister from Toulouse on April 30, he stressed that he was "truly anxious to get home" and had no intention of accepting the command. Circumstantial evidence suggests that when Torrens described the attitude of a "great personage" to the command of the American expedition as "abominable," he had Hill in mind.[25]

Murray also let it be known in no uncertain terms that he was not tempted by the offer of a division command either. Quite simply, compared to serving with Wellington, going to America was "sinking very considerably." In reality, Murray was trying to secure a position in Ireland. Not wishing to participate either, a relieved Pakenham wrote, "I think I have escaped America, and shall consider myself vastly fortunate in having been spared from such a service." It thus comes as no surprise that Wellington advised Bathurst that he was likely to be "disappointed" in his "expectations that some of the officers will go upon this expedition." Among the senior generals, only Clinton proved amenable, but his letter of acceptance certainly did not ring with enthusiasm.[26] Hard-earned reputations might easily be ruined in the United States.

The major generals being considered to lead the three brigades in each of the two divisions proved to be more receptive. Of the original six listed to take part, four undertook operations in North America—James Kempt, Frederick Robinson, Manley Power, and Robert Ross. That they were all relatively junior generals is revealed by the fact that the last three were promoted to major general on the same day in early June 1813.[27] Besides the call of duty, the opportunity to gain more laurels may have appealed to such ambitious officers. Wellington ruled out a fifth, Denis Pack, owing to wounds, even though Pack himself was prepared to go. Only Edward Barnes declined the offer of command.[28]

Two divisions, comprising eighteen regiments organized in six brigades, had been scheduled to accompany Lord Hill. By May 16, besides those drawn from other commands, the units from Wellington's army allocated to participate in this offensive included twelve infantry regiments as well as the 14th Regiment of Dragoons (see table 3.1).[29] Ross was nominated to command a brigade made up of the 1/40th, 5/60th, and 1/81st, although in the end none of these regiments accompanied him to America. His brigade was to form part of a division under Major General Kempt. Like Ross, Kempt had risen to national fame at the Battle of Maida in 1806. Apart from the 1/28th and 5/60th, all the other regiments nominated served at some point in the war with the United States.

Table 3.1. Adjutant General's Office, Toulouse, 16 May 1814, General Orders

The following Regiments being destined for a particular Service, are to be formed into Brigades and Divisions, as follows, and to be Commanded by the General Officers as set down for them.

Lieutenant General Lord Hill to Command		
First Division—Lt. Gen. Sir Henry Clinton		
Maj. Gen. Barnes	**Col. Keane**	**Col. O'Callaghan**
1/3rd (W) Canada	1/4th (W) Chesapeake	1/39th (W) Canada
1/27th (O) Canada	1/44th (O) Chesapeake	1/58th (O) Canada
1/37th (O) Canada	57th (W) Canada	85th (W) Chesapeake
Second Division—Maj. Gen. James Kempt		
Maj. Gen. Power	**Maj. Gen. Robinson**	**Maj. Gen. Ross**
1/5th (W) Canada	1/9th (W) Canada	1/40th (W) Louisiana
3/27th (W) Canada	76th (W) Canada	5/60th (W)
1/28th (W)	1/88th (W) Canada	1/81st (O) Canada
14th Regiment of Light Dragoons (W) Louisiana		

Key: This table includes the origins as well as the ultimate destinations for the units under consideration. (W) stands for Wellington units and (O) for those from other commands in the Mediterranean and United Kingdom.

At almost the same time that the command structure and composition of Lord Hill's expedition was being finalized in the south of France, back in London Lord Bathurst issued new instructions to postpone this organizational effort on May 18.[30] Three new "divisions" (essentially brigades) were identified for North America instead, only one of which was retained for service on the U.S. coast, the other two being directed to Canada. An additional four regiments were also designated to reinforce Prevost and provide him with an offensive capability. All these troops were to be sent off "under sealed orders to be opened at sea in order keep up the idea that a force is sent to the southern parts" of the United States, as Torrens put it in private correspondence. Lord Hill confirmed that it was government policy at the time to "keep up the idea of a large force going to America."[31] As a result, it was hoped to perpetuate the impression that towns and cities along the eastern and southern coasts of the United States were potentially threatened with attack. This ruse would hopefully assist the British goal of diverting American military resources from the frontier with Canada. Whether Ross would go to Canada or be part of the American operation had not yet been determined.

Word of the decision to postpone the main expedition at this stage and to substantially reinforce the British army in Canada instead took some time to reach the south of France. On May 27 the Earl of Dalhousie, who was in charge of military arrangements at Bordeaux, noted how "the former plan of expedition has been abandoned." It was evidently with considerable frustration that he informed Sir George Murray at the Quartermaster's Department that he had received correspondence from Bathurst "altering all the plan of the expedition." In turn, Murray, writing two days later, highlighted just how late in the day the decision to change the destination of so many of the troops had been received—some having begun to board ship. Among them were men that Ross was destined to command.[32] While the government had not given up hope that Hill could be persuaded at a later stage to lead a recast expedition to the South, whether he wanted to or not, the difficulties being experienced in finding a suitable overall commander, as well as two senior generals to lead the divisions, prompted a last-minute change of mind about troop deployments. In the end, as Torrens explained, "nearly the same extent of force is intended to proceed from the Garonne to Canada as a reinforcement to Sir George Prevost."[33]

A total of twelve regiments that had previously been scheduled to participate in the American expedition ultimately served in Canada, including eight Wellington regiments (see table 1).

It was against this disruptive backdrop that Bathurst identified Barnes and Ross as the prospective commander of the remaining brigade that would link up with Cochrane in Bermuda. Essentially, these troops were to form the vanguard of the expeditionary force that was ultimately to target the southern shores of the United States. The orders for this brigade were made out in the name of Barnes, who was senior to Ross on the army list. Torrens later recalled that Wellington was ultimately given the task of selecting a "separate brigade in charge of any officer whom he thought best calculated to conduct an enterprize for service upon the coast of America. His Grace named Major-General Ross."[34] Whether Ross was chosen in preference to or in place of Barnes, who had declined to serve in America, is unclear.

Reflecting the fact that redirecting substantial forces to Canada was an afterthought, it was to be June 3 before a "plan of campaign" for these reinforcements was sent to Governor General Prevost, reaching him by the second week of July. Prevost was informed that he was to receive 10,000 infantry "for the defence of Canada, or for the offensive actions on the Frontier to which your attention will be particularly drawn." Preparations for Hill's expedition having consumed Horse Guards and the Admiralty, Prevost was unfairly put under last-minute pressure to take the offensive. If he did not get a sufficient hint in this regard from his official instructions at this time, a further letter, which Bathurst wrote to him, made the government's expectations crystal clear. "I am bound in fairness to apprize you that if you shall allow the present campaign to close without having undertaken offensive measures against the enemy, you will very seriously disappoint the expectations of the Prince Regent and the Country." Prevost was given specific targets. Among the lengthy list of objectives were the destruction of Sackett's Harbor, achieving naval domination on Lakes Erie and Champlain, the retention of Fort Niagara, and restoring "Detroit and the whole of the Michigan Country to the Indians."[35]

Out of a total of 14,619 men from Wellington's army who were sent from southern France to serve in North America by June 6, only 1,270 infantrymen were allocated to Ross for seaborne diversionary operations. These were to be supplemented by 700 men from the 1/44th, artillery units, some 1,500 others comprising the 1/21st from the Mediterranean, and Royal Marines, making a total force of around 4,000 men. The rest of the troops from Wellington's command originally earmarked for Hill's expedition went to Canada instead under the command of Major Generals Kempt, Robinson, and Power. Canada, which had been the "cockpit" of the war to date, would remain the focus of British efforts at least until Hill undertook his projected expedition to New Orleans in December, considered the optimum time of year for operations in that region.[36] The responsibility for giving the United States a "good drubbing" had been transferred from Hill to Prevost. The actual allocation of additional military resources to him, however, far from justified such giddy expectations.

Ross's expedition may be characterized as an initial commitment to the government's southern strategy. When Lord Hill returned to London at the end of May, he revealed to his sister that he had been "told" that it was the *"particular wish* of [the] Government that I should go" to America, with plans made for Ross to link up with him at a later stage.[37] In the meantime, according to his orders, Ross's operations on the coast of the United States were of secondary importance, tying down U.S. military resources that might otherwise be used to engage Prevost's forces in Canada. The general's forces now constituting a radically reduced amphibious capability, no specific targets were identified by the government in London, contrary to Cochrane's expectations. While afloat, Ross was under the command of Cochrane, who was authorized to determine potential targets. The general, however, had the discretion to concur or demur with the vice admiral as he saw fit. He was also solely in charge once the troops made landfall. Instructions made clear that the relatively small size of Ross's force "will sufficiently point out to you that you are not to engage in any extended operations at a distance from the coast." Besides, Wellington noted that this expedition was not going to be easily supplied and regretted that it was the least provided for.[38] With many of these troops unpaid for some time, $200,000 had to be sent after Ross on board a frigate, not least with a view to satisfying such arrears; evidently, the men were expected to spend their wages on purchases on American soil. But the most crucial deficiency of all was the total absence of a cavalry capacity necessary for effective reconnaissance. Expectations of what Ross might achieve with his pocket-sized army were evidently underwhelming. Anyone who knew the general would have realized that he was never going to eat the "bread of idleness," to use his own words. Torrens was convinced that his "old friend Ross" would "act with more than common promptitude" when he reached North America.[39]

Plans for sending additional troops had been under discussion since January 1814. On a professional and personal level, Ross was only given a very short period of time to consider the offer of a command. Still recovering from the life-threatening wound that he suffered at Orthes in February 1814, he was arguably physically unfit for field command at that time. He could easily have declined serving in America on medical grounds without any stain on his honor. But it was not in his nature to shrink from a challenge. On May 14 Ross was offered command of a brigade—a prompt reply was requested. The following day he duly obliged in a typically ebullient fashion: "The offer of the command of a brigade in the Expedition about to proceed from Bordeaux to America is such that cannot be refused." Claiming that he had made a complete recovery from his injuries, the general made immediate plans to travel to Bordeaux. Officers who served with Ross in America maintained that Wellington had implored him to accept the command.[40] In reaching his decision, though, Ross had no idea that he would become the commanding officer of a discrete corps, such was the secrecy shrouding his mission.

Whether the general was as enthusiastic as his letter of acceptance indicates is another matter. His subordinate on the expedition, Colonel Arthur Brooke, indicated that Ross, still recovering from his wound, was far from pleased. An Irish barrister who knew him well also indicated that he accepted the command with a heavy heart, though "health and love oppose."[41] Steeped in an honor code, his keen sense of duty prevailed. It was a decision that came at an enormous personal price in terms of his domestic situation. Ross had to set sail without arrangements being finalized to transport his family back to the United Kingdom and left his ailing wife, whom he affectionately called "Ly," to see to these matters.

Ross sent his last comforting letter to his heartbroken spouse before departing from Pauillac, on the Gironde estuary. He was clearly a worried man. "Be therefore my Ly more cheerful. Do not look upon the black side of the picture but be *convinced* of our speedily meeting again, when our happiness will be heightened my Ly by our temporary separation. The care of our little fellow requires that every consideration should be had to your Health which must be lost if you yield to a Depression of spirits."[42] Known for his generosity, the general told her to purchase "everything" to the "*smallest* degree" that she needed and that "should the four hundred pounds not be sufficient draw four more." In a further attempt to raise her spirits, he resorted to his characteristic charm and wit. "The old master of the house in which I am billeted proposes paying you a visit. He is a pilot of this harbor and frequently goes to Bordeaux. His wife of about 60 has gained my heart so that my departure is lucky, the old gentleman is 74 so beware of his attractions." He also explained that two officers recently arrived from England reckoned that peace would soon be concluded with the United States.[43] The couple's separation, therefore, might last only a matter of months.

What Ross did not tell his wife was that the Quarter Master General's Department of Wellington's army had organized twelve months' supplies for his expedition. His correspondence throughout his American service betrays a man haunted by the state of his wife's mental health, perhaps believing that she was suicidal. Family records reveal that she later partially "destroyed her husband's correspondence in a passing fit of insanity." While some of his letters to her remain extant, none are known to exist from her to him. Besides her mental fragility, Elizabeth Ross was prone to ill physical health. General Ross's enduring concern throughout his expedition to America was the "sentiment of having acted an unkind part to my Ly in leaving her in a foreign country with careless servants about her."[44]

Fortunately for Mrs. Ross, senior figures in the army and navy looked out for her. Sir Henry Clinton tried to reassure Ross by saying that he had seen his wife "well" before he left Bordeaux. No doubt the arrival in the area of the 4th Division, including the 20th Regiment, cheered her somewhat. After that it was only left for Clinton to ensure that she could remain as long as necessary in the home that she had been occupying in Bordeaux. Housing, it appears, was the least of her troubles. Getting sea passage to England was much more difficult. That she had been stranded along with the spouses of other senior servicemen upset Rear Admiral Pulteney Malcolm, who was to accompany Ross to America. Worried about the general's wife, about whom he made representations to Lord Keith (probably in relation to transport to England), Malcolm wrote to his own wife, "should Mrs. Ross land at Plymouth be civil to her."[45]

Instead of making arrangements for her to return to the family seat of Rostrevor in Ireland, Ross wanted her to travel to Clifton, Bristol, where she was to stay with his brother's family. According to tradition passed down through the Ross family in Rostrevor, the general's wife had a "presentiment she would never see him again"— a spine-tingling sensation no doubt felt by many a soldier's spouse, although no less harrowing for that.[46]

Not only is it enlightening to understand Ross's state of mind at the prospect of his American expedition, but it is important to appreciate that of the troops and naval forces involved as well. Perhaps unsurprisingly, many in both services were reluctant to go. Among the troops assigned to the expedition was the 1st Battalion, 44th Regiment, commanded by Colonel Brooke, from County Fermanagh in the north of Ireland. The 1/44th had seen service in eastern Spain. When they reached Bordeaux on May 26, after a march from Tarragona totaling 526 miles, Brooke recalled remaining there for two days. Like many others, he was clearly thinking that they would soon see their friends and family at home. But what actually happened next was clearly a shock. After two more days of marching, the 1/44th found itself aboard ship, convinced that America was their destination. This had occurred "with but a few hours warning. All this, naturally could not be very agreeable, from the General [Ross] to the Drum Boy, although all were obliged to put on a good face." Some of the Royal Navy captains in the expedition were furious that they only discovered their destination from newspapers and army officers. Malcolm was absolutely livid. What made matters worse for him was his conviction "that there is not much in store for us" in America. How wrong he proved to be.[47]

While some of the older hands were fed up with war and hankered for home, some of the younger guns were keener for the fray. For eighteen-year-old Lieutenant George Robert Gleig of the 85th Regiment, son of the Bishop of Brechin in Scotland, peace promised poor promotion prospects and half-pay. Like many of his colleagues, in these circumstances he was keen to pursue his martial career. Besides, his regiment had not suffered such severe losses as other units, and the war with the United States afforded the opportunity to garner more laurels. Gleig's accounts of the campaign in America provide fascinating details on what transpired. But as Robin Reilly rightly cautions, he was a junior officer who was wholly unapprised of command decision making.[48]

For Captain Harry Smith, the proposed American expedition was a heaven-sent opportunity to try to secure promotion to major. Smith recalled being at Castel Sarrasin when Colonel John Colborne, commander of the 1/52nd, urged him to ride with him to headquarters in Toulouse to secure a position on the impending operation. When they arrived in time for breakfast, Colborne informed him that "my old friend Ross . . . is going. I will go and ask him to take you as his Major of Brigade." According to Smith, the general knew him during the retreat to Corunna. So by 4:00 P.M. the captain's involvement had been confirmed, and he returned to Castel Sarrasin "after a little canter of sixty-eight miles, not regarded as any act of prowess, but just a ride. In those days there were men."[49] Modesty was not one of Smith's virtues. His high opinion of himself and low opinion of others was marked.

Unfortunately for Smith, another highly talented young officer also considered the American expedition a welcomed opportunity for career advancement and vied with him for Ross's favor. This was Lieutenant George De Lacy Evans, deputy quartermaster general and an Irishman like his commanding officer. Ross was well pleased with his staff officers. Having initially described Smith as "sharp, active and intelligent," he remarked later that his brigade major "improves much with acquaintance." As it happened, a fraught relationship was to develop between Smith and Ross, accounting in no small measure for Smith's sometimes spiteful published account of the American campaign—a version of events cited by generations of historians without question even though it is riddled with inaccuracies. The key to understanding Smith's jaundiced recollection of events lies in the contrasting relationship that developed between Evans and Ross. In a letter to his wife, recalling that Evans had previously visited them during dinner in Bordeaux, the general lavished praise on his deputy quartermaster general as "an extremely intelligent, active fellow and an *Irishman.*" In a classic case of the kettle calling the pot black, Smith accused Evans of "burning with ambition."[50]

The careerist attitude of Gleig, Smith, and Evans gives an insight into the mindset of some of the "hirelings" in the British army, featured in the words of Francis Scott Key's "Star-Spangled Banner." These were professional soldiers, which made them so hard to beat. It gave them a decided advantage over the citizen-soldiers, the part-time militia, who made up the overwhelming majority of the U.S. forces they were to encounter.

Less pleasing for Gleig and other officers was the short notice of the order to proceed to embarkation and the requirement to get rid of their horses immediately. With just two days' warning, this was necessarily done at an "enormous loss." And with a shortage of ready money, the best that some officers and men could secure for their animals in a bartering economy was a plentiful supply of alcohol. A donkey, it was said, fetched a bottle of brandy. Ross meanwhile wrote to his wife prior to departing for America, giving her instructions about how to spend the money if his muleteer managed to get a "decent" price for his animals. Ever generous, Ross told her to give the muleteer a "few dollars" as he was a "*bona mano*" while "Hales" was to get an extra three or four dollars from the proceeds as he had looked after him well when he was wounded.[51]

None of the regiments in the fusilier brigade that Ross had commanded were considered for the expedition, probably owing to the high levels of casualties they had suffered during the latter part of the war with France. Ross's attachment to the 20th was not completely severed, however, as Captain Thomas Falls served as his aide-de-camp on the American expedition. Two privates from the 20th, Samuel Barber and Isaac Dodd, accompanied the general on board Malcolm's flagship, HMS *Royal Oak*, probably as his manservants.[52]

The 1/4th, 1/44th, and 85th were assigned to Ross's new command. They marched for Pauillac, a small port on the Garonne River near Bordeaux, at the end of May. As they passed a major army encampment, they were saluted with the strains of "The British Grenadiers" by the bands of the regiments that remained and given "three hearty cheers," which "gladdened" the ear of many men who would otherwise have dearly loved to return home, even for a short time. Last to board ship on June 1 was General Ross, who was accompanied by the faithful Captain Falls and Lieutenant Evans, soon to become his most indispensable staff officer. The following day, after being delayed by winds, the expedition set sail, sixteen vessels in all, while another ship was scheduled to follow with entrenching tools.[53] Sailing with sealed orders that were not to be opened until well out at sea, Ross did not know where he was destined. That his tiny army would make such an indelible imprint on world history must have been unimaginable at the time.

CHAPTER 4

"TOO LATE" FOR THE CHESAPEAKE

As British reinforcements made their way to North America, speculation ran rife in the press about their prospective operations. At the beginning of June 1814, *The Times* in London trumpeted that it would not be long before the British flag would fly in Washington. According to historian John R. Grodzinski, the impression conveyed by the government at the time, and by many historians since, was that a "red-coated juggernaut of elite" Wellington troops had been unleashed on the Americans. This was an exaggeration as the troops from the Peninsular army dispatched to North America only represented about a quarter of the duke's infantry.[1] That being the case in reality, the British government and public had high expectations of what could be achieved.

While it was an open secret that a force of some description was destined for the shores of the United States, Major General Ross and Rear Admiral Malcolm were told not to open their "sealed instructions" before they reached the Bay of Biscay. On June 10 Ross revealed in a letter to his wife that Bermuda was his destination, although she was urged to keep this information to herself "as the orders are secret," despite the fact that he was convinced that it was widely known in England where they were going. "Of what is to take place on my reaching Bermuda, I of course cannot inform you but still think that the trip back again will be the most likely consequence." These were not the sentiments of a man hell-bent on chastising the Americans. Ross was holding out hope that a peace deal would be brokered without him having to fight. In this respect he may have been influenced by Wellington's reported view that the expeditionary force might never have to set foot on American soil.[2]

Ross's main concern on his trans-Atlantic journey was the mental and physical well-being of his wife. The letters that he wrote her during the American expedition were repetitive, although this is less to do with the fact that he lacked a flair for original writing than due to his overwhelming concern for her welfare. Very much out of character with his normally self-assured, good-humored nature, his correspondence shows that domestic concerns weighed heavily on his mind. In the Azores on July 13, he took advantage of a ship traveling from the islands to write to his wife, expressing his hope to see her again before the end of the year.[3]

At times during the expedition, Ross was pensive and troubled. Besides his concern for his wife, he was still struggling with ill health following his near-fatal wounding at Orthes several months earlier. All the same, the general had an army to inspire and a relationship to forge with his colleagues in the Royal Navy. To these matters he attended with consummate skill during the voyage. In the first instance he had to win over Rear Admiral Malcolm, who had been looking forward to serving with his old friend, Lord Hill. Of his first encounter with Ross, the Scottish admiral's comment was short, certainly not sweet: "General Ross goes with me. I have just seen him. He is an Irishman." Despite this initial coolness, in no time at all the two men struck up a close personal relationship. Before long Malcolm noted how pleased he was with his army shipmates. Soon after he remarked that Ross was "highly distinguished as an active good officer." Of the Peninsular War veterans sailing with him on the *Royal Oak*, the rear admiral crowed that they would shortly show the Americans "what it is to have an enemy in their country. They have been so habituated to fight that they delight in it." Toward the end of June the convoy stopped off at St. Michael's in the Azores, where fresh supplies of cattle and vegetables were taken on board. Malcolm was unaware at this time that the rest of the troops originally allocated for the expedition had been sent off to Canada instead, a measure of the secrecy associated with the expedition. He told British consul general of the Azores, William Harding Read, that he should expect 10,000 men to follow.[4]

During the voyage, officers whiled away the time reading (Lieutenant George Gleig chose the ever popular *Don Quixote*), keeping diaries, playing draughts, writing a newspaper (the *Atlantic News*), or spending hours trying to harpoon dolphins.[5] One officer even brought along his dog. To raise morale, on July 19 Malcolm signaled an invitation to the officers to join him that evening. The visitors discovered the quarterdeck of his flagship turned into a theater. At 7:00 P.M. the curtain drew up and officers of the *Royal Oak* and the artillery performed "The Apprentice," followed by "Mayor of Garret." Afterward came music and dancing. With so few women on board, most of the officers danced as couples. Malcolm and Ross joined the fun.[6] As commanding officer of the troops, the general attended to such official duties with characteristic warmth and enthusiasm, helping forge a spirit of comradeship for the challenges that lay ahead.

Amid all the speculation that a large force was on its way, Vice Admiral Sir Alexander Cochrane sailed to Bermuda to rendezvous with it. In expectation of its imminent arrival, he penned a proclamation to the "Great and Illustrious Chiefs of the Indian Nations" on July 1 to solicit their military assistance, promising that "great Fleets and Armies" were on their way and that the Americans would end up begging for peace. Writing on the same day to Rear Admiral Cockburn, who was operating in the Chesapeake Bay, he revealed the reason for his optimism. An officer had arrived from England who informed him that Lord Hill was expected from Bordeaux with 15,000 men, soon to be joined by regiments based in the Mediterranean as well as others from England and Ireland. Relishing their prospective arrival, he also noted that he had as yet no directions from the government about prospective targets. Buoyant, his conviction that "with [the former slaves] properly armed and backed with 20,000 British troops, Mr. Maddison [sic] will be hurled from his throne" seemed on the point of being realized. This stated intention to solicit the help of slaves jangled frayed American nerves.[7] The senior British naval commander had also eagerly looked forward to serving with his highly talented nephew, the dashing Lord Thomas Cochrane. Lord Cochrane had been christened "Sea Wolf" by Napoleon for his daring attacks on French shipping, resulting in fifty captures in the Mediterranean alone, as well as for his part in British raids on the French coast. Before departing for American waters, however, Lord Cochrane was arrested in connection with a sensational fraud case just as he was about to set sail to serve as flag captain for his uncle.[8] It was to be a lucky escape for the Americans and a blow to Admiral Cochrane's plans.

While waiting in Bermuda on the army to arrive, Cochrane received two letters from Sir George Prevost dated June 1 and 2 that were to have a vital bearing on what happened when Ross arrived in theater. American forces had burnt the village of Dover and the hamlets of Turkey Point and Port Ryerse in the Long Point area of Upper Canada in mid-May. Prevost sent the vice admiral a copy of instructions that had been given to Lieutenant General Sir Gordon Drummond, ordering him to retaliate. He also requested the assistance of the Royal Navy in taking additional retaliatory measures.[9]

Prevost's correspondence in early June affirms his belief that the burning of the U.S. villages of Black Rock and Buffalo in December 1813 had revenged the earlier destruction of Newark by American forces, which had resulted in hundreds of civilians being left homeless in the middle of the severe Canadian winter. The new outrages at Long Point were important in shaping British retaliatory policy by the time Ross arrived. It is important to bear in mind that the British had been far from blameless in terms of torching American settlements in the intervening period, particularly in the Chesapeake Bay area.[10] That being acknowledged, from a British perspective, Rear Admiral Edward Codrington confirms that new American outrages in Canada, even after Prevost had tried to settle the score, were a crucial factor in Cochrane wishing to inflict the "severest retaliation." Neither had the burning of the parliament buildings of York (modern-day Toronto) or of civilian homes in Newark by the Americans been forgotten—they featured in the ongoing discussions among senior commanders.[11]

To some extent, earlier U.S. depredations had had a cumulative effect that governed Prevost's attitude by early June 1814. Canadian historian Donald E. Graves contends that the hardline approach adopted by Cochrane was critically influenced by "Prevost's request to retaliate for Long Point." Not that the vice admiral needed much encouragement on this score. Some months before receiving the governor general's request, however, as Graves also points out, Cochrane had already made his intentions clear to Cockburn, operating in the Chesapeake Bay. American "Sea Port Towns laid in ashes & the Country wasted will be some sort of a retaliation for their savage Conduct in Canada" and that revenge attacks should be "made near to the seat of their Government from whence those Orders emanated."[12]

Prevost's correspondence to Cochrane of early June was followed by his receipt on July 15 of an advance copy of the orders Lord Bathurst had given Ross.[13] Significantly in terms of retaliatory policy, Ross was told that "if in any descent you shall be enabled to take such a position as to threaten the Inhabitants with the destruction of their property, you are hereby authorized to levy upon them contributions in exchange for your forbearance." Military equipment, harbors, and shipping were to be either destroyed or confiscated. That towns and cities were to be razed in the event of a ransom not being paid was not mentioned explicitly, but this was the definite thrust.

Bathurst clearly meant that private property was also to suffer. This was not a novel departure in terms of government policy, for these orders mirrored those given to Colonel Sir Sidney Beckwith when he was operating in the Chesapeake area the previous year; Beckwith did not implement them.[14]

Embracing Bathurst's instructions to Ross in orders that Cochrane issued on July 18, naval officers were directed to "destroy and lay waste such Towns and Districts upon the Coast as you may find assailable." That same day he qualified these orders in a "Secret Memo" to his commanders, which authorized them to accept a ransom in lieu of destruction, although military installations and equipment would be destroyed regardless. Cochrane was even more specific in indicating that "private property" was only going to be "spared" in the event of "contributions" being paid. In general, the language employed in the "Secret Memo" was almost identical to that contained in the orders to Ross and Beckwith. In a memorial drawn up by Cochrane several years later, he specifically stated that the "secret Memorandum was founded by your Memorialist upon the Orders given by Earl Bathurst . . . for the Guidance of the Commanders of His Majesty's forces employed on the North Coast of America."[15]

While the ransom provision in the "Secret Memo" was not Cochrane's idea in the first place, as has been assumed, there is no doubt that he enthusiastically endorsed the idea. Often accused of being obsessed with securing prize money, the vice admiral was more than prepared to cash in on righteous indignation as the occasion offered—retribution or ransom suited him. Anticipating that this "species of warfare" would "accumulate much of the Enemy's property," HMS *Hebrus*, a transport ship, was sent to Cockburn for the "reception" of enemy property, and he was instructed to arrange for the erection of suitable storage space on Tangier Island.[16]

Cochrane's grand plans for wreaking destruction on coastal towns and cities, of course, were very much dependent on the arrival of a corresponding grand army. In expectation of this, he once more considered potential targets. In doing so, he firmly ruled out taking forts, believing that objectives could be achieved without "taking the Bull by the Horns" with its consequent loss of life. Philadelphia, Boston, or New York would require an assault force of 12,000 men. Vessels could be positioned within the range of Congreve rockets with which to bombard New York, unless a ransom could be secured.

Having participated in the capture of Philadelphia in 1777, Cochrane was fully aware of the tactical approach required to do so again. On July 14 he wrote to Bathurst to inform him that he had decided to stay in Bermuda until the troops arrived and had learned of the government's intentions in relation to prospective high-value targets. In the event of troops arriving soon, either Baltimore or Washington could be assailed: "They may be either destroyed or laid under contribution as the occasion may require." In anticipation of substantial reinforcements, Cochrane intended to give the Americans "a complete drubbing before Peace is made—when I trust their northern limits will be circumscribed and the command of the Mississippi wrested from them." The vice admiral was also evidently intent on holding New Orleans should he capture it.[17] But his strategic dreams were about to be punctured, at least temporarily.

Robert Dundas, Lord Melville, first lord of the Admiralty, wrote to Cochrane on May 22 to explain "all we have been able to place at your disposal at present in the way of military assistance." He was trying to soften the blow. Melville did not tell him that the real reason why so few troops had been sent to assist him was that Hill and other senior commanders did not share his enthusiasm to trounce the Americans. Nor did he reveal that eight Wellington regiments and several thousand troops arriving from the United Kingdom and the Mediterranean assigned to support him had been redirected to Canada. By mid-July the penny was dropping for Cochrane that the prospective arrival of troops was not going to "correspond with the numbers stated in the Public Prints," demonstrating yet again the importance of newspaper reports and the pitfalls of contemporaries relying on them. When Ross instead of Hill arrived at Bermuda in command of little over 2,500 men, there is no doubt that Cochrane was hugely disappointed, even dumbfounded. News from England led him and other senior naval commanders to think that Hill and up to 15,000 Wellington troops had been on their way and that the total amphibious force could number as many as 30,000 men.[18]

After linking up with Cochrane at Bermuda, Ross transferred his quarters to the vice admiral's flagship, HMS *Tonnant*, a powerful ship of the line. Before long, the relatively inexperienced major general was to be surrounded by no less than four admirals. These men, however, were not steering in one direction. Cochrane's main priority was to attack New Orleans later in the year, but Cockburn was obsessed with Washington, while Codrington was the most cautious of all. As for Malcolm, it was his stated view, "I shall be much better pleased if we make a dash at some place or other and then return home." What they all had, or were soon to have, in common was an admiration for Ross, both for his professional ability and for his congenial nature. Writing to his wife, the general was full of praise for Malcolm in particular and in a lighthearted manner acknowledged his onerous and unfamiliar position as overall commander of the troops on the expedition. "Nothing can exceed the friendly kindness of Admiral Malcolm whom I quit with considerable regret. He has expressed his wish that I should continue with him but circumstances requiring me being with the commander in chief I lament much my being such a Big Wig."[19]

A week after Ross reached Bermuda, another fleet of transports arrived from the Mediterranean under the command of Major General Gerard Gosselin. Ross was authorized to take his pick of one of Gosselin's battalions to participate in his mission. According to Cochrane, under instructions that were "found at Bermuda," the 1/21st Battalion, which had sailed from Italy, was assigned to the American expedition. Cochrane's letter hints that there was a problem over orders. Another account, written by a naval officer involved in transporting Gosselin's troops, details a chaotic situation at Bermuda as a frantic search was made to find the misplaced orders.[20] For a time Ross's position as commanding officer of the amphibious expeditionary force was in jeopardy.

On July 30 Codrington noted that "we are all extremely annoyed" to learn that Gosselin was "senior to Ross and neither a Wellington man, nor one who is known to the army. He may be a very good one [general], but he is not known to be so: and as Ross's division were made content with the trip merely by his coming at their head, it is a very unfortunate circumstance." Without the missing orders, it was assumed that Gosselin would "supersede" Ross and that the operation would have to proceed on that basis. On the following day Codrington was mightily relieved to report that the missing orders were found. Gosselin was sent on his way to Canada, this arrangement being "most agreeable to the Wellingtonian troops, who were again to serve under one of their own generals." In a similar vein Gleig commented of Ross, "as a colonel of a regiment, a general of brigade in Lord Wellington's army, his name had long stood high." Codrington had every confidence that Ross would lead his men "a la Wellington." According to Whitshed Keene, the longest-serving member of Parliament at the time, "if there was one man more likely than another to imitate Wellington, General Ross was that man. He did not say to his troops, *Go,* and do such a thing; he said *Come* and do it."[21]

The rumpus involving Gosselin is revealing in a number of ways. Not only does it show that Ross's reputation went before him with troops whom he had never previously commanded, but also a senior naval commander, Codrington, was equally pleased to be serving with him. The notion that he was leading crack "Wellingtonian troops," however, was far from accurate. Only two of his four units, the 1/4th and the 85th, were Wellington's men. And only the 1/4th had considerable experience in the Peninsular War. The soldiers of the 85th were not considered "peninsular fire-eaters." Having suffered heavy casualties during the first siege of Badajoz in May 1811, that regiment was sent back to England to replenish its ranks. It then served only in the latter stages of the Peninsular War, arriving at the end of August 1813, having been "re-officered" following serious internal discipline problems. The regiment suffered very light casualties in subsequent engagements, indicating that its recent battle experience was limited.[22] For other peninsular units, both these circumstances did little to increase the standing of the 85th. As for the 1/21st and 1/44th, as one of Wellington's men remarked, it "is no reflection on the courage" of these battalions "to say they were not as good soldiers as the veterans who had fought through so many glorious campaigns under the Duke of Wellington." When the 1/21st (Royal North British Fusiliers) joined the expedition in Bermuda at the end of July, it was observed that they were not in great shape.[23]

Malcolm was infuriated by the delay at Bermuda. Resuming his voyage on August 3, he was concerned that "our good and excellent general" was unwell. His hope was that "action will bring him about. . . . I like him much." This was the first of several occasions when Malcolm commented on Ross's ill health. Whether the general, like so many others, was suffering from the heat, from the wound he suffered at Orthes, or from a combination of both is unclear. Certainly, Ross admitted that he struggled with the climate. He was not the only one. Codrington, remarking on the heat being "somewhat oppressive," reported, "we are not particular as to dress: and some of the more formal might have stared at the Admiral, the General and the Captain of the Fleet sitting in conversation without their coats." Malcolm also reflected on the prospect of serving with

Cockburn, "the life of the cause. He is not a favourite of mine but he is a dashing officer." Many of the British officers in the army and navy had previous experience serving together.[24] Not that this was always an advantage as rivalries and personality clashes simmered during the expedition. Before long, if for different reasons, Malcolm and Codrington both wished that Cockburn would return to Britain.

During the delay at Bermuda, Ross took the opportunity to send a number of letters to his wife, the first one immediately after his arrival. He returned to the prospect for peace: "That it may shortly take place is my most hearty prayer and that my best Ly may be shortly restored to me is the sincere and ardent prayer of her truly attached Robert Ross." That continuing concerns about his wife's mental state weighed heavily on his mind were reinforced in a second letter two days later. "The care of our little children ought and must divert your thoughts from yielding to unpleasant thoughts." In an uncharacteristically brusque manner, he asked his wife to "recollect the many women whose miseries from adversity of circumstances must exceed yours." Given his domestic predicament, a man hoping to see his wife before the end of the year, Cochrane's longer-term plans to conquer and hold territory in Louisiana is likely to have been a source of considerable concern. Ross, by contrast, was much more disposed to immediate strikes, not least with a view to hastening an end to the war. And if he had to fight, the upside of being in command of the troops was the prospect of prize money. "Any advantage to be derived" from military action "will I trust fall to my lot and I should consider myself a most fortunate fellow but for the misery in which my Ly is involved. This reflection leaves a weight on my mind greater than I can express."[25]

Ross's correspondence to his wife while he was in Bermuda is also revealing in terms of the light it sheds on British plans, or the lack thereof, once the force arrived on the American coast. On July 26 the general noted that he would be heading in the first instance to the "Chesapeake where our proceedings will depend totally on circumstances." Four days later he again mentioned sailing for the Chesapeake, where he did not expect to stay more than a few days. Ross noted that "the climate" in the region, which "becomes unhealthy about the middle of next month will not permit a continuance ashore. We shall in that case probably go to the northward to which part particularly is not decided." In a similar vein on August 3, Admiral Malcolm recorded that he was "now steering for the

Chesapeake . . . , but we are too late for that particular place." That nothing spectacular was being planned by the British was reinforced in a letter written by Cochrane on August 11, just thirteen days before Washington was to be captured. The vice admiral informed Secretary John Croker at the Admiralty, "I cannot at present acquaint their Lordships of what may be my future operations, they will depend much on the information I may receive in this quarter."[26]

Ross, along with most of his staff officers, joined Cochrane in proceeding to the Chesapeake before the convoy carrying the troops left Bermuda. En route, plans were made to form an "artillery brigade" with one hundred seamen each from the *Tonnant, Albion, Dragon, Ramillies,* and *Ajax.* They were to be "exercised frequently in the use and the transportation of field pieces and also of small arms, and to be held in readiness to land and accompany the army whenever wanted." Proceeding to rendezvous with Cockburn, there was no sense whatever that Ross and Cochrane were preparing for a dramatic assault, least of all on Washington. Harry Smith later recalled being the "only staff officer left" behind with the rest of the troops and Admiral Malcolm. This was the first straw in the wind suggesting that Smith felt sidelined in the decision-making process. To compound matters, on July 25 his great rival for the general's attentions, Lieutenant George De Lacy Evans, had been appointed Ross's "military secretary."[27]

Given the massive let-down Cochrane had just experienced regarding the troops being made available to him, it is perhaps no wonder that he was indecisive in terms of how he would seek to utilize Ross's command. It seemed that the "confusion" that had to a large measure characterized British operations in the Chesapeake in 1813 was to be repeated. In theory Cochrane's predecessor on the American station, Admiral Sir John Borlase Warren, had come up with a potentially effective plan of action. In November 1812 Warren had proposed a diversionary attack on New Orleans to relieve pressure on British forces in Canada. He also contemplated using a "flying army" in attacks along the East Coast, Washington being among his projected targets. He believed the American capital could be attacked if the operation was undertaken with "celerity." Its capture, he argued, would "probably shake the union to its centre."[28] Implementing the strategy was another matter.

Even more than Warren, Cochrane was wedded to the idea of capturing New Orleans.[29] He initially considered that a very substantial expeditionary force would be required, although he later argued that as few as 3,000 troops could achieve success. Weather conditions suggested that December was the best month to launch an attack. The admiral's conundrum was deciding what to do with Ross's "little army" in the meantime. The key to understanding what happened next during the 1814 campaign essentially came down to "circumstances," as Ross indicated, as well as the drive and purpose of Cockburn, who was fixated with attacking Washington. At the end of June, he wrote to Cochrane, "I am decidedly of opinion that about the seat of government and in the upper parts of the Chesapeake is where your operations may be commenced to most effect."[30]

During the British attack on the West Indies island of Martinique in 1809, Cochrane relied on Cockburn at a critical moment. Governor of Guadaloupe since 1810, Cochrane had already been sizing up the most vulnerable strategic points in the United States. He realized even then that Washington could fall to a surprise attack. In 1814 it was to Cockburn that he once more turned to for a plan of campaign. On July 17 Cockburn responded to his invitation to advise the vice admiral about the commencement of operations once the army arrived. He considered a range of potential targets that included Annapolis, Norfolk, Baltimore, and Philadelphia as well as Washington. For Cockburn, the deciding factor in recommending an attack first on the U.S. capital was that these other objectives would "be more likely to fall after the occupation of Washington than that city would be after their capture." In other words, while defenses in the region were still so poorly organized, there was going to be one chance only to seize the plum political prize, the nation's capital, "always so great a blow to the government of a country."[31]

Cockburn's detailed plan of operations emphasized that the window of opportunity was also weather bound as the hurricane season was approaching. He suggested that the army should be landed at Benedict on the Patuxent River, from where "within forty-eight hours after the [troops'] arrival . . . , the city of Washington might be possessed without difficulty or opposition of any kind." The distance to the capital from Benedict was estimated to be less than fifty miles. While the major thrust of operations should be centered on the Patuxent, he recommended that "a tolerably good division" of ships "should at the same time be sent up the Potomac with bomb ships . . . which will tend to distract and divide the enemy" as well as "amuse Fort Washington," which guarded the river approach to the capital.[32] As for other targets under consideration, Cockburn stressed that there would be considerable difficulty in battering Fort McHenry outside Baltimore into submission and that this "time" should not be lost in "striking our first blow." While not actually recommending that an attack on Baltimore should immediately follow an assault on Washington, the city was best attacked from the Washington road as it had "no defense whatever in its rear."[33]

Historians have rightly emphasized that the strategy employed to capture Washington mirrored Cockburn's recommendations in so many ways. In evaluating his proposed tactics, it is important to bear in mind that the ease with which he predicted Washington was to be captured was predicated upon what he termed the "mighty and overbearing strength" that Cochrane had led him to expect. In other words, he was reckoning on up to 30,000 men, not the 3,500 or so "bayonets" who actually showed up. There was no "grand expedition," at least not yet. So much was going to depend on the attitude of Ross in circumstances that were very different to what Cockburn had been anticipating. As one of the admiral's biographers has noted, "without the army Cockburn's opinions were academic."[34] That is to say, much depended on what Ross decided to do since he had full discretion when it came to the deployment of troops.

CHAPTER 5

"Up Hill, Down Dale"

By the time Major General Ross reached the Chesapeake Bay in mid-August, American newspapers reverberated to the news that Lord Hill was daily expected. Under favorable sailing conditions, British correspondence could be sent from North America to London in about three weeks.[1] Depending on the weather—that is, sailing into the prevailing westerly winds—dispatches going in the opposite direction could take up to several months. In other words, there was a considerable time lapse between events occurring in Europe and Americans becoming aware of them. This communication black hole worked to the advantage of Ross's task force and played a key role in his decision making when he reached America.[2]

Having postponed Hill's "grand expedition," the government's strategy that it would be "politic" to keep up the impression of his impending departure for America proved to be highly successful. The deception worked with the assistance of the British and American press. News from Britain that Hill was on his way was duly reprinted by U.S. newspapers. The *Virginia Argus*, for example, carried a report on August 21 that it is "confirmed that Lord Hill has accepted the command in this quarter of the world and is to embark at Bordeaux. It is treating us with some respect to oppose to us so distinguished a general."[3]

By the end of July it was being reported in North America that Hill would command a force of 12,000–15,000 men. Republishing extracts from London papers, the U.S. press duly, and accurately, reported that the expedition was to be "independent" from military commanders in Canada. The *Boston Gazette* correctly stated that the invasion force had been increased to 18,000 men and that Ross was among the generals to take part. Another U.S. newspaper account that "30,000 bayonets" were to be sent reflected the expectations of British naval officers on station in the American theater. And the number of troops rose again to 40,000 and that "villages, and possibly cities" would be burned.[4] The reports carried in the American press were to have a key bearing on the way events unfolded when Ross landed on U.S. shores. The specter of Hill arriving preyed on the minds of the Americans, sapping morale.

Facing the prospect of seaborne attack, defensive preparations were undertaken to a greater or lesser degree along the Atlantic coast during the summer of 1814, building upon the work of the previous year. Baltimore, always a likely British target, was a flurry of activity, with more cause for concern than most others. Branded a "nest of hornets," the city was home to privateers that were the scourge of British merchant ships. Young John Pendleton Kennedy, a Baltimorean who later served as secretary of the navy, was thrilled by the stirring military preparations in the face of the expected British offensive. Among the sparse naval forces available were several vessels commanded by Commodore Richard Dale at Philadelphia. Kennedy was highly amused by a popular joke coined by Dale about the likelihood of an attack by Lord Hill. Someone said to him, "Well, commodore, there is news that Hill will soon be in the Delaware." "I shall be glad to see him," remarked the officer, "and the moment I hear that he is coming up, we shall have a brisk time—up Hill and down Dale."[5]

Fearing imminent attack, fortifications were hastily erected in many U.S. coastal cities. The military precautions undertaken by New Yorkers were hailed across the country. Many newspapers reported on the contribution of a "large band" of "Patriotic Butchers" who worked on the fortifications at Brooklyn Heights.[6] The Washington Benevolent Society in New York, a body of Federalist activists, also did their bit in very substantial numbers. Weavers, sawyers, cabinetmakers, saddlers, shoemakers, and plumbers pitched in. There was female patriotism too. An "Amazonian Corps" volunteered a day's work building breastworks. "Teachers with their juvenile scholars also turned out for a day's duty." The New York African Mutual Society for Relief played its part, while Italians and Frenchmen contributed as well. But the most prominent group of volunteers to mobilize were Ross's fellow countrymen, the Irish, the "Daughters" and "Sons of Erin."[7] This did not happen by chance.

On August 20 some 1,500 Irishmen gathered in "the Park" at 5:30 A.M., "desirous of appearing in their national character, arrayed against the British enemy." They were allocated to construction on the entire defensive works that day. Irish women labored too. Accompanied by two bands, they marched to Brooklyn Heights, waving U.S. and Irish flags. Just as significant as their industry was their motivation. As an Irish American newspaper in New York put it, "we have no interest but the safety of our country [the United States of America]: no ambition but to march with its defenders. Thrice happy, if in doing so, we may also avenge the wrongs of our dear and native land [Ireland]." A wave of embittered exiles came to the United States following the 1798 rebellion in Ireland, many of whom considered America's war with Great Britain as an opportunity to wreak vengeance. Meanwhile, on the British side, Ross's fellow Irishmen constituted a substantial portion of his army. The 1/21st (Royal North British Fusiliers) was nominally a Scottish unit, but almost half its enlisted men were Irish.[8]

Thanks to what the radical English newspaper editor William Cobbett lauded as the "tell-tale press of America," Ross and other British commanders were able to read all about the defensive preparations in New York and elsewhere in the U.S. press, which they consulted "daily," and they made plans accordingly.[9] Cochrane made a point of not only reading American newspapers but also forwarding them to the Admiralty. By the time the general reached the Chesapeake, the least prepared city along the East Coast, arguably, was Washington. And this despite the fact that from as early as June, President Madison anticipated a possible attack on the grounds of the "*éclat* that would attend a successful inroad upon the capital, beyond the intrinsic magnitude of the achievement." He recommended that a force of 10,000 men should be put in readiness for the city's defense. As a result of these deliberations, the Tenth Military District was created with a view to coordinating defensive arrangements in the Chesapeake Bay area.[10]

After much disagreement between the president and the secretary of war, John Armstrong, Madison decided to offer command of the new military district to Brigadier General William H. Winder, the nephew of the Federalist governor of Maryland. This pivotal state was "bitterly divided on the war" but was going to have to supply the majority of the militia in the event of a British strike on Washington.[11] By appointing his nephew to head the new military district, the administration hoped that Governor Winder would be more amenable to calling out the militia if circumstances demanded. That the people of the United States were not united behind the war effort was to play into Ross's hands.

Ross was to benefit too from the power struggles wracking Madison's administration. Secretary of State James Monroe and Secretary of War Armstrong were constantly at loggerheads. They were widely considered to be rivals for the presidency, with an election due in 1816. What is more, with "accumulating evidence of Secretary of War Armstrong's deceit, insubordination and incompetence," Madison, encouraged by Monroe, took him to task. Historian Ralph Louis Ketcham has argued that normally Armstrong would have been fired in such circumstances. With an apparently even greater British threat pending in the Chesapeake Bay area, however, replacing him at such a critical moment was not possible. Others have argued that the implication of the "massive reprimand" resulted in Madison essentially assuming control of the War Department. An expert in constitutional law, the commander in chief had little aptitude for military matters.[12] Armstrong, who dismissed the prospect that the British would attack the capital, sulked. The administration was at sixes and sevens during the crucial period before Ross arrived.

As for the man delegated to command American forces in the event of a British invasion, Brigadier General Winder was frenetically active but lacked tactical ability. A nominal army of 93,500 militiamen was theoretically available to him from fifteen states. Yet in the emerging crisis, he found himself only being able to call upon limited numbers from Maryland, Virginia, and Pennsylvania. In the weeks that followed, Winder's boundless energy was misdirected, and he developed no coherent plan to defend the nation's capital.[13] Major General Ross had indicated that he was going to be governed by "circumstances" when he reached the United States. That he was to face such an inept American commander proved to be another stroke of luck.

Hapless though he may have been, Winder ended up being right about one thing, at least in regard to Cockburn's strategic plan. Writing on July 9 to Armstrong, who did not bother to reply, the general observed that the British had carried out comprehensive reconnaissance in local rivers during the past year and "must be presumed to have such accurate information, that whatever expedition may be destined for these waters, will have a definite object, to the execution of which, on its arrival, it will proceed with the utmost promptitude and dispatch."[14] Attempting to fathom where the British would strike was his major problem—and to be fair, at the time the British themselves had not decided if or where they would attack. While Rear Admiral Cockburn had his heart set on Washington, his superior, Vice Admiral Cochrane, was more intent on eventually targeting New Orleans but even less certain about his intentions in the meantime, particularly when so few troops actually arrived. Meanwhile, Ross was an unknown quantity. He, after all, had discretion about how his troops would be deployed when he made landfall.

As Cockburn waited for reinforcements, he masked his burning desire to strike at Washington and wipe it off the map. For some months before the attack on the U.S. capital, *Niles' Weekly Register* in Baltimore was surprised that British forces in the Chesapeake, led by the "ruffian Cockburn," who had terrorized the area in a campaign of arson, rape, murder, and pillage the previous year, had been so inactive.[15]

Unknown to the newsmen, this resulted from the fact that Cockburn was playing a waiting game. In anticipation of substantial numbers of troops arriving, he was also relishing the opportunity to deal once and for all with Commodore Joshua Barney's Chesapeake Flotilla. The veteran Barney had spent the winter of 1813–14 recruiting sailors and building boats with the intention of attacking the British fort on Tangier Island. His fleet of small vessels was detected by the British and forced to seek cover in St. Leonard's Creek, an inlet on the north side of the Patuxent River. Here he and his sailors fought a dogged defense against a squadron commanded by Cockburn's subordinates. Catching the British off guard, the Americans launched a combined land-and-naval operation on June 26 that resulted in the flotilla managing to break out from the creek and move up the river to Benedict.[16]

While waiting on Cochrane and the army to arrive, Cockburn conducted a series of raids along the Potomac River to keep the Americans guessing about the route they might use in an attempt to seize the capital. As this policy of shadow boxing continued, a Royal Navy reconnaissance mission sailed up the Potomac in late July. One frigate managed to negotiate the tricky Kettle Bottom shoals, prompting speculation locally that Alexandria or Washington were among potential targets. Still, Armstrong was not the only one skeptical of an imminent attack on the District of Columbia. Dr. James Ewell, a prominent physician in Washington, was similarly convinced that the British were targeting the Chesapeake Flotilla, never imagining that they would attempt to capture the capital.[17]

While the Americans were struggling with how to respond to the British threat, it became clear that Cockburn would have a fight on his hands to persuade Cochrane, and to a lesser extent Ross, to proceed with an operation against Washington with the significantly diminished army arriving from Europe. Seasonally adverse weather in the region inclined them to leave the area without attempting a landing. Despite this, he was determined not to be put off. Lieutenant James Scott, whom Cockburn described as his "aide-de-camp," later recalled that a "plan was, I believe, submitted to the Commander-in-chief [Cochrane] by the Rear-admiral for the capture of Washington, notwithstanding the disappointment of the latter at finding only four, instead of twenty thousand men, were destined for the Chesapeake."[18]

When Cochrane and Ross arrived in the Chesapeake Bay, Cockburn briefed them about his shore operations with a battalion of marines, who had carried all before them. His account of these successes did not convince his naval superior and the general. Codrington documented the outcome of the meeting: "it is determined that we shall not stay here long enough to endanger getting sick." During the voyage from Bermuda to the Chesapeake, Ross contemplated striking a blow against the Americans as soon as possible, though not in that area, which was notorious to the British for the "Sickly Season" at that time of year.[19]

The dynamic of the situation changed when Ross agreed to undertake a reconnaissance with Cockburn in the intervening days until the troop convoy rendezvoused. Had Malcolm's transports not been becalmed for four days within one hundred miles of the Chesapeake and arrived sooner, this may never have transpired. The admiral took the army commander ashore to show him how "easy" it was to conduct warfare in the Chesapeake. Ross accompanied him on a raid against St. George's Island in the Potomac. Frederick Chamier, a midshipman on HMS *Menelaus*, participated in this operation. On making landfall Chamier stated that they "were commanded by Sir George Cockburn in person, and with him, as an amateur, was the gallant general Ross." The target of the mission was to destroy a factory. Ross directed the skirmishers and apparently demonstrated military tactics to the admiral.[20]

That Ross and Cockburn struck up what appeared to be an instant rapport has been explained as proceeding from the general being "sold" to the admiral's strategy by the ease with which these operations were conducted. This is correct to a degree. Oral tradition in General Ross's family indicates that he simply could not believe how little resistance his operations met from the Americans.[21] In the first instance, this persuaded him to stay longer than the couple of days he had anticipated. That the British were able to raid so far inland impressed him. Good soldier that he was, Ross wanted to see the lie of the land for himself. The fact that there was no sign of sickness among the Royal Marines who had been operating with Cockburn since the middle of July was regarded as significant.[22] What has not been appreciated before is that the positive chemistry that soon manifested itself between Ross and Cockburn had been previously cultivated during the Egyptian campaign in 1801, when they had served together.

Having managed to proceed a considerable distance toward Washington on one of these reconnaissance missions, with Cockburn's encouragement Ross first contemplated an attack on the capital once Barney's flotilla in the Patuxent was destroyed. The general readily agreed that an operation against Barney could be used as a pretext to land his army within striking distance of Washington without betraying this as the ultimate objective. Evans recalled that the American capital was being considered as a potential target as soon as Ross arrived in the Chesapeake.[23]

Cockburn had to work much harder to persuade Cochrane to sanction a joint army-navy operation to destroy the Chesapeake Flotilla, never mind targeting Washington. Cochrane later claimed that he endorsed a staged approach to capturing the capital that was to begin by an attack on the flotilla and included a diversionary operation by a squadron of Royal Navy vessels under Captain James Gordon up the Potomac. In reality, if the vice admiral had ever given any countenance to such a plan, his enthusiasm soon evaporated. According to Evans, Cochrane "disapproved of the movement from the neighbourhood of Benedict" and "decidedly dissented" from advancing on Washington. In other words, he was even reluctant to sanction a combined army-navy attack against Barney. Evans's view is supported by Codrington, who characterized the army's initial deployment ashore as "*merely . . . a demonstration* for which alone they are intended on this occasion." At most, the troops were to provide cover for a number of days in support of the attempt to destroy Barney's flotilla before reboarding.[24]

Ross for his part was keenly aware that he was responsible for land-based operations. Just before his men made landfall, he made a number of key decisions indicating that he treated the forthcoming operations much more seriously than an opportunity for the troops to stretch their legs ashore after a long voyage. He finalized arrangements to split his "division" into three brigades, commanded by Colonels Arthur Brooke, William Patterson, and William Thornton. Captain Harry Smith, major of brigade to this point, was appointed deputy assistant adjutant general, while Captains Henry Debbeig (1/44th), James McHaffie (1/21st), and Richard Gubbins (85th) were appointed "majors of brigade." These arrangements represented a statement of intent for the impending reconnaissance in force, with an initial aim to collaborate in the destruction of Barney's flotilla while keeping open the option of advancing on Washington should a favorable opportunity arise.[25] Ross was going to be guided by "circumstances," not the whim of Cochrane, who was notorious for changing his mind, nor Cockburn's obsession.

In preparation for landing, provisions for three days were cooked. Each man was issued three pounds of pork and two and a half pounds of ship's biscuit. As the waters became shallow and the larger ships and frigates began to run aground, the troops transferred to smaller vessels. Late on August 18 the first British boats reached Benedict, though too late to put the men ashore. On the day before debarkation commenced, Evans recorded that Ross asked him to draw up a proclamation to reassure local inhabitants that their private property would be safe, but Cochrane objected to this "as interfering with the retaliatory measures of severity demanded by the atrocities committed on the Frontiers of Canada."[26] Clearly from the start, there was serious disagreement between army and navy commanders about the conduct of operations in so far as they would affect private property and civilians.

Captain Duncan MacDougall, who would later become Ross's aide-de-camp, provides additional testimony of the battle of wills occurring in the British high command in relation to retaliatory policy. Cochrane, he reveals, told Ross that he had learned that the Americans had "wantonly burnt the town of Newark on a Canadian December night without any military object" and had destroyed the public buildings in York, the capital of Upper Canada. He impressed upon the general that Governor General Prevost strongly recommended "the indispensable necessity of retaliating, with a view of preventing the Americans from continuing to pursue a system of warfare so barbarous and indefensible." MacDougall recalled Ross's response, that he "had been accustomed to carry on war in the

Peninsula and France in a very different spirit, and that he could not sanction the destruction of private or public property, with the exception of military structures and warlike stores."[27] Whatever Cochrane might say to the contrary, Ross had no intention of exacting revenge on the civilian population for American excesses in Canada. Nor was he intending to destroy public buildings.

To cover the initial landing, a brig was anchored at Benedict on the morning of August 19, its broadside facing the shore, cannons loaded and pointed at the small town in case the Americans attacked. The British could hardly believe that no effort was made to resist the invasion. Codrington observed that rising ground along the Patuxent seemed so conducive for artillery emplacements. After the landings began, the afternoon was spent organizing the troops into three brigades. The First, or Light, Brigade, commanded by Colonel Thornton, comprised the 85th Light Infantry Regiment and the light companies of the 1/4th, 1/21st, and 1/44th. Also added to it were the "Colonial Marines"—the former Chesapeake slaves—along with a company of Royal Marines. Colonel Brooke of the 1/44th would lead the Second Brigade, made up of the 1/4th and 1/44th. Lastly, the Third Brigade, to be commanded by Colonel Patterson, included his own 1/21st, Marines, and approximately one hundred sailors to pull the fieldpieces. The British artillery was skimpy at best, with only one 6-pounder, two 3-pounders, and a rocket battery eventually seeing action. By an official reckoning of the troops at Benedict signed by Captain Smith, the total number ashore was 4,185 men. Subtracting those listed as sick, the effectives totaled 3,591.[28]

Issued with three days of provisions, British troops immediately tried to supplement their rations and provide a good "mess," a bonding feature of army life that revolved around a group of soldiers pooling their food and sharing a meal together. Observing the British was James Monroe, the secretary of state. He conceded that while the troops plundered the local area, not least of livestock, they did so "with respectful regard." The British were dependent on finding horses locally. On August 20 Lieutenant George Gleig and Lieutenant Garlike Philip Codd foraged in the local countryside. At four o'clock in the afternoon they were about to tuck into the meal they had prepared when suddenly, "the bugle sounded the assembly and we were obliged to leave our meal and fall in. The Brigade formed and moved to the road, when General Ross passed us, and we cheered him as he passed." From the start the British engaged in mind games. Evans was conscious that "Americans entertained at this period, the most exalted ideas of our irresistible Valor, and intrepidity." But they were wholly unaware that Ross had been incarnated as Lord Hill in the American mindset. As the march commenced, musicians struck up a popular tune, "See the Conquering Hero Comes," a hardly coincidental choice.[29] The British army was in its pomp, and Ross took every opportunity to demoralize his enemy.

From the American point of view, the arrival of the combined British naval and army force in the Chesapeake Bay in mid-August led to much speculation about intended targets. A report circulated on August 16 that the armada of almost fifty vessels signaled a British intention to destroy Washington. The *American and Commercial Daily Advertiser* in Baltimore predicted that the British would make a "dash" on the capital, although in doing so they would "never return" to their "Mother Country." But then there were a "thousand rumours" about the size of the enemy force, who commanded it, and its likely destination. Royal Navy command of the ocean left the entire U.S. eastern and southern seaboard vulnerable. As an American congressman put it at the time, the British thus could appear "no man can tell when, and no man can tell where."[30] The initiative very much rested with Ross, and it was a nightmare situation for Winder trying to anticipate British intentions.

William Jones, secretary of the navy, did what he could to bring reinforcements to the Chesapeake. On August 19 he wrote to Commodore John Rodgers at Philadelphia. Although uncertain if Washington or Baltimore was the intended target, he considered it of the utmost urgency to order Rodgers, with three hundred men, to Baltimore, where a detachment of U.S. Marines was scheduled to meet him. Writing to Commodore David Porter at New York on the same day, Jones summoned him and his crew to help defend the American capital. In the confusion and panic that prevailed as British troops landed, Rodgers noted that "owing to some shameful irregularity in the Post Office, your Letter, altho' it is dated the 19th. Inst., was not delivered until ten o'clock yesterday morning"—that is, August 22. By the following day Rodgers was at New Castle, Delaware, heading for Baltimore, still some seventy miles away. At 8:30 A.M. on the twenty-third, Jones wrote once more to Rodgers, directing him to Bladensburg instead to help defend the national capital, a distance of just over one hundred miles.[31] Rodgers and his men would not to arrive in time to help stem the British advance on Washington.

With an invading army so close, the mayor of Washington, James H. Blake, imposed a curfew in the city from ten o'clock at night beginning August 20. Citizens were asked to be on the lookout for spies. An incident involving an allegedly cross-dressing British agent was reported to have occurred on the twentieth. Several American newspapers as well as Vice President Elbridge Gerry detailed an incident involving a British officer supposedly visiting the U.S. capital disguised as a nun. He was later reputed to be Major Timothy Jones of the 1/4th. Not only had the nun called at the boarding house of Mrs. Suter in the city and "exclaimed against the vile British," but "she" had also sought information about American forces being assembled to resist them. This nun had the "impudence" to go to the President's House, where she "advised Mrs Madison repeatedly to move her person and effects." The First Lady, like others, was reported to have considered this person to be a spy. "This impudent scoundrel was tall and stooped to conceal his height."[32] During the war, there were numerous rumors that spies dressed as women visited the Executive Mansion. While a British spy may well have visited Washington at this time, it is unlikely that it was Major Jones.[33]

Despite the proximity of the British to Washington, Secretary Armstrong remained convinced that they would not attack the city. Baltimore, he believed, was going to be the target. The guessing game benefited the raiders as American forces were to be dispersed rather than concentrated for the defense of the capital, demonstrated in Secretary Jones's decision to send Rodgers to Baltimore while directing Porter to Washington. Driven to distraction, Winder was convinced at one point that Annapolis would be the objective, only to change his mind and reckon that it would be Fort Washington on the Potomac.[34]

While Armstrong dismissed the prospect of a British attack, others in the administration now feared the worst, including Armstrong's rival, James Monroe. The secretary of state, carrying the rank of colonel from his military service during the Revolutionary War, noted on August 18 that Washington was the more likely target for the British. He also called on the president and stated that "this city was their object." Madison agreed. He granted Monroe permission to undertake a reconnaissance mission with a troop of horse to observe enemy movements. "Exposed to capture," this has been termed "the most unusual mission ever conducted by a secretary of state." Monroe was accompanied for a time at least by a number of other gentlemen, including Dr. William Thornton, a prominent Federalist from Georgetown and architect of the Capitol.[35]

Why Ross met so little resistance from the very earliest stage of his operations may be explained to some extent by the dispersion of American forces due to uncertainty about where the British meant to strike. So far as the Virginia militia is concerned, for example, recent research has shown that substantial numbers were to be tied up shadowing Gordon's naval force as it simultaneously ascended the Potomac. In the face of an impending assault, one report in mid-August stated that many Maryland militiamen had not complied with orders to rendezvous for service at Baltimore and Bladensburg, some believing that they were under no legal obligation to do so. A matter of weeks before Ross's army arrived, in an uncannily accurate prediction, Commodore Barney reported on the palsied local militia, which he doubted would stay long enough to see the British before retreating. If only "100 *did* arrive, they would be looked upon as the Advance guard of 2000 more; no resistance would be made for fear of the arrival of the *supposed* main army which were following. . . . [B]efore the *real* number could be known the mischief would be done."[36] The prevailing belief among many of the militia that they would face overwhelming numbers of Wellington veterans under the command of Lord Hill deterred many others from doing their duty. Figuratively speaking, many Americans in the Chesapeake region were shell shocked at the prospect of facing a huge invasion force before a shot was even fired.

Colonel Allen McClane was one of the few Americans who discovered at an early stage that the British were commanded by Ross, not Lord Hill. He was also aware that British policy was to intimidate the populace by "reporting an overwhelming army." In this instance it was working. After Ross's force landed, McClane reported, "it was very common to see a white cloth stuck on a pole at a house, which was a signal of submission, that he found the roads crowded with men in arms running from the enemy to secure their property, but found none disposed to fight, or obstruct roads, &c., all panic-struck, believing the British reports."[37] It was exactly what Barney had feared. Hill's ghost expedition had spooked many Americans. Militia numbers were hemorrhaging. Events soon demonstrated that the lack of opposition to the initial stages of Ross's operations ashore emboldened the general to try his luck in getting closer and closer to the American capital, encouraging him to contemplate a "dash" for Washington.

CHAPTER 6

"THEY ARE NOT IN A CONDITION TO STRIKE AT WASHINGTON"

Safely disembarked at Benedict, Major General Ross proceeded with his reconnaissance in force. Initially, progress was painfully slow in the heat and humidity of a Chesapeake Bay summer, with the army moving no more than six miles on Saturday, August 20. Major George Brown of the 85th Light Infantry was entrusted with the job of reconnoitering the situation ahead. Lieutenant George Gleig described how the three brigades marched cautiously, with about 100–150 yards between them, as about fifty flankers swept the woods and fields to nearly half a mile from each. Owing to a shortage of horses for the junior officers, Gleig marched in the stifling heat along with his men. He was astonished that more troops fell out from the ranks owing to fatigue than he had ever seen during a march three times as long in the Peninsular War. The lieutenant attributed the attrition to the climate conditions as well as the men having had to spend so long aboard ship in cramped conditions.[1]

On Sunday, August 21, the army resumed its march at four in the afternoon. Ross traveled parallel to the Patuxent as best he could to maintain contact and support Cockburn's squadron of Royal Navy boats targeting Barney's flotilla, but the available roads were often miles from the river. Nevertheless, the line of march permitted Ross to meet Cockburn near Lower Marlboro, where Cochrane and Codrington joined them. The vice admiral was closely monitoring developments. He noted that it was going to take longer than originally anticipated, for Commodore Barney's Chesapeake Flotilla was moving as far as possible up the river to evade their pursuers. According to Lieutenant Evans, Ross was also aware at this stage that American forces were congregating near Bladensburg, where he believed they would position themselves on wooded hills nearby.[2] Even though the operation to destroy the flotilla had barely begun, Ross was keeping an eye on the bigger picture, including the possibility of an advance on Washington via Bladensburg.

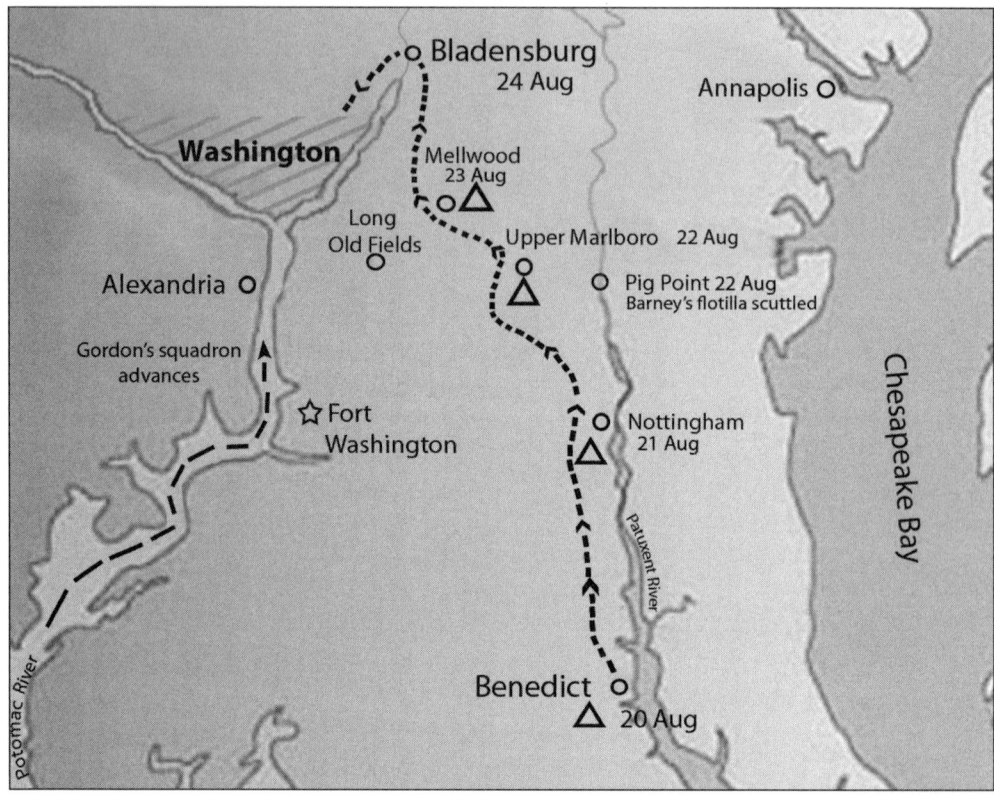

British Advance on Washington, D.C., August 1814. Map by Mark McCavitt. Copyright © 2016 by the University of Oklahoma Press

As the combined British forces approached Nottingham, some shots were fired at them. Lacking cavalry, Ross and a few other mounted officers set off in a vain pursuit of their attackers. Itching for action, this response was typical of Ross. To Walter Lord, though, it was "a rash thing to do but the General was always putting himself in dangerous situations—it was a mark of his leadership." Wellington was well known for similar escapades. Both commanders made a virtue out of being "on the spot," regardless of personal danger. Later, the British received reports that Barney's flotilla was eight miles away at Pig Point.[3]

Ross's army and Cockburn's squadron set off again at 7:00 A.M. on Monday, August 22. Four miles from Nottingham, American cavalry and artillery were spotted in a commanding position overlooking the road. Ross immediately pushed 300 light infantrymen under cover of woodland to fend off the enemy while the army continued marching. Shots were exchanged, and at the summit of the hill a column of 1,500 American infantry, escorted by mounted dragoons, were seen retreating in the direction of Washington. Because the primary function of Ross's troops at this stage was to provide cover for the Royal Navy gunboats, the Americans were not pursued. Besides, as Evans put it in his contemporaneous account of events at the time, "indecisive [actions] are to be avoided, partly with a view to encourage a General action."[4] Ross was keeping his eye on the bigger picture, a battle for the American capital.

During the march, the lie of the land precluded regular communication with Cockburn. It was only when huge explosions rang out that Ross and his men became aware that Barney's flotilla had been engaged. A glory hunter, Cockburn had ordered an immediate assault without coordinating with the land forces, personally leading the way. Ross may not have been pleased that his naval colleague unilaterally pushed ahead with an attack on what was meant to be a joint operation. As James Pack, one of the rear admiral's biographers put it, the "success in effecting the destruction of Barney's flotilla belonged to Cockburn alone." Proceeding without army support, it was a gamble that almost cost him his life. In one of the brief exchanges of fire that ensued, a party of Americans targeted the admiral, with two of the men coming very close to hitting their mark. In the end Cockburn was robbed of his chance to defeat Barney in battle. The flotilla was to be destroyed, but at the hands of the Americans themselves. Secretary Jones had instructed the commodore to do so should he be faced with overwhelming firepower and to proceed with his men to join the American army.[5]

Alerted by the sound of battle, Ross sent some mounted officers and artillerymen with rockets to lend what assistance they could, though they were ultimately not needed. While the fate of the flotilla was yet unclear, the army's advance stalled. As soon as its destruction had been confirmed, Ross lost no time in marching toward Upper Marlboro—that is, in the direction of Washington, not back to the ships. Codrington's correspondence makes it clear, though, that once Barney was neutralized, the army's "demonstration" was supposed to conclude. Ross later acknowledged that the resolution to disembark the army at Benedict had been taken by Cochrane and himself with the specific aim of supporting an attack on the flotilla. The decision to proceed farther at this point was his alone, having ascertained that "the Force of the Enemy to be such as might authorize an attempt at carrying his Capital."[6]

That same day, August 22, Ross's army reached Upper Marlboro, in the process successfully bamboozling the Americans about his ultimate objective by exercising the "perfect feint." The general led his troops in the first instance on a route leading them toward Fort Washington and the city of Washington from a southern direction, only to reverse their course and head toward Upper Marlboro. This bewildered the Americans. The capital could still be attacked from this direction, but the British could also strike instead at Baltimore or Annapolis. According to Lieutenant Evans, as British forces arrived in Upper Marlboro, a brief exchange of fire occurred with a retiring American column. Taking control of the village, Ross concluded a deal with its residents, who promised neutrality in exchange for protection. Far from demanding a ransom from them rather than burning their buildings, the general even offered compensation for what Evans described as an "irregularity" that took place during the skirmish. Ross then chose as his headquarters the home of a prominent local medical practitioner, Dr. William Beanes, one of the citizens who approached the British under a flag of truce. In his diary Gleig later recalled obtaining a bottle of milk from "our friend Dr Bean [sic]."[7]

Upper Marlboro's strategic location was particularly important. The British estimated that the shortest routes to Washington across a major bridge were eighteen miles and twenty-two miles via Bladensburg. Baltimore was thirty-eight miles away, while Annapolis was twenty-two miles distant. Each city had reason to feel under threat, especially with American military resources widely dispersed. While the British army remained stationary for some twenty-four hours, Gleig discerned that the general was hesitating about what to do next. There was, of course, justification for halting on purely physical grounds, some thirty miles having been covered in less than three days in sultry weather.[8] But there was more to it than this.

Unknown to anyone in Washington, Ross had not passed the point of no return and was not intent on attacking the city. Not only had he to weigh the prospects of a successful advance on the American capital, as well as securing his retreat, but he also had to consider the tactics of his enemy. The farther he moved away from his support ships, the more the moves were not all his to make. Major George Peter, an American officer who had been shadowing the British for some time, was undoubtedly correct in his assertion that a serious attack on their rear at this stage would have deterred them from attempting to reach Washington. Ross had signaled that he was going to be governed by circumstances, which remained favorable as American tactical mistakes played into his hands. Nevertheless, the general had good reason to be cautious, not least as he was conscious that an assault on Washington "completely overstepped the intentions, and was wholly uncontemplated by [his] government," as Evans put it. To strike at the U.S. capital, while operating more than fifty miles from the main fleet, would be fraught with danger. Defeat could have had catastrophic consequences for Ross as the commanding officer. The prospect of facing a court-martial for exceeding his orders may well have crossed his mind.[9] As he confessed in a letter to his wife, "at the moment the Attempt was made upon the City of Washington, I felt an apprehension of the Consequences of Failure."[10]

Having only taken three days' supplies with them, the British were living off the land. On arriving in Upper Marlboro, Private John Corbett of the 85th Regiment was delighted to come across a one-and-half-acre field of potatoes. Corbett filled a haversack as the ravenous troops soon dug up the entire crop. Entering a nearby house, he found a ham, "and we made a good mess." According to a copy of a captured order drawn up on Ross's behalf at the time by Captain Harry Smith, the general was furious with his officers for failing to deal with stragglers and marauders.[11]

Meanwhile, the longer the general waited, the greater the danger. While not doubting that Ross was in two minds about proceeding—indeed, he had wisely reserved judgment all along about the feasibility of an attack on Washington—the traditional explanation for how events unfolded at this time may be questioned. To some extent it was not that Ross had become fainthearted without the support of Cockburn; he just was waiting on him. And the general was waiting too on the marines, seamen, and marine artillery that he deemed necessary to reinforce his "little army."[12] During the voyage to the Chesapeake, sailors had been drilled in the use of artillery and small arms for land-based operations as a 500-strong "artillery brigade" "to be held in readiness to land and accompany the army whenever wanted." If ever there was a time when Ross needed his small force to be augmented, this was it. Besides, food supplies had become a major problem, not just in relation to advancing on Washington but in terms of making provision for an eventual, possibly hurried, retreat as well.[13]

As it happened, Ross was left clicking his heels at Upper Marlboro for longer than he would have wished, waiting on Cockburn's reinforcements. In the meantime he was rightly concerned that the Americans might outmaneuver him. Sound strategic, operational (manpower), and logistical (supplies) considerations existed to give him pause for thought. If Ross was to attempt to seize Washington, a rapier-like thrust would be required. He would have to push on as quickly as possible once it became clear that the capital was to be his target and attack it before American forces could be concentrated. As the general considered his options, some of his officers urged caution, owing to the dangers of being cut off or even attacked at night, while others encouraged him to continue to Washington.[14] The column was now only sixteen miles away from the U.S. capital and still had not been seriously challenged.

Evans was one of the most vehement advocates of proceeding. He recollected years later that some of his colleagues on the general's staff were convinced that the admiral's presence could prove crucial in reaffirming Ross's resolve to proceed. While the prospective British operation to capture the U.S. capital hung in the balance, Cockburn spent the rest of August 22 securing prizes and enormous amounts of tobacco off Pig Point. Two army staff officers took the initiative and set off to find Cockburn, bringing with them an extra horse for the admiral.[15] There is more than a hint in Evans's account that he approved of this action—indeed, he may have been its instigator and was perhaps even personally involved. Intriguingly, he later described his role in the advance on Washington as "altogether peculiar and unexampled." Besides Ross, he claimed that only Cockburn was aware of this contribution.[16]

Cockburn, along with his aide-de-camp Lieutenant James Scott and Captain James Wainwright, arrived at Upper Marlboro in the early hours of August 23. No marines, marine artillery, or seamen accompanied them.[17] Cockburn observed of his deliberations with Ross that it was quickly resolved to proceed with an attempt to capture Washington. Evans concurs that agreement was soon reached but that the decision was the general's. While the delay has often been portrayed as a crisis of confidence on Ross's part, this is an exaggeration. There is no reason to doubt, however, that Cockburn's encouragement tipped the balance in favor of proceeding with the advance. In the discussions that reportedly took place between the commanders, the admiral reiterated his view that Washington was there for the taking. Not only would the seizure of the U.S. capital be considered an achievement of international significance, but he also wagered that the American government would be willing to pay a handsome ransom to save their public buildings from destruction.[18] In order to make it happen, Ross requested that Cockburn immediately send for the marines, marine artillery, and seamen.[19]

Cockburn wrote to Vice Admiral Cochrane explaining that he had heard that Ross had occupied Upper Marlboro on the evening of August 22. Arriving early the following day, he explained that he came to "learn" of the general's "future plans," finding him "determined (in consequence of the information he has received and what he has observed of the Enemy) to push on towards Washington." The use of the word "towards" rather than "to" is interesting as it indicates that Ross was willing to pursue his probing mission and to be guided by the situation he encountered on the ground. In an account published years later, John S. Skinner, the American officer for prisoner exchange, recalled that Ross had told him that the operation to capture Washington was "not part of their fixed design," that it had only been finally resolved upon after Barney's flotilla was destroyed. In advocating that the advance should continue, Cockburn was supposed to have recommended to "push on, so far as to feel their strength, at any rate, and if circumstances require it, we can fall back to the shipping." Again, the use of the word "circumstances" is far from coincidental, given that Ross himself had used the term to describe how his operations would be governed. Evans confirms the phased nature of British objectives. Had just the destruction of the flotilla been achieved, the decision to disembark the army would have been considered worthwhile.[20]

Delighted to finally have a chance of taking the U.S. capital, Cockburn informed Cochrane that he intended to accompany Ross and afford him all assistance possible. Spirits were buoyant among Royal Navy personnel after the destruction of Barney's flotilla. Importantly, Cochrane was reassured that the expeditionary force was in good health. The commander in chief was respectfully requested to permit HMS *Hornet* to proceed as far as Nottingham with essential supplies—bread and spirits. Scott was ordered to take news of the decision to attack Washington to Cochrane.[21]

As Ross summoned all the assistance he could, he was aware that the Americans were reported to have twice the number of troops available to them—and increasing all the time. On the other hand, his enemy was considered to be poorly led and disciplined. The British general nevertheless had to make contingencies for his retreat. In this respect Captain John Robyns and the 250 Royal Marines who had accompanied Cockburn when he pursued Barney's flotilla were vitally important. Appreciating that Upper Marlboro was located at a strategically important location and wary of being cut off in his rear, Ross determined to secure the village to facilitate a possible avenue of retreat. Robyns and his men were ordered to set up a defensive position at the courthouse and tasked with gathering stores. Carrying out the latter duty proved surprisingly easy. According to American officer Colonel Allen McClane, who was monitoring British movements, not only were Robyns and his men undisturbed, but also local people brought in plentiful supplies.[22]

Ross's options were also affected by what his enemy was doing, or more to the point, not doing. On the morning of August 23, with the British still at Upper Marlboro, President Madison reviewed American troops at Long Old Fields. Pleased with what he saw, he penned a note to his wife, Dolley, telling her that morale was good. Earlier in a military briefing, Secretary Armstrong had assured the president that at most the enemy would attempt a hit-and-run attack on the capital. Moreover, Brigadier General Winder informed Madison that the British had no cavalry and no artillery. Reassured, the president tried to console the First Lady by saying that "they are not in a condition to strike at Washington." His only nagging worry was that the "temerity" of the British "may be greater than their strength."[23] Little realizing it, in Ross the Americans faced precisely such a daring commander, a man well used to facing superior odds.

Events in the capital had already taken on a life of their own. The previous day money was removed from the banks and orders issued for the removal of government records.[24] Senate Clerk Lewis Machen testified to chaotic scenes in the American capital, where panic and raw terror were taking hold. One correspondent involved in evacuating children eight miles outside the district described the road as crammed with women and children the whole way: "I never saw so much distress in all my life as today." As people began to fear the worst for the capital, recriminations had already begun. Dolley

Madison reported on the "hostility" toward her husband and that "disaffection stalks around us." Despite the personal risks he ran, it was a measure of political divisions that Madison's American adversaries mocked him at the time: "James the 1st has taken the field in person." With the British army on the march, Mayor Blake issued an appeal for "all able-bodied Citizens remaining here, and all freemen of color," to go to Bladensburg to construct fortifications considered necessary by Brigadier General Winder. Four to five hundred volunteers turned out. Blake later praised the patriotic conduct of the free blacks.[25]

Still there was no attempt to erect defenses in Washington itself. For critics at the time, the obvious place to defend was the Capitol. According to Colonel McClane, that is precisely what Secretary Armstrong urged on August 23. He also recommended using adjacent private buildings for defensive purposes. His plan was not adopted. On the same day, according to a friend of the president, New York banker Jacob Barker, Secretary Armstrong also relayed a proposal to blow up the Capitol to prevent it from falling into British hands. Declining the proposition, Madison was reported to have said, "it would have a better effect in arousing the nation into resistance for the enemy to do it."[26]

That morning local newspapers attempted to calm fears by assuring readers of the unlikelihood of a British advance on the city, and that in any case there were sufficient men to successfully ward off an attack. At midday Winder was informed that the British still had not moved out of Upper Marlboro. With 6,000 men at his disposal, the American commander finally contemplated seizing the initiative. Just as he permitted himself to dream of winning a stirring victory, the British army moved out of Upper Marlboro.[27]

Having made his arrangements with Cockburn, Ross pressed ahead with the army at 4:00 P.M. on Tuesday, August 23. He continued to mask his intentions by first heading in the direction of Washington, then swinging toward Alexandria. A detachment of Americans engaged the British. Major Peter of the D.C. Militia artillery had set up his battery of six artillery pieces, supported by Captain John Stull's "riflemen," who were in fact armed with muskets. Just prior to the arrival of the British advance party on the scene, with General Ross typically in the vanguard, Peter had been ordered by Winder to retire. No sooner had he done so than Ross and other officers appeared. Peter directed Stull to open fire.[28]

Peter maintained for decades afterward that had these "riflemen" been actually armed with rifles instead of muskets, then the British general would have been shot and the advance on Washington abandoned. A British officer confirmed that the Americans fired a volley at Ross, the musket balls coming close to hitting their target. To cover his retreat afterward, Peter ordered several artillery salvos, which the British also confirmed had been aimed very accurately. Since Ross had landed five days previously, "incredibly," as Walter Lord remarked, "this was the first American artillery to fire on the enemy." The British returned fire, and the American detachment retreated to Long Old Fields.[29]

The invaders then made camp for the night near Melwood, the estate of Ignatius Digges (close to present-day Andrews Air Force Base). Even then the Americans could not be sure that Ross was about to strike at the capital city. Was this just another feint before the raiders retraced their steps the short distance to Upper Marlboro and headed elsewhere? As the British settled down for the night, they were being watched by Secretary of State Monroe as they "slung their kettles." It was time for the troops to eat and perhaps make tea.[30] But they were far from idle or complacent.

Lieutenant Colonel William Wood of the 85th Regiment later confided that on both August 22 and the following day, British officers were seriously concerned that they could have been surrounded, attacked, or cut off. The possibility of being forced into a humiliating surrender crossed the minds of some. Ross and his officers, professionals that they were, based their dispositions and expectations on what they thought their enemy's strategy should be. On this count they were justifiably apprehensive that they were in a vulnerable position. While marking time until the additional marines, marine artillery, and seamen could catch up, Ross contemplated a daring nighttime raid on an American camp three miles away. The assault was aborted when it was discovered that the enemy had not only been substantially reinforced but also had moved camp five miles farther away. Meanwhile, Cockburn's seamen and the marine artillery succeeded in joining the army overnight.[31]

In the prevailing situation, when the two armies were camped so close to one another, it is no surprise that each side feared a nighttime assault. As it happened American encampments were disturbed on the nights of both August 22 and 23 by jittery sentries opening fire. At Long Old Fields on the twenty-second, shots were fired when a drove of cattle arrived in the camp. The following night things were just as bad in the camp at Bladensburg, where troops from Baltimore were assembling. A soldier in the 5th Regiment recalled that there were two false alarms that the British were advancing on them within five minutes of each other. A few minutes after the second alarm, the men were ordered to march to Washington. They had hardly gone more than a mile when they were ordered to halt, with the troops remaining under arms until morning. Not surprisingly, the men were exhausted.[32]

Following Winder's orders to retreat, the District of Columbia Militia encamped at the Washington Navy Yard. It was a long night for the commanding general, who did not know which way the British might come. The enemy could cross the Eastern Branch of the Potomac (now the Anacostia River) by several bridges: a lower bridge, an upper bridge called Stoddert's Bridge, and a third upstream at the old tobacco port of Bladensburg. If the enemy came by way of Long Old Fields, Winder knew they would attempt to cross by means of one of the lower bridges. He decided it would be prudent to post an infantry unit at the lower crossing and to burn Stoddert's Bridge. He made arrangements with Captain Thomas Tingey, the British-born commander of the Navy Yard, to destroy the span. Between 3:00 A.M. and 4:00 A.M., visible to the British pickets ten miles away, a red glow colored the sky as flames leapt up from the burning bridge.[33]

Unknown to the Americans, a dramatic last-minute hitch occurred for the British plans. While the two go-getters, Ross and Cockburn, were preparing to risk everything in a daring assault on Washington, a contrasting chemistry existed between the two more cautious commanders, Cochrane and Codrington. According to the latter, the vice admiral had decided that he wanted the land-based operation terminated forthwith and was not, it seems, pleased with Cockburn's unauthorized decision to accompany Ross in pressing ahead for Washington. Writing on the day Barney's flotilla was destroyed, August 22, Codrington responded to news of this success by penning a stinging commentary. In comments directed at Cockburn, he emphasized how much he despised "humbug and boasting." He accused the rear admiral of not knowing "what arrangement is, and yet he pushes himself into such a position as to make everything subservient to his self sufficiency." Codrington concluded by expressing a wish that Cockburn would return to England. Rumors even reached Britain that Codrington and Cockburn eventually ended up not being on speaking terms, an accusation Codrington denied.[34] As it happened, it was on that very day too that Cochrane received English newspapers that detailed the fraud trial at the Old Bailey in London involving his nephew, Lord Cochrane. While he hoped the young man would be proven innocent, the "poor Admiral" confided to Codrington that the "horrid business . . . [had] caused me so much uneasiness."[35] With his family name in disgrace in London, he was even less disposed to incur additional disrepute by sanctioning a risky raid on Washington.

Ross received notification of Cochrane's opposition to the land-based operation in the early morning hours of August 24. This communication had the effect of prompting a last-minute crisis in terms of decision making, at least according to Scott. His version of events is that he found Cockburn and Ross asleep when he returned. Having roused them, Cockburn had to browbeat the nervous general into proceeding. "It is too late—we ought not to have advanced—there is now no choice to us. We must go on." Claiming that he had arrived in camp at 2:00 A.M., Scott noted that there was a long period of animated deliberations that ended with the "eastern sky" becoming "tinged with the blush of day" as Ross finally struck his hand against his forehead. "Well, be it so," he exclaimed, "we shall proceed!"[36]

Scott's version of events at this time has dominated the historical narrative. In what has been portrayed as a second so-called crisis of confidence in less than twenty-four hours, Ross was characterized once more as a weak-kneed commander. All too often accepted at face value, at the very least Scott's account should be scrutinized. Whereas he recalled finding Ross and Cockburn asleep on his return, the rear admiral claimed in his "Memoir of Services" that he was in the act of imploring the general to push ahead with his mission when he received Cochrane's order to abort. Newly unearthed evidence from Evans's unpublished "Memorandum of Operations" also contradicts Scott in more substantive matters. According to Evans, Cochrane's letter was received at daybreak on August 24. He portrays Ross as poised to pounce on Washington and giving Cochrane's recommendation short shrift. If his timing is correct, that Scott returned at daybreak rather than at 2:00 A.M., then the discussion about what to do next did not last long. The army resumed its march on Washington between 5:00 A.M. and 6:00 A.M.[37]

What is not in doubt is that Cochrane's communication presented a major difficulty, particularly if the attempt to take Washington ended in failure. The vice admiral's vacillation during these operations exasperated both army and navy officers. Knowing which whim to follow proved extremely difficult. Rear Admiral Malcolm testified to his frustration with Cochrane, whom he described as "so very unsteady" and that he "contradicts his own orders daily." In a similar vein he recalled in another letter home that his commanding officer "carries certain notions too far and talks much of them but never defines them in his orders. We are therefore obliged to judge for ourselves and I endeavour to be correct." Cochrane was well known for being hard to contend with. Lord Keith, a senior figure in the Royal Navy at the time, described him as "a crack-headed, unsafe man."[38]

Ignoring Cochrane's request, Ross and his army set out on the final stage of its march directly toward Washington. They were to be guided by two spies secured by Evans. This route was taken to mask the general's true intention to proceed by Bladensburg and to encourage the Americans to destroy the major bridges across the Potomac, hoping to avoid them being used to cut him off should he be forced to retreat. When the army reached the junction of the Bladensburg and Washington roads, thirty mounted artillery drivers pursued an American cavalry patrol for some two miles on the direct route to the capital, blowing their trumpets and making as much noise as possible with a view to convincing the Americans that the entire British army was intending to seize the major bridges. Having sold another decoy, the column then moved with all speed toward Bladensburg, which was known to be the location of the closest fordable part of the Eastern Branch of the Potomac.[39] What followed was a race against time for both the British and Americans.

Major General Robert Ross, unknown artist. Courtesy Stephen Campbell.

Mrs. Elizabeth Ross, original pencil drawing, artist unknown. Courtesy Francis De Courcy Hamilton.

Lieutenant General Sir George De Lacy Evans, G.C.B., photograph by Roger Fenton, 1855. Courtesy Library of Congress, Prints and Photographs Division, LC-USZC4-9309.

Sir George Cockburn, G.C.B., Rear Admiral of the Red and One of His Majesty's Lords of the Admiralty, by I. J. Halls, Esq., engraving by Charles Turner, 1819. Rear Admiral Cockburn poses against a background of buildings burning in Washington. Courtesy Library of Congress, Prints and Photographs Division, LC-DIG-pga-02909.

James Madison, by John Vanderlyn, 1816. Courtesy the White House Historical Association, White House Collection 968.627.1.

William Henry Winder, engraving by Charles Balthazar Julien Fevret de Saint-Mémin, 1804. Courtesy Library of Congress, Prints and Photographs Division, LC-USZ61-1899.

Commodore Joshua Barney, by Charles Willson Peale, ca. 1788. Courtesy Library of Congress, Prints and Photographs Division, LC-USZ62-395.

Dolley Madison, by Gilbert Stuart, 1804. Courtesy the White House Historical Association, White House Collection 944.1737.1.

John Sioussat, unknown artist. Sioussat was the president's servant who proposed to booby trap the Executive Mansion and who later contested British claims that they found a banquet at the residence. Courtesy the White House Historical Association, White House Collection.

George Washington, by Gilbert Stuart, 1797. This portrait was saved from being destroyed or captured by the British at the instigation of Dolley Madison. Courtesy the White House Historical Association, White House Collection 800.1290.1.

The Fall of Washington . . . or Maddy in Full Flight, engraving, ca. 1814. This cartoon pours ridicule on President James Madison for fleeing from the British. Courtesy Library of Congress, Prints and Photographs Division, LC-DIG-ppmcsa-3112.

101

Captain Henry Shaw, unknown artist, ca. 1814. This miniature of Capt. Richard Henry Shaw, 1/4th Regiment, is displayed in a bookcase in the residential quarters of the White House. Shaw is reputed to have set fire to the residence. Courtesy the White House Historical Association, White House Collection 998.1775.1.

The President's House, by George Munger, ca. 1814. This depicts the mansion after the fire. Courtesy the White House Historical Association, White House Collection 2001.1800.1.

A View of the Capitol after the Conflagration of the 24th August 1814, engraving by George Munger, ca. 1814. This image includes a representation of the burnt shell of the Sewall-Belmont House. Courtesy Library of Congress, Prints and Photographs Division, LC-DIG-ppsca-30570.

Watercolor and wash depicting a waterfront fire, probably the burning of the Washington Navy Yard, on the Eastern Branch of the Potomac River, Washington, D.C., by William Thornton, ca. 1815. Courtesy Library of Congress, Prints and Photographs Division, LC-USZC4-5716.

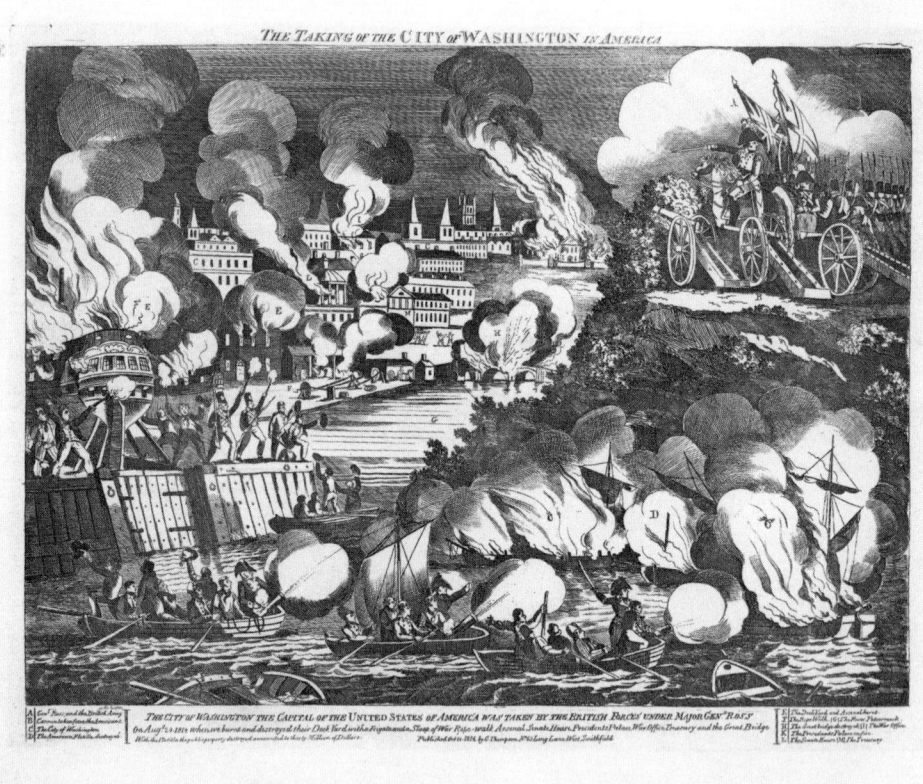

The Taking of the City of Washington in America, wood engraving, 1814. This composite image shows the British operation to destroy Commodore Barney's flotilla, Ross's victory at the Battle of Bladensburg, and the burning of the public buildings in Washington as well as the Navy Yard. Courtesy Library of Congress, Prints and Photographs Division, LC-DIG-ppmsca-31113.

Capture of the City of Washington, London, 1815. This is a British representation of events after Ross's advance party was attacked as it entered Washington. It shows General Ross directing his forces to burn the President's House, Capitol, and the Sewall-Belmont House (from which shots were fired that killed the general's horse and several of his men as he attempted to negotiate the surrender of the city). Courtesy National Archives.

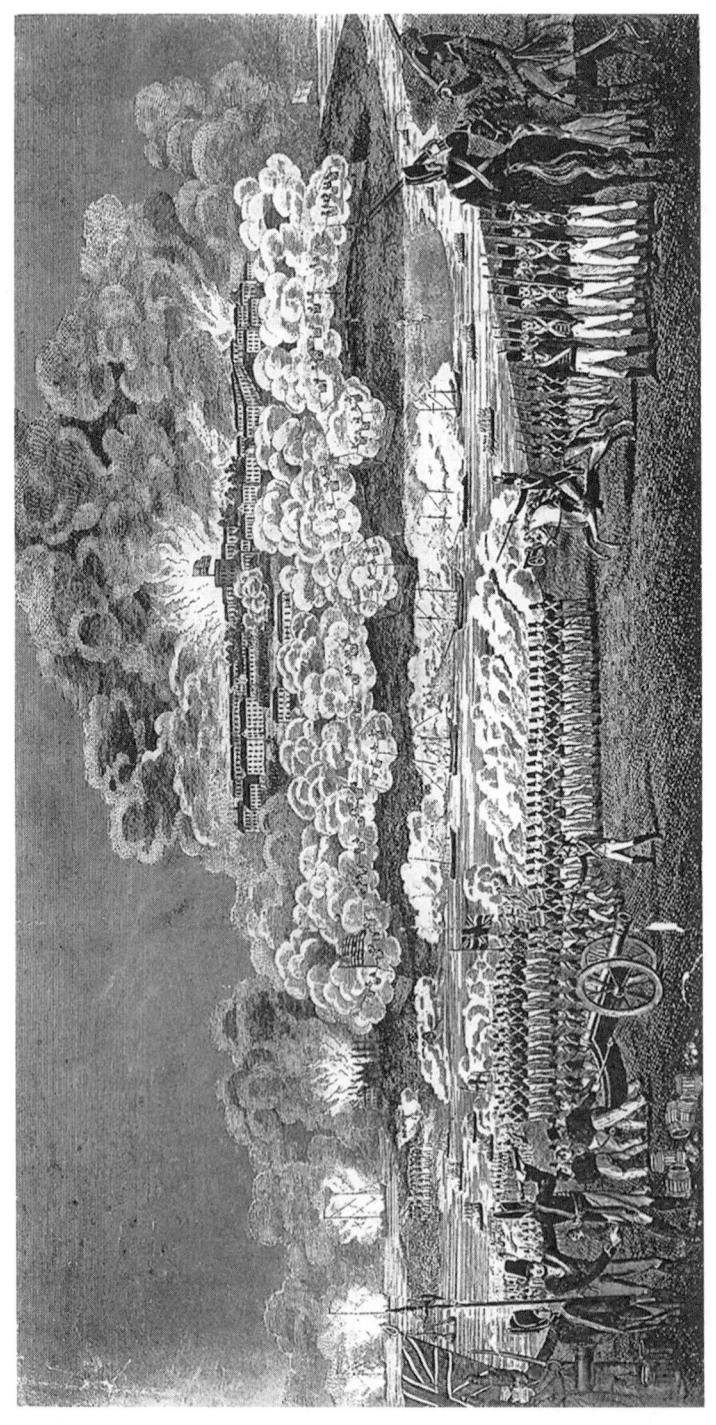

Washington. A Representation of the Capture of the City of Washington, by the British Forces under the Command of Major Gen. Ross and Rear Adm. Sir G. Cockburn, August 24, 1814, engraving, ca. 1815. This British depiction of the capture of the U.S. capital, created in 1815, greatly exaggerates the physical size of the city and the fighting involved in its seizure. Courtesy Library of Congress, Prints and Photographs Division, LC-USZ62-44919.

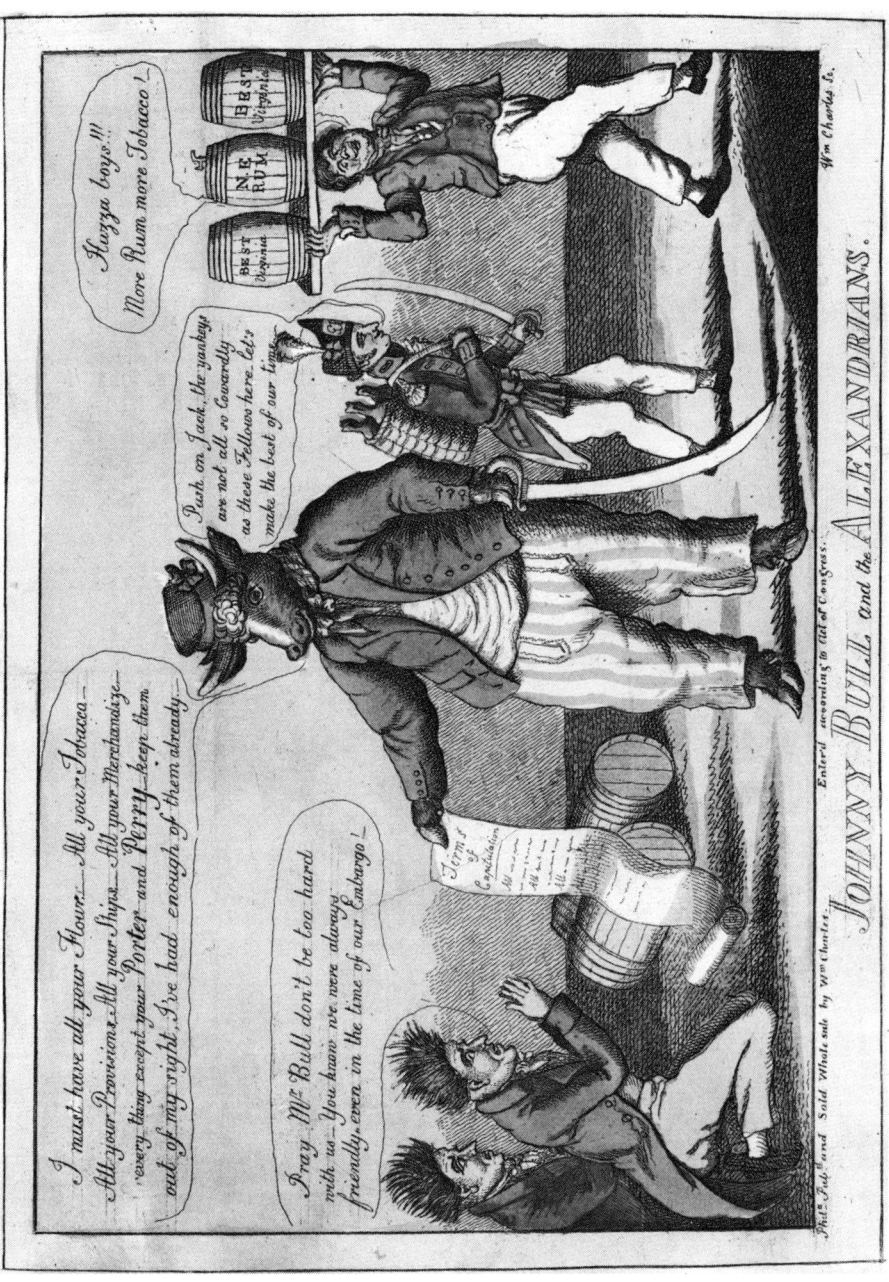

Johnny Bull and the Alexandrians, etching by William Charles, 1814. This cartoon depicts the ransom demands of Captain James Gordon's Royal Navy squadron. Courtesy Library of Congress, Prints and Photographs Division, LC-DIG-pga-05639.

Francis Scott Key, wood engraving, n.d. Courtesy Library of Congress, Prints and Photographs Division, LC-USZ62-53017.

Death of General Ross at Baltimore, by Alonzo Chappel, ca. 1859. This illustration portrays Ross facing the enemy when he was shot. Courtesy Library of Congress, Prints and Photographs Division, LC-USZ62-7718.

The Death of General Ross, near Baltimore, as Soon as He Perceived That He Was Wounded He Fell into the Arms of a Brother Officer, engraving by G. M. Brighty, ca. 1816. By the trajectory of the Congreve rocket fired by his British comrades, this version of Ross's death indicates that he had turned his back to the enemy when he was mortally wounded. Courtesy Library of Congress, Prints and Photographs Division, LC-USZ62-100670.

John Bull and the Baltimoreans, etching by William Charles, ca. 1814. This image shows Ross being shot by riflemen concealed in bushes. Courtesy Library of Congress, Prints and Photographs Division, LC-USZ62-7431.

Ross of Bladensburg coat of arms. Courtesy Christopher T. George.

Ross Monument, Rostrevor, Northern Ireland. Courtesy John McCavitt.

CHAPTER 7

HIGH NOON AT BLADENSBURG

Ross stole a march on the Americans when he pushed his men headlong for Washington in grueling climatic conditions. Time was of the essence. And while the British were en route for the U.S. capital from early in the morning of August 24, Secretary of War Armstrong was even then assuring Mrs. Madison that there was "no danger." It also took some time for General Winder to be convinced that Ross was marching on the capital by way of Bladensburg. The British feint earlier that day had left him uncertain as to their intentions. The American commanding officer eventually realized that the British were indeed on their way to the capital via Bladensburg, where the Eastern Branch of the Potomac could be forded. Following consultations early that day with President Madison and members of his cabinet, Winder was left in a "high state of excitement." Under enormous political pressure, he confided to an aide, "I am but a nominal commander," the president and Armstrong having "interfered with my intended operations, and I greatly fear for the day."[1] As Ross began his final advance toward Washington, U.S. civilian and military authorities were still at sixes and sevens.

At approximately 10:00 A.M. reports confirmed that the British were advancing to Bladensburg. Winder mobilized his forces to march out to join up with the Baltimore militia already there. In an extraordinary oversight he gave no thought to incorporating Commodore Barney and his four hundred navy men or Captain Samuel Miller and his 113 U.S. Marines in the defense. These forces had been left to guard a lower bridge on the Eastern Branch, where the president consulted with Barney. Realizing that a considerable number of the sailors were "tall, strapping negroes," Madison queried whether the African Americans would run from the British. Barney replied, "No sir . . . they don't know how to run: they will die by their guns first." Convinced, the commander in chief ordered Barney to Bladensburg and then galloped off.[2]

The men available to Winder were mostly militia from Maryland and the District of Columbia. While it had originally been planned that Virginia would furnish 2,000 militia for the defense of Washington, none ultimately took part in the upcoming battle. Supply difficulties and incompetence resulted in 700 troops of the 60th Regiment of Virginia Militia under Colonel George Minor remaining in the capital. Most exasperatingly of all, by the time an armory clerk insisted on counting and recounting flints to be issued to them, Minor's men were too late to offer assistance. More than 1,500 other Virginians were occupied shadowing Captain James Gordon's squadron as it ascended the Potomac, a diversionary strategy that was working well. Meanwhile, none of the projected 5,000 militia from Pennsylvania materialized—Winder's letter of August 18 requesting them was not received by state authorities until August 23.[3]

By the time they arrived in Bladensburg, Ross's troops were in poor shape. As the redcoats had been sweltering in scorching temperatures along sunbaked, dusty roads, the heat began taking its toll. Although he allowed the men to refresh themselves at a stream, stragglers soon littered the roadsides after the march resumed. The British general could afford little let up as he dashed for Washington, even as men fell dead from heatstroke in the ranks on what was reported locally to be the "hottest day ever felt." Ross realized, however, that the less time the Americans had to congregate their forces, the fewer would be British casualties—and the greater the chance of taking the American capital. Forced marches in such grueling conditions were by no means unusual in warfare of the period. During the Peninsular War, rifleman Edward Costello recorded men dying on the march during the "melting"' month of July. During Napoleon's advance to Moscow in September 1812, French troops dropped dead from heat. It was also far from a pleasant duty that day for Ross and Rear Admiral Cockburn. The column was ambushed by riflemen on several occasions on the way to Bladensburg. Ross also, and unknowingly, was being specifically targeted. In later years it was claimed that Brigadier General William G. Belknap, father of William Worth Belknap, a future U.S. secretary of war (1869–76), was "a youth in the War of 1812, and with a cousin endeavored to ambush and kill general Ross near Bladensburg."[4]

Just as the British were not in an ideal condition to fight, the Americans assembling at what was to become a haphazard front line on the Washington side of the bridge at Bladensburg had problems too. Lieutenant Colonel Joseph Sterett's troops had arrived from Baltimore the day before and were exhausted from the heat. False alarms throughout the night had also resulted in the men getting little rest. An earthwork erected for heavy cannon had to be altered at the last minute to suit the 6-pounder cannon actually deployed by Colonel Decius Wadsworth because the parapet was too high. Major William Pinkney, in command of the rifle companies defending the bridge, realized that there was no time to alter the parapet along its whole length. Some effort was made, though, to conceal the cannon with brushwood. Fifty yards behind these gun emplacements, in an orchard, the blue-uniformed 5th Maryland Regiment anxiously awaited the arrival of the invaders. One militiaman, Ensign George Hoffman, arrived there exhausted and famished just before combat commenced. He recalled that the troops were so ravenous they broke their line to get apples before they were dismissed.[5]

As the Americans waited for the British, Pinkney was alarmed to see the 5th Regiment march away from his men to the other side of the orchard and reform some 500 yards away. Unknown to Pinkney, courageous but meddlesome Secretary of State Monroe, thinking he could improve the troop positions, had ordered the change.[6] Brigadier General Tobias Stansbury had positioned his brigade of Maryland militia, including regiments commanded by Lieutenant Colonel Jonathan Schutz and Colonel John Ragan, in the orchard with a view to supporting Pinkney and the artillery, which had a commanding view of the bridge. Proud of his role in the War of Independence, the secretary of state reveled in being called "Colonel Monroe" and could not resist the temptation to act as a military "tactician." He was also responsible for directing the U.S. Regiment of Light Dragoons, under Lieutenant Colonel Jacint Lavall, to a ravine to the rear of Stansbury's brigade where more than 300 men congregated, unable to see never mind join in any developing action.[7] Once again, American mistakes were playing into Ross's hands.

A "false alarm" occurred in American ranks when Colonel William Beall's troops from Annapolis marched into Bladensburg shortly before Ross's redcoats.[8] When the men realized that they were Americans and that Winder had arrived as well, the army raised three cheers. Beall's men tramped to a position in the rear. American troop deployments were disorganized. The men were all congregating on the Washington side of the Eastern Branch (in modern-day Cottage City and Colmar Manor), having withdrawn from the town of Bladensburg on the opposite bank. Winder failed to take control of even those troops he nominally commanded, admitting as much three days later in an apologetic letter to Armstrong. As a Baltimore correspondent put it at the time, the "rapidity of the enemy's march" was the key factor that "prevented the proper junction of our army." By noon, there was simply no time for the American general to improve his positions. A dust cloud rose over Lowndes Hill to the south of the town: this time the British *were* coming. And they were coming "rapidly" and in "very fine style," as an American field commander noted. The British officers, according to one report, maintained the momentum, driving the troops forward with their swords as the men gasped for breath. These officers would soon risk life and limb leading their soldiers in battle. As the column of redcoats appeared, the bright sunlight glinted on bayonets that were already fixed, perhaps with a view to unnerving the inexperienced American militiamen.[9]

Armed with two pearl-handled dueling pistols, President Madison arrived at Bladensburg, an area infamous as the "dueling ground" of Washington, and almost literally bumped into Ross and the British at high noon.[10] Cheers greeted Madison's party as they galloped along the road, heading "straight for the bridge, and the British." William Simmons, an American scout, managed to warn him in the nick of time. The president and his entourage reined in and turned around. They had assumed that a party of horsemen they had seen in the village were Americans. Instead, as Simmons was to testify, the horsemen were British—the lead elements of the invading army.[11]

Turning back toward their own forces, the presidential party soon found Brigadier General Winder. Secretary Armstrong had earlier predicted how the battle would go, bluntly informing Madison that the militia would be beaten. Winder was equally pessimistic about the prospects for success. Even before the fighting started, he was heard to remark to some of his men, "when you retreat, take notice you must retreat by the Georgetown Road." Apart from its effect on morale, this instruction was yet another tactical mistake. If the troops retreated along the Georgetown Road, they could not be reformed with the D.C. militia on the Washington Road. Winder's defeatism was becoming a self-fulfilling prophesy.[12]

Unsurprisingly, the presence of the president and cabinet bolstered morale, at least initially. As James Wilkinson put it at the time, "every eye was immediately turned upon the chief, every bosom throbbed with confidence, and every nerve was strung with valour." Monroe was especially confident of victory. According to a contemporary British account, the president "addressed the American army previous to the battle of Bladensburgh [sic], and recommended them to do their duty and fight well for the honour of their country, kill and make prisoners of all the Britishers."[13]

At the outset of the battle, Madison was with Winder to the rear of Stansbury's line. In other words, the president was just behind the American front line, some 500 yards from the bridge at Bladensburg. Apart from the day Lincoln was almost shot nearly fifty years later in July 1864 at Fort Stevens in Washington, D.C., during the Civil War, this was the only occasion when an incumbent U.S. president was on an active battlefield as commander in chief. Madison was in decided danger. Several U.S. newspapers recorded at the time that the president, the secretary of war, and the secretary of state "were in view of the enemy when they advanced." A private letter from a British participant claimed that "officers of the 85th distinctly" saw the president. Had there been "any cavalry on the spot," the correspondent goes on, "Madison might have been taken prisoner." The president had been known to don a "huge cockade" to identify himself as the commander in chief.[14] While there is ample testimony that the British were aware of Madison's presence on the battlefield, it cannot be categorically stated that Ross knew this before the battle began, thus influencing his tactics in an attempt to pull off a sensational coup by capturing the president.

Ross's army began assembling on Lowndes Hill in Bladensburg around noon, ready to attack the American lines. The troops halted there for some fifteen to twenty minutes. The Second Brigade closed up in time to be factored into his tactical planning, while the Third Brigade lagged in the rear. Lieutenant George De Lacy Evans recorded that the "impatience of the troops to reach the expected scene of action" had "caused an interval of more than a mile between each" of the three brigades. Contrary to the uncritical acceptance accorded to Captain Harry Smith's representation of Ross rushing into battle helter-skelter without having a "good look," other accounts indicate that the British general took time to carefully survey the American positions. Hanson Catlett, a U.S. army surgeon, testified to Congress later that some British "officers were seen observing us from the opposite heights." Indeed, Ross later paid tribute to the advice of Captain Thomas Blanchard of the Royal Engineers for his assistance in sizing up the American positions. The pressure on the British commander was immense as an immediate decision whether to advance or retreat was required. As Peter Snow has written: "Ross was playing for the highest stakes. Defeat would mean an almost certain court martial."[15]

Lieutenant Colonel William Wood of the 85th Regiment provided interesting details of the British deliberations about what to do next, advance or retreat.[16] He stated that Ross assembled some of his senior officers in a house on Lowndes Hill, the upper story of which "completely overlooked the first line of American troops, with the reserves then in sight." The U.S. positions appeared to be "formidable." Working on the wrong assumption that the enemy troops were fresh while his own men were exhausted, Ross discussed his options with his officers, including whether to retreat. That the enemy was discovered to be composed mainly of militia was the vital factor governing the decision to press ahead with the attack.[17]

With no small degree of exaggeration, Ross later wrote in his dispatch that the "Enemy was discovered strongly posted on very Commanding Heights formed in two Lines" on the opposite side of the river.[18] The American front line was composed of the Maryland militia, while there was supporting artillery and riflemen congregated near the bridge. Evans, Ross's military secretary, observed that the second American line was on the crest of the hill leading from Bladensburg toward the American capital. About a mile away, it comprised Barney's flotilla men, U.S. Marines, D.C. militia, a few hundred regulars, and several units of Maryland militia. Ross reckoned that the Americans numbered between 8,000 and 9,000 men, double his own force. His experienced military eye would have quickly noted, however, that there were yawning gaps in the enemy lines. Many units were still in the process of taking up their positions, while others were arriving. Ross also observed breastworks with a battery in the center of the enemy's forward positions. Spanning the river to Bladensburg stretched a narrow wooden bridge.[19] As Ross looked at it, there were no American defenses to the left of the bridge, where the deeper water was not fordable. If the British forced the bridge and proceeded along the road to Washington, the entire right flank of the American front line would be exposed. In deciding to launch an attack before all of his troops had reached Bladensburg, Ross concluded that he could exploit the disorganized enemy line and seize a bridgehead across the river.

Ross's great strengths included his ability to read the ground and to quickly seize an opportunity. He also thrived in adversity.

He made his name tackling greater odds, not least at Krabbendam (1799), Maida (1806), and Roncesvalles (1813). As the general considered what to do, an officer reportedly asked him, "What will be said of us in England, if we stop now?" Ross is supposed to have responded, with typical tongue-in-cheek bravado, "if it rain militia, then . . . we will go on."[20] As the president feared, the British commander "may be bound also to do something, and therefore to risk everything." In truth, having come so far, *could* Ross turn back? Despite his official dispatch describing the American positions as formidable, his private opinion differed. The general later confided to Rear Admiral Malcolm that "three thousand men well posted would have obliged him to retreat."[21]

Colonel Arthur Brooke recorded Ross's plan of attack in his diary. Colonel William Thornton's First Brigade, comprising the 85th Regiment as well as the light companies of the 1/4th, 1/21st, and 1/44th, would take the lead in storming across the bridge. The Second Brigade, made up of the 1/4th and 1/44th and commanded by Brooke, was to follow. The 1/44th was tasked with sweeping away American resistance on the front line, while the 1/4th prepared to push on toward the second line. The Third Brigade, which included the 1/21st and a battalion of Royal Marines, would be held in reserve. Brooke's evidence about proceedings in the initial phase of British operations at Bladensburg is wholly at odds with that of Captain Smith. Often cited by historians, Smith was strongly critical that Thornton, soon followed by Ross, charged off to attack the Americans, leaving him to wait on the Second and Third Brigades with only vague instructions.[22]

Before the main British thrust into Bladensburg, the advance party from the 1/4th and 85th, led by Major George Brown and supported by the mounted artillery drivers, charged into the village. A fortified mill close to the bridge was found abandoned.[23] An officer of the 1/4th recalled that when this "advanced guard" went into the town, the Americans opened up a heavy fire from the opposite side of the bridge, raking the road, forcing the British to find shelter among the houses. Only a small number of redcoats entered Bladensburg in the first instance. In vain, the American scout Simmons attempted to get his countrymen to "reserve their fire for a few minutes" until it could do more damage against the main army, just then "coming down the hill." Bad as the situation was for the British, it could have been worse. They were surprised that the Americans had not taken the opportunity of using local buildings as cover to hold them back for several hours at least.[24]

Ross has been criticized for insisting that his lead units storm across the bridge at Bladensburg rather than ford the river farther upstream. His decision was correct, though, as Brigadier General Stansbury later explained. He had earlier ordered forty horsemen with axes to cut down the bridge and was appalled to discover that this instruction had not been carried out. Recognizing that the British could still have "forded the stream above," the destruction of the bridge "would, in some degree, impede their progress, and give our artillery and riflemen more time and opportunity to act with effect against them." In other words, the British would have been more exposed to American fire fording the river than in crossing the bridge. Modern military historian Ronald J. Drez, agrees. He describes fording a river under enemy fire as the "worst of all possible tactical situations."[25]

Thornton's brigade formed up to storm across the bridge. As the British troops advanced, they came under artillery and rifle fire. Captain Benjamin Burch had brought a total of five 6-pounders of the Washington Artillery Company onto the field. In yet another sign of the belated and hurried manner in which many American units took up their positions, Burch recalled that he had "dismounted, and took charge of my pieces, and in a few moments we opened fire." Founded by James Hoban, the Irish architect of the Executive Mansion, the Washington Artillery Company was comprised mostly of Irishmen from Georgetown. These "Irish artillerymen" wrought havoc on British troops, many of whom were also Irish.[26] The Baltimore artillery and Wadsworth's battery blasted the enemy too, with Wadsworth reserving his fire until the redcoats filled the bridge. Lieutenant George Gleig recalled that when these guns opened up, "almost an entire company was swept down." American cannon and rifle fire had taken a devastating toll on the British who had been unable to get close enough to return fire with their much-shorter-range muskets. The first attempt to cross the bridge had been repelled.[27]

The American bombardment forced Thornton's men to take cover among the houses, where they continued to come under attack. Cannonballs perforated the sides of buildings. Practiced in light-infantry tactics in America in the days of the War of Independence, as Matthew Spring has demonstrated, British troops in general were trained to skirmish according to the lie of the land, acting independently and taking what cover was offered. During the Peninsular War, British soldiers used cover as necessary. At the Battle of Talavera in 1809, troops were ordered to lie down when they came under artillery fire.[28] Honed by years of recent experience fighting the French, the men of Ross's light brigade were simply resorting to standard tactics after coming under fire at Bladensburg.

The bridge had been strewn with British dead and wounded. The Americans "gave three loud huzzas." One soldier of the 85th, a Scotsman who had seated himself on the steps of a house and whose arm, shattered by roundshot, dangled now by a fiber, shouted back, "Dinna halloo, my fine lads, you're no' yet out of the wood! Wait a wee, wait a wee, wie your skirling!" Meanwhile, Private Corbett of the 85th took some comfort from the fact that he and his comrades had been ordered to take cover in a storehouse, where they availed of the opportunity to fill their canteens with whiskey.[29]

Major Pinkney, commander of the Baltimore riflemen, recalled that when the first assault on the bridge was driven back, the British did not renew the attack straightaway; a long interval ensued. Before attempting to storm the bridge once more, Ross deployed Congreve rocket launchers, which set up near a warehouse. To the mostly untested Americans, this was a frightening "new weapon."[30] The rockets arched over the river in a "snaking swirl of smoke." British accounts indicate that they also utilized one 6-pounder and two 3-pounders in the battle.[31] From the start, Ross's men were heavily outgunned in artillery.

When the British opened fire with their rockets and cannon, President Madison and his cabinet secretaries witnessed what then unfolded from just behind the front line. The initial salvo of rockets proved to be completely inaccurate. Captain Henry Thompson, 1st Baltimore Horse Artillery, could clearly see that none of the weapons struck American lines. If the first salvo of Congreves was harmless, the wholly unpredictable flight of the missiles served a vital purpose in terms of unnerving the militiamen. Prone to changing direction with no warning, the rockets "trailed flame and smoke, made a fearful noise and blew up with a thunderclap, showering shards of metal or case shot on those in their vicinity." After a few well-aimed rounds of American artillery fire targeted the rocket launchers, they stopped firing for a time. Winder, for all his disorganization, did not lack courage. He tried to rally his men by calling out to them not be afraid—the rockets were harmless. Yet he advised the president to move back.[32]

Exactly when Madison retired from the battlefield has hitherto been misrepresented. A report quickly circulated that he saw the first rocket launched by the British "and instantly retreated. He was seen gliding down a hill, and was watched until he went entirely out of sight." His alleged rapid departure was soon called the "flight of Madison."[33] Before long he was caricatured in an American poem as the winner of the "Bladensburg races:"

> And still, as fast as he rode on,
> 'Twas marvellous to view
> How be outrode the CABINET,
> And eke the troopers too.[34]

The reality, however, is that Madison took enormous personal risks on that Wednesday, the day General Ross almost captured him before the battle even began. In fact, by remaining on the battlefield, the president continued to run risks.

Winder later testified that the first three or four rockets "passed very high above the heads of the line." Thereafter they were fired in a more horizontal direction. James Monroe saw rockets "fall near the President," a contention supported by another contemporary American account. Madison stood his ground, but many of the militiamen did not. The rockets now passing very close above the heads of Schutz's and Ragan's troops, composing the center and left of Stansbury's line, a "universal flight of these two regiments was the consequence." Managing to rally about forty men, Ragan pitched from his horse and was taken prisoner. That substantial numbers of the Americans on the front line were spooked by the Congreve rockets is hardly surprising. After all, an entire brigade of French troops "panicked" and fled under rocket fire at the Battle of Leipzig in 1813.[35]

Apart from being terrorized by the rockets, the Americans on the front line were also conscious, as Stansbury noted, that a British "flanking party, concealed by the banks and bushes, was pushing up the river to turn our left." The number of British troops who forded the river is a matter of some dispute, though it is clear some did.[36] Whatever the size of this flanking force, Ross was engineering a pincer movement to attack both flanks of his enemy's front line, and thus only a matter of time before his seasoned regulars prevailed. It is vitally important to bear in mind too that the Americans thought they were facing overwhelming numbers of British regulars led by Lord Hill. "Fevered imaginations" ran wild in this regard. "Intelligence" had reached Winder the day before the battle that the British force advancing on Washington comprised 10,000 men.[37]

At about the same time as British forces fanned along the river and crossed the ford, about one o'clock, they also made ready to charge across the bridge once more. Bladensburg was a piecemeal battle, not a set-piece action. From a British point of view, it was fought according to Ross's penchant for light-infantry tactics, utilizing terrain and the initiative of his troops. A map drawn by a British officer shows the rocket brigade deploying on the approach to the bridge and then in the middle of it, perhaps suggesting that further salvos of rockets preceded the renewed attempt to cross. Knowing that Ross had ordered the 1/4th and 1/44th to form up and follow him, Thornton rode forward on his gray horse. Lieutenant Scott noted that the colonel "dashed forward, followed by his gallant regiment, in a manner that elicited enthusiastic applause" from the British commanding general. As soon as the leading company of the 85th advanced, American fire cut down seven men. Thornton and his troops pressed ahead regardless, Gleig recording that they ran over the bodies of their own dead and wounded. This time, as a Baltimore paper recorded it, when the British troops fell, their comrades "merely threw them out of the way." Running in small groups at full pelt, Thornton's men made it to the other side. In the operation to seize the bridge, Major Brown, commander of the British advance, was wounded "severely in the groin" by a musket ball. Thornton was soon followed across by Ross as well as the Second Brigade, Colonel Brooke recording that his men came under heavy fire as they deployed prior to advancing on the Americans.[38]

Ross's key initial objective had been achieved, getting across the river in sufficient numbers to enable an assault on the American positions. But the hardest fighting had yet to come.

CHAPTER 8

"Hero of Bladensburg"

When Ross's men successfully reached the eastern side of the Eastern Branch of the Potomac by means of the bridge as well as fording the river further upstream, the moment of truth arrived for the American militia. Trepidation permeated their ranks. An American officer who was overheard giving orders to provide blankets to carry off the wounded soon found his men had taken to their heels instead. Before taking flight as the British advanced, Ensign George Hoffman of the First Regiment of Maryland Militia noted that his company had opened fire. Indeed, according to an American eyewitness, James Wallace, a blaze of fire, smoke and roar of gunfire erupted along the American line.[1]

After the smoke cleared from the volley fired by his company, Hoffman looked around him. To his evident astonishment, he saw his comrades tumbling over a fence in their haste to retreat. Then a cannonball hit the ground directly in front of him before bouncing over his head.[2] In this early stage of the battle, Secretary of War Armstrong, who had done so little to preempt the British attack, pointed out to President Madison the "disorder and retreat of a part of the first line, soon after that action began, and stigmatise[d] it as base." Americans and British observers afterward poked fun at the militia for the swiftness of their flight. "Never did men with arms in their hands, make better use of their legs."[3] Indeed, for the speed of his own retreat, Armstrong was later caricatured as "Legstrong."[4] It is clear, however, that some of the American militia and artillery on the front line mounted stiff resistance, if only for a short time.

After crossing the river, the British troops reformed and advanced in line, coming under heavy fire. The redcoats charged up the hill at the Americans who had retreated, a substantial number of whom withdrew in a disciplined manner, firing frequent volleys as they pulled back. So even after coming under attack from Congreve rockets and artillery as well as facing a frontal assault by British infantry, there were elements of the inexperienced militia in the forward positions who performed gallantly. Many of these men belonged to

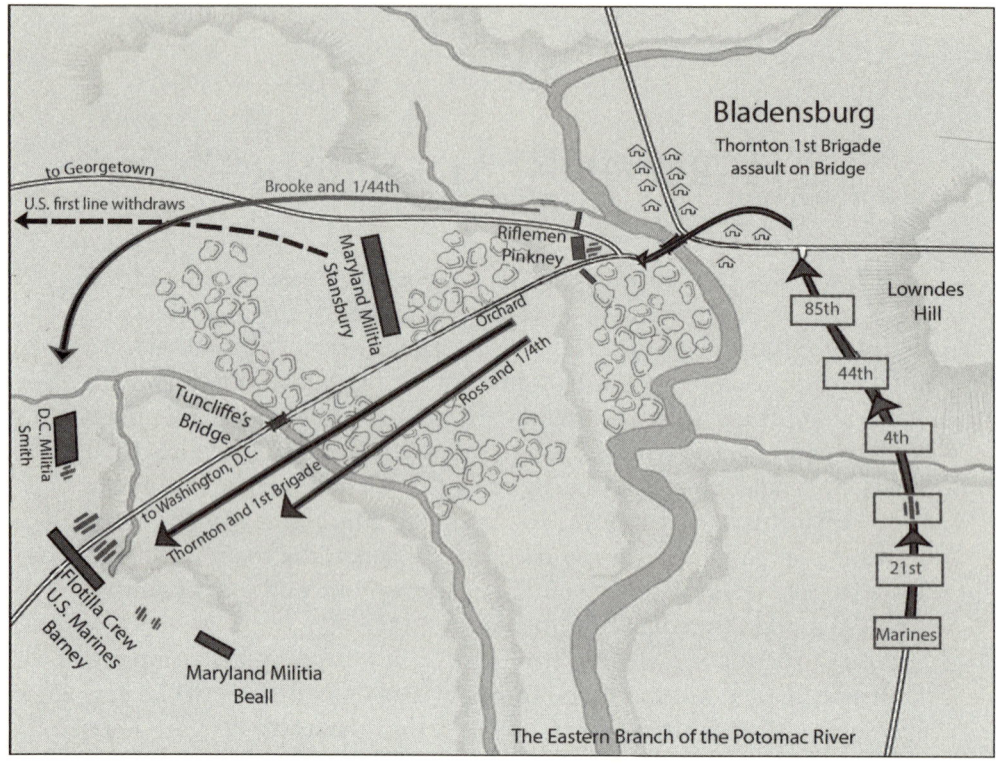

Battle of Bladensburg, August 24, 1814. Map by Mark McCavitt. *Copyright © 2016 by the University of Oklahoma Press*

the 5th Maryland Regiment from Baltimore. On two occasions these militiamen staggered the British advance. As the battle raged, forty British artillery drivers on horseback, nicknamed "Cossacks," charged the American guns. Six rank and file were wounded in this action, along with four horses killed and eight wounded. A couple of Colonel Wadsworth's cannon were soon captured, while the artillerymen of one Baltimore battery were forced to withdraw. The 5th Regiment, however, maintained the fight. Meanwhile, some British troops were able to take some cover in the orchard earlier occupied by American forces. Under inaccurate fire, their officers nonchalantly picked apples from the trees.[5]

Monroe's earlier decision to withdraw Stansbury's brigade from the orchard before the fighting commenced was now proving to be a critical mistake. The British were not able to find shelter there but did utilize it to screen a flanking movement. General Winder directed American artillery to fire on a barn in the lower part of the orchard where British forces were believed to be congregating. He then observed a heavy concentration of troops using the cover of the orchard to advance along the Washington Road. This was Colonel Thornton's First Brigade. Soon it was in position to flank the 5th Maryland, which was ordered to retreat. Having until this stage acted with resolution, the Baltimore men fled in disorder. Lieutenant Colonel Joseph Sterett, commander of the 5th, later testified, "we were outflanked and defeated in as short a time as such an operation could be performed." In the end, according to one of his privates, John Pendleton Kennedy, the regiment was driven off the field "with the bayonet."[6]

When it appeared that the American front line positions were about to be overrun, Winder issued an order for a general retreat from this part of the battlefield. Meanwhile, the American commander tried to direct the retreating militia along the Washington Road to reform at a second line with the D.C. militia, additional units of Maryland militia, some regulars, Commodore Barney's sailors, and U.S. Marines. But as they had been earlier instructed, the militiamen mostly fled down the Georgetown Road, pursued by the British 1/44th, which had by this stage crossed the river too. Writing afterward, James Monroe claimed that the presidential entourage "retired after our little batteries were carried, and the left of our line broken." Even then, instead of returning to Washington, Madison moved to behind the line anchored by Barney's guns.[7]

As the battle unfolded, the psychological effect on unseasoned American militia of British regulars advancing despite destructive fire was telling. A British officer claimed that he was later informed that the Americans were completely unnerved, "that it was of no use staying there to be shot, for the Britishers did not mind being killed at all." Armed with muskets having an effective range of 100 yards at most, British infantrymen were trained not to fire until having closed in on the enemy. As the redcoats kept coming, even to the very "mouths of our cannon," the Americans were forced to retreat. As they withdrew, British artillery peppered the woods with grapeshot. It is not clear if they used their own or captured American cannon, or both, for this purpose. The British had not only successfully crossed the river but also were routing the first American line. Throughout the fighting, according to a young midshipman from the brig HMS *Espoir*, General Ross "behaved most gallantly, riding through the ranks, cheering the soldiers." Before these mopping-up operations were completed, fighting had already broken out at the second American line, situated about a mile to the rear of their forward positions.[8]

The location of this second position was determined by Secretary of State Monroe's decision to order Colonel Beall's 800 militia from Annapolis to occupy rising ground on the present site of the Fort Lincoln Cemetery, south of the Washington Road. Maryland militia under the command of Lieutenant Colonel Jacob Kramer formed up in front of Beall. Brigadier General Walter Smith placed his D.C. militia on a rise on the opposite side of the Washington Road, behind a small stream spanned by a wooden bridge known as Tuncliffe's Bridge. Supporting Smith's men were regular troops of the 36th U.S. Infantry under Lieutenant Colonel William Scott and companies of the 12th and 38th U.S. Infantry.[9]

Taking up positions too were Joshua Barney and his flotilla men plus 113 U.S. Marines under Captain Samuel Miller, who had been placed under Barney's command.[10] With his men following behind, the commodore had just made it to the second line as the British attempted to storm across the Eastern Branch. He positioned his forces in the middle of the second line, establishing two 18-pounders directly on the Washington Road and three 12-pounders to his right, where Miller's marines were stationed. Some of the sailors, including Charles Ball, an African American, were assigned to work the guns, while the others joined the marines in serving as infantry. With his ad hoc brigade and batteries in place, Barney provided formidable firepower. But his forces arrived too late and were too far back to stem the British advance across the river. Also arriving on this section of the battlefield was the Georgetown Light Artillery under Major George Peter. Francis Scott Key, an aide to General Smith, directed the artilleryman to position his guns at a location the major later maintained would have restricted his operational effectiveness. Peter ignored Key's instructions, choosing instead a position to the left of Barney as the next best location to provide a commanding view of the road.[11]

As the 1/44th continued to pursue American forces of the first line along the Georgetown Road, Thornton led the First Brigade along the Washington Road toward the second American line. With the benefit of hindsight, Lieutenant Gleig considered this move risky, believing that the colonel should have waited until the rest of the army came up in support. In their haste to proceed, Thornton's men cast off their knapsacks to lighten their load. It is not clear if Ross authorized this advance or if the colonel made the decision himself, using his initiative as he would have been expected to do. Either way, the initial isolated attack on the second line failed.[12] The responsibility for this ultimately rested with Ross as the commanding general. The 1/4th was not yet in position, as he had earlier planned, to lend support to the First Brigade. By pressing ahead, Thornton possibly was lulled into a false sense of confidence or simply wished to maintain the initiative. Whatever the explanation, the First Brigade was soon shocked by unexpectedly severe resistance.[13]

As they approached Tuncliffe's Bridge, which traversed a ravine south of present-day Lincoln Cemetery, the British came under fire from Kramer's militia. Forcing the Americans back, Thornton pushed farther up the road, approaching the District of Columbia boundary, where Barney had positioned his batteries. Taking aim at the dense column of British, the naval artillery opened up with an 18-pounder, which cut down the leading ranks. Lieutenant Colonel Wood of the 85th Regiment recollected that Barney's battery swept the road and staggered the progress of the column. Three times the British regrouped and advanced before the carnage had become so great that the remaining troops abandoned direct attack, taking cover in the ravine as their officers made plans for flank attacks.[14]

With the fighting at its height, "the president had a full view of the conflict," according to his friend Jacob Barker, a New York banker. Madison observed the slaughter caused by the naval guns as "the fire from Barney's guns made perfect lanes through the ranks of the enemy, but . . . the troops filled the voids thus created, without turning to the right or to the left to see whether their companions had lost a head, a leg, or an arm." The disciplined conduct of Ross's redcoats in the face of withering fire finally convinced the president that regular troops were far superior to a citizen army—that in retrospect, Winder stood no chance.[15]

Having taken cover in the ravine under heavy bombardment, the British were first of all intent on flanking Barney's right. Deploying from the woods into an open field, Thornton led his men to within fifty yards of the American positions when the 85th were stunned by a devastating volley. Three 12-pounders serviced by Miller's marines had opened such a destructive fire that the British fell back. Barney's guns also continued to take their toll. It was at this point that Thornton encountered the stiffest resistance. In the face of ferocious fire, nevertheless, the colonel led his men bravely onward, only to be cut down when a musket ball slammed into his leg, splintering the bone high up in his thigh. Having been removed to the side of the road, he was then hit by grapeshot that tore asunder his jacket. Tasked with attempting to sweep aside Beall's militia with a view to turning the American right, Lieutenant Colonel Wood, the commander of the 85th, also fell, suffering four severe wounds. Emerging from the ravine, the British light infantry also came under heavy fire from Beall's militia.[16]

The 85th already had incurred casualties in the early stages of the battle on entering the town of Bladensburg and in charging across the bridge. Now the new, surprisingly fierce resistance at the second American line took a fearful toll on its officers. Captain John Knox noted that this phase of the action had barely lasted fifteen minutes when there were three field officers down and "8 or 9 others of the 85th sprawling on the ground. . . . Thinks I, by the time the action is over the devil is in it if I am not either a walking Major or a dead Captain." By the time the battle ended, many of the officers of the regiment, who had led the charge with "Hurrah! Gallant 85th! Push forward for the honour of Old England!" had reportedly been killed or wounded. Besides two killed, eight were so seriously wounded that they had to be left at Bladensburg.[17]

The success they were having against the British regulars caused the seamen and marines to shout "Board them! Board them!" They charged the enemy, waving their cutlasses in the air, and forcing the British to retreat. The commodore claimed that both the 85th and 1/4th gave way before his men, though it was only the 85th that had been forced to fall back; Ross had yet to arrive in support of the 85th with the 1/4th. Gleig estimated that the British advance was checked in this part of the battlefield for half an hour. Indeed, the First Brigade just held on to their position at the ravine.[18]

While the First Brigade was thus pinned down and leaderless, Ross's whereabouts are unclear. What is certain is that the general had not gone galloping off to the "head of Thornton's people" at the very start of the battle, as Captain Harry Smith's highly inaccurate version of events alleges.[19] Ross was not present during these initial assaults on the American second line. It was soon clear, however, that he was summoning forces to not only lend support to the embattled brigade but also to press on to victory. Driven to tears of frustration at seeing his comrades "totally unsupported," Gleig was greatly relieved when Ross arrived at a "critical moment" with reinforcements from the 1/4th. On the general's taking control, the lieutenant recalled that "charge, charge, was the only word of command issued." In doing so, he did exactly the opposite of General Winder, who ordered retreat after retreat in the battle. There was more to Ross's actions than rousing cheerleading and individual heroism. Once more he was endeavoring to flank the Americans on both sides as he was able to bring additional forces to bear. Congreve rockets were also deployed here, Rear Admiral Cockburn directing the fire of the marine artillery.[20]

Significantly, accounts of this phase of the battle do not indicate that the Americans, most of whom were militia, were spooked by the rockets to the same degree as their countrymen in the first line. Accurate return fire targeted the British rocket launchers. "Mr. McDaniel" of HMS *Tonnant* was severely wounded. Describing these events, Lieutenant James Scott recounted that while Cockburn gave instructions for the artilleryman's care, "a musket-shot passed between the Admiral's leg and the flap of his saddle, cutting the stirrup leather in two, without doing any injury to him or the horse." Cockburn dismounted. As an aide and a marine tried to lash together the stirrup leather, the marine was killed.[21] The admiral survived unscathed—such is the fine line between death and glory on the battlefield.

As Ross prepared to press home the attack on the second line, the disorganized manner in which the disparate American units had taken the field hampered their ability to resist. As the British drew closer, Lieutenant Colonel Scott's regulars of the 36th Infantry, along with companies of the 12th and 38th Regiments, were discovered to be in the line of fire of Major Peter's battery. Scott was ordered to fall back from his original position. In the process an opportunity to bring the regulars' firepower to bear in the battle was lost. When British troops emerged from the ravine on the right in an attempt to flank the American left, they were permitted to come within "pistol range" of the regulars, who "remained, without orders to fire." At this key moment the U.S. troops received a "peremptory order" to retreat. They followed their orders and ended up not firing a single shot in the battle. The withdrawal of the regulars was a crucial factor in forcing the artillery of Major Peter to retire as well. Having completely routed the Americans on the

Georgetown Road, additional British troops under Colonel Brooke were also beefing up the attack on the American second line and soon threatened to overrun Peter's position. The major withdrew his guns.[22] The D.C. militia now came under the British sights.

The sense that the American positions were crumbling was reinforced when Ross spurred the 85th to renew its attack on Beall's militiamen, who soon took to their heels. Gleig later recalled that when the Americans "gave way, one brave fellow tried to stop them by waving the flag he carried." He fired three times as Gleig advanced directly toward him in his bid to capture the colors. Wounded, the American militiaman dropped the flag, although not before his third shot grazed the lieutenant's thigh.[23] But there was to be no glory for the militia involved in this stage of the fighting, only ridicule. As Charles Ball memorably put it, "the militia ran like sheep chased by dogs." Commodore Barney later registered his disgust that the militia made virtually no resistance before retiring from the battlefield. Whether in this instance it was because Beall could not persuade his men to withstand a bayonet attack by the British or that he obeyed an order from Winder to retreat, his militiamen retreated in disorder, exposing the right and rear of the position occupied by the marines and Barney's guns. Some of Ross's men seized a commanding position on the hill that flanked Barney and Miller, allowing hundreds of British to fire down on them. At this juncture a sharpshooter shot the commodore's horse from under him.[24]

Meanwhile, having made its way across from the Georgetown Road, the 1/44th attempted to outflank the American left, where Brigadier General Smith's D.C. militiamen were stationed. These units fired a number of volleys, but they were out of range. The fighting now had reached the tipping point. Witnessing the British beginning to flank the American second line on both the right—when they seized the hill from Beall—as well as on the left, Winder ordered Smith to retreat to prevent his force being destroyed or forced to surrender. The District militiamen were furious with this decision, some shedding tears, some cursing.[25]

Having succeeded in subjecting Barney's position to flanking fire, Ross moved in for the kill with his most battle-hardened troops, the 1/4th. If there was ever a man cut out to lead by example in a bludgeoning attack, it was Ross, still sporting the unhealed scars of the serious neck wound incurred in leading a similar attack against the French at Orthes. Once more, at Bladensburg the general advanced under murderous fire, exhibiting again the exceptional personal bravery that was the principal hallmark of his career. An officer of the 1/4th observed that the Americans "opened one of the tremendous volleys of musquetry and artillery that could possibly be imagined." Ross reportedly later said that Barney's first gun "laid ten of his men in the dust."[26] Nevertheless, he and the 1/4th pressed on.

With supporting U.S. forces taking flight or retreating and the British closing in, Barney's ammunition-wagon drivers drove off in panic. The British continued to pour fire into the commodore's battery. According to an American artilleryman, one of the flotilla men who had been shot "picked the bullet out of the wound in his shoulder, handed it to me, requesting me to remove his belt which was pressing the wound, and then with the utmost sangfroid continued to fight." Sailing Master John Adams Webster's horse was shot through the head and a ball pierced his hat. A musket ball shattered U.S. Marine commander Captain Miller's arm. Other American sailors were struck down, two of them killed. Then the commodore received a musket ball in his thigh. Running out of ammunition, taking fire on its flank, and faced with being overrun by a full frontal assault from Ross and the 1/4th, the American center was on the verge of annihilation. The battle had been decided.[27]

Barney ordered his men to spike the guns and retreat. Three officers attempted to help him from the field; faint through loss of blood, the commodore sank to the ground. But the guns were not spiked, for some of the men evidently continued the fight. Both British and American accounts concur that the 1/4th, with Ross at their head, bayonet charged Barney's position to the very "muzzles of the guns" and seized them. Some of the flotilla men were bayoneted as they held fuses in their hands. That the commanding general had played a leading role where the fighting was fiercest is reflected in the fact that his dead horse was seen "lying not many yards from the wreck of the gallant Commodore's guns." Capturing the artillery, the British then turned them on the Americans.[28]

Few American military commanders emerged with much credit from the Battle of Bladensburg, sometimes referred to as the "trial of souls." Joshua Barney, however, garnered respect in the United States as the "Champion of Bladensburg."[29] And what of President Madison by the time the battle ended? A poem entitled "Battle of Bladensburg," which appeared in 1815 in the Georgetown *Federal Republican*, indicates that "upon the hill stood Madison" during the fighting involving Barney, until the commodore "hit the ground." British sources agree that the president remained on the battlefield until Barney's position was overwhelmed. "A letter from a gentleman who was present at the capture of Washington" claimed that "P. Madison was close to Commodore Barney when the latter was wounded and taken, and owed his escape to his own insignificant appearance." That Ross and Cockburn were overheard later that day expressing regret that they had failed to capture the president was perhaps more than wishful thinking. In his infamous "race" from Washington into Virginia, a turnpike man allegedly witnessed Madison riding "at about nine miles an hour, whipping his horse with all his might."[30] That the president eventually fled the battlefield is true, but it was precisely because he remained there for so long, at the risk of capture, that required him to make good his escape with such expedition.

In the aftermath of the battle, according to an account published some years later, while lying on the ground badly wounded in the arm, Captain Miller's pockets were rifled through by a British soldier. Seeing a ring on a finger on his wounded arm, the soldier threatened to cut off the digit and then tried to pull the ring off without success at first, though in doing so reopened the wound. The fresh blood lubricated the finger so he could remove the ring. Coming upon the wounded marine captain, Ross was "particular in ordering every attention to be shown to him." When Miller told the British commander what had happened, the general reportedly responded: "Tell me his name. He shall be instantly shot! The orders are peremptory in any such case of outrage offered to a wounded soldier." While the American apparently knew who the culprit was, he declined to report him to Ross.[31]

Unable to escape too, Commodore Barney was captured. When Lieutenant Scott encountered the celebrated American veteran, Barney told him that a corporal of the 85th Regiment was the first one to discover him, "to whom he offered his watch and well-lined purse" if he would agree to stay with him. The corporal "refused both, saying his wounded situation was a sufficient protection."[32] A similar account of Barney's capture was printed in the *Belfast Newsletter* in October 1814. Interestingly, this version provides the additional information that Barney requested that the soldier be called from the ranks as he wished to present him with his watch. The soldier declined the offer on the grounds that Barney was a prisoner.[33] The honorable conduct of the British corporal toward the commodore set the tone for a series of cordial exchanges between the British and Americans immediately after the battle.

Following his capture, the wounded naval officer was introduced to Ross and Cockburn. The chivalrous, if candid, conversation was recorded in Barney's memoir. In a heartfelt manner, the general said, "I am very glad to see you, Commodore!" Wounded but undaunted, Barney replied with great pluck: "I am sorry I cannot return you the compliment General!" Smiling, Ross turned to Cockburn. "I told you it was the Flotilla men!" Agreeing now, the rear admiral remarked, "they have given us the only fighting we have had." After conversing with the commodore, Ross conferred briefly with Cockburn. Barney testified that the general then told him he was paroled and that he would be conveyed to any place he wished. Barney chose the tavern in Bladensburg.[34] He and his men certainly merited Ross's acknowledgment for how hard they had fought. But this often quoted exchange does little justice to some of the other American military units engaged at Bladensburg.

In the annals of the U.S. Marines, the performance of Captain Miller and his men at Bladensburg is highly regarded. Barney later apologized to Captain Alexander Sevier of the marines, who had been wounded in the battle, for not acknowledging him in his report, having mentioned only those whom he had actually seen in action. The commodore assured him that "your not being mentioned in my report will not diminish the glory yourself and the other officers of the marine corps acquired. . . . [P]resent my respects to Lieutenants [Benjamin] Richardson, [William] Nicol, [Charles] Lord and [Edmund] Brooke, who so ably assisted on that memorable day."[35] In addition, Major Pinkney's riflemen distinguished themselves in helping repel the first British assault on the bridge over the Eastern Branch. Besides Barney's guns wreaking havoc on the British, so too had those of Captain Burch and Colonel Wadsworth at the bridge over the river, while Major Peter recorded years later, "I was the *first* to meet the enemy, and the *last* piece of artillery fired at the battle of Bladensburg was from my battery." A Mr. Custis of Arlington, a relative of George Washington, assisted in loading the last round despite being disabled in one hand by rheumatism.[36]

As for the British, casualties from the battle totaled 64 dead and 185 wounded. The bloodiest fighting occurred when Ross and the 1/4th seized Barney's guns. The King's Own, as this unit was known, lived up to the reputation they had earned in Iberia as fierce fighters—this was reflected in the fact that they suffered the heaviest casualties, including 24 killed and 63 wounded. Indeed, 33 men of the 1/4th were so badly hurt that they had to be left behind in Bladensburg when the British retreated to their ships. These were commanded in the battle by Major Alured Faunce, whose horse was shot from under him. Not far behind in terms of killed and wounded, though, was the 85th Regiment, with 15 killed and 64 wounded; 40 of its wounded had to be left behind in Bladensburg.[37]

On the British side, the action took a heavy toll on officers in the 1/4th and 85th particularly, with three killed and twenty wounded. It would be no exaggeration to say that British success on the day can be put down in some great measure to the caliber of officers serving under Ross, ten of whom later reached the rank of general: Colonel William Thornton, Lieutenant Colonel William Wood, Major George Brown, Lieutenant William Williams, Lieutenant Frederick Gascoyne, and Lieutenant Henry John French, all of the 85th; Major Alured Faunce of the 1/4th; Colonel Arthur Brooke of the 1/44th; and staff officers Lieutenant George De Lacy Evans and Captain Harry Smith. Evans particularly distinguished himself during the fighting, having possibly two horses shot from under him.[38] But it was the courageous conduct of the British commander that caught the eye of friend and foe alike.

Charles Ball, one of Barney's flotilla men, could not help but "admire" the conduct of British officers in leading their fatigued men. He singled out Ross for particular praise. "I thought then, and think yet, that General Ross was one of the finest looking men that I ever saw on horseback." As Hezekiah Niles, a Baltimore newspaper editor, was prepared to admit, "that general *Ross* was a brave man, no person will be disposed to deny and that he was a 'dashing' officer must be admitted from the character of his attack at Bladensburgh." On the British side, Ross's bravery hugely impressed his men. While there is no doubt that he had at least one horse killed under him, a number of reports indicate that the figure could have been as many as three.[39] According to Henry Torrens at Horse Guards, by the time the battle ended, the commanding general "had no less than four musket balls through different parts of his clothes." Little wonder that both British and American newspapers referred to Ross as the "Hero of Bladensburg."[40]

CHAPTER 9

TO BURN OR NOT TO BURN

Having won the Battle of Bladensburg, Ross could afford his tired troops little respite before making the final push for Washington. From his point of view, it was vital to maintain the initiative, thereby preventing the Americans from regrouping and mounting another stand to protect the capital. This is precisely what his adversaries attempted to do, however vainly. The retiring American army had been repeatedly ordered to stop and reform, only for countermanding orders to be issued. They fell back again and again. The troops were convinced that at the very least a desperate last effort would be made to defend the Capitol. Reaching the site, General Winder was joined by Secretaries John Armstrong and James Monroe. Armstrong once again advocated occupying the legislature and nearby houses utilizing the regulars of the 36th and 38th Infantry Regiments as well as the flotilla men and marines. Fearing that his force would be isolated there, while the British could roam at will throughout Washington, Winder's view that the scattered forces should proceed beyond Georgetown prevailed.[1] In the end Montgomery Courthouse (present-day Rockville) became the rendezvous point. The capital was to be abandoned to whatever fate the British had in store for it.

Despite the order to retreat, not all American military personnel left Washington. Mordecai Booth, a clerk at the Navy Yard, noted that many militiamen took refuge in their own homes. Wearing civilian clothing, it would have been easy to melt away in this fashion.[2] Booth recorded that he witnessed gathered near the Capitol a contingent of 250–300 U.S. Marines and flotilla men before the British arrived, the marines now commanded by Captain Samuel Bacon. Also among the group, Booth recognized Sailing Master John Geoghegan, a highly experienced flotilla officer. The flotilla men did not regard themselves as under Winder's command and thus were not bound by the general's order to retreat.[3] At the very least they were loitering with intent. Ross was right to suspect that he might face further resistance.

After pausing to eat at between five and six o'clock in the evening, Ross advanced with his 3rd Brigade, which had not been involved in the battle that had ended around two hours earlier, for the roughly five-mile march to Washington. The behavior of some African Americans who had gathered on the Washington Road, believing that the British victory would free them, amused the redcoats. The slaves made fun of big-talking American officers who they said were among the first to flee from the battlefield. Meanwhile, the two brigades that had been engaged were either resting, carrying the wounded to Bladensburg, or burying at least some of their dead.[4]

Ross was determined to capitalize on his advantage in order to seize Washington. Energized by the battle and by victory, the general took up his customary position at the head of his troops. In the excitement of the campaign, his problems with his health and coping with the oppressive heat paled into the background. Capturing an enemy capital, after all, was a "soldier's dream." And there may well have to be more fighting to come before the city was his. A local newspaper reported that the British proceeded cautiously, fearing ambush or that the battle to decide the fate of the city had yet to be fought.[5]

The remaining people in Washington dreaded the arrival of the British. Shrieking women and crying children mortified Thomas McKenney, an aide to D.C. militia commander Brigadier General Smith, as straggling soldiers streamed through the streets of the city. Dr. Ewell, a highly regarded physician who remained with his wife and daughters, was equally concerned for the women of the capital. The sense of foreboding was accentuated by the sight of Secretary of War Armstrong, his aides, and throngs of gentlemen stampeding along thoroughfares, some bawling out: "Fly, fly! the ruffians are at hand! If you cannot get away yourselves, for God's sake send off your wives and daughters." His wife in convulsions and his daughters wailing, the doctor was petrified that the British would run amok in the city, defiling its womenfolk. But this was not to be a repeat of events at Hampton, Virginia, on June 25, 1813, when the debauchery of British forces brought great shame on British arms.[6] Although Ross was absolutely determined to ensure that the civilian population was not to be harmed, there can no doubt that the female population anticipated the enemy's arrival with outright terror.

Before moving into the city, in a statement of intent the British general made arrangements to ensure that private property and citizens were to be respected. Ross summoned Major Norman Pringle of the 1/21st soon after the army arrived at the outskirts of Washington. He ordered him to take command of one hundred rank and file to act as the advanced guard entering the capital. Pringle was further instructed to place sentries at various points, send out regular patrols, and prevent soldiers and seamen entering the city or local homes.[7]

As the British column advanced on Washington, it was preceded by local guides. With the defeat of the American army, it is possible that more local people were prepared to assist the victorious invaders, particularly if they were paid. Proving his worth in so many respects, the irrepressible Lieutenant Evans had also been recruiting scouts. This hardly endeared him to his rival, Captain Harry Smith, who claimed that he was in charge of intelligence gathering. Evans secured the services of Joseph Gray, an African American from Washington.[8] That the work was risky was reflected in the level of payment per day, which Gray claimed to be forty dollars. Gray was to become a trusted member of Ross's entourage.[9]

The British army reached Washington around dusk, sunset occurring before 8:00 P.M. Accounts vary whether there was still daylight or if it was dark by the time Ross's advance guard entered the city, although these need not necessarily be considered contradictory accounts. Michael Shiner, a young African American slave, later recalled that he was on Capitol Hill when he heard the tramp of the approaching British. When he saw them, "they looked like flames of fier all red coats and the stoks of ther guns painted with red ver Milon and the iron work shind like a spanish dollar." It is possible that Shiner saw the bayonets of the approaching troops glistening in the last rays of sunlight. The key points are that the British paused before entering the city, and darkness descended rapidly that evening.[10]

A critical point in proceedings had been reached. Would the Americans offer further resistance? And in seizing the city, what did the British intend to do there? To burn or not to burn, that was the question. Having detailed Pringle and his men as his "provost guard," Ross now had to ascertain if there was going to be further fighting or whether the city would be surrendered. In warfare of the period, civic leaders customarily presented themselves to formally surrender to the victorious general with a view to ensuring the safety of its inhabitants and property. This is clearly what the British expected.

According to Rear Admiral Cockburn's aide, Lieutenant Scott, the British sounded a parley again and again, but in each instance it was ignored. A trumpeter accompanied the British advance force entering Washington, more than likely for this very purpose.[11]

As at Moscow in 1812, when the Russians deprived Napoleon of his big moment by not formally surrendering the city, the federal and civic authorities in Washington confounded the British by making no attempt to negotiate terms of capitulation. Leading citizens of Upper Marlboro had already negotiated with the invaders, and delegations from Alexandria and Georgetown were subsequently to do so. This did not happen at the U.S. capital. In the days leading up to the fall of Washington, Mayor James Blake was under pressure from some citizens to be prepared to meet the enemy with a flag of surrender. Blake said that he preferred to die in the city's streets. In any case he believed that the matter was one for President Madison, the cabinet, and General Winder. Afterward Blake also implied in a letter to the Washington-based *National Intelligencer* that the president approved of his decision to leave the city without surrendering it. Certainly this is how several commentators interpreted the mayor's remarks.[12]

That no formal capitulation occurred cannot be put down to an oversight as pandemonium ensued in the aftermath of the American defeat at nearby Bladensburg. This was a calculated political decision taken at the highest level—and in advance. In this respect the reported reaction of Mrs. Madison to the "contribution" negotiated by Alexandria authorities to avoid that city being burnt, homes and all, by Captain James Gordon's naval squadron a few days later is surely significant. In her view the Alexandrians should have opted for their town to be destroyed instead.[13] While the political calculations underpinning the decision to avoid a formal surrender are understandable, Mayor Blake was derelict in his duty to the citizens remaining in Washington by exposing them to the dangers often attended by the arrival of a conquering army.

Acting under the same instructions as Gordon, there is strong evidence that Ross attempted to secure a "contribution" in lieu of destroying the public buildings in Washington as his orders permitted, although military stores and installations would have been burned regardless. From the British point of view, a ransom would be a bonus to the capital being forced into a humiliating surrender, the political damage already done and the military glory achieved.

The rules of war of the era promoted "profit and patriotism."[14] Prize money for such captures would be due to the military and naval personnel according to established rules, both officers and men benefiting. Prize paydays were an accepted norm in military life. Capturing the American capital city offered the prospective of a lucrative purse. Indeed, British records reveal that the seizure of property and vessels on the Patuxent River, as well as "booty" in the simultaneous British naval operation up the Potomac as far as Alexandria, resulted in substantial payments to Ross's estate. Two instalments, £1,774 and £389, were paid. To get a sense of the values involved, Ross's yearly wage as a major general amounted to £1,383.[15] Better for the British to barter than burn. To some extent too, the general was bluffing as he had no intention of burning public buildings, let alone private houses. The refusal of the Americans to negotiate was wholly unconventional, bewildering the British.

Not wishing to send his troops into the city by storm and risk atrocities, Ross was keen to take precautions in case American forces decided to mount a last-ditch effort to defend Washington. The British general, however, had lost his trusted commander of the advance, Major George Brown, who remained in Bladensburg seriously wounded. In the darkening night Ross and Cockburn, with men on either side of them, rode into the outskirts of the city at Capitol Hill. Ross was reportedly riding his favorite horse, Roslin.[16] In addition to sounding the parley to discuss terms by drum and trumpet, the British stated later that they carried a flag of truce.[17] Not surprisingly in the circumstances, with military and government officials fleeing in advance of the arrival of the British, evidence from the U.S. side in relation to this sequence of events is nonexistent.

As Ross's party approached the Capitol and passed the large, illuminated house owned by U.S. diplomat Albert Gallatin (known today as the Sewall-Belmont House), a number of armed Americans reportedly shouted, "here come the English bugers." A volley of shots rang out. Two British soldiers, corporals in the 1/21st, were killed, and perhaps three other soldiers wounded.[18] British army records show that the two slain corporals of the 1/21st were Scotsmen, John Anderson from Ayr and James Donaldson from Paisley. Ross himself narrowly missed death or serious injury. His horse, however, was mortally wounded; the mount of the trumpeter was also shot. The assailants reportedly cheered at their success.[19]

Several British officers reported that the firing came not only from the Sewall-Belmont House but also from other nearby houses as well as from a party of up to three hundred Americans based at the Capitol, although it is not clear if they were believed to be occupying the building or just on its grounds. Whatever the truth of the matter, Ross ordered the 3rd Brigade to fire a volley of shots at the Capitol, with a view to deterring further resistance. This action reinforces the impression that the British believed they had come under fire from the hallowed corridors of the U.S. legislature.[20] This was suppressing fire. Ross was not the type to insult American institutions.

Most of the evidence that the Capitol had been used for military purposes comes from the British, although it is not entirely one sided. Washington resident Mary Hunter later recalled telling British officers that gunpowder had been stored there. It is more than possible that American forces had begun to stockpile powder in the building when they were told to rendezvous there after the retreat from Bladensburg. Indeed, Secretary Armstrong had recommended turning the Capitol into a fortress immediately after the battle and suggested utilizing adjacent houses too.[21] In the end it may be no surprise that enraged American troops, appalled at the decision not to defend the city, ended up doing precisely what Armstrong suggested.

No American account confirms that shots had been fired at the British from the Capitol. More than one, though, concurs that the shooting came from more than one property. Washington socialite Margaret Bayard Smith, although not present in the city on that day, wrote that four or five houses in the neighborhood of the Capitol were destroyed by the British after men had fired on "the English as they were quietly marching into the city." Several other American sources confirm that the British were fired at from a number of buildings that were subsequently set on fire. Tomlinson's Hotel was among the premises burnt. In his diary Michael Shiner describes how the British found guns and ammunition there after the shooting incident. There are grounds for believing that shots had been fired from it.[22]

According to Congressman Charles Jared Ingersoll, who investigated events in the area at the time, other houses burned by the British were not near the Sewall-Belmont House. One of them was General Washington's "house," a reference to the long-dead president's rental houses on North Capitol Street, "the unprovoked destruction of which General Ross much regretted when informed of its ownership." While agreeing with Ingersoll that when the British learned of the property's association with the first American president they reportedly expressed their deep regret, the *New Bedford Mercury* noted that the structure had been set on fire because the British had been shot at from it.[23]

Some American accounts at the time and since have maintained that only the shot that killed Ross's horse was fired, that no shots came from the Capitol, and that there was no British flag of truce. Ingersoll, who subscribed to these views, nevertheless called the person who fired from the Sewall-Belmont House a "caitiff"—a cowardly wretch. It was a "murderous shot" for which the congressman conceded "Sewall's house was justly laid in ruins." Margaret Bayard Smith described the shooting at Ross as an "outrage." Meanwhile, a report in the *New Jersey Journal* declared that the general's horse was "improperly killed under him." And the *Federal Republican*, printed in Georgetown, on August 26 recorded that when the British commander reached the Sewall-Belmont House, "Gen. Ross, at the head of his troops, halted, expecting that the city would propose terms of capitulation. While in this situation, a shot . . . killed the horse on which Gen. Ross rode." All these American accounts imply that the attack contravened the conventions of warfare. According to a local newspaper at the time, this "wanton firing" was precisely the type of incident that could have been avoided had Mayor Blake done his duty properly.[24]

In the years since the British occupation of Washington, debate has raged about the identity and number of people who shot at Ross and his advance guard. One version indicates that the assailants included "blacks." It was even speculated at the time that an unidentified woman fired the shot that killed Ross's horse, though a resident of Dowson's Row in the area, Mr. Hickey, was also named as the culprit. In the main, as far as individuals connected with the shooting incident are concerned, much contemporary evidence points the finger at a hairdresser of either French or Irish descent.[25]

Walter Lord observes that most people attributed the attack on Ross to an Irish barber named Dixon, also known as Dickson. "Chief barber" to Congress for more than twenty years, for some he was a Figaro type, a talkative and good-humored man. The *National Intelligencer* in Washington preferred to describe him as "the most pugnacious knight of the razor we have ever known." Afflicted by lameness, Dickson could not serve in the militia. Apparently enraged by the American retreat from Bladensburg, he was reputed to have fired a musket at General Ross. Reports are contradictory about whether or not he was captured. Another version of the shooting incident records that a Mrs. Peter recognized the gunman as a "worthless hairdresser. . . . [T]he British soldiers were so enraged they would have torn him to pieces—but Ross remarked he was certainly too worthless to live—but he might live *here.*"[26]

While Dickson may well have been involved in the attack on Ross, it is clear that he was far from the only one who opened fire on the British. After all, a volley of shots rang out, not just a single report. Surviving testimony about who else opened fire on Ross and his party confirms the involvement of some of the flotilla men who had remained in the Capitol area.[27] After the war a claim for compensation for the damage done to the Sewall-Belmont House was lodged with the U.S. Senate on the basis that some of the flotilla men used it as a military base to attack the British. According to the affidavit, while most of the flotilla men escaped, three were captured. Not until 1847 was compensation granted after a witness came forward to validate the claim.[28]

Even after the shots rang out, Ross tarried in the hope of negotiating a deal. Evidence indicates that the Capitol and other buildings were not torched immediately. For example, U.S. Navy clerk Mordecai Booth reconnoitered Capitol Hill after the British arrived and before he met Captain Tingey at the Navy Yard at 8:20 P.M. Having set out for Tomlinson's Hotel, Booth did not record that it or any other building was on fire when he arrived in the area. His timeline of his movements until he saw the Capitol burning suggests that it was set ablaze around 9:00 P.M. Father McElroy, from a vantage point at Georgetown, took a precise note in his diary when he saw the Capitol on fire, "9:06."[29]

Events in Washington between 8:00 and 9:00 P.M. had a critical bearing on the decision whether or not the public buildings would be burnt. What is not in doubt is that the British were eager to offer surrender terms. The disgraced Secretary Armstrong later observed that when the redcoats entered the city, they put a price on the ransom for the public buildings and sent an emissary to attempt to negotiate with an appropriate U.S. authority. Armstrong named Dr. William Thornton, architect of the Capitol, as the sole American involved in these negotiations. As for President Madison, according to Armstrong's version of events, he contemptuously rejected the proposition. In terms of Thornton's alleged role as an intermediary, he only returned to Washington on August 25, the day after the burning of the public buildings had begun. It has also been questioned how contact could have been made with the president. One critic of Armstrong maintained that Madison had already crossed the Potomac into Virginia by the time the British arrived and was incommunicado to both friend and foe. The whereabouts of the chief executive that night, however, is far from clear. Paul Jennings, the president's "valet," a slave, later testified that he found him waiting to cross the Potomac at the Georgetown ferry about sunset.[30] The timeline provided by Jennings does not prove that the British managed to get in contact with the president by means of a go-between, although it is not beyond the bounds of possibility. The weight of the extant evidence, however, does not support Armstrong's contention that Ross managed to contact Madison.

The attack on Ross and his advance guard indicated to the British that the Americans were not going to negotiate. This impression was reinforced just after 8:20 P.M. when Captain Thomas Tingey, commandant of the Washington Navy Yard, abided by his instructions to torch the premises rather than let military stores and vessels fall into British hands. This was a painful task. Having lost his wife several months earlier, the English-born Tingey now lost the Navy Yard he had done so much to establish. Property and military equipment burnt there by the Americans included storehouses (multiple buildings), the frigate USS *Columbia* (outfitted and ready for sea), the sloop USS *Argus* (13 guns), the frigate USS *Essex* (nearly ready for sea), the hull of the frigate USS *Boston*, and the hull of the frigate USS *General Green*. French Forrest of Washington, who later rose to the rank of commodore and served in the Confederate navy, was entrusted with destroying the newly built *Argus*. Tingey was aware that the British were at Capitol Hill at this time, although it was only after setting the Navy Yard ablaze that he noticed the Capitol on fire as well.[31]

Meanwhile, there was outrage in British ranks at the attack on General Ross, a hero to his troops. Dr. Ewell, whose home Ross later used as his headquarters, was told by British officers that had the general been killed, "it would have been impossible to have restrained the soldiery, who idolized him, from committing the most horrid outrages, both on our city and its inhabitants." Lord Bathurst, the secretary for war at the time, believed that "by the laws of war . . . the lives and property of all the people of Washington were forfeited." And yet despite being fired upon in contravention to the codes of warfare he valued so highly, Ross was soon heard to call out to his men to "spare the lives and properties of the inhabitants" of the city.[32] But for Ross, a massacre might have ensued.

In the decision-making process that followed the shooting, the general's aide-de-camp, Captain Duncan MacDougall, recollected that it was only after being "warmly pressed," implicitly by Rear Admiral Cockburn, that Ross agreed to burn the public buildings of Washington "for the purpose of preventing a repetition of the uncivilized proceedings of the troops of the United States." It is also clear that Cockburn was pressuring the army commander to burn the entire city, private dwellings and all. Ross has been portrayed as "soft" and pliable, Cockburn supposedly managing to win the general over to his line of thinking repeatedly. This depiction of the relationship between the two senior British officers, however, sits at odds with what transpired on this occasion. The admiral's wish to raze the city in the hope that the American capital would be moved to a more antiwar location in the north did not prevail. Highly regarded among friend and foe for his "humanity," Ross was not going soft in refusing to burn private property but instead was taking a tough stance. As a result, he has been regarded as "the publicists' very model of a moral major general."[33]

From a personal point of view, the British commander may well have been more concerned with the fate of his favorite steed, Roslin, than with his own well-being.[34] The "assassination" of the horse is recorded as having a marked effect on the army, requiring "all the energy and severity of discipline to prevent retaliation." At the animal's funeral, according to one account, "there was scarcely a dry eye in the ranks." It was later also reported that Ross attributed his actions at Washington to the killing of his horse.[35] The nub of the issue was the circumstances in which Roslin was shot. For Ross, it was an "uncivilized" breach of military etiquette as he attempted to negotiate an orderly surrender of the city. An officer and a gentleman, one who played things by the book and valued chivalry, he would have considered the attack on himself and his men under a flag of truce as an affront to the codes of honorable warfare. And in this respect it is worth bearing in mind his unforgiving attitude soon after toward Dr. Beanes of Upper Marlboro, who would be accused of violating a neutrality agreement. Matters of honor between "gentlemen" mattered immensely in that era.

Having previously expressed his aversion to burning public or private property, Ross followed his orders, at least in so far as burning the public buildings in Washington was concerned. In the circumstances it appears that he recollected his earlier exchanges with Vice Admiral Cochrane when the naval commander had urged him to retaliate for American outrages in Canada, not least the burning of the public buildings in York. Cochrane's assertion that the Americans pursued "a system of warfare so barbarous and indefensible" would have struck a chord now with the general. His earlier objection to burning public buildings on the grounds that he had been used to waging the war with France in an altogether different spirit had been confounded by the wholly unconventional conduct of the Americans. The French would never have opened fire on a flag of truce. To some extent Ross had become persuaded of Cochrane's line of thinking. In conversation at Washington with Dr. Ewell, the general reportedly justified the burning of the public buildings as retaliation for what had happened in York. Ingersoll records too that "Ross continually deplored the tragedy which he said he had to perform, occasioned, he added, by the Americans burning the British capital in Canada."[36]

CHAPTER 10

COURTEOUS CONFLAGRATOR

Circumstances on the ground when he arrived in Washington proved to be the decisive factor that convinced Ross to finally agree to obey his orders, at least in part, and burn the public buildings. The British general had no intention of abiding by Vice Admiral Cochrane's recommendation to "lay waste" the city that now lay at his "mercy," private property included. As the man who captured Washington, Ross in large measure dictated what ensued during the brief British occupation of the U.S. capital. Elaborating on his whereabouts and actions while in the district is thus instructive. Completing the work of destruction was not the only thing occupying his attention. The commanding general was also examining his range of options about his next military move. From his point of view, managing to seize Washington with such a tiny force was wholly unexpected.[1] What to do next was equally challenging—maintain an offensive or secure a safe retreat.

The Capitol was the first public building to be set ablaze. It has been alleged that before doing so Cockburn proposed a motion from the Speaker of the House's chair: "Shall this harbor of Yankee Democracy be burned? All for it say 'Aye!'" It was unanimously carried. A number of American accounts of the rear admiral's conduct during the short British occupation portray him as delighting not only in the destruction but also in mocking the American president. He was said to have boasted of personally setting fire to the Capitol and the President's House. Less well known is his courteousness to many Washingtonians. No matter how complimentary he was to American ladies, he was aware that they despised him. In effect, not only were views of Cockburn's behavior affected by his demonic reputation but also by comparison to the "humane" Ross, a commander whom a travel writer of the period reported was regarded as a "universal favourite" in the American capital.[2]

The Capitol, as it turned out, was not so easily torched. The British used improvised combustible materials. In the south wing, after parts of the building were set alight, the heat was so fierce that the arsonists were forced to withdraw. Some rooms escaped the inferno. The north wing was more extensively damaged because there was more wooden material to fuel the blaze as well as the books and furniture of the Library of Congress. On learning that these books had been destroyed, Ross expressed his regret to Dr. Ewell, remarking that he did not "make war . . . against letters." Ewell's published recollection of events, which details his dealings with senior British officers, is the primary source of information regarding the British general's conduct while in Washington. For the doctor, fair-minded Americans would consider Major General Ross to be a "magnanimous enemy." His representation of Ross's activities was by no means unchallenged at the time. The Washington-based *National Register*, in a stinging review of Ewell's publication, claimed that the British general was asked to spare the library but dismissed the request on the grounds that "we have no time to be trifling with books."[3]

Besides the hallowed halls of Congress being set in flames, a number of private buildings in the Capitol Hill area were ablaze too. Some were deliberately fired by the British, who believed that they had been fired upon from them when Ross entered the city, including the Sewall-Belmont House, Tomlinson's Hotel, and possibly others. A small number of homes caught fire accidentally when flames and cinders from the Capitol billowed toward nearby structures in the strengthening breeze. In some cases it is impossible to be sure which homes were set on fire deliberately or caught fire accidentally. Evidence in relation to George Washington's townhouses is mixed in this respect. Whatever the reasoning, their destruction may have had an added personal sadness to Ross given that his uncle had served with Washington during the 1755 expedition under General Braddock to Fort Duquesne (present-day Pittsburgh). In total, according to two local newspapers, during the time British forces were in the capital, six private buildings were destroyed.[4]

Shortly after the Capitol was set on fire, Ewell saw lights in the windows of his house on nearby Carroll Row. His heart sinking, the doctor thought the British had set his home ablaze too, but these were just reflections from the burning Capitol. His house had, however, been pillaged by the troops. On arriving at his door, the doctor recorded that Ross came up to him as he had overheard that his house had been robbed and "in a tone that will forever endear him to me as a perfect gentleman," the general expressed his regret for what had happened. Not realizing that they were at Ewell's home, the British commander asked him which house was his and he would have it guarded. "This is my house, sir," said Ewell. With "amiable embarrassment" Ross told him, "Why, sir, this is the house we had pitched on for our headquarters." The general then offered to remove his baggage elsewhere. When the physician insisted otherwise, Ross indicated that he would trouble him as little as possible and that any room would suffice. Ewell proceeded to show him to his own bedroom. Ross declined to accept the offer for some time and tried to persuade his host to bring his wife back home. "I am myself a married man, have several sweet children, and venerate the sanctities of the conjugal and domestic relations."[5]

In the main, Ross's conduct was reserved, even subdued, during his time in Washington. That he was far from a well man may account for this, at least in part. Besides not having fully recovered from the wound he incurred at Orthes some months earlier, he had had at least two horses shot from under him on this momentous day. He had also been hit by four musket balls during the battle that, while not wounding him, must have caused serious bruising. Meanwhile, Dr. Ewell's detailed account provides a fascinating insight into the general's attitude and state of mind. Never once did he hear the British commanding officer utter an offensive remark about the president or the U.S. government "but often expressed the deepest regret that war had taken place between two nations so nearly allied in consanguinity and interest. I can, moreover, truly say I never saw the sunbeam of one cheerful smile on General Ross all the time he was in Washington. His countenance seemed constantly shrouded in the close shades of a thoughtful mind."[6] The general's melancholy mood has often been explained as proceeding from his abhorrence at implementing orders he found distasteful. And there can be no doubt that the British commander abided by them with very considerable reluctance. Ross's disconsolate demeanor also proceeded from a nagging worry about his wife's well-being. Vice President Elbridge Gerry indicated afterward that he had heard that the general, a "young and amiable man," was deeply troubled about her.[7]

After the Capitol was set on fire, the troops then marched to the President's House. William Gardner was an eyewitness to events on Pennsylvania Avenue when, at ten o'clock at night, a party of one hundred men were marching to the White House, as it was often called even then.⁸ The troops were accompanied by four officers on horseback to whom Gardner appealed to protect civilians and private property. Ross and Cockburn pledged to do so and advised local citizens to remain in their homes. By implication, this would prevent troops from plundering an otherwise empty dwelling. Yet British assurances that private property and citizens would be respected did little to diminish the raw fear as a night of unfathomable horror ensued for those citizens who had not fled. Before burning the President's House and the Treasury, Ross reportedly made arrangements for either supper or coffee at Mrs. Suter's boarding house at the corner of F Street and opposite the Treasury Department.⁹

As with the Capitol, some British officers depicted the White House as a military installation in an attempt to justify its destruction. According to one account, it "had been converted into a military post, and, before we entered the city, was garrisoned by a company of infantry, with two pieces of artillery." Providing similar details, Lieutenant James Scott described it as the enemy "head-quarters." That there were two artillery pieces stationed in front of the mansion was confirmed by an American witness, William Simmons. The White House was in reality far from the "head-quarters" of U.S. forces. That being acknowledged, as Ingersoll also admitted, its "large hall" stored "munitions of war." Evidently, some consideration had been given to defending the building. Much as Dolley Madison may have wanted cannon to be placed at every window of her "Castle" to make a last-ditch resistance, events did not transpire that way. She also quickly rejected the suggestion of her hot-tempered servant "French John" Sioussat to booby trap the building.¹⁰

In reality, American troops had long since abandoned the President's House before the British arrived. Some hours earlier Navy Yard clerk Mordecai Booth visited the mansion during a reconnaissance mission and found on duty a single officer on horseback. When the British arrived they found it abandoned, its contents already rifled through by local "rabble." This has been termed "looting" in many accounts written from both British and American perspectives. But a report in the *Federal Republican* at the time paints a different picture. President Madison returned to the mansion for a time on his way back from Bladensburg. On leaving it for the last time, he reportedly "told the people they might have whatever they could save in his house" before the British arrived. Whether by invitation or not, it is clear that locals took substantial amounts of property from the Executive Mansion. A young American girl, Mary Ingle, witnessed an inebriated British officer ordering a subordinate to get him a drink of water in a silver "goblet of old Jimmy Madison." Before a hand judiciously was put over her mouth, the young girl blurted out, "No Sir, that isn't President Madison's goblet, because my father and a whole of lot of gentlemen have got all his silver and papers and things and have gone."[11]

When the British reached the President's House, they reportedly found an abandoned coach at the front door. It was described with great exaggeration by one soldier as the "American state coach and horses." Earlier with great pluck, Dolley Madison had remained at the residence, determined to prevent as many priceless items as possible from falling into enemy hands even as the British were momentarily expected, according to the slave-servant Paul Jennings.[12] In these dramatic moments, in her own mind and in the view of others present, there was no doubt that she appeared to be risking capture by delaying her departure until she was assured the famous portrait of George Washington would be saved. As it turned out, while the occupants of the First Lady's coach reckoned they heard the voices of British soldiers pursuing them, Ross and his men did not in fact arrive for a number of hours. The portrait was indeed saved, though it was not cut from its frame as it is often said. Sioussat and Thomas McGaw, the Irish gardener at the President's House, were responsible for hacking it from its outer frame. And contrary to popular perception, Mrs. Madison did not depart with the portrait stashed in her coach. The painting was entrusted to Jacob Barker and his friend Robert G. L. De Peyster.[13]

While Mrs. Madison was understandably anxious that the British would seek to capture her, Dr. Ewell's account of conversations with General Ross indicate that she had nothing to fear from the chivalrous general. A courteous conflagrator, the British commander was alleged to have remarked that he would not have burnt the White House if Mrs. Madison had "remained at home"—that he did not make war on "ladies." Not only did he regard her very highly but he also stated that he would have preferred to "protect, than burn a house which sheltered such an excellent lady." Described by the U.S. vice president at the time as a "genteel, well behaved man" and by at least two Americans who crossed paths with him during his expedition as the "perfect gentleman," is it stretching things too far to accept him at his word in this respect?[14] Perhaps.

Before setting fire to the White House, the hungry and thirsty British troops and sailors ate the dinner that had been prepared for the president and his entourage, with Ross reportedly drinking to "his Majesty's health at the head of the table." Major Norman Pringle of the 1/21st recorded what was on the menu: "ducks, geese, hams, turkeys, buffalos' tongues, and buffalos' bumps." This so-called presidential victory meal has exercised historians in the two hundred years or so since its serving. Certainly, British accounts written at the time concur that they believed a celebratory dinner had been prepared for Madison. Writing to his brother-in-law Ned Glascock, to whom he often corresponded in a jocular fashion, Ross remarked that "so unexpected was our entry and capture of Washington: and so confident was Maddison [sic] of the defeat of our troops, that he had prepared a supper for the expected conquerors." Finding a table laid for forty people, the general was amused that the British consumed the "fare" instead and that "the health of the Prince Regent and success to his Majesty's arms by sea and land, was drunk in the best wines."[15]

For many years, American versions of this event accepted the testimony of Sioussat, who disparaged claims that a meal had been prepared. In a letter composed in 1848, however, Dolley Madison admitted that "when the British did arrive they ate up the very dinner and drank the wines that I had prepared for the President's party." Had the Americans succeeded in repelling the British at Bladensburg, there is little doubt that this meal would have been transformed into a victory celebration, regardless of whether or not this had been the original intention. There is every reason to believe that the First Lady, in her customary manner, would have thrown the doors of the Executive Mansion open for such an occasion. Certainly, John Pendleton Kennedy of the Baltimore militia had brought along his dance pumps, hoping to be invited to the expected victory ball. Although not present on the occasion, Lieutenant William Stanhope Lovell of the Royal Navy claimed that "General Ross, Rear-Admiral Cockburn, and all the field officers of the to-be-captured army, were to have been invited: but they forgot the advice of Mrs Grundy in her cookery book, 'Catch your hare first.'"[16]

By contrast to events elsewhere in Washington, where Ross insisted on respect for private property, he permitted "souvenir-hunting" in the White House before the building and its remaining contents were consumed by flames. Lieutenant Scott was tempted by snow-white fresh linen in the president's dressing room. A report carried in British newspapers recorded that one soldier made off with Madison's knives, forks, and plates in a table cloth, while a Mr. Urquhart took the president's dress sword. Those involved reveled in gossiping among themselves about what was taken.[17]

According to Walter Lord, one account even has Ross stuffing his pockets "full of Madison's old love letters," as the general was reputed to have stated it. Frustratingly, it is not clear from Lord's sources what the reference for this is; there is no corroboration for this allegation.[18] An account published in the *Quebec Gazette* on September 22, 1814, reported that Rear Admiral Cockburn acquired Madison's hat and "love letters." It seems likely, therefore, that over time Ross came to be attributed with the actions of Cockburn in this respect. Not that the general was beyond a bit of trophy hunting himself. A sword reputedly belonging to the president and a cane belonging to his wife were sold at auction from the Ross estate in the 1940s.[19]

In contrast to events at the Capitol, where sailors were primarily responsible for setting the building ablaze, soldiers were prominent in burning the Executive Mansion. In modern times, a miniature portrait of Captain Henry Shaw of the 1/4th, who is reputed to have started the fire, is displayed in a bookcase in the residence quarters of the U.S. president.[20] Lieutenant George Pratt also has the dubious distinction of orchestrating the destruction of the building. Most remarkably of all, a messenger sent by the French ambassador, Louis Serurier, to General Ross found the British commander in one of the rooms collecting all the furniture he could that was to be burned. While there is no other evidence to confirm this version of events, it is by no means inconceivable that Ross was prepared to lend a hand, given that he was never one to ask another man to do something that he was not prepared to do himself. He had hoped, however, to spare Dolley Madison's expensive pianoforte, worth $485, the British commander and his wife, after all, being keen musicians.[21] Vice President Elbridge Gerry related a story that when the general "entered the President's House, he touched an elegant piano there, said it was a pity to burn it, and proposed to have it removed into the yard, to give someone an opportunity for saving it for Mrs Madison." With the building already in flames, Rear Admiral Cockburn returned to the room where the piano was located and hastened the officers out—the building and roof were ablaze.²² To describe Ross as a reluctant arsonist would be an understatement.

Nevertheless, before retiring for the night, the Treasury Building was also torched. General Ross and ten officers then returned to Mrs. Suter's, where according to Ingersoll, a supper had been hastily prepared. The officers, in a jovial frame of mind, snatched a quick meal with no liquor or wine. Perhaps they had already consumed enough champagne at the President's House. Cockburn is said to have had the candles blown out, preferring to eat by the "light of the burning palace and Treasury." In conversation, the British officers were heard regretting that Madison had escaped, bragging that they had wanted to show him and his wife off in England. Even more disappointing was the failure of Captain James Gordon's naval squadron to make its appearance at Alexandria, within sight of Washington. Delayed by adverse winds and having to negotiate the Potomac's troublesome shoals, the British flotilla did not anchor off Alexandria until Sunday, August 29, four days after Ross's army decamped from Washington.²³

During the reported supper, an interesting exchange was supposed to have taken place between Ross and Cockburn that sheds light on the contrasting attitudes of the two men to that evening's destruction as well as on who was calling the shots, the assertive admiral or the supposedly submissive general. An officer came to inquire whether the War Office was still to be burnt. "Certainly," replied Cockburn. "It will be time enough in the morning," said Ross, "as it is now growing late, and the men require rest." The general's view prevailed. Then the rear admiral mentioned a nearby bank that also should be destroyed. Ross enquired from Mrs. Suter if the bank was private or public. She believed it to be private, given that it was located in a private house. It escaped the flames.²⁴

A previously unconsidered account of what transpired at Mrs. Suter's lodging house, written by Vice President Gerry and based on conversations with lodgers there, casts a somewhat different light on these proceedings. In part it flatly contradicts Ingersoll's portrayal of what transpired, that Ross called at Suter's for coffee, not dinner, for example. In the end it is impossible to be certain whether the general called there for supper or for coffee. While there is no doubt that marching most of the day, fighting a battle, and burning public buildings built up a hearty appetite, would the officers really have had two meals in such a short space of time?²⁵

Before settling down for the night, the British came upon the offices of the *National Intelligencer*. According to Lieutenant Scott, the newspaper had "taken the lead, and given the key-note to the republican press, in vilifying England and the English." The editor, Joseph Gales was "an Irish renegade," so the British believed. The premises were about to be torched when a number of ladies approached Cockburn and asked him not to burn the building in case the fire would spread to their properties. The order was immediately rescinded, but a party of sailors volunteered to pull the house to the ground, doing so in a couple of hours. Another version of the same incident indicates that Ross's view prevailed over the admiral's. In this telling, the building was not burnt because the general was informed that the premises provided a sole source of income for a widow.[26]

It was to be late in the night of August 24 by the time the British operation had finished. Cockburn was reported at the time to have "concluded his victorious and destructive orgies of that memorable day and night, with the coarse luxury of lust in a brothel."[27] As for Ross, he returned to his quarters at the home of Dr. Ewell. Before the momentous day ended, he issued a communication to the army expressing his hearty approbation of their conduct in the "brilliant action of the 24th."[28] Around the same time Ross retired for the night, an hour-long thunderstorm started about midnight, with torrential rain falling. An American witness indicated that "one of the most dreadful storms of thunder and lightning ever known in Washington, met and lighted on the British invaders, dimming and quenching their malicious fires." It was as if Divine Providence had come to the assistance of the Americans. In reality, while the fires may have damped, they were not completely extinguished. Not only did they continue to smolder overnight but residents and invaders alike also were to be disturbed by the sound of seven or eight major explosions at the Navy Yard. The British speculated that these resulted from large magazines being ignited by the flames. Some fires were reportedly still burning two days later.[29]

Overnight, Major Pringle with one hundred men stood guard. At 8:00 A.M. on the morning of August 25, after a marathon stint of duty that witnessed Pringle and his company marching sixteen miles in the sweltering heat from dawn on August 24 and then undertake a twelve-hour overnight sentry shift, they were finally relieved. Pringle was delighted to report that when he was ordered to return to camp, Ross personally thanked him for undertaking this duty. What is more, the major was proud to recall that "a great many other inhabitants of Washington, thanked the General and the soldiers for *the protection they had afforded them* from the marauding attacks *of their own countrymen.*"[30] Testimony provided by American writers at the time concurred that most of the pillaging that occurred during August 24–25 was done by local looters. Lists of properties supposedly plundered by the British therefore must be treated with caution because it is not clear whether the invaders or locals were responsible.[31]

On the whole during the short British occupation, Ross's men behaved in exemplary fashion, wholly in accordance with the example set by their chivalrous commander. In later years Major Pringle became embroiled in a very public controversy about the conduct of British troops in the American capital. He rejected claims made by a British writer, James Stuart, that troops proved impossible to restrain and that a substantial amount of private property was destroyed.[32] The weight of evidence overwhelmingly supports Pringle's refutation of such charges. It is important to try to set the record straight about precisely what happened in Washington during the British occupation. While some of the evidence is hearsay, there is no reason to doubt that there were isolated incidents of indiscipline.

Captain Duncan MacDougall, Ross's aide-de-camp, mentioned many years afterward that his commander compensated a woman who had several hundred dollars taken from her. Similarly, Dr. Ewell documented that his home had been plundered by the British. Ross reportedly had several of his men flogged for indiscipline. An American soldier witnessed two soldiers based at Bladensburg being flogged for theft. A contemporary American account written by William Gardner for the *Federal Republican* claimed that during the short British occupation, Ross was informed that a British soldier was in the act of robbing people. The culprit was apprehended by an officer sent to investigate. Gardner recorded that he had been told that the offender was paraded and shot, though he did not witness the execution himself. Even Ross did not escape allegations of misconduct either. The *National Register* carried a story by the "Critical Society, Washington" that one citizen "had his horse taken from him by this very liberal British general."[33]

While a comprehensive survey of period American newspapers sheds much additional light on events in Washington at the time, it is important to weigh the information carefully. The correspondents who made the allegations against Ross, it should be borne in mind, were intent on discrediting Dr. Ewell's highly favorable account of the personal conduct of Ross and Cockburn while they were in the American capital. In terms of the punishments the general was alleged to have meted out to some of his men, there is no doubt that he insisted on the highest levels of discipline. Conventional methods of punishment at the time included flogging and, where necessary, execution. Throughout his career, however, there is nothing in meticulous British army record keeping that confirms that he ever had a man flogged, much less executed. Had capital punishment been meted out in Washington, there would have been a paper trail, proceedings of a court-martial, for example. Still, there is every reason to believe that his troops were aware that misconduct could have dire consequences. Soldiers in the 85th Regiment in particular would have needed no reminding of what such actions could lead to. Shortly before the unit was attached to Ross's brigade, a private was executed for breaching the Articles of War when he committed a number of robberies and seriously assaulted a French citizen.[34]

While there may remain questions about the methods Ross used to maintain high levels of discipline, there is no doubt that he generally succeeded in doing so. The anti-Madison *Federal Republican* claimed that the British army's "respect to private person and property" was "unexampled in the annals of war." In one of its first publications after the destruction of its offices, even the rabidly pro-Madison *National Intelligencer*, though modifying its original view that private property had in general been "scrupulously respected," still concluded that the British were much more respectful of private property than local looters. Ross's success in preventing his troops from running amok resulted in part from sensible precautions in terms of where he stationed the main body of his men. The 3rd Brigade was encamped on Capitol Hill, where the general had his quarters, while the remainder of his army was kept outside of downtown Washington at Maryland Avenue and Fifteenth Street, about 1.5 miles from the Capitol.[35]

From the start of August 25, the British were busy completing the destruction of public buildings. The War Office building, which also contained the Department of State, was set ablaze by sailors and soldiers.[36] The only public building to be spared was the Patent Office after representations were made to officers that it contained numerous privately owned models. Later that same morning British forces went to the Navy Yard, where they endeavored to complete the destruction begun by the Americans themselves. A story later carried in *The Times* in London suggests that Ross visited the Navy Yard, describing a report on its contents as having been provided by "the General." The Marine Barracks and the nearby Commandant's House were still intact when they arrived. Tradition has it that the British did not burn these buildings because they respected the fighting qualities that the U.S. Marines had displayed at Bladensburg.[37] The true explanation appears to be less glamorous. Because the Navy Yard was located in one of the more built-up areas of Washington, Ross was persuaded by local people not to endanger local properties by burning the barracks. Lieutenant George De Lacy Evans alludes to his presence at the Navy Yard when he afterward noted that the "conciliatory measures adopted by General Ross" enhanced his humane reputation when he decided not to burn the barracks owing to the inevitability that the prevailing wind would have resulted in flames spreading to nearby homes.[38]

With fires raging in various parts of the city, another storm contributed to the apocalyptic nature of events. A hurricane, or perhaps a tornado, struck Washington about midday on August 25.[39] Trees were torn up, homes were destroyed, and timber beams and brickwork flew like feathers in the air. Many people lay flat in an attempt to avoid injury. A British officer and his horse were dashed to the ground when they turned a corner into the teeth of the wind. Writing of Ross's actions during the storm, American historian Allen Clark has described him as "gallant in war and gallant to women," specifically mentioning an incident that occurred during this storm. The camp of the British army was reportedly by the spring close to the Abraham Young Mansion, then occupied by a Mrs. Gibson. Ross and several other officers took shelter there from the elements. Mrs. Gibson, fearing her house would be destroyed, ran out into the garden and held fast to a fence. The British general, risking his own safety, rescued her.[40]

Until the morning of August 25, Ross's operations went comparatively well. This good fortune was not to last. A major accidental explosion occurred at the arsenal at Greenleaf Point as a detachment of British soldiers and marines were undertaking its destruction. Mary Ingle recalled that the blast took place in the middle of the storm. "Our hearts stood still lest it should mean deadly conflict between the enemy and our dear ones." According to one account, a discarded cigar was thrown down a well where, unknown to the British, gunpowder had been deposited, although there is no evidence to indicate that this was a trap laid by the Americans. Other theories for the freak accident abounded. Captain Mortimer Timpson of the Royal Marines, who was caught up in the explosion, believed that it resulted from an attempt to destroy an American gun by placing another at right angles to it and that the ignition in the well was caused by sparks flying in the wind.[41]

Whatever the reason, there is no doubt that a massive explosion occurred. Bodies were seen flying into the air, and others were reported to have been buried alive under tons of debris. Captain Timpson was among the men who rocketed into the air. Dr. Ewell was one of the American physicians who tended many of the injured and estimated that as many as thirty were killed and forty-seven were mutilated. An official British army accounting put the number of seriously wounded who had to be left behind at Washington at forty-four, including seventeen Royal Marines, twelve rank and file of the 1/21st, seven members of the Royal Artillery, six Royal Marine Artillery, and two members of the 85th Light Infantry.[42]

The survivors of the explosion were brought to Capitol Hill, where a hospital was established, joining the Union Jack that had earlier been triumphantly erected there. Dr. Ewell recorded Ross's reaction on seeing the wounded. "I never saw more endearing marks of sympathy than were exhibited on the countenance of General Ross," he wrote. When the general expressed his concern to the doctor about what was to become of the men who were too badly injured to be moved when the army pulled out, Ewell reassured him that he would do all in his power to look after them. Close to tears at one point, Ross gathered himself, spent some moments in silence, and then enquired whether mattresses and refreshments could be obtained for the wounded in Georgetown. Ewell assumed from this comment that Ross intended to march to Georgetown to destroy Foxhall's Foundry, where cannon were manufactured for the army.[43] Indeed, it is possible that had Gordon's squadron hove in sight, Ross may well have targeted the foundry.

Feeling exposed to attack, a "peace deputation" from Georgetown approached the British either very early in the day of August 25 or conceivably the previous night. At breakfast time on the twenty-fifth, Dr. William Thornton implored Charles Carroll to accompany him to meet the British, suggesting this on the basis that Carroll had already participated in the Georgetown deputation and was therefore familiar with some of the officers. The men had offered to surrender the town to Ross if he agreed to spare their homes. A group of townsmen from nearby Alexandria also arrived in Washington that day to negotiate with the British. According to Evans, the Alexandrians solicited the protection of private property in return for their "neutrality," terms that were accepted.[44]

More detail has survived of the negotiations with the Alexandrians because Dr. Ewell claimed that he heard every word of what transpired. Cockburn was initially keener to find out if Captain Gordon's squadron was within sight of Alexandria. On being informed that it had not been spotted, the admiral conceded that he would negotiate, that the British needed provisions and would pay a fair price for them. Ewell's account of this meeting is also interesting in so far as Ross was not present. Washington socialite Margaret Bayard Smith later claimed that the shooting that had killed Ross's horse had a major bearing on his conduct in the city. "I imagine Genl. R. thought that his life was particularly aim'd at, for while his troops remained in the city he never made his appearance."[45] As the long-established British hate figure for Americans at the time, there is no doubt that accounts of the occupation of Washington often focus on the words and deeds of Cockburn. Ross was by no means as anonymous in terms of his presence in the city as Smith claimed, though there are grounds for conceding her point that the general was not as conspicuous as the admiral.

Given that Ross was absolutely determined to preserve discipline among his troops, he appears to have spent more time with them than out and about in the city. What is more, there is also evidence that he may have returned to Bladensburg during the day on August 25. An American prisoner of war from the 5th Maryland Regiment held there recalled seeing him in the town.[46] It is possible that Ross returned to Bladensburg to visit his wounded troops. It was certainly not out of character for him to have done so.

Around midday on August 25, a substantial American force was seen on the opposite bank of the Potomac, sending a patrol toward Georgetown. To prevent them coming over from Virginia, the British burnt the Washington side of the Long Bridge over the river. As events transpired, no American force launched a counterattack. A single horseman, John Lewis, a great nephew of George Washington, exchanged words and fire with British sentries and was shot dead.[47] While British forces continued to complete the destruction of public buildings as well as some privately owned ropewalks that produced navy material, Ross was busy planning his next move.[48]

In terms of his military options, whatever the British commander was going to do, he would have to do it quickly. Remaining stationary was fraught with danger. That the Americans would regroup and counterattack was a reasonable assumption. Should he decide to maintain the offensive, proceeding to Baltimore presented a tempting target if he were to march northeast directly overland. Lieutenant Evans, his military secretary, recorded at the time that that option was under discussion while they were in Washington. This was decided against on the basis that Cochrane had already tried to stop the expedition to the American capital and that Ross was not in a position to assume that the necessary naval support would be available.[49] The alternative was withdrawal.

Ross's preferred option was to link up with Captain Gordon's squadron, then making its way up the Potomac. That this was under serious consideration was reflected in Cochrane's decision on August 26 to direct Captain John Hanchett to proceed up the Potomac on board HMS *Dictator* to apprise Gordon that the army had reached Washington and may seek to retreat along the banks of the river in conjunction with him.[50] In many respects, however, Ross was not the master of his own destiny. He certainly could not control the weather. There was no way of telling, for example, how badly the recent storm had damaged or would delay Gordon's squadron. As it happened, some of these vessels had been unmasted and driven aground.[51] With no sign of Gordon, Ross opted to withdraw to his naval support on the Patuxent via Upper Marlboro, where he had stationed a substantial force of marines. The aftermath of the freak storm, which caused so much damage locally, also afforded him the chance to get a head start on his would-be pursuers.

To confuse the Americans about their true intentions, the British engaged in mind games, spreading rumors that Annapolis and Baltimore were their next targets. Prior to decamping, Ross deployed the Light Brigade, consisting of the 85th Regiment and the light companies of his other units, in a maneuver that threatened Georgetown. He deliberately kept up the impression to the last minute that he intended to take the surrender of Georgetown. The brigade would remain in this menacing position until close to nightfall, at which time it was to withdraw and follow the rest of the army to Bladensburg. As at Roncesvalles in the Pyrenees in 1813, Ross ordered his men to heap fresh fuel on campfires as he opted for a nighttime retreat, leaving his wounded to the mercy of the enemy. An American writer at the time branded it a "midnight flight."[52] In light of what had just transpired, this was a small crumb of comfort for the Americans.

In summary, as Ross pulled out, what was the degree of destruction left behind in a capital city that in 1814 contained, at a conservative estimate, just over 500 buildings? The groundbreaking work of historians Ralph Eshelman and Scott Sheads shows that some twenty premises, including public buildings, were burnt by the British during their occupation, some of which caught fire accidentally. This represented 5 percent of the structures in the city at the time. Other fires, including several bridges and the initial ones at the Navy Yard, were started by the Americans themselves. In itemizing the relatively small number of buildings destroyed by the British, no attempt is being made to minimize the significance of the actual destruction by Ross nor to underestimate the terror experienced by citizens in the capital and for miles around. The fires in multiple buildings in the Navy Yard alone helped convey the impression that the entire city was on fire.[53] In reluctantly agreeing to torch the public buildings, the British commander only followed his orders to the minimum. He was entirely discriminate in the buildings he ordered destroyed. Ross disobeyed his orders by absolutely refusing to burn private property, with the exception of the premises used to attack him and his men.

Contrary to mistaken popular perceptions at the time and since, the whole city of Washington was not burned. For a fateful moment, Major General Ross held the U.S. capital and its citizens at his mercy. Although strange as it may seem to the modern eye, there is much reason to believe that by the standards of the day, he acted in a merciful fashion. By the laws of war, the attack on Ross and his men as they entered under a flag of truce laid the city open to a fearful retribution. In the end, as a story published in a Washington, D.C., newspaper thirteen years later observed, it was to Ross's "forbearance and generosity we owe it, that a single house was suffered to remain in the City of Washington. He stripped war of many of its horrors—he waged it gallantly, at the command of his sovereign, but he was nobly generous."[54]

CHAPTER 11

"FEELINGS OF MOST ACUTE MISERY"

As the British army pulled out of Washington, the coup that Ross pulled off in capturing the U.S. capital was tinged with regret. A lucrative prize payday had been missed when the Americans made no effort to offer a "contribution" to save their public buildings.[1] The British general was also rueful that he was not marching straight for Baltimore, just fifty miles away, a city that was vulnerable to attack from the direction of Washington. In making arrangements for the withdrawal, he proceeded on the basis that he was likely to be attacked. As Steve Vogel has observed, "it seemed inconceivable that the Americans would not mount a counterattack."[2]

With the city under curfew from 8:00 P.M. on the evening of August 25, the British army retreated toward Bladensburg, pulling out between 9:00 and 9:30 P.M. Left behind were forty-four non-commissioned officers and rank and file too seriously wounded to be moved following the explosion at Greenleaf Point, all under the charge of a Sergeant Robert Sinclair of the 1/21st. These soldiers feared retribution from the angry citizens of Washington. When Dr. Thornton, a city magistrate, visited them, the sergeant asked for protection for his men.[3] It turns out that they had good reason to fear the worst.

Dr. Ewell, who had been tending to these men, was worried not only that the wounded British prisoners would be killed but also that his own life was in danger. Describing those baying for blood as immigrants, "not Americans," he was astonished that "they were the very countrymen of those wounded prisoners." That Irishmen featured prominently among them is distinctly likely. Among British newspaper reports of what transpired in the battle for Washington, the *Times* noted that the stiffest resistance came from "Irish rebels" in American ranks.[4] A "Statistical Description" of Washington published in 1816 reveals that almost half of the city's population of just over 8,000 were Irish—and Gaelic speakers at that—with many of them unable to speak English. Such immigrants hated the British. In one of Washington's streets at the time was a sign with the inscription, "Peter Rodgers, sadler, from the green fields of Erin and tyranny, to the green streets of Washington and liberty."[5] In the end Ewell was fortunate that a number of prominent local citizens supported his humanitarian endeavors, and the danger passed. The physician was struck by how the British wounded cared for one another. American children also helped by bringing "scraped lint" to the hospital.[6]

The road to Bladensburg was negotiated without any major difficulty. The Third Brigade led the way, followed by the Second, with the First (Light) Brigade taking up the rear, a reversal of the order in which they had marched to Washington. This did not happen by accident. The rearguard is the most important position in a retreat. To Ross, it made sense for his light troops, adept at skirmishing, to take on that task. As the column came close to Bladensburg, the moon rose to reveal a horrifying sight—unburied bodies littering the battlefield.[7]

During the pause at Bladensburg, Lieutenant George Gleig paid a quick visit to the British wounded in town. Besides their physical sufferings, some were "deeply affected at the thought of being abandoned by their comrades, and left to the mercy of their enemies." Officers and men whose wounds were very serious were under the care of an assistant surgeon to the 1/44th as well as two hospital mates. According to George Henry Calvert, gold was left behind to pay for all their needs. He also visited the British officers during the halt in Bladensburg. Describing William Thornton as a "very pleasant man," he remarked that "if a bullet is not an obstacle, I am sure that Colonel Thornton will become one of the most important generals." The colonel duly rose to the rank of general but died at the age of sixty-one from a bullet—his own.[8]

As for the British wounded there, concerns about maltreatment at the hands of Americans proved to be misplaced; they were cared for with kindness. In so doing the Americans reciprocated the generous treatment afforded their own captured and wounded by Ross. Colonel Ragan, who had been taken prisoner at Bladensburg, managed to return to Baltimore on parole by the start of September. "He states as we understand that those of our countrymen who experienced the same misfortunes with himself, are treated with the same kindness, and suffered to return home on their parole."

The chivalrous relationship between the British and the Americans was typified by Joshua Barney's conduct in assuming responsibility for prisoner exchange. The commodore not only honored the exchange arrangements he negotiated with Ross but also became good friends with the wounded Colonel Thornton, the two men having shared a room.[9]

Anxious to put as much distance between himself and a possible pursuing force, Ross proceeded with his overnight withdrawal. His deception plan worked, allowing his army a fifteen-hour head start before it even became known in Georgetown that the British had pulled out. Just because we know in retrospect that there was no major force pursuing him does not mean that Ross was not correct to take elaborate precautions. Some Americans hoped and believed at the time "that the enemy's troops now in Washington will never regain their ships. They will be conquered or captured!!!"[10] This was not to be the case.

Unaware that no major effort was being made to harry him, Ross pushed on through the night, even as his exhausted men were at times almost asleep on their feet. The only major difficulty the British encountered on their way back to Benedict resulted from nature, as the pioneers were kept busy clearing away fallen trees that blocked the road. A number of bridges also had to be repaired, though it is not clear if these had been destroyed by the Americans or were damaged by the storm. When the army set out from Bladensburg, it was preceded by sixty cattle procured by the Commissariat Department. A welcome supply of meat it may have been, but driving this herd at night was far from easy. What is more, moving along dark, narrow pathways, the army was in danger of losing its way. This was only avoided, according to Captain Harry Smith, owing to exhausted troops throwing flour from their haversacks, thereby marking the way for those who followed. By daylight, he reckoned that the army had not proceeded three miles beyond the town, though probably an underestimate. Gleig, by contrast, no doubt exaggerated in claiming that the army had covered some eighteen to twenty miles overnight. What is certain is that progress was far from rapid.[11]

The British halted between 7:00 A.M. and 8:00 A.M. on August 26 for a five-to-six-hour rest. Ross later acknowledged that this fatiguing overnight march resulted in a number of men falling out of the ranks. British army records show that a high proportion of those who either deserted, went "missing," or were "taken prisoner" during the retreat to Benedict occurred during this night march. These included twenty-eight men from the 1/21st and fifty from the 85th Regiment, who were described as "taken prisoner."[12] On this date too, thirteen men of the 1/44th went "missing." The 1/4th lost the least men on the way back, although five men "absented on the march" on August 25.[13] Given that the retreat occurred almost totally unmolested by pursuing forces, it may be more accurate to describe many of those listed as missing, taken prisoner, or absent on the march as deserters.

As the British withdrawal continued, dysentery swept through the ranks. The surgeon of HMS *Melpomene* treated many men who took ill. Eighteen miles had been covered between roughly 9:00 P.M. on August 25 and 8:00 P.M. on August 26, equating to one mile per hour. On the whole the British could not believe their luck once again that the retreat was so uneventful, even "leisurely." Henry Torrens at Horse Guards in London wrote Vice Admiral Cochrane that "the conduct of the Americans in allowing the Army—so inferior in numbers and without cavalry—to retreat unmolested is quite inexplicable, and proves beyond a doubt the extent to which your daring enterprise had created a panick." Unknown to Ross, Hill's phantom expedition was still working in his favor. Rumors abounded that Lord Hill was on his way to Washington with substantial reinforcements. A letter received in Philadelphia from Baltimore dated August 26 stated, "we have positive assurances that Ld. Hill has arrived, and that the British army received him at Bladensburgh [sic] with three cheers." Another paper reported that Hill had arrived there with the "main army" of 10,000 men.[14]

By sunset on August 26, the British reached Upper Marlboro. En route, large numbers of slaves approached the column, the men offering to become soldiers or sailors in return for their freedom. According to Gleig, few were given the opportunity, attributing this to Ross's insistence on protecting private property, thereby implying the general condoned slavery. Another British officer, "Old Sub," recollected that substantial numbers of slaves following the army from Washington were taken on board the fleet, some of whom became private servants to officers while the rest were sent to Tangier Island, presumably to be enlisted. After the fall of Washington, Cochrane addressed a letter to Lord Bathurst in which he indicated that the general and himself were in agreement about the advantages of black troops. Evidence also shows that Ross was determined to look after the long-term interests of a number of African Americans who proved their worth as guides during the operation, not the least of whom was Joseph Gray. For a time, Gray was employed as his servant. Lieutenant George De Lacy Evans later wrote that it had been the intention of General Ross to have applied at Bermuda or Halifax for support for all those in a similar situation to Gray, who had "abandoned" their country but who could be useful in terms of "espionage" in the event of a new war with the United States.[15]

The army left Upper Marlboro the next day and marched as far as Nottingham, arriving early on August 28. They discovered a Royal Navy brig there, presenting its broadside to any pursuing force. A Royal Artillery officer, George Laval Chesterton, described the scene as the victorious general was "greeted with vociferous cheers from the well-manned yards of the brig." The salutation was taken up by the sailors on the gunboats, barges, and captured vessels swarming the river. The exhausted troops joined in, thereby prolonging "this merited welcome." Ever the professional, while the army was at Nottingham, Ross sent his most trusted staff officer, Evans (proving his worth once again as an experienced dragoon), along with a body of horsemen back toward Upper Marlboro to determine whether any American forces were in pursuit.[16]

The general need not have worried. The white citizens of the U.S. capital had other things on their mind, not least the fear of a slave revolt. Besides, by August 27 Washington was being threatened once more, this time by the approaching Royal Navy squadron led by Captain Gordon. The city was again vulnerable after U.S. Army captain Samuel T. Dyson, commander of Fort Washington, situated on the banks of the Potomac River blew up the post rather than engage the British. James Monroe feared that the capital was on the brink of being captured a second time. Anchoring at nearby Alexandria, Virginia, Gordon demanded, and received, a "contribution" in exchange for his "forbearance" in not destroying that town. He was acting under the same instructions as General Ross and Rear Admiral Cockburn. But the Common Council of Alexandria failed to persuade Gordon to "pay the same respect to private property that Admiral Cockburn and General Ross had done at Washington, that by their conduct they had immortalised their names."[17] The controversy surrounding the ransom that Gordon demanded in accordance with his orders has cast a shadow over his extraordinary operation. Sailing abilities of the highest order were required to negotiate the tricky shoals of the Potomac with such large vessels.

While the army itself was not engaged during its retreat, two incidents of note involving stragglers occurred. The most famous one happened after the British column had departed Upper Marlboro on August 27. A group of citizens led by former Maryland governor Robert Bowie as well as General Ross's erstwhile friendly host, Dr. William Beanes, seized British stragglers and deserters scavenging the neighborhood in search of food. The apprehended soldiers were sent off to captivity in Queen Anne's Town because some of the citizens of Upper Marlboro wanted to release them, fearing British retaliation. One deserter, Tom Holden, was discovered in the doctor's garden trying "to steal refreshments." Historian Donald G. Shomette attributes the involvement of Beanes with the party of volunteers as an attempt in part "to save face for his earlier friendly reception of the enemy."[18] Whatever the reason, his decision to get involved resulted in serious consequences for the elderly doctor.

Evans and his horsemen, ordered on a reconnaissance mission by Ross to Upper Marlboro, came upon Holden, who had escaped from his captors and passed himself off as a straggler. Quickly thinking on his feet to avoid being shot for desertion, he informed his comrades that the inhabitants of Upper Marlboro, led by Dr. Beanes, had "risen in arms," seizing others like himself, "put some of them to death, and made others prisoners." A vengeful party of some fifty to sixty British horsemen then descended on the village in the middle of the night. Beanes and a number of others were seized, and Evans threatened to raze it if the captured troops were not returned. The threat of dire consequences had the desired effect. By the following morning five stragglers were released. Evans freed some of his American prisoners in return, but Beanes and a few others were taken off to the British fleet.[19]

Over the years, there has been considerable puzzlement concerning why Dr. Beanes was singled out for what appeared to be particularly harsh treatment. That he was one of the citizens of Upper Marlboro who had previously agreed to a neutrality pact with Ross is essential to an understanding of what transpired. The general was reputed to be "unforgiving in matters of honor."[20] He bridled at impropriety or injustice. This is the key to understanding his treatment of Beanes just as it is essential to knowing why he risked his career over a controversy involving a pig in Malta in 1801 as well as his decision to burn the public buildings in Washington after he was fired upon under a flag of truce.

Francis Scott Key was to be charged with securing the release of Beanes. Key's brother-in-law, Roger Brooke Taney, admitted that something happened when the British were in Upper Marlboro that bound Beanes not to take up arms against the British. When Governor Winder later appealed to the British general for the release of the physician, he vouched that Beanes had not wittingly breached the codes of war. It was also clear to Brigadier General John Mason, U.S. commissioner for prisoners, that the basis for his detention was for violating "propriety" inasmuch as he was one of the citizens who "met them [the British] under a flag on their first approach and was under engagement to . . . refrain from acts hostile to them." That Beanes was considered to have breached the terms of the neutrality pact agreed with the British under a flag of truce at Upper Marlboro is confirmed by William Hill's recollections of a conversation he had with Ross on board HMS *Tonnant*. The general signaled that he only agreed to pardon the doctor when he was informed of the chivalrous treatment of British soldiers left at Bladensburg, "not from an opinion of his not being justifiably detained.[21]

The incident involving Dr. Beanes was not the only such occurrence during the retreat. Reportedly, British prisoners had also been taken by pursuing American cavalry units. Some of the captured men were stragglers, while others may have been deserters. A Colonel Cross had assembled a party of ten to twelve men with a view to picking up British stragglers near Upper Marlboro on August 27. Initially, it was reported that Cross led a blood-curdling bayonet charge that resulted in some troops surrendering, though a later account discredited this exciting version. Eight redcoats did indeed surrender at this time, though, being either indifferent to their fate or simply too exhausted to resist.[22]

The British army's retreat toward its shipping nevertheless proceeded unchallenged. On August 28 after a good night's sleep, there was a feeling among some of the troops that they would continue their march to the fleet. Perhaps reassured by Evans's reconnaissance, Ross realized that there was no danger of a meaningful American pursuit and so further rested his weary troops. With the Patuxent River teaming with small vessels, there was time to remove prize property from Nottingham, principally flour and tobacco. Sick and wounded men were also evacuated on the boats.

Finally, late on August 29 the British arrived back at Benedict. The following day, as the regiments marched to their reembarkation point, the sailors greeted them with raucous cheers. A jubilant Captain Robert Rowley crowed that "Ross and Cockburn have immortalized themselves."[23]

Contemporary records indicate that Americans felt humiliated by the defeat at Bladensburg, by the capture of their capital city, and that no last-ditch defense had been mounted. More than anything, it was the lack of fight shown in defending Washington that rankled Americans at the time, especially "the stigma which this event will necessarily . . . affix on the national character," as one commentary put it, not the defeat of a largely civilian militia at the hands of a regular army. To make things worse, there was much anger that Ross was permitted to retreat unchallenged. This view was epitomized by Speaker of the House Henry Clay, one of the U.S. peace negotiators in Ghent. Clay wrote irritably: "The loss of public property gives me comparatively no pain. What does wound me to the very soul is, that a set of pirates and incendiaries should have been permitted to pollute our soil, conflagrate our Capital, and return unpunished to their ships!"[24]

The British were delighted that they had managed to return to Benedict almost entirely without incident. The progress of a force of some 4,000 men retracing its steps along the same route by which it came resulted in local devastation.[25] The army, after all, was living off the land—and very well at that. Fed "like fighting cocks," according to one soldier, each day afforded an abundance of pigs, sheep, beef, and veal as well as milk and vegetables. Americans along this route complained of numerous outrages.[26] In his haste to regain his ships, Ross was unable to prevent stragglers from marauding in the countryside.

By August 30 the main body of the British army had safely reembarked without setting eyes on the enemy during the retreat. The cheers of the navy at the signal achievement of Ross's diminutive command had barely died down, and the euphoria of completing his expedition had hardly sunk in, than Ross was brought back down to earth with a shuddering thump. After much anxious waiting, on his return to the fleet from Washington, he finally received letters from his ailing wife, dated June 16 and 26. Admiral Codrington reported that the general was unsettled to learn that she was still in France at the time they were written "and very unwell." Of the general and his wife, Codrington had been "told no two people could be more attached."[27]

In his response to these letters, Ross remarked that his "perusal" of them "has completely overwhelmed me and I declare to you that were it in my power to leave the Army I would without hesitation fly to you." His wife's "melancholy" condition, about which he had been worrying for some time, was evidently every bit as bad as he feared. How deeply it affected him was revealed in the very first line of his letter to her, which reveals the momentous news that his army had taken Washington. "It is my best loved Ly with feelings of the most acute misery that I take my pen to write to you."[28]

Acknowledging his wife's predicament, the general urged her to steel her mind to cope with it. Ross reassured her that his own health was holding up; even the oppressive heat did not bother him so much while ashore, owing to "great occupation." In some measure he tried to cheer her up with news of his capture of Washington, revealing his astonishment that his expedition had been "crowned with a success that I had no reason to expect." And in further testimony to the political value of choosing the capital as a target, he emphasized that his operation would hasten an end to the war. He told her, "They [the Americans] feel strongly the disgrace of having had their Capital taken by a handful of men and blame very generally a Government which went to war without the means or the abilities to carry it on." Captain Harry Smith, the bearer of his official dispatch, he assured his wife, would call on her at Clifton and give a fuller account of what happened. The war, Ross believed, "cannot last long we then meet my Ly never again to separate."[29]

Writing a day later to his sister-in-law, Maria Ross, the general admitted that in normal circumstances his military success in capturing the American capital "would make me probably one of the happiest soldiers in the service were my joy not completely damped by the melancholy letters I have received from my dearest Eliza ["Ly"]. They have given me more affliction than the success of our operations have afforded me satisfaction." He reiterated that if he had been a position to "quit the army I should not for a minute hesitate in flying if possible across the Atlantic." To his sister-in-law he also was more forthright in acknowledging that the heat was taking a toll on his health.[30]

Meanwhile, the general's well-being was clearly a source of concern to Rear Admiral Malcolm, who noted on September 1,

"General Ross is not very well. I sincerely hope that he will soon be strong again. We have great confidence in his ability. He is a most excellent man and understands his business perfectly." The U.S. agent for prisoner exchange, Colonel John S. Skinner, saw Ross some days later and described his "uncicatrixed [neck] wound." This indicates that the serious injury he received at the Battle of Orthes in February had not completely healed. Worried too that the general may not have been fit to continue in command, Captain Smith shared his concerns with Torrens at Horse Guards when he returned to London.[31]

Despite his condition and anxious to maintain the initiative while the U.S. government remained in disarray, Ross was already contemplating another dramatic, if high risk, attack. Major Richard Gubbins, temporarily in command of the 85th, noted on August 31 that he was getting his regiment ready for "further service and immediate operations." According to Lieutenant G. G. MacDonald, R.N., Ross asked Cochrane to attack Baltimore; Evans recorded that the general made this proposal on September 1. The vice admiral would have none of it, citing concerns about the "sickly season." Instead, he intended to go to Rhode Island, where the troops could set up winter quarters. With much reluctance, Ross agreed. Buoyed up by the stunning success at Washington, Cochrane hoped that not only would reinforcements arrive by the start of December but also that New Orleans would be captured by the following spring. His intention was to "drive the Americans out of Louisiana beyond the Spanish boundary—all this may be accomplished before the month of March and the keys of the Mississippi placed in the custody of Gt. Britain." The admiral was reported to have boasted that he not only intended to eat his Christmas dinner in New Orleans but to spend the carnival there as well.[32]

Clearly, the two commanders were at cross-purposes about their joint operations. To Ross, a man who dearly wished to speed home to be with his ailing wife, Cochrane's plans were going to tie him down in America for much longer than he had hoped, perhaps longer than his wife could endure. Possibly influenced by domestic concerns, the general wanted to capitalize on his coup de main in capturing Washington by delivering a coup de grace at Baltimore.[33] If Ross succeeded in capturing that "nest of hornets," the ramifications could have been enormous. Henry Torrens at Horse Guards believed that a few more such triumphs could force the Americans to sue for an immediate peace.³⁴ For the time being, however, Cochrane had decided not to attack Baltimore.

Evidently unaware of Ross's differences with Cochrane, Captain Rowley indicated that in the warm afterglow of British success at Washington, "I do think it impossible for more perfect unanimity to exist than does at this moment between Army and Navy." While waiting on Gordon's safe return from his foray on the Potomac, and as plans were being made for the expeditionary force to sail north to Rhode Island, the British celebrated their success with "regular Balls, Dinner parties, Pick Nicks on shore," with the "bands serenading in the woods." The dances were mainly held on Malcolm's flagship, HMS *Royal Oak*.³⁵

Cochrane having ruled out a proposal to attack Baltimore that was put to him on September 1, four days later Rear Admiral Codrington reported that the main fleet was due to leave the Chesapeake when the vice admiral changed his mind and "assented to another operation here at the wish of the General and Cockburn." It was a measure of his infuriatingly vacillating nature that Cochrane quickly had second thoughts about the wisdom of doing so. Instead, Cockburn was ordered to sail to Bermuda on September 5. The next day Cockburn had sailed less than ten miles on his voyage to Bermuda when he was signaled to return to the fleet. The capricious Cochrane, who once changed his orders three times in half an hour, had on this occasion changed his mind for a third time in a matter of days. He now agreed to attack Baltimore.³⁶ While there is no record of what happened during this short interval, it is highly likely that Ross pleaded with him to seize the moment.

The reasoning behind Cochrane's final resolution to attack Baltimore was explained by Evans in his memorandum of operations in the Chesapeake, dated September 7. Recently published American newspapers had been received the previous day that conveyed in "such strong Colours the General alarm, and defenceless state of Baltimore." This information explains the vice admiral's dramatic change of plan.³⁷ Rear Admiral Codrington confirmed that the receipt of these newspapers was a vital factor in the decision-making process. From September 2 to September 6, the troop ships had been stationed off Drum Point, which happened to be the location where a Mr. Hopewell lived, a Federalist who regularly supplied the British with newspapers. Cochrane decided, however, that the attack could not proceed until the squadron of ships under Captain

Gordon returned from Alexandria—Gordon's squadron included bomb ships that would be needed for the assault. Evidently fearing that Gordon had gotten into severe difficulties, the expeditionary force sailed twenty miles up the Potomac in preparation for a "rescue mission," though in the end this was not necessary.[38]

In eventually conceding to Ross's wish to strike Baltimore, Cochrane may also have had domestic considerations in mind—tempted by a high-profile opportunity to restore his family name. Writing on September 3, he confessed that "the brilliant success" in the capture of Washington "has roused me a little from the most severe depression of spirits I ever suffered, the recent occurrences at home of the shameful conduct of some of my near relatives has hurt me beyond what I can possibly describe, having brought up Lord Cochrane." News of the imprisonment of his nephew in London on fraud charges had wounded him deeply. Ever in two minds, the vice admiral later made it plain that the decision to target Baltimore was "contrary to my opinion but extremely urged by the General to which I reluctantly consented but to preserve unanimity between the two services." Cochrane's justifiable concern was that there were insufficient troops for the operation.[39]

Which American newspapers the British consulted is not clear, but reports were indeed emanating from Baltimore that the city was teetering on the brink of capitulation. This was particularly apparent in the immediate aftermath of the defeat at Bladensburg. Correspondence abounded that no attempt would be made to defend Baltimore. A letter dated August 25 reported that wounded were streaming into the city and the victorious British were on the march, due to arrive in thirty-five hours. "There is, at the moment, a contest between civil and military powers—*the former are for sending a capitulating embassy, but the military men will not consent.*"[40]

As it turned out, the arrival of Commodores John Rodgers and David Porter played an important role in steadying American nerves. Writing to Secretary of the Navy William Jones from Baltimore on August 27, Porter confirmed the reports that demoralized residents were disinclined to defend the city. Before long he declared that efforts to bolster its defenses had succeeded, and "the citizens of Baltimore have recovered from their panic." Major General Samuel Smith, the commander in Baltimore, also played a key role in stiffening resolve. Captain Benjamin Howard challenged the notion that the city would have surrendered but for Porter, regarding this as an injustice to General Smith. The presence of Commodore Oliver Hazard Perry, victor at the Battle of Lake Erie in September 1813, also helped assuage frayed nerves. According to L. P. W. Balch, a militiaman from Virginia, Perry was "tranquil as an unruffled lake: no low passions seemed to have disturbed his bosom: modest, dignified, seemingly unconscious either of his worth or his fame." By September 1 a local newspaper described Baltimore as "very calm. . . . The men, without distinction of party act *like men*."[41] Whether and how hard they would fight when faced with a determined attack by Ross's victorious army was another matter.

The failure of the British to press home their advantage with a more immediate assault on Baltimore not only afforded the Americans time to strengthen defenses but also to rejuvenate spirits that had been sagging. Maryland militia captain James Piper believed that Ross mistakenly decided to rest on his laurels instead of striking while many of Baltimore's defenders were profoundly anxious. He attributed this to the British general's pompous attitude, which cost him his best chance to attack the city.[42] As Ross suspected, Baltimore was there for the taking in the days immediately after his triumph at Washington. The ineptness of the militia's defense of the U.S. capital and the lack of any harassment of the army during its retreat had an important knock on effect, indicating to Ross that a subsequent attack on Baltimore might present the same relatively easy task. Unknown to Captain Piper, the general had been frustrated by Cochrane in his initial design to drive home his advantage. But delayed though the assault might be, Ross was now determined to put Baltimore's resolve to the test.

CHAPTER 12

"WE HAVE LOST OUR GOOD GENERAL"

The British attempt to capture Baltimore was to be a two-pronged operation. The Royal Navy would seek to neutralize Fort McHenry, which commanded the seaward approach to the city, while Major General Ross advanced by land along the North Point Peninsula. Army operations began in the early hours of September 12, known afterward in the Baltimore area as "Defenders Day." As at Benedict, the landing of the troops was covered by a brig with cannons pointed ashore. A British officer reported that despite the fact that there was no sign of the enemy, the brig "sent a shot into the wood which must have given a terrible shock to some innocent tree." The redcoats soon leapt from the long boats back onto the Maryland shore. Taking no chances, they immediately dropped to a prone position.[1] Yet again, to the amazement of the British, the Americans did not oppose their landing. Major General Samuel Smith, U.S. commander at Baltimore, had decided not to meet the invaders at the water's edge.[2]

Ross soon learned that the Americans had been building defensive positions about three miles away at Humphrey's Creek. Once again, as at Bladensburg, in an effort to disconcert his opponents, the general advanced with his light troops and the First Brigade, commanded this time by Major Timothy Jones of the 1/4th, leaving Colonel Arthur Brooke to supervise the rest of the disembarkation. This time, however, Ross was deprived of the services of 85th Regiment's talented officers who had led the advance to Bladensburg but were wounded in that battle. This was to have a telling effect on the unfolding operation. Not only was Colonel William Thornton missing as commander of the light troops, but Major George Brown was also unavailable to lead the advance guard as he had done so effectively on the way to Bladensburg. The British again were handicapped by the lack of cavalry, not least for reconnaissance.[3]

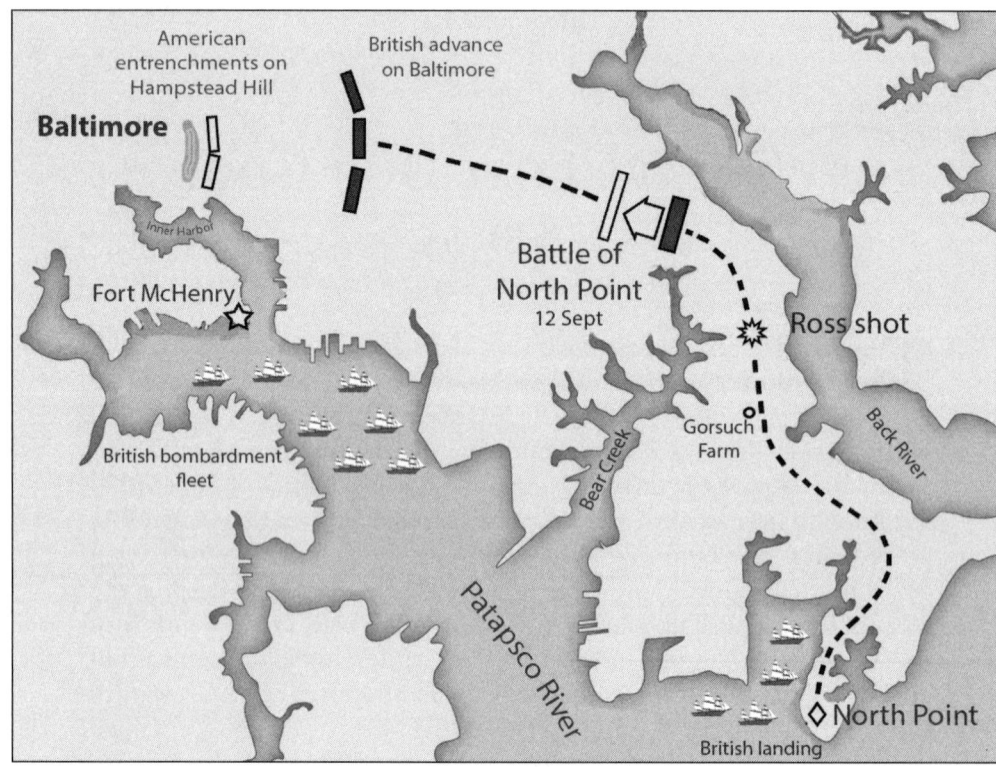

British Operations around Baltimore, September 12–15, 1814. Map by Mark McCavitt. Copyright © 2016 by the University of Oklahoma Press

While three British companies were pushed forward to screen the army's approach, Lieutenant Gleig noted that no dedicated "advance" was formed and "placed permanently under the command of a distinct leader." One of the lead units was the light company of the 1/4th. Lieutenant Francis Fitzgerald MacNamara of the Royal Marines later claimed that he undertook similar duties when he "commanded a company of undisciplined Black Men." Without a commander of the advance whom the general could wholly depend upon, Gleig recorded that Ross was even more tempted to take a forward role as the British marched toward Baltimore.[4] As Wellington had earlier written of Sir John Hope, Ross was inclined to want to manage the skirmish line.

Rather than wait and try to resist the British at the formidable defenses in Baltimore, General Smith sent a substantial force to feel out the enemy at North Point. Brigadier General John Stricker volunteered his City Brigade for this task. This command consisted almost entirely of Baltimore militia, but also included some militia companies from Hagerstown, Maryland, and Pennsylvania. Hysteria seems to have been whipped up among residents that the British intended not only to despoil the city but also to defile its womenfolk. Hezekiah Niles, a local prowar newspaper editor in Baltimore, later called Ross the "leader of a host of Barbarians . . . devoted [to expose] the populous city of Baltimore to rape, robbery and pillage."[5] The widely reported respect that the British general had ensured for private property and citizens in Washington did not impress the Baltimoreans, who feared dire and bloody calamity.

General Smith had long anticipated that the British would land at North Point. Having been mobilized on September 11, Stricker and his militiamen would march down Patapsco Neck that day and camp for the night near the Methodist meeting house. He elected to engage the enemy just south of there, where the peninsula narrowed between Bear Creek and Back River. Stricker's force totaled 3,185 men in five regiments: the 5th, 6th, 27th, 39th, and 51st Regiments of Maryland Militia. By their own reckoning, the British would land at North Point with 4,419 men, not counting sailors, who probably brought the total force to upward of 5,000 men.[6]

While the landing site was predictable and afforded the Americans the opportunity for advance planning, it is readily understandable why the British disembarked at North Point. As Lieutenant Evans explained, should the enemy choose to try to stem the British advance along that peninsula, the Royal Navy could outflank them using the rivers on either side. Certainly, the Americans were conscious of this danger. On the morning of September 12, Stricker ordered his riflemen to the skirts of a thick, low pine wood beyond a blacksmith's shop, miles ahead of his main line at Bear Creek, with a view to engaging the forward troops of the enemy, known to be moving quickly up the main road. But the men panicked and retreated when they thought the British were landing on the Back River's shore on the eastern side of Patapsco Neck to cut them off.[7]

When he got to Humphrey's Creek, Ross was surprised to find the hastily prepared defensive positions abandoned, though his forces captured a handful of American dragoons there. The rapidity of the British advance might certainly be one reason for Stricker's apparent inability to get sufficient forces to these entrenchments in time to offer any sort of meaningful resistance. While Ross pushed ahead, the disembarkation of the rest of his army proceeded. Making landfall, the troops moved under cover of a wood since men were dropping in droves owing to the heat. Brooke later came across Ross and Rear Admiral Cockburn sitting on the steps of a house, probably at Robert Gorsuch's farm, and learned that he was to wait there until the rest of the troops came up. The colonel recorded in his diary that the general was keen to reach a particular, though unspecified, point that day, with a view to advancing the following morning to Baltimore.[8]

Meanwhile, at the Gorsuch farm, General Ross interrogated the three dragoons captured at Humphrey's Creek. They told him that as many as 20,000 defenders awaited him in Baltimore. American artillery, they volunteered, numbered up to one hundred pieces, manned by seamen who knew how to use them. According to Gleig, the "General heard all this with a countenance which never once varied in its expression." When he was finished questioning the prisoners, Ross ordered the bugle sounded, and the troops prepared to advance once more. His interrogation of the three captured dragoons may have led him to conclude mistakenly that he would encounter no more than light resistance before he reached the main entrenchments in Baltimore. While at Gorsuch's farm, Ross enjoyed a leisurely breakfast.[9]

On learning that the assembled Americans were largely militia, Ross, legend has it, declared, "I don't care if it rains militia, I will sup in Baltimore tonight or in hell." To date, the historical record can only trace these utterances to a combination of two remarks attributed to the general, their sources dating from 1863 and 1878, calling into serious question their credibility. New evidence locates these comments, or variants of them, much earlier. On September 24, 1814, *Niles' Weekly Register* in Baltimore referred to Ross as the man who did "not care if it rained militia."[10] As for him saying that he would sup in Baltimore, James Rees in 1836 said of Ross that this "accomplished and generous officer remarked in a moment of excitement, that on a certain evening he would sup at Gadsby's, in Baltimore, or in hell!" Gadsby's Hotel, where the stagecoach stopped, was located on Baltimore's Hanover Street.[11]

Of these "bombastic remarks" alleged to have been made by Ross, it has been suggested that they would be more in keeping with Rear Admiral Cockburn's character than the general. That being acknowledged, there are now stronger grounds for believing that the general did indeed utter the comments attributed to him, although whether it was one statement or a conflation of two remains unclear. In a certain sense it may have been a case that they were simply the jocular remarks of a quick-witted Irishman.[12] It is entirely possible, of course, given what he had seen of the performance of the American militia to that time, that he simply did not rate them highly as an adversary. Indeed, it may have been the main reason why he was prepared to risk attacking Baltimore, despite being heavily outnumbered. That the American militia were little better than a "military mob" prone to "confusion" was a view shared by some Americans as well at the time, including the Committee of Vigilance and Safety of Baltimore. Regardless of the merits of Ross's famous quip, it soon returned to haunt him.[13]

As for the captured dragoons at Gorsuch farm, they had only told Ross about the defenders in the entrenchments some eleven miles ahead. They had not mentioned that Stricker's brigade was less than four miles away. On learning that a small force of British troops were "enjoying" themselves at Gorsuch's farm, Stricker was outraged. "Insulted at the idea of a small marauding party thus daringly provoking chastisement, several of my officers volunteered their corps to dislodge it." Whether his officers were as keen for the fight as the general intimated is another matter. When he sent the riflemen and some other units back down the neck, it was characterized as a "Forlorn Hope" mission. This force consisted of 150 men of the 5th Regiment under Major Richard Heath and 70 riflemen, among them Captain Edward Aisquith's rifle company, which had been on the front line at Bladensburg.[14] What happened next, the skirmish in which General Ross was mortally wounded, has ever since provoked controversy.

From a British point of view, accounts vary whether he was facing the Americans when fatally wounded or when he turned his back and was returning alone to bring up the column. Some British writers also contended that Ross was effectively assassinated by a gunman using a tree for cover. There was more than a hint too by a number of fellow officers at the time that Ross had thrown his life away by taking unnecessary risks. In this respect he can be compared to Major General Isaac Brock, who was killed at the Battle of Queenston Heights on 13 October 1812 leading what Mackay Hitsman and Donald Graves have described as an "unsuccessful and hurried counter-attack" at the head of one hundred men.[15] In reconnoitering so far ahead of his column with an advance unit, Ross was doing the job of a company commander.

Evidence provided by Cockburn and Lieutenant Scott of the Royal Navy concurred that the general was returning by himself to the main column when he was shot. The suggestion that Ross's career ended so ingloriously "cantering to the rear" incensed Evans, his military secretary, who maintained that the general was facing the enemy when he was struck, a version confirmed by American witnesses. That Ross was accompanied at the time is verified in a number of accounts that record that he fell into the arms of an officer or officers riding by his side. Both Captain MacDougall, his aide-de-camp, and Captain Edward Crofton of the Royal Navy were named in this respect, with Crofton confirming that he had been by the general's side.[16]

The charge that Ross made a basic tactical mistake and lost his life needlessly at the head of his troops emanated from Rear Admiral Cockburn. Just prior to the skirmish, Cockburn became concerned that the general had pushed too far forward from the main column with only fifty or sixty men, and he had just pointed out this mistake to the army commander when the shooting began.[17] Once again, Evans objected strongly to the insinuation that a man of Ross's military experience required a naval officer to school him in the basics of his profession. According to the lieutenant, Ross was accompanying just one of a number of reconnaissance patrols pushed out to the front and flanks of the advancing army. Other British and American participants confirm Evans's claim in this respect. The wisdom of Ross risking his life in this matter seems not to have occurred to his military secretary. Bemoaning the death of the highly popular general, Vice Admiral Cochrane remarked that his "only Fault was that of exposing his own Person more than was necessary for a General to do."[18] Ross lived by the mantra of being "on the spot"—and died by it.[19] The surprising thing is not so much that he lost his life in this fashion near Baltimore, but that he had not been killed before then, either at Bladensburg or in the host of battles fought against the French.

So far as the allegation that Ross was assassinated is concerned, both the British and Americans at least agree that the person who shot him hid in or behind a tree.[20] That the Americans took cover in the natural terrain to fire upon the British was not denied by

Captain Benjamin Howard, who was involved in this skirmish. Howard, however, rejected out of hand the British accusation of foul play. Whatever the truth about the circumstances in which General Ross was shot, during subsequent engagements that day, the British showed little mercy to American snipers discovered hiding in trees. One officer reported that they "were shot from their perches at leisure."[21]

The favorite Baltimore legend is that Privates Daniel Wells and Henry Gough McComas, aged nineteen and eighteen, respectively, and members of Aisquith's Rifle Company, were the militiamen responsible. They were reputed to have fired simultaneously. But the controversy has been protracted and is not as cut and dried as the legend would have it. An account by the son of a Corporal Hulse of Aisquith's Rifle Company, published in 1889, claims that his father was shown a bullet that McComas, described by a contemporary as a "tall, slender youth of emaciated form," had made from melting some old silver. The elder Hulse not only claimed that he handled this silver bullet but also that he saw McComas load it and was only thirty feet away from him when he fired, killing the British general.[22] Debate has continued for more than two centuries as to whether Ross was hit by a round from a rifle, a musket ball, or buck and ball. A British officer remarked at the time that the "honour of the feat has been claimed by at least a half hundred pretenders." A letter written by British Army Surgeon Alexander Baxter has recently come to light, giving details of Ross's wound and death. Writing on September 17, 1814, Baxter reports that Ross's mortal wound was caused by a musket ball that "was found deeply embedded in . . . the last dorsal vertebra." The ball passed through the general's right arm just above the elbow and entered his torso, fractured the fifth and sixth ribs, "passed through the Diaphragm, and wounded the right lobe of the Liver, passing deep and dividing the vena porta, which may have thrown its blood into the right cavity of the Thorax which was found filled with Blood."[23]

Ross did not die straight away but, according to Baxter, lingered in extreme discomfort for three hours, passing in and out of consciousness before expiring. Baxter states that the general spoke more than once about his wife and children and asked that all the money in his pockets be given to those who carried him back to the ships. The signs were immediately ominous to his comrades. Colonel Brooke, the next-most-senior army officer, recorded in his diary that

Lieutenant Evans galloped up to him to relay the fateful news. On being hit, Ross reportedly cried out, "send immediately for Colonel Brooke." Before passing away some hours later, the general is supposed to have issued instructions to Brooke.[24] This representation of a dying Ross attending to his military duties till his dying breath is suspiciously romanticized. In his diary Brooke noted that he ended up facing an American army with no inkling of the general's intentions. And in his official dispatch about the Battle of North Point, Brooke remarked that Ross survived just long enough to commend his young family to the "protection of his King and Country." In a letter of condolence to the general's brother, the Reverend Thomas Ross, Rear Admiral Cockburn stated that the general had been mortally wounded about midday. Ross handed Cockburn "a locket from his bosom, saying give that to my dear wife, and tell her I commend her to my king and my country," shortly before his death.[25]

Whatever the reason why Brooke was not privy to Ross's strategy, Lieutenant Evans enjoyed the general's confidence. Indeed, later reports in England stated that when the subsequent Battle of North Point was fought, the British were not directed by Brooke but by Evans. It was not just a matter of Ross being impressed by this highly talented young officer. In Brooke's own correspondence at the time, the colonel acknowledges that in preparing to assault Baltimore, he was influenced by the views of Cockburn and Evans that the American positions could be turned and that he had shown the lieutenant a note received from Vice Admiral Cochrane. Evans's influence with senior officers was widely understood. Peter Bowlby, an officer in the 1/4th, reported that owing to the fact that Brooke was not "a literary man," he "had one of his staff write the dispatch which was pronounced to be one of the most beautiful ever written." By implication, it was Evans who "did not fail to speak highly of himself." Quoting the Irish saying "small blame to him," Bowlby described the young officer, as "both poor and clever." Later in his career Evans would command a division during the Crimean War.[26]

The mortal wounding of Ross understandably shocked his men, who idolized him. As Captain William De Bathe of the 85th put it, "we have lost our good general," a comment that perhaps had as much to say about his amiable personality as his generalship.[27] The key to Ross's success in forging such bonds of loyalty and respect, after all, lay in what Cochrane described as his "system of cordiality." At the time, Evans did what he could to conceal the general's prostrate body from the troops. It is clear, however, that they knew what had happened. Gleig realized something had gone terribly wrong when he saw the general's riderless horse stampeding, its saddle bloodstained.[28] Lieutenant Gordon Gollie MacDonald was haunted by the sight of not only witnessing such a gallant officer dying but also seeing his "magnificent black Horse" by his side, "the Animal actually appearing as if conscious of his loss." Ross's deep attachment to his horses, such a distinguishing feature of his life, was equally apparent as he died.[29]

After he was wounded, General Ross was reportedly laid for a short time under the shade of an oak tree. An attempt was then made to take him back to the fleet for attention. When it was proposed to transport him on a rocket wagon, the general refused, supposedly saying that he "would not deprive his men of a weapon so important to their success." There are some grounds for believing that Ross was initially carried on a makeshift stretcher made from two fence poles to Poplar Heights, about a mile and a half away. At this point his attendants were reported to have commandeered a cart, horse, and some blankets, perhaps from the home of Abraham Stansbury.[30] Cockburn was later reported to have said that he believed Ross might have been saved had he been more comfortably conveyed back to the fleet rather than being jolted on a cart.[31]

According to Baltimore tradition, the British general died at a poplar tree on a local landmark known as Poplar Heights by Gorsuch's farm, where he and Cockburn had enjoyed breakfast hours earlier. Lieutenant Philip Haymes, naval aide-de-camp to the general, reportedly heard his last words. At 9:00 P.M. on September 12, Haymes boarded HMS *Royal Oak* with Ross's corpse. The ship's log book for the following day reads in part: "Expended 129 Gallons of Rum to preserve the Corpse of Major General Ross."[32] He thus truly was conveyed to his grave in a barrel of rum, as legend has maintained.

As might be expected, Ross's death had an important bearing on the unfolding Battle of Baltimore. Outnumbering Stricker's brigade, Brooke succeeded in winning the Battle of North Point. Some British accounts of the action belittle the resistance offered by the Americans, with Lieutenant Scott describing it as a rerun of the Bladensburg Races. This was an exaggeration. The militia put up much stronger resistance at North Point than they had done at Bladensburg. Suffering some 350 men killed and wounded, including 49 dead, headed by General Ross himself, the British had been given a taste of the heavy casualties they could expect should they decide on a full-blown assault on the American defenses.[33]

The next objective for the British was Baltimore itself. In the city spirits sank when news spread that Stricker's brigade had been defeated. The sight of wounded men and "flocks of fugitives" arriving compounded the sense of dread. Some years later a visitor to the city reported that the people did not deny that they were prepared to flee if the British had pressed ahead with an attack on Baltimore. And while it bristled with fieldworks, men, and artillery, the defenses were far from impregnable, according to Evans. Surveying a series of fortified heights, he reckoned that a concentrated attack in two or three columns on one of them would have compromised the rest.[34]

A vital officer in the British chain of command, Evans documented at the time that Brooke had determined on a night attack, targeting the city's eastern defenses on Hampstead Hill, also known as Chinquapin or Loudenslager's Hill, centered on present-day Patterson Park. New research indicates that Baltimore's "ramshackle, pieced together city defenses" were indeed vulnerable. After the Battle of Baltimore, improvements were required, not least on Hampstead Hill.[35] Whether the British would have succeeded in their attempt to storm the city is a moot point.

Initially reluctant to sanction the operation against Baltimore, Vice Admiral Cochrane warmed to the idea. Perhaps sensing that Ross and Cockburn would garner the acclaim for the successful attack on the American capital, he thrust himself—and his family—center stage at Baltimore. Cochrane transferred his flag to the *Surprize*, his son's ship, during the naval bombardment of Fort McHenry, an attack immortalized in the lyrics of Francis Scott Key's "Star-Spangled Banner." Having blown cold, then hot, over the prospective attack, Cochrane's enthusiasm waned once more when he learned of Ross's death. Lieutenant Scott of the Royal Navy recalled being sent by Brooke to Cochrane to request a simultaneous naval and land attack. In the end the vice admiral was not prepared to take additional risks. Perhaps the news of Ross's death shattered any confidence he may have had that the operation could be successful, though he initially encouraged Brooke to press ahead. With the general's loss, however, there was less reason to risk vital naval and land forces that could be used for his cherished attack on New Orleans. Besides, before the campaign had begun, the vice admiral stated that he was firmly opposed to capturing forts owing to the losses that would be sustained. Whatever the reason, Cochrane subsequently informed Brooke that he could not expect naval cooperation and clearly indicated his opposition to continuing the offensive.[36] The colonel felt he had no option but to retreat.

While the American resistance at Fort McHenry proved historically and memorably brave in the face of apparently overwhelming odds, with the "rocket's red glare" and "the bombs bursting in air" as Key described it, the fort's survival was in truth owed to Cochrane's reluctance to press home the naval attack at the risk of heavy casualties and damage to his vessels. His decision to withdraw provoked considerable recrimination within British ranks. That the navy bombarded Fort McHenry from a distance enraged Evans. This was not the level of cooperation that had been promised to General Ross. Rear Admiral Malcolm, confirming that Cochrane's letter to Brooke prevented the attack, revealed that this decision had been "much discussed since and with warmth by individuals." And there was no mistaking, the army in unison blamed Cochrane.[37]

It was not just a case of the two services indulging in a blame game. Malcolm's correspondence after the failure of the attack on Baltimore indicates very clearly that Cochrane had a lot to answer for and that Codrington, captain of the fleet, "has a difficult task" in dealing with the vice admiral. Their relations soon became increasingly fractious.[38] Meantime, Midshipman Robert Barrett recollected that as the fleet sailed away from Baltimore, "sullen discontent was displayed and malevolent aspersions cast upon our veteran chief, by men, even, who stood high in the Service."[39]

It was not just Cochrane who drew criticism. While there was a certain custom of British officers not wishing to speak ill of the dead, particularly when it was the highly popular Ross, at least one senior commander, Codrington, questioned the wisdom of the operation. Cautious by instinct, he had tried in vain to dissuade the general from proceeding with an attack when its "only chance of success was in the panic of the enemy, the probability of which was gathered merely from the American papers." Blaming Cockburn and Evans for influencing the army commander in this regard, Codrington went on to register his surprise that "so sensible a man as General Ross should be led away" by reports of American weakness. In reality, Baltimore turned out to be a "very different place from what that hearsay led us to believe." In a rather obvious reference to Ross, he went on to remark that there were only so many "wonders" that "heroism" could achieve.⁴⁰

That a defeatist mentality prevailed in Baltimore after the fall of Washington, it is worth pointing out, was more than just hearsay. Nevertheless, in alluding to the influence of newspaper reports on British military planning, Codrington draws attention to an important point. Rumors carried in print that Lord Hill commanded a massive amphibious operation played a hugely important role in cowing American resistance, leading to the capture of Washington. In a role reversal, press reports of defeatism in Baltimore lulled British commanders into a false sense of security, only for them to discover at their cost by the time they attacked that they were going to have a tougher fight than they expected.

Rear Admiral Malcolm, who had struck up such a friendly rapport with Ross, signified in his correspondence to his wife that he would rather not have targeted Baltimore. Cochrane had not been persuaded. Malcolm reckoned, however, that "as we were so close," an all-out assault should have been undertaken that would have been successful, though with heavy losses. Recriminations were running rampant. To rub salt in the British wounds, as they sailed away from Fort McHenry, Barrett wrote that "the Americans hoisted a most superb and splendid ensign on their battery"—the Star-Spangled Banner—firing a gun at the same time in a defiant gesture. Looking back at the city, the British witnessed "the reflection from Baltimore of an illumination of the city to celebrate its deliverance."⁴¹

There was much speculation at the time and since about how differently things might have worked out had Ross lived. Captain Howard was convinced that Ross would more than likely have pressed ahead with an attack, though the American officer believed that it would have failed. The British for their part were equally confident that they could have prevailed. Ross's reported comments after he was shot perhaps revealed his anticipated tactic. The soldiers were to hold their fire, and use the bayonet.⁴² Perhaps as in Egypt in 1801, Ross had been contemplating a nighttime bayonet attack. Certainly, Brooke had determined upon this tactic, targeting the city's eastern defenses at Hampstead Hill. Aware that the general was being criticized in some quarters for undertaking the operation against Baltimore in the first place, Evans not surprisingly was certain that Ross would have seized the city had he lived. The military secretary was not the only one who shared this view. "Old

Sub" insisted that this was the "universal belief throughout our little army, that had General Ross survived, Baltimore would have been in our possession within two hours of our arrival at the foot of Clinkapin [sic] Hill."[43] Flushed by his victory at Bladensburg, Ross may well have been tempted to go for broke in attacking Baltimore. On the other hand, as his sensible approach toward advancing on the U.S. capital had shown, he was more than prepared to order a retreat should he find the odds stacked against him. At a key point in the Battle of Sorauren (1813), it is worth recalling, Ross ordered his brigade to retreat when its position became untenable.

For some, and not only on the British side, Ross's death proved to be pivotal, not just to the survival of Baltimore, but for the future of the United States. For George Douglas, whose letters chronicled events in Baltimore at this critical time, the "raw and undisciplined" troops had "saved Baltimore, & perhaps America." Senator Robert Goldsborough, who was visiting the area during the crisis, reported that Baltimore owed its survival to the shot that killed General Ross. L. P. W. Balch, an American militiaman serving in the city at the time, concurred with this opinion. In his travels shortly after the war, John Duncan Morrison recalled visiting Baltimore and examining the remains of defenses erected to resist the British. Unimpressed, afterward he remarked that a rifleman had saved the city. "It might seem that an individual bullet could be of but little avail as to the result of a battle—it can kill but a man; but when that man is a commanding officer, and such an officer as Ross, the bullet that kills him is decisive of the day." For Lieutenant Gleig, the British operation was undermined by the death of Ross, "its mainspring and director." It was a measure of how his fellow officers in both the army and navy regarded him that they immediately raised "£1,000 for a monument" to his memory.[44]

After his death in Maryland, arrangements were made to give Ross a funeral fit for a hero in Halifax, Nova Scotia.[45] Why Ross's body was not sent back to Ireland remains something of a mystery, not least as it was only owing to his death that Captain Bruce, in charge of HMS *Raven*, sailed home with dispatches detailing events at Baltimore.[46] Local lore in Halifax relates that "as a mark of a hero, his troops drank from his funeral keg" en route to his burial.[47] Similar tales are told in Baltimore. Saddled with organizing the general's funeral, Rear Admiral Codrington confessed that he wished it were over.[48]

On learning that HMS *Tonnant* and other vessels were sailing into port on September 28, Sir John Sherbrooke, lieutenant governor of Nova Scotia, made preparations for dinner but canceled them when he learned of Ross's death. The following day the general was buried in what was to become the largest public funeral of the war in Halifax. Accounts of a highly emotional service for Ross indicate that his death continued to have a numbing effect on the army and navy. To his credit, Codrington arranged a ceremonial spectacle that enthralled the assembled throngs attending from town and country alike. The harbor teamed with shipping, including about one hundred transports and seventeen ships of the line. Lady Sherbrooke described the services, which began at three o'clock with an "amazing crowd" in attendance. "The coffin was landed at the King's Wharf from the *Tonnant*; minute guns being fired from the ship during the time it was waterborne and when it landed." Another contemporary account noted how troops paraded four deep with weapons reversed. Then the "massed bands of many regiments filled the air with the sound of mournful martial music—troop after troop in varied regimentals, cavalry, artillery, line soldiers, Highlanders, pass, and then the sailors of the fleet—then a splendid concourse of staff officers in flashing uniforms, scarlet and gold—then an object, on which every eye was riveted, the bier, and on it the coffin of the dead hero." Soldiers lined the streets the entire way. During the proceedings, the general's "war horse," it was said, "seemed to seek his master in the crowd." Many sobbed. Ross's aide-de-camp stepped forward, broke the general's sword in two, and threw it on the grave. Proceedings ended with a salute being fired and then the procession reformed, "and the brave General Ross was left alone in his glory, sleeping in the quiet Halifax church-yard."[49]

CHAPTER 13

RAMIFICATIONS

Robert Ross would never know how his operation to capture the capital of the United States was received in Britain or what its military and political ramifications would be. The *Federal Republican* in Georgetown suspected at the time that "it will hardly be credited by Englishmen. Even here it is still considered a dream." On September 10 William Cobbett, a pro-American newspaper editor in Britain, noted the "deep regret" of the *Times* that the American war had lingered for "so many months without being distinguished by any memorable stroke."[1] That was all about to change, literally overnight.

Ross's staff officer, Captain Harry Smith, and Captain John Wainwright, R.N., carrying the military and naval dispatches, respectively, from the Chesapeake, arrived in London at midnight on September 26 with news of the British triumph. Wainwright went to the Admiralty, while Smith went to Downing Street to lodge his correspondence. The Admiralty instantly became abuzz with activity, and contact was made that night with the *Times*. That the capture of Washington was considered a sensation was revealed in its edition of September 27. "We stop the press to announce the receipt of the following most important intelligence from America"—publishing what it described as an "exclusive"—a bulletin from the Admiralty revealing details of the successful operation to the public for the first time.[2] In the immediate aftermath of the capture of Washington, jockeying for credit had already begun between the army and navy.

If Smith missed out on the *Times* scoop, this was to be more than compensated for when he returned to Downing Street the following day. Lord Bathurst informed him that the Prince Regent wished to see him straightaway. During the conversations, Smith heard the celebratory firing of guns in London. Indeed, guns were fired in Hyde Park and at the Tower on three successive days at midday.[3] Surveying British newspapers at the time, Troy Bickham concludes that the "response in Britain to the attack on Washington bordered on euphoric." Some Englishmen believed that the entire city had been destroyed, not just its public buildings. And they were delighted with that. As the *Courier* put it, "war America would have; and war she has got. . . . Washington is no more."⁴ The *Public Ledger* predicted that Baltimore, Boston, Philadelphia, and New York could be turned into smoldering ruins before the end of the year. The *Post* regretted that Ross had not torched more private property. As for the *Sun*, it compared the "victory with Wellington's greatest successes," even going so far as to state it as "full and perfect in all its parts."⁵

The "peace minded" *Spectator* and the *Morning Chronicle*, the leading Whig opposition newspaper, were in harmony in characterizing the capture of Washington as a "brilliant dash." The burning of the public buildings did not serve to dampen the attitude of the *Morning Chronicle*. While this action was to be regretted, it was considered restrained retaliation for Americans destroying villages in Canada. Having broken the story with the last-minute changes to its edition of September 27, the *Times* salivated about it the following day, pouring scorn on President Madison and mocking him for fleeing from the battlefield.⁶

And it was not only London that celebrated news of the capture of Washington. The *Caledonian Mercury* reported that the momentous news was saluted by the firing of guns at Edinburgh Castle, with the ships at Leith Roads doing likewise. Reports of the British victory were translated into French, German, and Italian. Twelve people were wounded when a magazine exploded in Heligoland during celebrations marking the news. Such was the jubilant reaction in Britain that it prompted William Cobbett to remark, "it was the common notion, that a Vice-Roy was about to be sent thither to represent, and govern in the name of your Royal Father."⁷ This jingoistic reaction was wholly at odds with military reality, though, for the British simply did not have the capability to recapture their former colonies. Yet that is not to deny that at this juncture there was a reasonable expectation that the American expedition could realize further military success and strategic gains before the war was brought to a conclusion.

The British in Canada were elated too. The *Montreal Herald* gloated about the Capitol being destroyed. "Those horse-whipping, kicking, spitting, tarring and feathering Hottentots, will not have a suitable place wherein to cover their heads in the ensuing extraordinary Session." The term "Hottentot" was no throwaway remark but was intended as deeply insulting. In the early nineteenth century, this was not only used to refer to a South African people called the Khoekhoe but was also employed as a reference to the "lowest stage of human development and the basest form of existence and morals."[8]

And friends of the general celebrated in the neighborhood of his beloved Rostrevor, where some thirty local gentlemen held a victory dinner at the inn in the village. Bonfires and illuminations marked the occasion. Plans were being made for a welcome-home dinner for the victorious general. Glasses, plates, and dishes had been bought at considerable expense in Dublin, and a band of musicians was being organized. Meantime, wits in Britain were having a field day. Recalling Ross's visit to Mrs. Suter's boarding house in Washington, one newspaper quipped that "when Gen. Ross supped at Washington, instead of asking *what's to pay?* he ought rather have enquired *what's the damage?*" The Irish general Ross was hailed as a national hero, the "Gallant Hibernian."[9]

While there was widespread euphoria, Ross's actions in burning the public buildings did not win universal approval in Britain and Ireland. Among the fiercest critics were the *Leeds Mercury* and the *Liverpool Mercury*, with the latter, a vehicle for some of the war's main critics, wondering what world reaction would be to a foreign army burning palaces in London. The most ferocious criticism in the immediate aftermath of the destruction occurred in Ireland, where memories were still fresh, and raw, following the ruthless repression of the United Irishmen movement during 1797–98. The *Irish Magazine*, a radical newspaper linked to the rebel cause, likened the "savages in British pay" who burnt Washington to the "burnings" of the "Orange savages in Ireland."[10] Dissenting voices there may have been, but they were largely drowned out by the cacophony of celebration.

As far as the British government was concerned, Ross's success was greeted gleefully. Lord Liverpool, the prime minister, took it upon himself to forward a copy of the *London Gazette Extraordinary*, published to mark the successful operations of the army and navy on September 27, to the Duke of Wellington in Paris. On the same day, Lord Bathurst sent off a message to Wellington in which he stated that the "conduct of Major-General Ross does great credit to your Grace's school." Clearly delighted, the duke was reported to have held a celebratory dinner or ball, although ambassadors from allied powers did not attend.[11] The British foreign secretary, Lord Castlereagh, also in Paris, reputedly bragged that the British would soon control New Orleans and Louisiana. The British provided the American peace commissioners at Ghent with copies of newspapers revealing the fall of Washington. "Let them feast upon Washington" crowed an exhilarated Lord Liverpool.[12]

Congratulating Vice Admiral Cochrane, the prime minister promised to do all in his power to assist future operations.[13] Unaware at the time that Ross was dead, news about the capture of Washington prompted a major reevaluation in London of his role. Changing military priorities during the summer of 1814 had already resulted in Ross, instead of Lord Hill, being earmarked to realize Cochrane's military objectives in the Gulf of Mexico. Hill's "grand expedition" was postponed again. Instead, what was described as a "little expedition" comprising some 2,000 troops sailed on August 24 under the command of Major General John Keane to reinforce Ross. By coincidence, this was the very day that Ross won the Battle of Bladensburg. An extra unit, the 1/40th, was sent separately to make up for any losses that may already have been incurred. Besides additional troops, heavy artillery was also sent to enable Ross to hold a position in the United States.[14]

On September 27, the day news of Washington's capture broke in London, plans were immediately made to send Ross two more units from Britain. The two selected comprised Wellington veterans. The 1/7th, 1,000 strong, had served in Ross's brigade during the Peninsular War, while the 1/43rd, also 1,000 strong, formed part of the famous Light Infantry Division. Arrangements were also put in place to assign two West Indies–based black regiments to serve under Ross. His army thus having been tripled in size, a second general was now also considered necessary to accompany the additional troops, Major General John Lambert being so appointed. In sum, within two days of news arriving in London of the fall of Washington, Bathurst wrote to Ross to inform him that he was to command a force of 10,000 troops, including two subordinate generals. Bathurst also emphasized that "this force is placed very much at your discretion as to its employments," thereby recalibrating the army commander's role at the expense of Cochrane. Ross was on course to be granted a commission as "Commander of the Forces," a truly independent command.[15]

Blissfully unaware that Ross was dead, Henry Torrens at Horse Guards reckoned at the end of September that the general would be handsomely rewarded for his coup at Washington. Perhaps reflecting where primary credit was being given in London for the operation's success, Ross was almost immediately singled out for a knighthood; the insignia was forwarded to his widow, her will documenting that she possessed his Cross of the Order of Bath. It was to be several months later before Rear Admirals Cockburn, Codrington, and Malcolm were similarly honored, when a long list of knighthoods were announced.[16] That Ross would soon be ennobled occurred at the time to Vice President Elbridge Gerry, who speculated that the triumphant British general would be created "Lord Washington." Anticipating too that Ross would be raised to the peerage, the *Irish Magazine* was thankful that a rifle ball had robbed "the Orangemen of a Saint, and the hospital of incurables [House of Lords] of a new Peer."[17]

Oblivious of Ross's death, speculation in Britain about where his next "dash" would take place reached fever pitch. In the end, by the time Harry Smith found "poor Mrs. Ross in the highest spirits at the achievement of our arms under her husband . . . , at that very moment of her excessive happiness he was in a soldier's bloody grave." The sky-high expectations for Britain's new national hero were shattered. A realization that the Americans were not about to be "drubbed" into submission took hold in London. Ross's death coincided with the British naval defeat at the Battle of Lake Champlain and the consequent military reverse at the Battle of Plattsburgh, as Sir George Prevost's invasion of the United States from Canada foundered. The same vessel that carried the dispatches from the Chesapeake announcing Ross's death also conveyed American newspapers that broke the story that their countrymen had won a major victory at Lake Champlain. Meanwhile, Lieutenant General Sir Gordon Drummond had to abandon the siege of Fort Erie that same month.[18] Such depressing news from North America punctured the mood of optimism in Britain following the capture of Washington.

Elation among Ross's friends and admirers at the general's victory at Bladensburg in Rostrevor now turned to despair.[19] The general's wife, his beloved Ly, was reported to be residing at Clifton, near Bristol, when she heard the news; her mother and sister comforted her. Ross's poignant remarks in relation to his wife as he died pulled at the heartstrings of many in Britain. What was not known by the public were the trying personal circumstances that lay behind these sentiments—the general's profound worry and nagging sense of guilt about his wife's illness. The *Times* was moved by the fact that "his last sigh was devoted to the tenderness of domestic affection. So should fall a hero, and a man. We have seldom perused, the melancholy annals of war seldom afford, so touching and yet so exalted a picture."[20]

For the second time in three weeks, Ross was to be the central character in a *London Gazette Extraordinary*. Having previously sparked national celebrations, news of his death occasioned national grief. The Duke of York, the commander in chief, was reported to be profoundly upset. It was also a source of regret, in military and diplomatic terms, not least to the prime minister. In conjunction with the humiliating failure of Prevost's operations, a swift end to the war with the British having a decisive upper hand was no longer in sight.[21]

In these circumstances Lord Liverpool's government was faced with a choice, pursuing either "conquest or compromise." Ross's stirring campaign inclined toward conquest, while Prevost's failure toward compromise. It was a measure of the significance of Ross's success in capturing Washington that not only had additional forces been assigned to his expedition but also a senior general would be required to replace him. On October 17, the day news broke in London that Ross had been killed, the importance attached to this development at the highest levels was evidenced by both the prime minister and the secretary for war visiting Torrens at Horse Guards to discuss a suitable replacement commander. They agreed to appoint Major General Sir Edward Pakenham, Wellington's brother-in-law.[22]

Not only did Lord Liverpool rue the loss of Ross, but also government and military correspondence in London makes it plain that Sir George Prevost was to suffer badly by comparison as the British government determined what to do next. The prime minister accused Prevost of mismanaging his campaign and regretted sending so many troops to Canada instead of allocating them to Ross. Had he done so, he reckoned the British might have taken every substantial American city south of Philadelphia.[23] Hindsight, of course, is a wonderful thing. And in his ringing endorsement of Ross, Liverpool was forgetting one thing, a more senior general would have been given command of such a large force, relegating Ross to his originally conceived position as a brigade commander in a larger seaborne operation.

As for Prevost, he was subjected to a chorus of condemnation and a clamor for his replacement. A correspondent writing to the *Morning Post* was most scathing of all. Military objectives would have been realized "*had any Wellingtonian, even of the rank of corporal commanded*" instead of Prevost. "General Ross, with a handful, has done wonders. Here with four times his force we have done infinite mischief to ourselves, and elevated the hopes of the enemy beyond bounds." While far from blameless for the way events transpired, as Donald E. Graves has remarked, Prevost was unfairly made a "scapegoat" for British military failure during the Plattsburgh Campaign in the early autumn of 1814. That his career ended "under a cloud" has detracted from his signal achievement in defending the Canadas with scarce resources.[24]

Before long, pressure built up for Wellington not only to take overall charge of military operations against the Americans but also to act as a minister plenipotentiary who could negotiate peace terms. Besides, with his life apparently under threat in Paris, it has been argued that the American war offered a pretext for permitting him to return from the French capital. While supposedly not objecting to going to North America, the Iron Duke doubted that he would be successful without British control of the Great Lakes. He stated bluntly to the prime minister that the military situation did not support an insistence that the Americans should cede territory as the price for peace, thereby rejecting the notion of *uti possidetis* as the basis for the end of the war, each nation retaining what territory they held at that point. Wellington's well-known advice to the government is often considered to be the tipping point when London conceded that it was not possible to hold out for territorial concessions from the Americans. It has been argued, however, that Wellington essentially "avoided the North American command."[25] If so, he was following in the footsteps of Hope, Hill, and Murray before him.

Besides the sobering advice offered by Wellington, domestic political pressures were also taking their toll on the government, as demonstrated by the feisty debates on the Prince Regent's speech at the state opening of Parliament on November 8.[26] Extracts from these debates have often been cited by historians analyzing British reaction to Ross's capture of Washington. It has been argued by historian George Dangerfield in *The Era of Good Feelings*, for example, that "after a brief and somewhat shamefaced celebration the British themselves condemned" the burning of the public buildings. While there is a degree of validity in this view, it overstates the case.[27] Far from backtracking on the issue, the Prince Regent lavished praise on General Ross and the conduct of British forces in Washington and placed on public record the sense of national loss at Ross's death. Even William Cobbett, a key member of a small, if vocal, minority in opposing the war with the United States, acknowledged in his *Political Register* that the "language of the principal London prints has been, from that day to this, in perfect harmony with the tenor of this [the Prince Regent's] speech."[28]

Contemporary British reaction to Ross's operations should be considered in two distinct phases, the initial response to what occurred in the American capital followed by the changed circumstances when news of the general's death shocked the country three weeks later. The key shift in opinion about what had occurred at Washington was not a wholesale change in attitudes but a decision by the Whig opposition in Parliament to criticize the conduct of what now seemed to be an unwinnable war. Basing their views on a selective reading of American newspapers, these members argued that what occurred at Washington had backfired, uniting the American people for the first time behind the war.[29] Whether the Whigs would have adopted this stance had Ross been alive and on the offensive is another matter. Their agenda was very much driven by a desire to end the war, and so to end the income tax, a temporary wartime measure.[30] The Liverpool government, by contrast, stood by what had occurred in the American capital. That it stood by Ross too was reflected in the motion to erect a national monument in his memory, a proposal tabled in the House of Commons a matter of days later.

In criticizing what occurred in Washington, the Whigs carefully avoided blaming Ross and enthusiastically joined in the parliamentary tributes paid to the fallen commander. The motion to erect the national monument in his honor was unanimously carried at the conclusion of the debate. It was warmly endorsed by two prominent Whig politicians, both Irishmen: George Ponsonby, leader of the Whigs in the House of Commons, and Whitshed Keene, the longest-serving MP (and known as "Father of the House"). Ponsonby spoke movingly, not least on behalf of Ross's wife, while Keene acknowledged a longstanding acquaintance with General Ross as well as his father.[31]

Writing to George Canning at the end of December 1814, Lord Liverpool emphasized how eager he was to bring the war to an honorable end. While Wellington had agreed to command the army in the forthcoming campaign, the Iron Duke reckoned that the only important strategic target that the British could hope to capture and hold was New Orleans, although the climate there was unhealthy. In an evident reflection on Ross's capture of Washington, the prime minister went on to remark that the British had the capability to land at various parts of the U.S. coast, "destroy some of their towns, or put them under contribution; but in the present state of the public mind in America it would be in vain to expect any permanent good effects from operations of this nature." In mentioning the "public mind in America," Lord Liverpool was effectively conceding to the Whig accusation, based on their skewed analysis of U.S. newspaper accounts, that the raid on Washington had been counterproductive. Previously, Liverpool had argued that he had "seen much stronger justifications of the conduct of our forces at Washington, which had been published in America, than any that had been published even in this country."[32]

While the government was contemplating resorting to radical plans to secure acceptable peace terms, the reality was that in tandem with these developments, the strength of the British hand at the peace negotiations in Ghent had been weakened by the failure of the attack on Baltimore, which had cost Ross his life, and especially by Prevost's setback in New York. That the Americans had at one point accepted a British ultimatum in relation to their Indian allies was largely due to Ross's raid on Washington, at least according to Henry Goulburn, one of the British delegation negotiating with the Americans. At the time, as Dangerfield has pointed out, observers in Ghent reckoned that the odds on the United States surviving the capture of its capital were not good.[33] The political calculations underpinning Ross's capture and brief occupation of Washington were having an effect, at least temporarily. As the *National Advocate* in New York put it afterward, "The real negotiators of the British government are COCKBURN, and ROSS, and HILL." The failure to burn Baltimore or hold Plattsburgh, according to Goulburn, immeasurably weakened the British hand.[34]

Partly as a result of misreading the U.S. reaction to the capture of Washington, when the Treaty of Ghent was signed on Christmas Eve, 1814, the British effectively let the Americans off the hook.[35]

Aware of their own setbacks, the Liverpool government did not appreciate the full consequence of Ross's short, sharp, successful, campaign, regardless of his death. Owing to the communications time lapse, it was as if Britain and the United States were living in parallel universes. When the key decision making about ending the war was taking place in London, it was based on inaccurate and outdated information from North America.

After the capture of Washington, the American economy and government was in danger of collapsing.[36] With a hammer blow expected in subsequent months at New Orleans, the British setbacks in September 1814 were believed to be no more than a stay of execution. As Henry Adams remarked, the "symptoms of approaching failure in government were not to be mistaken, and the capture of Washington, which was intended to hurry the collapse, produced its intended effect. . . . [T]he Government was prostrate and New England was practically independent." High-risk strategy that it may have been, in targeting Baltimore, Ross was seizing the moment to bring the U.S. government to its knees. The possibility that Washington would no longer remain the capital city was seriously discussed in Congress.[37] Had the general abided by his orders and burned the entire place, Washington's days as the capital of the United States may well have been numbered.

In the six months after Ross captured Washington, a political crisis prevailed, and the United States of America teetered on the brink of a political precipice that some feared could result in disunion, possibly civil war. The reaction in the United States to the capture of Washington has often been gauged by the sentiments of American newspapers. In evaluating the response of the press to this event, it is worth bearing in mind Jeffrey Pasley's observation that "newspapers were the republic's central political institutions, working components of the party system rather than commentators on it." It is true that many American newspapers trumpeted the theme of unity in the immediate aftermath of the capital's fall, a war that had once only enjoyed partisan support had become national, they argued. These sentiments were drawn upon by British opponents of the war at the time and by many historians since who have argued that Ross's operation unified Americans behind what had previously been called "Madison's War." Even President Madison's arch-critic, Alexander Hanson of the *Federal Republican*, reputedly showed solidarity. As the *Baltimore Patriot* put it at the time, "party spirit" was to be "sacrificed . . . upon the altar of patriotism."[38] In the face of impending doom, American journals resorted to songs and poems to stir the nation—most famously manifested by Francis Scott Key writing "The Star-Spangled Banner" about the rescue of Baltimore from the heretofore successful British.

Blood-stirring metaphors filled many pages. "'Tis indeed an electric shock, striking fire into our bosoms! It lights up the flame of patriotism, and makes us feel as our fathers felt." Comparisons were made with the low points of the American War of Independence. As the *National Advocate* put it, "the nation has seen darker days than these. From the flames of the Capitol a light has flashed over the land, and rekindled the fire of patriotism in almost every bosom."[39]

And to some degree, the rhetoric was matched by action. Evidence shows increased military preparations in the United States following Ross's raid on Washington as Federalists proved more willing to rally to a war of defense, having previously rejected the offensive war that was launched by the United States against British North America. Considerable efforts continued to mobilize and to erect defenses, particularly in the big coastal cities that were vulnerable to attack. Initiatives were taken in many cases at state level rather than in collaboration with the federal government, which lacked the resources to function properly.[40]

To a certain extent, the capture of Washington united Americans in adversity. But that is only part of the story. Bitter party rivalry persisted. This was evidenced in the American press and later in Congress. Papers supporting Madison's Democratic Republicans suspected that their Federalist political opponents were in league with the British. Many Federalist newspapers, for their part, concentrated their fire after the fall of Washington not on the British, but on President Madison and his administration. The claim that even Hanson of the *Federal Republican* rallied to the president needs to be tempered. Despite remarking on September 2 that the "fight will now be for our country, not for a party," his badgering of Madison remained every bit as intense. In the same edition, Hanson considered who was "really guilty" for the "fall of the Capital . . . JAMES MADISON IS THE CAUSE OF THIS." Not many weeks were to pass before the *Federal Republican* branded the flight of the president and his cabinet from the battlefield the "Bladensburg Races." The *Washingtonian* a few days later warned that the union was on the verge of collapse. "We will never forget, that the worst enemies of our country are those who invited and provoked the British to point their cannon at our doors."[41] In the Federalist press, the bitterness toward President Madison was intense, with virtually not a word about Ross and his British army.

Attacks on the administration raged like wildfire across parts of the country. The *Delaware Gazette* referred to the "imbecility and folly of our rulers." The *Vermont Mirror* compared the president to the notorious Roman emperors Nero and Caligula. And there were still examples of the conflict being characterized as "Madison's War." For the *Portsmouth Oracle*, "if Mr. Madison could live a thousand lives or die a thousand deaths he could not live long enough nor die often enough for the disgrace he has brought upon us."[42]

Meanwhile, the reaction of the *Boston Spectator* to the capture of Washington is fascinating. Rejecting the "insidious appeals to our patriotism" by the administration, the British were characterized not as mindless arsonists but as a "discriminating enemy." Ross's actions were portrayed as "magnanimously" giving the lie to "the impostures, which our rulers propagate. They do not make war on unoffending citizens—they have proved, in the most striking and honourable manner, that they have not come for conquest or to deal vengeance on individual citizens." That Ross and his troops had proven themselves to be merciful enemies while they were in the U.S. capital was a view shared by the *Federal Republican* when it opined that the British had been in a position to "dispose of the lives and fortunes of us all, though their clemency spared both." One of the main reasons why Federalists were disposed to view the actions in Washington so favorably resulted from relief that the British had acted with restraint in response to what they described as American provocation and "atrocities" in Canada.[43]

Before this crisis ended, which did not happen before news emerged of Andrew Jackson's victory at the Battle of New Orleans on January 8, 1815, the president lost most of his cabinet, finding himself isolated politically. John Armstrong's pressured resignation as secretary of war was soon followed by the departure of William Jones at the navy and George W. Campbell at the Treasury. With Vice President Gerry soon to die as the crisis took its toll, only Secretary of State and Acting Secretary of War James Monroe and Attorney General Richard Rush remained from Madison's cabinet at the time Ross attacked. It was a measure of the seriousness of the situation that his administration managed to survive in the aftermath of the British raid.[44]

While historians have made pointed references to the Whig criticisms of British actions in Washington in Parliament, at almost the same time Federalists mercilessly attacked the Madison administration over the fall of Washington in Congress.[45] These congressmen reflected the rhetoric of the Federalist press. Representative Cyrus King from Massachusetts not only branded the president the "destroyer of Washington" but also caricatured him as "Nero" fiddling while the capital burned. The administration, King claimed, had "exasperated" the British. Repeatedly describing Madison as "Your President," he dismissed the notion that America had been united as a result of British operations as a "feeble though insidious cry." Madison and his cabinet were lampooned several times for winning the Bladensburg races. The possibility of civil war was aired openly by several congressmen. These debates echoed to the sound of "crisis."[46] The shattering blow delivered by Ross to the young Republic was still resounding even after his death, and despite the American victories at Lake Champlain and at Plattsburgh.

Facing thousands more British reinforcements, either already sent by a government buoyant after Ross's success or preparing to embark, and with an attack on New Orleans imminent, Congress did not authorize raising additional regular troops for the new campaign in 1815. Attempts to persuade lawmakers to pass a conscription bill or secure the necessary finance to conduct a truly offensive war failed. The Federalists, meanwhile, kept up their attacks on the Madison administration throughout this late-war crisis, culminating with the Hartford Convention, which met from December 15, 1814, until January 4, 1815, and from which Democratic Republicans at the time believed would emerge a "New England federation."[47] Rumblings of civil war stirred even louder.

With a new campaign in 1815 apparently looming, the United States was fortunate to have James Monroe as secretary of war. He formulated a more effective land-based strategy, although there is some doubt whether he would have been able to resource it with men and money. Congress had, however, proved amenable to supporting a novel departure in terms of naval strategy, passing a bill to build "twenty armed fast sailing cruisers, to cripple and destroy the British commerce." Two squadrons of cruisers, to be commanded by Commodores David Porter and Oliver Perry, were fitted out to attack targets in the West Indies and British home waters.[48]

In the wake of the burnings at Washington, there is evidence that the Americans were prepared to retaliate in kind in British territories. Philip Freneau testified to a mood for revenge in "On the Conflagrations at Washington," a contemporary poem. "Supposing *George's* house at Kew Were burnt (as we intend to do)."[49] American naval capacity may not have rendered London a potential target, but isolated coastal targets were another matter. Tasked with "illuminating the British channel" with his "flying squadron," Commodore Porter recorded in his memoir that "it was just as well" that peace intervened and "we had no opportunity to indulge in acts of retaliation." *Niles' Weekly Register* reported in November 1814 that an American privateer from Baltimore raided Harbor Island in the Bahamas, burning or plundering twenty-seven houses. This was justified as an act of retaliation for the burning of the Capitol. *Niles* raised the prospect that the cruisers authorized by Congress might also engage in such retaliatory attacks and could land marines from time to time on the coasts of Scotland or Ireland, where hundreds of towns were vulnerable to attack or even burning.[50] The *Register* was pointed in referring to Scotland and Ireland only in this regard, not England; that Cockburn was Scottish and Ross was an Irishman may not have been coincidental in this context. It is against this background that two reports, one British and one American, emerged in subsequent years of a plot to burn General Ross's home village of Rostrevor should be judged.

The reported plan for a retaliatory attack on Rostrevor was first mentioned in a book written by William Bailey that was published in Washington in 1826. A privateer was to convey attackers who would burn the picturesque village—including Mrs. Ross's home. A reference to the supposed plot featured again in print a number of years later, in 1834, when a bitter public row broke out between a British writer, James Stuart, author of *Three Years in North America*, and Major Norman Pringle of the 1/21st about the conduct of British troops in Washington. This account carried similar details of the proposed operation. Both reports contained much accurate local knowledge.[51] By the time Ross died, greatly exaggerated fears of attack by American privateers resulted in the Royal Navy convoying merchant vessels traveling from the important port of Newry at the head of Carlingford Lough, on the shore of which Rostrevor was nestled.[52] To date in the war, as the research of Brian Arthur and Andrew Lambert has demonstrated, the perceived privateer threat greatly exceeded the actual damage caused to British commercial interests. Whether this would have remained the case had the war continued, in light of the large numbers of privateers fitting out to take the war to British waters in the aftermath of Washington, is a moot point. Having traveled to Boston to purchase cruisers, Commodore Perry failed in his objective. Writing on Christmas Day, 1814, he revealed that all suitable vessels had been bought up as privateers.[53]

In sum, Ross's campaign on the shores of the Chesapeake Bay lasted less than a month, but its immediate ramifications were huge, politically and militarily. That it threatened the very existence of the American political experiment for a time is little appreciated. Lionized as a new national hero, Ross, through his success at Washington, had an important bearing not only in reconfiguring British strategy toward preparations for a large-scale assault on New Orleans but also in influencing the timing and complexion of the Treaty of Ghent, which brought the war with the United States to a conclusion.

Epilogue

In the introduction we suggested that Robert Ross has become a forgotten general. To some extent, of course, the prominence accorded to what happened at Washington in 1814 was bound to have diminished with time as subsequent events in British and American history occurred. This was to happen sooner in Britain, not least because of the profile of the Battle of Waterloo (1815).[1] Subsequently, the events of the War of 1812 were to pale into relative obscurity too in the United States when the Civil War broke out in 1861. That being acknowledged, it is nevertheless surprising that Ross should have disappeared into an historical void. To sustain this view, it is worth highlighting and evaluating the extent to which Ross was initially memorialized in Britain and Ireland as a national effusion of grief and adulation prevailed, if only for a short time. But the repercussions of Ross's actions loomed larger and longer on the American stage, where he remained a high-profile figure, even in death, for some time.

Poetry was a popular medium that attempted to catch the mood of the nation when news of Ross's death reached Britain. There were various representations of him as a British and an Irish hero.[2] Some poets likened him to other British commanders who had died in battle, including James Wolfe, Horatio Nelson, Ralph Abercromby, and John Moore.[3] Common touchstones noted that Ross was brave to a "fault" and that he uttered his last words about his wife and family. In contrast to the considerable corpus of praise poetry occasioned at the time, Samuel Taylor Coleridge considered writing an "Ode on the Death of General Ross," but he apparently never finished it. He intended to "utter a voice of lamentation on the *moral* war between the Child and the Parent Country."[4]

With Ross's fame having soared to new heights and the manner in which the dying general bequeathed his family to the nation earning widespread sympathy, it is not surprising that the British government granted a pension for life to Elizabeth Ross and her children.[5] Rather than accepting the knighthood that had been conferred on her husband, Mrs. Ross had another idea in mind. Heartened by the grant of the pension, she wrote to Lord Bathurst to thank him and also requested that he intercede with the Prince Regent on her behalf to add "Ross of Bladensburg" to her children's names.[6] The Prince Regent not only duly obliged but also went further by including Elizabeth herself and all her children's descendants as entitled to being called "Ross of Bladensburg."

The patent granting the augmented surname to Ross's family made it clear that it was accorded not just for his service in America but also in recognition of his achievements throughout his military career. His performances at the Battle of Maida (1806), during the retreat to Corunna (1808–1809), and at the Battles of Vitoria (1813), the Pyrenees (1813), and Orthes (1814) were all acknowledged. The features of the augmentation of arms included a "Hand grasping the Colours of the United States of America the Staff broken" in memory of his victory over American forces at Bladensburg.[7] Mrs. Ross later named her family home "Bladensburg" in Rostrevor. As fate would have it, she lived on the opposite side of the road in the village from Caroline Penelope Hamilton, sister-in-law of the Duke of Wellington. Hamilton was the sister of Major General Ned Pakenham, Ross's successor, who was killed at the Battle of New Orleans in January 1815.

While at the time Pakenham may have been the most high-profile British general to serve in North America during the War of 1812, Major General Isaac Brock remains the "best known hero" on the British side, or more accurately, from a Canadian point of view. Brock, like Ross, had fought in the Helder Campaign in 1799. His service in British North America was to provide the platform for the general's main claim to fame, and it was there that he next saw combat in 1812, falling that year at the Battle of Queenstown Heights on August 3. The contention by Wesley Turner, Brock's recent biographer, that "no person on the British or Canadian side from the War of 1812 became memorialized as immediately and as much as Isaac Brock" is not fully true.[8] In the short, though not the longer, term, that distinction belongs to Ross as evidenced not least by the remarks of the Prince Regent, the British government, and sentiments in the press.

That Ross garnered the most contemporary praise of any British general serving in the War of 1812 owes much to his success in capturing Washington. It also led to inflated assessments of his ability.

To rate him on a par with Wellington, for example, is a gross exaggeration. C. S. Forester's assertion that he was "perhaps the most brilliant of Wellington's brigadiers" is not without some foundation. But there would have been quite a list of rival contenders for this accolade, several of whom served in the War of 1812 too. Major Generals James Kempt, Manley Power, Frederick Robinson, and Thomas Brisbane were all seasoned campaigners with the Iron Duke, officers whom he described as "the best of their rank in the army." Based in Canada, however, they did not have the opportunity to demonstrate their talents, blaming Governor General Prevost for failing to capitalize on their experience.[9]

What makes Ross stand out from the other Wellington generals who served in North America is that he was the only one to succeed with an independent command, though even this needs to be qualified since he did not have a commission as "commander of the forces." His achievement in the United States stands in marked contrast to Pakenham's signal failing at New Orleans in January 1815. And yet Ross's relative success should not be overestimated either. In reality he only led a small-scale diversionary force with limited independence about choice of targets. His seizure of the U.S. capital resulted in the British government radically reappraising his assignment, with the decisions being made to triple his complement of infantry, assign two major generals to serve under his command, and accord him much greater autonomy in terms of selecting objectives. This would have been the real test of his leadership credentials had he lived to prove his mettle one way or the other. In that sense Captain Harry Smith, who was often unjustifiably critical of the general, was correct.[10]

It was against a background of Ross's celebrity at the time that Colonel Brooke was delegated some two years after the general's death by fellow army officers to petition for a medal "in the name of Washington or Bladensburg" to be awarded to the officers involved in the capture of the American capital. Lord Bathurst refused the request, informing him that the government had decided not to grant any more medals and was not prepared to make an exception.[11] Noting that a regiment had been granted the battle honor "Niagara," Brooke then asked that the four regiments involved should be permitted to have a battle honor, either "Washington or Bladensburgh [sic]." This was soon granted for three of the regiments, the 1/21st being the exception, since only its light company had been involved in the battle. In 1854, a year after Sir George De Lacy Evans became the regiment's colonel, Queen Victoria consented to "Bladensburg" being added to the regimental color of the 21st Royal North British Fusiliers.[12]

Evidently, the esprit de corps that prevailed among the units involved in the Chesapeake Campaign was strong and enduring. The famous U.S. general Winfield Scott was in Paris in September 1815 when some of the officers of regiments involved in the capture of Washington organized a banquet to commemorate the event there. Angered Americans in Paris retaliated by holding a dinner on January 8, 1816, to mark the first anniversary of Andrew Jackson's victory at New Orleans.[13]

The national monument to Ross voted by parliament was eventually placed in St. Paul's Cathedral in November 1821 at a cost of £1,575. According to a London newspaper at the time, Britannia is depicted "absorbed in grief at the loss of a favourite hero." Promoting Ross as a role model to officers and men, the imagery conveyed the impression of "humane, compassionate manliness." Progress had also been made on two monuments to his memory in the family seat of Rostrevor. In 1815 the *American Beacon* ran a story on a memorial commissioned by the 20th, or "Maida," regiment to the memory of their former commanding officer; they had raised £300. On receiving news of his death, "the regiment appeared at church in mourning on successive Sundays for a month." Their monument, including a bust of the general, was to be erected to his memory when the new church in Rostrevor opened. A second, more prominent monument was completed in Rostrevor by 1826, a 100-foot obelisk that remains a dominant feature of the shoreline. A number of local meetings were held to set up a committee, raise funds, and discuss its location. The father of Lord Castlereagh, the British foreign secretary, was included among the subscribers.[14]

Discussions took place between the local committee and Colonel William Thornton, who had led the First (Light) Brigade during the British attack at Bladensburg. It appears he was acting on behalf of army and navy officers who had raised a subscription to erect a monument to their fallen comrade in the immediate aftermath of his death. As a result of the consultations, they resolved to combine the two funds. Agreement having been reached in that regard, discussion ensued with Mrs. Ross. But she found herself in a difficult position, for the general had expressed a "particular objection" to any such tribute earlier when the widow of one of his close comrades erected a memorial for her late husband. Ross expressed his disapproval in the strongest terms at the time and, according to his son, David, "took that occasion to request she would remember his sentiment if ever similarly situated." His preference was for "simplicity."[15]

Under the original proposal, the committee suggested erecting a memorial in Rostrevor on the exact spot where the general had chosen to build his "country residence." This was confirmed in correspondence from Mrs. Ross, who described "the situation for a house, with an approach to it, had been decided upon and the trees on the hill planted with reference to the beauty of the whole." As General Ross himself had planted the trees, she was loath to see them felled to make way for a monument. Besides, she hoped one day that her son would build a home there. An adjoining site was eventually chosen. The first caretaker of the Ross monument was Andrew Robb. He had participated in all the major battles involving the 20th Regiment from 1799 to 1814 and was later "one of the funeral party" when Napoleon was buried at Saint Helena in 1821.[16] When the fanfare associated with these tributes in Britain and Ireland died down, Ross soon faded from the popular consciousness as the Battle of Waterloo took center stage.

So far as the situation in the United States was concerned, Ross's short campaign resulted in an outpouring of song, poetry, and artwork. He was to have an influence on U.S. government policy and politics for some time as well. Most immediately, and yet enduringly, it may be argued that Ross, and certainly his actions, are critical to an understanding of the lyrics of "The Star-Spangled Banner," written at the time by Georgetown lawyer, poet, and lyricist Francis Scott Key—the song that in 1931 became the U.S. national anthem. Certainly, the link between Ross and the future anthem occurred to the editors of the *Baltimore Patriot* when the paper mentioned the general's death and quoted from Key's lyrics. The paths of these men had crossed on three occasions. Key was a participant in the Battle of Bladensburg and was profoundly influenced by the destruction of the public buildings in Washington. He was evidently deeply worried by the prospect that Baltimore could be captured and destroyed—with potentially far-reaching effects on the young Republic. Subsequently, General Ross dined with him on board the HMS *Tonnant* after Key and John S. Skinner had arrived via a "flag of truce" ship to try to secure the release of Dr. Beanes, who had been taken prisoner following the incident in Upper Marlboro during the British retreat from Washington. The dinner had almost ended when Skinner discovered that "the plainly dressed officer next on his right, the most reserved gentleman at the table, was no other than Gen. Ross."[17]

Aware of Ross's ability as an audacious field commander, Key was greatly relieved when he saw the "Star-Spangled Banner" flying after the repulse of the British onslaught by sea and land. In writing the words of his song, he was inspired by events during the bombardment of Fort McHenry as well as the land assault at North Point, which cost Ross his life. He was also influenced by the earlier proceedings at Bladensburg and Washington. This background of preceding American reverses is essential to understanding the sense of deliverance evoked in his song.

Maddeningly, Key has left little record that helps explain his lyrics. There are grounds for believing that the British general featured prominently in his consciousness as he contemplated the words. In a conversation with a fellow lawyer, Key testified to the third occasion when his path crossed with Ross. He described the fallen commander's body being brought on board ship and accurately detailed the nature of the general's wounds. And he remarked too how distraught the British were by news of Ross's death, their hearts filled with "the most unaffected sorrow."[18] Recalling, it seems, the dinner that he shared earlier with Ross and other senior British officers, it is arguable that it was the fallen general who Key had particularly in mind when he wrote of the British casualties:

> And where is that band who so vauntingly swore
> That the havoc of war and the battle's confusion,
> A home and a country should leave us no more!
> Their blood has washed out their foul footsteps' pollution.

As Americans listen to the words of their national anthem to this day, it should remind them of the time that Ross seized their capital city and threatened the very existence of the nation by his subsequent attack on Baltimore. That the Star-Spangled Banner yet waved "o'er the land of the free and the home of the brave" was a closer call than many might imagine today.

Ross features in a host of contemporary American poems too. Richard Emmons weighed in on the theme of national danger in 1827 with the publication of his popular poem, *The Fredoniad, or,*

Independence Preserved: An Epick Poem on the Late War of 1812. He also highlighted the importance of the British general in a separate work entitled *Defense of Baltimore and the Death of General Ross*. Philip Freneau, regarded as the "Father of American Poetry," likewise penned a number of poems that featured Ross, including "Royal Consultations, Relative to the Disposal of Lord Wellington's Army" and "On the Naval Attack near Baltimore." Another poem, "On the Conflagrations at Washington," deals directly with the capture of Washington. Freneau too specifically addressed the British general in a poem entitled "The Death of General Ross."[19]

As for artists, within just over a fortnight after the British commander's death, Andrew Duluc, who claimed that he had "seen fall in battle one of the oppressors of our liberty"—that is, General Ross—was advertising a print called *First View of the Battle of Patapsco Neck*. Ross is portrayed falling off a white horse, even though he was riding a black one at the time of his shooting.[20] A plate entitled *Battle at North Point and Death of Genl. Ross* dates from 1817. While drawn some years later, Alonzo Chappel's painting *Death of Genl. Ross at Baltimore* is perhaps the best-known and most dramatic artistic representation of Ross's mortal wounding.[21]

Extraordinary, large-scale illuminated representations of Ross's shooting were created immediately after he was killed and in the decades that followed. Many of them celebrated his death. At the end of December 1814, the *Boston Gazette* carried a notice announcing "an exact representation of the late Gen. Ross . . . in the manner in which he was honourably conveyed to Halifax." In other words, his body was to be depicted immersed in rum at the Roman Museum in Newberry Street. The illuminated spectacle also featured an accompanying band of musicians.[22]

In July 1815 Baltimore's *American and Commercial Daily Advertiser* proclaimed the existence of a "Grand Panorama," featuring "An Elegant Painting of the Battle of North Point; or the death of General Ross" by a Mr. Burdett. Covering 230 square feet of canvas, it was a representation of "the general after falling from his horse, his wound exposed to view." The advertisement noted that "this painting has been exhibited in the Washington Gallery, Philadelphia, to crowded houses." In the same year a separate large-scale painting of the death of Ross by a Mr. May was also on display in the Appollodorian Gallery in Philadelphia, which boasted that the representation of the general was based on an actual miniature.[23]

Ross also featured among the London Cabinet of Wax Figures exhibit on display in the Shakespeare Gallery, New York, in 1821. Two years later a public notice announced that on September 12–13, 1823, on the anniversary of the Battle of Baltimore, the front of Baltimore Museum (also known as Peale's Museum) would feature an illuminated transparency of the death of General Ross.[24] By 1829 he was still a celebrity in the Baltimore area. In that year an American veteran of the battle was charging twenty-five cents admission—children half price—to see his large oil painting, *The Advance Guard of the Baltimore Brigade and Death of General Ross*. As part of a commemoration of the Battle of New Orleans in early January 1832, the "Death of General Ross . . . in two splendid attitudes" was on display at Baltimore Museum. Just over a year later he featured among the statues in the American Museum of Wax Statues and Living Animals in Front Street, Philadelphia.[25]

This lingering American fascination with Ross is not surprising, given that his actions still affected presidential affairs for some time after his death, not least by casting a shadow (in more ways than one) on the inauguration of James Monroe as president in 1817. Previously held indoors, the event was held outside because the Capitol was still being repaired following its burning by the British. Ross's brief visit to Washington thus played at least some part in establishing a tradition of outdoor inaugurations. The new president recalled events from three years previously in his inaugural address. Monroe made a major commitment to defend the American coast and inland waterways from invasion. He clearly had Ross's raid on Washington in mind when he justified the projected expense by reminding his audience of the dangers posed by an enemy possessing a powerful naval force "aided by a few thousand land troops." In the aftermath of the War of 1812, fortifications were erected along the East Coast.[26]

Before his inauguration day ended, Monroe was to be reminded once more of General Ross. When the president was reading his speech, a turkey buzzard reportedly picked up part of the skull of Ross's horse, which had been killed on the night he entered Washington, and dropped it later near a bridge over a stream. As Monroe returned from the ceremonies, his horses were spooked by the skull and "came very near baptising his new hatched dignity by running off the bridge and thereby emptying him into the stream," according to Dr. William Thornton, architect of the Capitol, who also had acted as an American intermediary with the British during their short occupation of the capital. After becoming president, Monroe embarked on a tour of the United States in 1817, during which he visited the Baltimore area, including the spot where the general was shot.[27] That he was scarred by events involving Ross until his dying day is revealed by Monroe' agitated state as he lay "emaciated" on his deathbed. In his final days he was haunted by a nagging sense of guilt for the crucial role he had played in forcing his political rival, John Armstrong, to step down as secretary of war after Washington was captured.[28]

Monroe's successor, John Quincy Adams, also visited the location where the British general had been shot. He was shown an oak tree that had been hit by more than twenty British musket balls. That the "wounded tree" was regarded to be significant in the incident was reflected in the fact that the president picked up six white oak acorns. A keen horticulturalist, Adams planted them in the grounds of the White House, where they took root the following spring. More controversially during this same visit, the president raised a toast to the militiamen who killed the general: "Ebony and Topaz. General Ross's Posthumous Coat of Arms and the Republican Militiamen who gave it." This proved to be a political mistake, capitalized upon by his adversaries during the 1828 presidential contest, considered by some as the "dirtiest" campaign in American political history, and playing some part in costing Adams his chance for reelection. Even at the time, he realized that the meaning of his toast would be lost on many of his audience and prepared an explanation. In essence, Ross was considered to be Ebony, the "Spirit of Darkness," and the militiamen who killed him were Topaz, the "Spirit of Light." The trouble arose in part because of the "far-fetched allusions" and the "unsatisfactory explanation" that the president gave at the dinner. His political opponents used this to maximum advantage in portraying Adams as out of touch. Equally, whether feigned for political purposes or not, there was much outrage that he insulted the memory of an honorable enemy. Like his British army contemporary who served in Canada, Major General Brock, Ross was much "admired by his American foes."[29]

The president's sentiments engendered so much notoriety that there was even an "Ebony and Topaz" song. Some defended the toast, justifying it as the "sentiment of every true American" and signally "appropriate to the place" where it was tendered. The president was widely criticized and ridiculed, however, for his comments about the "bullet which sped to his [Ross's] heart and made his wife a widow and his children orphans." The *United States Telegraph* in Washington took a particular interest in the controversy. One of its editions carried a commentary that condemned him for "reopening the wounds of grief in his [the general's] afflicted relatives."[30] Several others remarked that Adams must have been drunk at the time. Not only was the controversy damaging to the president's reputation at the time but it also dogged him throughout the 1828 election.[31]

Despite his actions at Washington, it is clear that many Americans at the time respected General Ross. Perhaps the most remarkable tribute accorded him by an American adversary was the trip to Ireland undertaken by George Stewart, captain of the 5th Regiment of Maryland Militia, who fought against him at Bladensburg and was wounded at the Battle of North Point on the same day the British commander was killed. Stewart visited the general's family in Rostrevor and paid tribute to Ross's gallantry.[32]

Less surprisingly, there is also a considerable body of American testimony that condemned Ross and his actions. He was branded at the time as a "conflagrator" and "incendiary, or legalized firebrand," for burning the public buildings in Washington. Hezekiah Niles was prepared to admit that Ross was a courageous soldier, even a "dashing" commander, as his conduct at Bladensburg had demonstrated. But "here his merits, if these things are merits, appear to have an end, for his after-conduct was barbarous." Similarly, while not questioning the general's bravery, the *National Advocate* commented that the destruction he was responsible for in Washington warranted him being described as a "savage."[33]

By the second half of the nineteenth century, Ross had receded from the popular consciousness on both sides of the Atlantic, the annual Defenders' Day celebrations in Maryland proving the main exception. With time, even such hostile American views of Ross as perpetuated in Baltimore were moderated. In 1909 the *Baltimore Sun* published a story about the visit paid to Ross's tomb in Halifax, Nova Scotia, by Thomas G. Hayes, a former mayor of Baltimore, in which he stated that "there is no doubt that General Ross was a brave and honourable soldier." Several years later, at the centenary of the Battle of Baltimore in 1914, the same paper carried an article by Francis B. Culiver entitled "Gen. Robert Ross' Grandson Sends Cordial Greetings" and recalled that Ross was "painted by some of the old chroniclers as an inhuman monster and in our childhood days we were wont to regard him as a cruel, bloodthirsty, relentless, ogre." Culiver was now prepared to describe the general as a "Gentleman and a Soldier."[34]

In more modern times, a handful of striking reminders of his role in capturing Washington are worth mentioning. It may be recalled that a putative plot to burn Rostrevor was conceived during the War of 1812, but no attack materialized. There was an American "invasion" of sorts of the Rostrevor area, though not until the Second World War. Large numbers of U.S. troops were stationed in the locality prior to D-Day in 1944. The Ross family mansion in the village was to be used by the British army, with Americans stationed elsewhere. According to oral tradition in the village, a passing U.S. Army tank took a potshot at the general's monument, though missing its target.[35] In the late twentieth century, another British commander named General Ross paid a visit to the American capital. This time he was made welcome at the official residence of the commandant of the U.S. Marine Corps, which had been spared in 1814. This was Lieutenant General Sir Robin Ross, commander of the Royal Marines, and a descendant of Major General Ross's brother, Thomas.[36] All involved were conscious of the historical background.

As for Ross's imprint in Britain and Ireland to this day, it is a measure of how much this one-time "national hero" receded from the popular view that even his obelisk in Rostrevor had suffered from neglect and vandalism. Taken into public ownership by Newry and Mourne Council in recent years, the monument and grounds were restored to their original splendor and reopened as a tourist attraction in 2008. The restoration of his monument has also coincided with a revival of interest in this largely forgotten British general, inspired in large part by the bicentennial of the War of 1812.

With commemorations in full flow, the portrait of the British general belonging to his Rostrevor descendants featured in a major War of 1812 exhibit at the Smithsonian Institution's National Portrait Gallery during 2012–13. The published catalogue described Ross as a "hardened veteran of far flung battles in France, Egypt and Spain" who "commanded his men to victory at the Battle of Bladensburg, followed by the capture and burning of Washington. In both cases Ross was noted for his honorable behavior towards prisoners, residents and private property."[37] Reunited with Rear Admiral Cockburn, if only in portrait form, at the exhibit for the first time in nearly two hundred years, it is a measure of how times have moved on that one of the curators of the exhibit expressed her sadness when it ended and the portraits of Ross and other British participants returned home. "When was the last time we were sorry to see the British go?"[38]

Notes

Abbreviations

ADM	Admiralty Papers, National Archives, Kew
Bluett Diary	Diary of Midshipman J. C. Bluett, Royal Navy Museum, Portsmouth
Brooke Diary	Arthur Brooke Diary, Ulster American Folk Park, Omagh
CO	Colonial Office, National Archives, Kew
Evans Memorandum	Lt. George De Lacy Evans, Memorandum of Operations on the Shores of the Chesapeake in 1814, NLS, Adv. MS., 46.6.6. fols. 1–28
GWU	Special Collections Research Center, Estelle and Melvin Gelman Library, George Washington University, Washington, D.C.
HL	Hartley Library, University of Southampton
LC	Library of Congress, Washington, D.C.
LMC	Library of the Marine Corps, Archives Branch, Quantico
MHSL	Maryland Historical Society Library, Manuscripts Division, Baltimore
MP	Malcolm Papers, Clements Library, University of Michigan (microfilm)
NAM	National Army Museum, London
NARA	National Archives and Records Administration, Washington, D.C.
NLS	National Library of Scotland, Edinburgh
NMM	National Maritime Museum, London
"Old Sub"	Anonymous, "Recollections of the Expedition to the Chesapeake and against New Orleans in the Years 1814–1815"
PC	Privy Council, National Archives, Kew
PRO	Public Record Office, National Archives, Kew
PROB	Probate, National Archives, Kew
PRONI	Public Record Office of Northern Ireland, Belfast
TCD	Trinity College, Dublin
Timpson Memoir	Capt. Mortimer Timpson Memoir, Royal Marine Museum, Portsmouth
WO	War Office, National Archives, Kew

Introduction

1. Ingersoll, *Sketch*, 168.
2. The 1/21st Regiment joined the invasion force at Bermuda, having sailed separately from the Mediterranean.
3. *Morning Chronicle* (London), 1 Oct. 1814; *Poulson's American Daily Advertiser* (Philadelphia), 30 Aug. 1814; De Jomini, *Art of War*, 385–86.
4. Snow, *When Britain Burned the White House*, 2. For Steve Vogel, "the capture of Washington by the British took its place as one of the boldest military feats of the age." See Vogel, *Perilous Fight*, 398.
5. Hickey, *War of 1812*.
6. Lord, *Dawn's Early Light*, 37; Adkins and Adkins, *War for All the Oceans*, 419.
7. Hickey, "'War Hawks,'" 727, 740; Bickham, *Weight of Vengeance*, 15; Hickey, "1812: The Old History and the New." U.S. newspapers afforded Sir George Prevost, governor general of British North America, much valuable information. See Hitsman and Graves, *Incredible War of 1812*, 128.

Chapter 1

1. "Description of Rosstrevor," *Newry Magazine* (1815): 108.
2. Writing to his brother, C. S. Lewis remarked, "That part of Rostrevor which overlooks Carlingford Lough is my idea of Narnia." See Fiona Campbell, "If You Didn't Find Narnia in Your Own Wardrobe," *Guardian*, 4 Dec. 2005, http://www.guardian.co.uk/travel/2005/dec/04/unitedkingdom.cslewis.booksforchildrenandteenagers. The authors wish to thank Peter Fitzsimmons for this reference. The place name "Rostrevor" is older than the Ross family's ownership of land in the area and has nothing to do with the family, though there is disagreement about its origin.
3. P. Carr, *Portavo*, 64–65; *Mourne Observer* (Newcastle, N. Ireland), 7 July 1983; Lowry, *Hamilton Manuscripts*, 111, 165, and app., lxvi; Johnston-Liik, *History of the Irish Parliament*, 6:190–93. George Ross married Ursula Hamilton.
4. Maguire, "Major General Ross," 117; *Morning Chronicle* (London), 3 Oct. 1814; Johnston-Liik, *History of the Irish Parliament*, 3:57, 6:190–93; *Gentleman's Magazine* (London), 85, pt. 1 (1815): 203; J. Ross, "Ross of Bladensburg," 443; George, *Scots in Maryland*, 64.
5. Washington to Dinwiddie, 18 July 1755, CO 5/46. The authors are grateful to Kevin Chambers for this reference.
6. Brumwell, *Paths of Glory*, 328; "Description of Rosstrevor," 108.
7. Ross's birthplace is listed as "Dublin," but there is a gray area in terms of birthplace entries in Trinity records. "When not the father's home, it is frequently . . . that of the maternal grandfather." See Entrance Book to Trinity College Dublin, 1769–1825, 66, TCD, Mun/V/23/4; and Burtchaell and Sadleir, *Alumni Dublinenses*, xii. The general's grandson claimed that he was born in Rostrevor. See J. Ross, "Ross of Bladensburg," 443. See also *Belfast Newsletter*, 11 Oct. 1814. The proposed original

inscription for the monument erected by the 20th Regiment to his memory in Kilbroney Parish Church, Rostrevor, mentioned that it was "to perpetuate his Worth in the Place that gave him birth." This is by no means conclusive either as the regiment originally proposed to erect this monument in Dublin. See *American Beacon* (Norfolk, Va.), 31 Oct. 1815; and Officers of the 20th Regiment to Christopher Moore, 13 Oct. 1814, PRONI, D2004/1A/4/11. In 1816 a correspondent to the *National Intelligencer* in Washington who was married to a woman from Rostrevor also claimed that the general was born in the village. See reprinted story in *Alexandria (Va.) Herald*, 13 May 1816.
8. Maguire, "Major General Ross," 117.
9. Ibid.; Longford, *Wellington*, 18. The Duke of Wellington's mother was beside herself about her son's future: "I vow to God I don't know what I shall do with my awkward son Arthur." He was "food for powder and nothing more."
10. Memoirs of the period abound with references to Don Quixote as soldiers tilted at the windmills of military glory. Capt. Sir John Kincaid was inspired with dreams of chivalry and in his "devotion to the cause would not have yielded to Don Quixote himself." Kincaid, *Rifle Brigade*, 180.
11. Maguire, "Major General Ross," 127; Longford, *Wellington*, 16; Dixon, *Lady Morgan's Memoirs*, 299. Note that Wellington was three years younger than Ross. See Longford, *Wellington*, xv.
12. Genet-Rouffiac and Murphy, *Franco-Irish Military Connections*, 104. Between 1755 and 1790, 449 pupils attended, including 261 foreigners, of whom 51 were Irish, coming "second" only to the English. When he left Angers in 1786, Wesley was "reported on by M. de Pignerolle as an Irish lad of great promise." Corrigan, *Wellington*, 5–6.
13. Entrance Book to Trinity College Dublin, 1769–1825, 66, TCD, MUN/V/23/4; Examinations Returns Register, 1771–97, TCD, MUN/V/27/3, fols. 118–20; *London Literary Gazette* (1820): 542; Board Register, 17 Jan. 1784–6 Oct. 1810, TCD, MUN/V/5/5, fols. 63–65.
14. M. Elliott, *Wolfe Tone*, 31, 34; Heron, *Constitutional History of the University of Dublin*, 152–54; Journals of the Historical Society, 1782–88, TCD, MUN/SOC/HIST/5 and 6.
15. Memorial of Capt. Robert Ross, n.d. [1795], WO 31/36; Inspection Return of His Majesty's 25th (or Sussex) Regiment of Foot, Gibraltar, 2 Dec. 1789, WO 27/65; "Memoir of Major General Robert Ross," 117; D. E. Graves, *Fix Bayonets*, 14, 25; Bunbury, *Narratives*, vii, xii.
16. D. E. Graves, *Fix Bayonets*, 15.
17. Tidridge, *Prince Edward*, 34, 49, 54; Beatty, *English Royal Family of America*, 198; *Army List*, 1790, 101.
18. Tidridge, *Prince Edward*, 54–56; Monthly Return of the Several Corps in the Garrison of Gibraltar, 1 July 1791, WO 17/1779; Log Book, HMS *Resistance*, 22 May 1791, ADM 51/758; Muster, HMS *Resistance*, 29 May 1791, ADM 36/11005; Prince Edward to Sir George Yonge, 1 June 1791, WO 1/287; Yonge to Lennox, 14 July 1791, WO 4/1001; *Army*

List, 1792, 83. The authors are grateful to Kevin Chambers for highlighting the connections between Ross and Prince Edward.
19. *Quebec Gazette*, 18 Aug. 1791; Adjutant General to the King, 8 July 1793, WO 3/11; Proceedings of Several General Courts-Martial Held at Quebec, 1793, WO 71/166; Beatty, *English Royal Family of America*, 187.
20. Monthly Returns of His Majesty's 7th Regiment, 1 Oct. 1794, 1 May 1795, WO 17/105; Memorial of Capt. Robert Ross, n.d. [1795], WO 31/36; Maguire, "Major General Ross," 117. One of Ross's brothers, James, is believed to have drowned at sea, though the date is uncertain. A Lieutenant Ross of the *Doris* drowned in 1801. See *Naval Chronicle* 6 (July–Dec. 1801): 345.
21. Ross to Graham, 20 Feb. 1796, WO 31/43; *Army List, 1799*, 576; *London Gazette*, 8 May 1798; *Morning Post* (London), 19 Dec. 1798.
22. Wolfe Tone, *Life of Theobald Wolfe Tone*, 1:177. It is believed that the dinner took place at Arnos Vale, the home of Thomas Mercer. See Ó Muirí, "Newry and the French Revolution," 110.
23. Bardon, *Ulster*, 229; M. Elliott, *Catholics of Ulster*, 248.
24. *London Gazette*, 8 May 1798.
25. Information courtesy of undated handwritten notes by Robert Linden, local historian of Rostrevor.
26. "Local Jottings," n.d., National Library of Ireland, MS 2223, fols. 311–13.
27. Luddy, *Drennan-McTier Letters*, 83.
28. Robert Johnson to Lord Downshire, 23 Feb. 1799, PRONI, D607/G/86.
29. Cannon, *Historical Record of the Twentieth*, 75; Steevens, *Reminiscences*, 8; Cole, *Memoirs of British Generals*, 2:299; Fedorak, "British Amphibious Operations," 143; B. Smyth, *Lancashire Fusiliers*, 1:186; G. Smith, *Life of Colborne*, 18–19.
30. G. Smith, *Life of Colborne*, 8, 15; Letters and Dispatches, 10 Sept. 1799, Manley Power Collection, NAM, 1973-02-8, photocopies. See also Ray, *Regiment of the Line*, 61.
31. Ray, *Regiment of the Line*, 63; G. Smith, *Life of Colborne*, 15; Letters and Dispatches, 10 Sept. 1799, Manley Power Collection, NAM, 1973-02-8; Steevens, *Reminiscences*, 10; Bunbury, *Narratives*, 9; B. Smyth, *Lancashire Fusiliers*, 1:192, 195, 319.
32. Torrens to Vansittart, 11 Nov. 1814, WO 3/608; Hansard, *Parliamentary Debates*, 29:180; Bunbury, *Narratives*, 38–39.
33. T. Bartlett, *Ireland*, 217; Downing, *Narrative*, 30–31. One soldier recalled being stationed in Clonmel, County Tipperary, describing its inhabitants as the "worst in Ireland. Many of our men were fired at while on sentry." Cooper, *Fusilier Cooper*, 11.
34. Robert Emmet's failed attempt to seize Dublin Castle in 1803 proved to be the "last gasp of the rebellion of 1798." See T. Bartlett, *Ireland*, 244.
35. B. Smyth, *Lancashire Fusiliers*, 1:319; Cole, *Memoirs of British Generals*, 2:299; Cannon, *Historical Record of the Twentieth*, 75.
36. Fedorak, "British Amphibious Operations," 144; D. E. Graves, *Fix Bayonets*, 66–74; Steevens, *Reminiscences*, 26; Downing, *Narrative*,

65; B. Smyth, *Lancashire Fusiliers*, 1:198; Power to Clephane, 20 June 1801, WO 31/115.
37. Fox to Hobart, 3 July 1801, WO 1/300; Keith to Nepean, 21 July 1801, ADM 1/404; D. E. Graves, *Fix Bayonets*, 74; Macksey, *British Victory in Egypt*, 145; Log Book, HMS *La Minerve*, June–July 1801, ADM 51/1353; "A History of the British Army in Malta," Malta Family History, http://website.lineone.net/~stephaniebidmead/Chapter123.htm.
38. Bunbury, *Narratives*, 152; R. T. Wilson, *History of the British Expedition to Egypt*, 2nd ed. (London: printed by C. Rowarth, 1803), 203–204; B. Smyth, *Lancashire Fusiliers*, 1:202.
39. B. Smyth, *Lancashire Fusiliers*, 1:202, 203; G. Smith, *Life of Colborne*, 30; Downing, *Narrative*, 91; D. E. Graves, *Fix Bayonets*, 50–51; Lane-Poole, "Sir Richard Church," 18. Note that Sir John Moore was also wounded on this expedition.
40. D. E. Graves, *Fix Bayonets*, 73, 77.
41. G. Smith, *Life of Colborne*, 33, 35–37; B. Smyth, *Lancashire Fusiliers*, 1:204; Statement of the Service of Lt. Col. Robert Ross, 26 Sept. 1809, WO 25/748.
42. Chapmen, *Register Book of Marriages*, 14(2):271; "Description of Rosstrevor," 109; *Dublin University Magazine* 37 (Jan.–June 1851): 493; Steevens, *Reminiscences*, 37; Maguire, "Major General Ross," 118; Hall, *British Strategy in the Napoleonic War*, 102; B. Smyth, *Lancashire Fusiliers*, 1:204.
43. G. Smith, *Life of Colborne*, 39, 44; Steevens, *Reminiscences*, 41. The term "amiable" is used to describe Ross on the inscription on the obelisk erected to his memory in Rostrevor.
44. Ross to Villettes, 21 Oct. 1814, PRONI, D2004/1/4/11; Villettes to Ross, 30 May 1804, ibid., D2004/1/4/1.
45. Villettes to Ross, 26 July 1804, D2004/1/4/2; Ross to unknown, 26–27 July 1804, D2004/1/4/3.
46. Seddal, *Malta*, 320; Rose, *New General Biographical Dictionary*, 79; Ross to Ball, 14 Sept. 1804, PRONI, D2004/1/4/5.
47. Ross to Ball, 14 Sept. 1804, PRONI, D2004/1/4/5; Ball to Villettes, 14 Oct. 1804, ibid., D2004/1/4/10.
48. Ross to Ball, 10 Oct. 1804, PRONI, D2004/1/4/8.
49. Ball to Villettes, 14 Oct. 1804, ibid., D2004/1/4/10; Ross to Villettes, 21 Oct. 1814, ibid., D2004/1/4/11; J. Ross, "Ross of Bladensburg," 443.
50. B. Smyth, *Lancashire Fusiliers*, 1:205; Davies, *Moore's Peninsular Campaign*, 14; Steevens, *Reminiscences*, 39.
51. Ross to Greenwood and Cox, 28 Feb. 1805, Ross Letter Book, NAM, 1992-06-184; "Baptisms Performed by Rev. D. P. Cosserrat," Malta Family History, http://website.lineone.net/~stephaniebidmead/baptism.htm; Hopton, *Battle of Maida*, 63–64, 84, 92; Mansfield, "Maida, 1806," 9.
52. Bunbury, *Narratives*, 237; Steevens, *Reminiscences*, 45.
53. Hopton, *Battle of Maida*, 60, 96, 126; *Morning Chronicle* (London), 6 Sept. 1806; Bunbury, *Narratives*, 246–47, 248; B. Smyth, *Lancashire*

Fusiliers, 1:213–14; Torrens to Vansittart, 11 Nov. 1814, WO 3/608; J. Moore, *Diary*, 113.
54. Hopton, *Battle of Maida*, 119, 127; *Morning Chronicle* (London), 18 Sept. 1806; *Caledonian Mercury* (Edinburgh), 25 Sept. 1806.
55. Hopton, *Battle of Maida*, 129, 160; D. E. Graves, *Fix Bayonets*, 97; Steevens, *Reminiscences*, 46, 253; Duke of York to Ross, 25 Feb. 1808, PRONI, D2004/1A/1/3.
56. Amyot and Windham, *Speeches in Parliament of . . . William Windham*, 1:5; G. Smith, *Life of Colborne*, 52.

Chapter 2

1. Memorial to Duke of York, 9 Feb. 1807, Ross Letter Book, NAM, 1992-06-184; Fox to Gordon, 12 Feb. 1807, PRONI, D2004/1A/1/1; *London Gazette*, 20 Feb. 1808; B. Smyth, *Lancashire Fusiliers*, 1:220. The promotion occurred "without purchase," i.e., without paying £3,500 for a promotion at this level. See Memoranda, 21 Jan. 1808, WO31/245; and Clephane to Duke of York, Mar. 1808, WO 31/249.
2. G. Smith, *Life of Colborne*, 63.
3. Blakeney, *Boy in the Peninsular War*, 242–43.
4. "Influenced by sentiments of affection similar to those which unite the members of a family with their parent," the 20th Regiment raised a subscription for a monument in Rostrevor to the memory of their former commander. See *American Beacon* (Norfolk, Va.), 31 Oct. 1815.
5. G. Smith, *Life of Colborne*, 67.
6. B. Smyth, *Lancashire Fusiliers*, 1:221; Inscription on Vault of Elizabeth Ross, PRONI, D2004/1A/1/2.
7. Holmes, *Wellington*, 108; Fletcher, *Wellington's Regiments*, 17–24; Steevens, *Reminiscences*, 52.
8. Moon, *Wellington's Two-Front War*, 16–17, 21; Muir, *Britain and the Defeat of Napoleon*, 51–59; Longford, *Wellington*, 102–105; Kieran, *Corunna*, 7; Dalrymple, *Memoir*, 81. At this time a corps could refer to a formation of troops comprising more than one division or to any body of troops.
9. Steevens, *Reminiscences*, 56.
10. Longford, *Wellington*, 105; D. E. Graves, *Fix Bayonets*, 171; Steevens, *Reminiscences*, 60–63; Carter, *Medals of the British Army*, 48; Coss, *All for the King's Shilling*, 172; Costello, *Rifleman Costello*, 24.
11. Steevens, *Reminiscences*, 63, 69, 70; Blakeney, *Boy in the Peninsular War*, 49–51.
12. B. Smyth, *Lancashire Fusiliers*, 1:320; J. Moore, *Diary*, 576.
13. Steevens, *Reminiscences*, 75; Report upon the Claims of the 20th Regiment of Foot . . . in the Years 1808 and 1809, WO 30/5. Ross submitted claims for one horse valued at £31 and another at £26.
14. Steevens, *Reminiscences*, 75–77; Blakeney, *Boy in the Peninsular War*, 100; B. Smyth, *Lancashire Fusiliers*, 1:240.
15. Muir, *Britain and the Defeat of Napoleon*, 74; Lord, *Dawn's Early Light*, 38. Ross, considered a "splendid commanding officer . . . ,

lost fewer men on the retreat than any other line regiment bar one." Haythornwaite, *Corunna*, 61.
16. *Derby Mercury* (England), 9 Feb. 1809; Maguire, "Major General Ross," 118; Duke of York to Ross, 30 Sept. 1810, PRONI, D2004/1A/1/7; Steevens, *Reminiscences*, 79; B. Smyth, *Lancashire Fusiliers*, 1:241. Despite vessels being available to evacuate the British army, Moore was buried at Corunna, not shipped back to England. This development is of some interest in relation to the reasoning behind Ross's later burial in Halifax, Nova Scotia, instead of his body being repatriated.
17. In early January 1809 Ross was informed that it was "unfortunate that just at this time, when your presence at home was so much to be desired for the arrangement of your family affairs, you should be called off." Correspondent to Colonel Ross, Dublin, 7 Jan. 1809, PRONI, D2004/1A/2/2.
18. Ross to Blacker, 24 June 1810, PRONI, D2004/1A/2/7. Writing from Rostrevor in July 1810, Ross acknowledged that he would require an "extension of my leave." Ross to Blacker, 6 July 1810, ibid., D2004/1A/2/10.
19. Maguire, "Major General Ross," 118; W. Carr, *Rosstrevor*, 25; "Description of Rosstrevor," *Newry Magazine* (1815): 107; J. McCormick to Colonel Ross ("or if absent, Mrs. Ross"), 7 Jan. 1813, PRONI, D2004/1A/2/32. Mrs. Ross continued to spend the summer season at what became known as Ghann Cottage for many years after her husband's death. See *Dublin Penny Journal*, 8 Aug. 1835. The "cottage" later served as a "Family hotel." See *Belfast Newsletter*, 18 May 1867.
20. B. Smyth, *Lancashire Fusiliers*, 1:242; Steevens, *Reminiscences*, 84; Adkins and Adkins, *War for All the Oceans*, 280; Muir, *Britain and the Defeat of Napoleon*, 101, 103; Fedorak, "British Amphibious Operations," 143.
21. Steevens, *Reminiscences*, 84; Walcheren Prize-Money Correspondence, 16 Jan. 1813, PRONI, D2004/1A/1/9; Field Return of the 20th Regiment of Foot, 19 May 1810, WO 27/98; B. Smyth, *Lancashire Fusiliers*, 1:215; *Morning Post* (London), 16 Aug. 1810.
22. Steevens, *Reminiscences*, 85; Proposition for Granting Royal Bounties to the Widow and Family of the Late Maj. Gen. Robert Ross, 20 Jan. 1815, WO 43/359; B. Smyth, *Lancashire Fusiliers*, 1:245; Bartlett and Jeffery, *Military History of Ireland*, 308; William Todd Jones to unknown, 29 May 1811, PRONI, D671/C/12/66.
23. Ross to Leigh, 14 Nov. 1810, Ross Letter Book, NAM, 1992-06-184; Torrens to Ross, 30 Apr. 1812, WO 3/602; *Freeman's Journal* (Dublin), 26 Dec. 1839; *Belfast Newsletter*, 28 Jan. 1857.
24. Vestry Records, Kilbroney Parish Church, Rostrevor, 25 Mar. 1811. The authors are grateful to Robert Linden for his handwritten notes from the vestry records.
25. Talbot Glascock Esq. in Account with Col. Robert Ross, PRONI, D2004/1A/2/31; Clippings, GWU, Gelman Library, Special Collections, Ross Papers, Box 1:17.

26. Torrens to Ross, 23 Aug. 1812, WO 3/603; Torrens to Ross, 8 Oct. 1812, WO 3/603. For Torrens's position, see Black, *War of 1812*, 149.
27. *Morning Chronicle* (London), 13 Oct. 1812; B. Smyth, *Lancashire Fusiliers*, 1:246; Steevens, *Reminiscences*, 86.
28. A son, Robert, was baptized in Lisbon on 19 February 1813. Proposition for Granting Royal Bounties to the Widow and Family of the Late Maj. Gen. Robert Ross, 20 Jan. 1815, WO 43/359.
29. D. L. Graves, *Midst of Alarms*, 153; Steevens, *Reminiscences*, 89–90; D. E. Graves, *Fix Bayonets*, 120; D. E. Graves, *Dragon Rampant*, 199.
30. Wellington to Ross, 1 May 1813, Wellington, *Dispatches*, 10:338.
31. B. Smyth, *Lancashire Fusiliers*, 1:321; Torrens to Wellington, 3 June 1813, Wellington, *Supplementary Despatches*, 7:626–27.
32. Longford, *Wellington*, 208–10; Coss, *All for the King's Shilling*, 135; Torrens to Vansittart, 11 Nov. 1814, WO 3/608; Hansard, *Parliamentary Debates*, 29:181–82; Gold Medals and Crosses Awarded during the Peninsula War, WO 100/16.
33. Maguire, "Major General Ross," 118; Muir, *Britain and the Defeat of Napoleon*, 267; Proclamation of Marshal Soult, 23 July 1813, Wellington, *Dispatches*, 10:576–78.
34. B. Smyth, *Lancashire Fusiliers*, 1:322.
35. Longford, *Wellington*, 217; Cole to Wellington, 27 July 1813, PRO 30/43/63/3.
36. B. Smyth, *Lancashire Fusiliers*, 1:347; D. E. Graves, *Dragon Rampant*, 202; Cooper, *Fusilier Cooper*, 82.
37. B. Smyth, *Lancashire Fusiliers*, 1:368–69; Oman, *Peninsular War*, 6:618. Another officer from the 20th recalled that Ross specifically called upon Captain Tovey. Ibid., 349. Tovey contradicted in certain respects an account of his bayonet charge that was written by Captain Kincaid. See ibid., 366–67. John Fortescue agrees about the rarity of a bayonet fight. See Fortescue, *History of the British Army*, 254.
38. Cooper, *Fusilier Cooper*, 83; *Sessional Papers of the House of Lords*, 40:98.
39. D. E. Graves, *Dragon Rampant*, 202; Oman, *Peninsular War*, 6:219, 619.
40. Groves, *Historical Records of the 7th or Royal Regiment of Fusiliers*, 144; Cooper, *Fusilier Cooper*, 83.
41. Oman, *Peninsular War*, 6:622–24; B. Smyth, *Lancashire Fusiliers*, 1:346. Bainbrigge wrongly dates events at Roncesvalles as 28 July instead of 25 July. See D. E. Graves, *Dragon Rampant*, 202.
42. B. Smyth, *Lancashire Fusiliers*, 1:350–51; Cooper, *Fusilier Cooper*, 84.
43. Longford, *Wellington*, 30, 218–19, 266–67; Snow, *To War with Wellington*, 2, 230.
44. B. Smyth, *Lancashire Fusiliers*, 1:354, 355, 360; Steevens, *Reminiscences*, 105; *Freeman's Journal* (Dublin), 6 Sept. 1838; Wellington to Bathurst, 1 Aug. 1813, Wellington, *Dispatches*, 10:576–89; Napier, *English Battles and Sieges in the Peninsula*, 360.
45. D. E. Graves, *Dragon Rampant*, 212; B. Smyth, *Lancashire Fusiliers*, 1:362; Cole to Wellington, 4 Mar. 1814, PRO 30/43/74. Ellis assumed

command on several occasions before Ross became involved with the fusilier brigade and took over when the general was badly wounded during the Battle of Orthes in February 1814. See D. E. Graves, *Fix Bayonets*, 242.
46. Steevens, *Reminiscences*, 109; *London Gazette Extraordinary*, 16 Aug. 1813; Wellington to Bathurst, 1 Aug. 1813, Wellington, *Dispatches*, 10:576–89; *Morning Post* (London), 6 Oct. 1814; Hansard, *Parliamentary Debates*, 27:68.
47. D. E. Graves, *Dragon Rampant*, 209, 212. Ellis was wounded on no less than eight occasions and died at Waterloo. See D. E. Graves, *Fix Bayonets*, 137.
48. Groves, *Historical Records of the 7th or Royal Regiment of Fusiliers*, 146–47; Steevens, *Reminiscences*, 106; B. Smyth, *Lancashire Fusiliers*, 1:361, 362; Hansard, *Parliamentary Debates*, 29:183.
49. B. Smyth, *Lancashire Fusiliers*, 1:322; Waggett to Ross, 13 Oct. 1813, PRONI, D2004/1A/1/14; Grant of Freedom of Cork, 11 Sept. 1813, PRONI, D2004/1A/1/13.
50. This sword is in the possession of Stephen Campbell, Rostrevor, a descendant of General Ross.
51. Steevens, *Reminiscences*, 107; Blakeney, *Boy in the Peninsular War*, 300–302; *Freeman's Journal* (Dublin), 6 Sept. 1838.
52. D. E. Graves, *Dragon Rampant*, 215, 218–19; George, "Family Papers of Maj. Gen. Robert Ross, Diary of Col. Brooke," 313; Cooper, *Fusilier Cooper*, 98.
53. Bell, *Rough Notes by an Old Soldier*, 147, 150; Beatson, *Wellington and the Fall of France*, 192, 229; Daniel, *Journal of an Officer in the Commissariat Department*, 286; *Baltimore Sun*, 29 May 1849, 6 Sept. 1908.
54. D. E. Graves, *Dragon Rampant*, 219–20; Cooper, *Fusilier Cooper*, 101. For the manner in which smoke shrouded battlefields at the time, see D. E. Graves, *Where Right and Glory Lead*, 38.
55. Fortescue, *History of the British Army*, 510; Beatson, *Wellington and the Fall of France*, 192; Longford, *Wellington*, 227.
56. D. E. Graves, *Dragon Rampant*, 220; Bell, *Rough Notes by an Old Soldier*, 149.
57. Hansard, *Parliamentary Debates*, 27:354; G. Smyth, *Biographical Illustrations of St. Paul's Cathedral*, 69.
58. G. Smyth, *Biographical Illustrations of St. Paul's Cathedral*, 69. Normally, Wellington was "stinting when it came to praise." See Coss, *All for the King's Shilling*, 42.
59. Horsfield, "Recipients of the Army Gold Cross," 175; Crowe, *Village in Seven Hills*, 30.
60. Clipping, GWU, Gelman Library, Special Collections, Ross Papers, Box 1:17; Mrs. Ross to Roger Hall, June [no year], PRONI, D2004/1/14/5.

Chapter 3

1. Dudley and Crawford, *Naval War of 1812*, 3:72–74.
2. Bathurst to Wellington, 28 Jan. 1814, Wellington, *Supplementary Despatches*, 8:547. For the currency of the term "grand expedition" on both sides of the Atlantic, see *Caledonian Mercury* (Edinburgh), 18 June 1814; *Hull Packet*, 21 June 1814; *Aberdeen Journal* (Scotland), 22 June 1814; *Palladium of Liberty* (Morristown, N.J.), 15 Sept. 1814; *New York Evening Post*, 16 Sept. 1814; *American and Commercial Daily Advertiser* (Baltimore), 21 Sept. 1814; *Niles' Weekly Register* (Baltimore), 25 Sept. 1814; and *Dedham (Mass.) Gazette*, 25 Nov. 1814.
3. Arthur, *How Britain Won the War of 1812*, 117. The British did not recognize the Louisiana Purchase. See Reilly, *British at the Gates*, 342–44; and Dangerfield, *Era of Good Feelings*, 75.
4. See WO 1/141, 1/142, 1/144.
5. Lambert, *Challenge*, 305, 306; R. Morriss, *Cockburn*, 98; Mahon, *War of 1812*, 344.
6. Hickey, *War of 1812*, 1–3; Bickham, *Weight of Vengeance*, 4.
7. Hickey, *Don't Give Up the Ship*, 140. For Prevost's long official title, see Hitsman and Graves, *Incredible War of 1812*, 25–26.
8. Adkins and Adkins, *War for All the Oceans*, 402.
9. After Waterloo Wellington remarked, "if I had the army which we broke up at Bordeaux, the battle would not have lasted for four hours." Timbs, *Wellingtonia*, 59. He was less than complimentary on a number of occasions about his troops, contributing in no small manner to their enduring reputation as the "scum of the earth." See Coss, *All for the King's Shilling*, 3.
10. Muir, *Britain and the Defeat of Napoleon*, 240; Bickham, *Weight of Vengeance*, 135, 163–65; Lambert, *Challenge*, 305. For Ross's views on the war, see chapter 4.
11. Bayard, *Papers*, 318. Setting back America's development by fifty years was reported to be the stated goal of Rear Admiral Cockburn, operating in the Chesapeake area. *Niles' Weekly Register* (Baltimore), 28 Jan. 1815.
12. Mahan, *Influence of Sea Power*, 2:332; *Cobbett's Weekly Political Register* (London), 5 Nov. 1814; Torrens to Clinton, 14 Apr. 1814, WO 3/607 enc85; Vogel, *Perilous Fight*, 259. See also Zuehlke, *For Honor's Sake*, 273.
13. *Cobbett's Weekly Political Register* (London), 17 Sept. 1814. See also Bickham, *Weight of Vengeance*, 135; and Lambert, *Challenge*, 314. For the vengeful attitudes of various public prints in Britain toward the Americans, see Bickham, *Weight of Vengeance*.
14. *Cobbett's Weekly Political Register* (London), 16 July 1814; Lord, *Dawn's Early Light*, 43; George, *Terror on the Chesapeake*, 66; Bickham, *Weight of Vengeance*, 161–65; Grodzinski, *Defender of Canada*, 325n18.
15. Torrens to Murray, 14 Apr. 1814, Wellington, *Supplementary Despatches*, 9:58; Cochrane to Bathurst, 14 July 1814, WO 1/141. See also Vogel, *Perilous Fight*, 28.

16. Hansard, *Parliamentary Debates*, 9:1115; Insurrection Act accessed at http://www.encyclopedia.com/doc/10245-InsurrectionAct.html (no longer available); Torrens to Hewitt, 20 Aug. 1814, WO 3/607; Fletcher, *Wellington's Regiments*, 145–46, 150, 152–56, 158, 161–63, 167, 169, 171–72, 174–76, 179–80, 182–83. In mid-April 1814 Lord Bathurst wrote to the commander of British forces in Sicily, Lord William Bentinck, instructing him to reduce military spending immediately, not least by not reengaging soldiers whose period of service had expired. See Bathurst to Bentinck, 14 Apr. 1814, WO 6/57.
17. Bathurst to Prevost, 14 Apr. 1814, CO 43/23; Bunbury to Croker, 15 Apr. 1814, WO 6/153; Bathurst to Wellington, 20 Apr. 1814, WO 6/32; D. E. Graves, "Redcoats Are Coming," 14. The 1/6th and 1/82nd were originally selected for the American expedition. See ibid.; Duke of York to Wellington, 20 Apr. 1814, HL, WP1/410; and Bathurst to Wellington, 20 Apr. 1814, WO 6/32.
18. Torrens to Clinton, 18 May 1814, WO 3/67; Bathurst to Wellington, 14 Apr. 1814, HL, WP1/409. The "independent" nature of the expedition was also stressed by Torrens as well as in correspondence to the Commissariat Department of Wellington's army. Torrens to Clinton, 18 May 1814, WO 3/67; Harrison to Herries, 6 May 1814, WO 1/853.
19. Chandler, *Napoleon*, 181–84; Harrison to Herries, 6 May 1814, WO 1/853; Cochrane to Melville, 2 Jan. 1814, NLS, Cochrane Papers, MS 2574. See also Forester, *Naval War of 1812*, 202.
20. Lambert, *Challenge*, 25; Cochrane to Melville, 27 Apr. 1812, NLS, Cochrane Papers, MS 2574; Reilly, *British at the Gates*, 264.
21. D. E. Graves, "Redcoats Are Coming."
22. Harrison to Herries, 6 May 1814, WO 1/853. See also Bathurst to Bentinck, 14 Apr. 1814, WO 6/57.
23. Donnett to Melville, 26 July 1814, WO 1/142; Dudley and Crawford, *Naval War of 1812*, 3:132–35.
24. Bathurst to Wellington, 14 Apr. 1814, HL, WP1/409; Wellington to Clinton, 14 May 1814, Wellington, *Dispatches*, 12:6; Torrens to Thornton, 11 May 1814, WO 3/607.
25. Oman, *Peninsular War*, 7:510; Hope to Bathurst, 2 May 1814, WO 1/142; D. E. Graves, *Fix Bayonets*, 172; Snow, *To War with Wellington*, 10; Bathurst to Wellington, 27 Apr. 1814, Wellington, *Supplementary Despatches*, 9:42; Sidney, *Life of Lord Hill*, 286; Torrens to Thornton, 11 May 1814, WO 3/607.
26. Murray to Wellington, 1 May 1814, Wellington, *Supplementary Despatches*, 9:57; Torrens to Murray, 18 May 1814, WO 3/607; Reilly, *British at the Gates*, 147; Wellington to Bathurst, 5 May 1814, Wellington, *Dispatches*, 12:2–3; Clinton to Wellington, 15 May 1814, HL, WP1/415.
27. Duke of York to Wellington, 14 Apr. 1814, Wellington, *Supplementary Despatches*, 9:82–84. Kempt, Power, and Robinson served in Canada. See Hitsman and Graves, *Incredible War of 1812*, 215–16. For the

promotions of Barnes, Power, and Robinson to major general on 4 June 1813, see *List of the Officers of the Army, 1821*, 12–13.
28. Wellington to Pack, 28 May 1814, Wellington, *Dispatches*, 12:28–29; Torrens to Barnes, 1 Nov. 1814, WO 3/608. For Robinson's letter accepting the offer of a command, see Robinson to Wellington, 4 May 1814, HL, WP1/414. See also Pack to Wellington, 16 May 1814, ibid., 415.
29. General Orders, 16 May 1814, HL, WP1/439; D. E. Graves, "Redcoats Are Coming"; Fletcher, *Wellington's Regiments*.
30. Preparations continued to be made for Hill to undertake operations in America later in the year. Under a revised plan of operations being considered in early August, Hill was to take charge of 11,000 men. Torrens to Hill, 6 Aug. 1814, WO 3/607.
31. Bathurst to Wellington, 26 May 1814, Wellington, *Supplementary Despatches*, 9:109–10; State of the Troops, 6 June 1814, ibid., 137; Torrens to Clinton, 18 May 1814, WO 3/67; Sidney, *Life of Lord Hill*, 239. When a prospective expedition to be led by Lord Hill was postponed again in August 1814, Torrens remarked that "the expectation of an enterprise under his Lordship should be kept in the publick [sic] mind." Torrens to Hewitt, 20 Aug. 1814, WO 3/607.
32. Dalhousie to Murray, 27 May 1814, Wellington, *Supplementary Despatches*, 9:118; Dalhousie to Murray, 30 May 1814, NLS, Murray Papers, Adv. 46.3.5; Murray to Wellington, 29 May 1814, Wellington, *Supplementary Despatches*, 9:115. Lieutenant Gleig of the 85th recalled that he "slept on board" on the night of May 29. Gleig, "Diary," in C. Barrett, *85th King's Light Infantry*, 116.
33. Torrens to Clinton, 18 May 1814, WO 3/67. Rear Admiral Malcolm, who was in charge of transporting Ross's "division" of troops to the coast of the United States, informed Vice Admiral Cochrane that it was "at first intended that all the troops ordered to America were to sail together but that was changed." Malcolm to Cochrane, 29 June 1814, NLS, Cochrane Papers, MS 2574, fols. 140–41.
34. Bathurst to Wellington, 18 May 1814, Wellington, *Supplementary Despatches*, 9:85–86; Torrens to Vansittart, 11 Nov. 1814, WO 3/608.
35. Hitsman and Graves, *Incredible War of 1812*, 214, app. 1; Fitz-Enz, *Final Invasion*, 50–52; Bickham, *Weight of Vengeance*, 169; Grodzinski, *Defender of Canada*, 147.
36. State of Divisions, 18 May 1814, Wellington, *Supplementary Despatches*, 9:119; State of the Troops, 6 June 1814, ibid., 137; George, *Terror on the Chesapeake*, 186n72; Weber, *Neither Victor Nor Vanquished*, 32; Donnett to Melville, 26 July 1814, WO 1/142.
37. Sidney, *Life of Lord Hill*, 286, 288–89. For more on these plans, see chapter 13.
38. Dudley and Crawford, *Naval War of 1812*, 3:72–74; Wellington to Bathurst, 11 June 1814, Wellington, *Dispatches*, 12:53. Even then it is a measure of the scale of the logistics involved that more than 500,000 musket-ball cartridges and almost 55,000 flints were sent. Return of Ordnance, Ammunition, 28 June 1814, LC, Cochrane Papers, MS 2336.

39. Memorandum for the Quarter Master General, June 1814, Wellington, *Dispatches*, 12:48–49; Dalhousie to Wellington, 28 June 1814, Wellington, *Supplementary Despatches*, 9:150; Hart, *New Annual Army List* (1840), 248; Torrens to Thornton, 30 Sept. 1814, WO 3/608. For Hitsman and Graves, "Ross had every intention of conducting more than a mere marauding operation." Hitsman and Graves, *Incredible War of 1812*, 240.
40. *Baltimore Patriot*, 29 May 1849; Fitzroy Somerset to Ross, 14 May 1814, GWU, Gelman Library, Special Collections, Ross Papers, Manuscripts, Box 1:3; Ross to Fitzroy Somerset, 15 May 1814, HL, WP9/2/2/45; Austin, "Letters of Elbridge Gerry," 511.
41. Brooke Diary; "On the Lamented Death of General Ross," *Derby Mercury* (England), 8 Dec. 1814. See also George, "Family Papers, Manuscripts, Box 1:3 of Maj. Gen. Robert Ross, Diary of Col. Brooke," 300–316.
42. Ross to Mrs. Ross, 10 June 1814, PRONI, D2004/1A/3/1. A small number of wives and children accompanied the brigade. Gleig, *Narrative of the Campaigns*, 68; Brooke Diary; Malcolm to Keith, 1 June 1814, ADM 1/158; D. L. Graves, *Midst of Alarms*, 158.
43. Ross to Mrs. Ross, n.d. [written as Kevin Chambers points out before Ross embarked for America at Pauillac, near Bordeaux], PRONI, D2004/1A/3/1.
44. Murray to Torrens, 19 May 1814, NLS, Murray Papers, Adv. 46.3.19, fol. 119; Francis John Oldfield to Anna Oldham, 15 Feb. 1877, in possession of Francis De Courcy Hamilton, descendant of General Ross; McCormick to Ross, 3 Feb. 1811, PRONI, D2004/1A/2/16; Ross to Mrs. Ross, 1 Sept. 1814, ibid., D2004/1A/3/8. Mrs. Ross later spent time in Italy for health reasons. Fanny Pieri to Mrs. Ross, 19 Jan. 1821, ibid., D2004/1/16/16.
45. Clinton to Ross, 27 June 1814, PRONI, D2004/1A/1/15; Malcolm to Mrs. Malcolm, 29 May [1814], NLS, Murray Papers, Acc. 13175, Box 1, loose papers; Ross to Mrs. Ross, 10 July [sic, June] 1814, PRONI, D2004/1A/3/3. As Kevin Chambers has indicated in correspondence to the authors, this last letter appears to be misdated. It was written "off Cape Finisterre" shortly after clearing the Bay of Biscay early in the voyage, light winds having slowed the fleet's progress.
46. Maguire, "Major General Ross," 120; D. L. Graves, *Midst of Alarms*, 205.
47. Brooke Diary; Malcolm to Mrs. Malcolm, [May] 1814, MP; Malcolm to Mrs. Malcolm, 7 June 1814, NLS, Murray Papers, Acc. 13175, Box 1, loose papers Malcolm to Cochrane, 26 June 1814, NLS, Cochrane Papers, MS 2574, fols. 140–41.
48. Gleig, *Narrative of the Campaigns*, 6; Reilly, *British at the Gates*, 147.
49. H. G. Smith, *Autobiography*, 1:182–83.
50. Ross to Mrs. Ross, 10 June 1814, PRONI, D2004/1A/3/1; Ross to Mrs. Ross, 22 June 1814, ibid., D2004/1a/3/2 Ross to Mrs. Ross, 22 June 1814, ibid., D2004/1a/3/2; H. G. Smith, *Autobiography*, 1:206. Evans

had only transferred to the Quarter Master General's Office on 13 March 1814, having previously served with the 3rd Dragoons. See List of Officers Serving in the Quarter Master General's Office, 25 Mar. 1814, NLS, Murray Papers, Adv. 46.5.5, fols. 254–55.
51. Gleig, *Narrative of the Campaigns*, 38; Gleig, "Diary," in C. Barrett, *85th King's Light Infantry*, 116; "Old Sub," 444; Ross to Mrs. Ross, [May] 1814, PRONI, D2004/1A/3.
52. Ship's Muster, HMS *Royal Oak*, 1 July–31 Dec. 1814, ADM 37/5135.
53. "Old Sub," 444; H. G. Smith, *Autobiography*, 1:193; Log book of HMS *Royal Oak*, 1, 2 June 1814, MP; Keith to Croker, 2 June 1814, WO 1/735.

Chapter 4
1. *Times* (London), 2 June 1814; Grodzinski, *Defender of Canada*, 161.
2. Bathurst to Wellington, 28 May 1814, Wellington, *Supplementary Despatches*, 9:85–86; Ross to Mrs. Ross, 10 July [sic, June] 1814, PRONI, D2004/1A/3/3; Glover, *Wellington's Voice*, 177–78.
3. Ross to Mrs. Ross, 10 July [sic, June] 1814, PRONI, D2004/1A/3/3; Maguire, "Major General Ross," 120; Ross to Mrs. Ross, 13 July 1814, PRONI, D2004/1A/3/4.
4. Malcolm to Mrs. Malcolm, 17 May 1814, MP; Malcolm to Mrs. Malcolm, [May] 1814, MP; Malcolm to unknown, 7 June [1814], NLS, Murray Papers, Acc. 13175, Box 1, loose papers; Malcolm to Cochrane, 26 June 1814, NLS, Cochrane Papers, MS 1574, fols. 140–41; Malcolm to unknown, 20 July 1814, MP; Read to Commissioners of Victuals, 24 June 1814, National Archives, Kew, Foreign Office 557/2; *Gentleman's Magazine* (London), 148, pt. 2 (1828): 286.
5. Gleig, *Narrative of the Campaigns*, 65; Gleig, "Diary," in C. Barrett, *85th King's Light Infantry*, 118, 125; "Old Sub," 445. Sir John Kincaid noted that "keeping journals" was one of the "usual amusements" at sea. Kincaid, *Rifle Brigade*, 2.
6. Memoir of Capt. Peter Bowlby, 4th (or The King's Own) Regiment of Foot, NAM, 2002-02-729; Gleig, *Narrative of the Campaigns*, 67–68. Brooke says that he "gave the ladies of the fleet a ball" on board his ship the night before the play on the *Royal Oak*. Brooke Diary.
7. Proclamation to the Great and Illustrious Chiefs of the Indian Nations, 1 July 1814, National Archives, Kew, Foreign Office 1/139; Extract from the *Bahama Gazette*, 24 July 1814, in *Repertory* (Boston), 31 Aug. 1814; Lord, *Dawn's Early Light*, 44; Dudley and Crawford, *Naval War of 1812*, 3:129–30; George, *Terror on the Chesapeake*, 66. Bathurst's instructions to Ross told him not to encourage a slave revolt.
8. Adkins and Adkins, *War for All the Oceans*, xxvi, 237, 471. See also Lambert, *Challenge*, 306.
9. D. E. Graves, "Why the White House Was Burned," 1108, 1112; Prevost to Drummond, 1 June 1814, LC, Cochrane Papers, MS 2326; Prevost to Cochrane, 2 June 1814, ibid.
10. Hitsman and Graves, *Incredible War of 1812*, 194–95. Cockburn had been "laying seaports in ashes and wasting the country for some time now." See Vogel, *Perilous Fight*, 34.

11. Codrington, *Memoir*, 313; Adkins and Adkins, *War for All the Oceans*, 414; MacDougall letter, *Times* (London), 25 May 1861.
12. D. E. Graves, "Why the White House Was Burned," 1112, 1114.
13. Postscript, 15 July, to Cochrane to Bathurst, 14 July 1814, WO 1/141. See also Codrington, *Memoir*, 310.
14. Dudley and Crawford, *Naval War of 1812*, 2:325, 3:72–74. The similarity in these orders is noted in D. E. Graves, "Why the White House Was Burned," 1114n91.
15. Dudley and Crawford, *Naval War of 1812*, 3:140, 141; Memorial of the Honourable Sir Alexander Inglis Cochrane, 30 Mar. 1816, PC 1/4102.
16. Dudley and Crawford, *Naval War of 1812*, 3:141–42.
17. Ibid., 132–35; Cochrane to Bathurst, 14 July 1814, WO 1/141.
18. Lord Melville to Cochrane, 22 May 1814, NLS, Cochrane Papers, MS 2574, fols. 130–31; Dudley and Crawford, *Naval War of 1812*, 3:132–35, 152–54; R. Morriss, *Cockburn*, 87, 100.
19. Snow, *When Britain Burned the White House*, 15; Malcolm to unknown, [7 June 1814], NLS, Murray Papers, Acc. 13175, Box 1, loose papers; Ross to Mrs. Ross, 30 July 1814, PRONI, D2004/1A/3/7.
20. Bathurst to Ross, 6 Sept. 1814, WO 6/2; "Narrative of the Naval Operations in the Potomac," 472–73.
21. Codrington, *Memoir*, 312; Gleig, *Subaltern*, 123; North American Station, Letters from Codrington, 30 July 1814, NMM, COD/7/1; *Annual Register, 1815*, 36. For further details of Keene, see chapter 13.
22. D. E. Graves, "Redcoats Are Coming," 12; Latimer, *1812*, 523; Fletcher, *Wellington's Regiments*, 179; Hansard, *Parliamentary Debates*, 30:49; Cooke, *Narrative of Events*, 218–19. According to Gleig, the 85th was chosen for the American campaign because it "had not suffered so severely as many other corps." Gleig, *Narrative of the Campaigns*, 5.
23. "Old Sub," 344; Malcolm to Mrs. Malcolm, 3 Aug. 1814, MP.
24. Malcolm to Mrs. Malcolm, 3 Aug. 1814, MP; Ross to Maria Ross, 2 Sept. 1814, PRONI, D2004/1A/3/9; North American Station, Letters from Codrington, 13 Aug. 1814, NMM, COD/7/1; Malcolm to Mrs. Malcolm, 3 Aug. 1814, MP. Brooke returned home on leave from Egypt in 1801 on board HMS *Ajax*, commanded at the time by Alexander Cochrane. See Brooke Diary.
25. Ross to Mrs. Ross, 24 July 1814, PRONI, D2004/1A/3/5; Maguire, "Major General Ross," 120; Ross to Mrs. Ross, 30 July 1814, PRONI, D2004/1A/3/7.
26. Ross to Mrs. Ross, 26 July 1814, PRONI, D2004/1A/3/6; Ross to Mrs. Ross, 30 July 1814, ibid., D2004/1A/3/7; Malcolm to Mrs. Malcolm, 3 Aug. 1814, MP; Dudley and Crawford, *Naval War of 1812*, 3:189–90.
27. *Tonnant* at Sea, 4 Aug. 1814, *Tonnant* Memo Book, No. 1, NMM, COD/6/4; H. G. Smith, *Autobiography*, 1:195; Declared Accounts, 25 July 1814–25 Aug. 1815, National Archives, Kew, Audit Office, 1/496/109.
28. Lord, *Dawn's Early Light*, 49; George, *Terror on the Chesapeake*, 39; Mahon, "British Command Decisions," 53; R. Morriss, *Cockburn*, 87; Warren to Croker, 21 Feb. 1813, ADM 1/4359.

29. Hitsman and Graves, *Incredible War of 1812*, 237.
30. Latimer, *1812*, 252; Cockburn to Cochrane, 25 June 1814, NLS, Cochrane Papers, MS 2574, fols. 135–39.
31. R. Morriss, *Cockburn*, 61; Cochrane to Melville, 27 Apr. 1812, NLS, Cochrane Papers, MS 2574; Dudley and Crawford, *Naval War of 1812*, 3:137–39.
32. Dudley and Crawford, *Naval War of 1812*, 3:137–39. Ralph Eshelman pointed out when reviewing a draft of this book that the distance to Washington via Bladensburg was longer.
33. Dudley and Crawford, *Naval War of 1812*, 3:137–39.
34. Ibid., 152–54; R. Morriss, *Cockburn*, 100.

Chapter 5

1. The *Bramble*, a dispatch vessel, reached England in twenty days from the Chesapeake. See *Niles' Weekly Register* (Baltimore), 16 Apr. 1814.
2. The communications black hole later had disastrous consequences for the British at the Battle of New Orleans in 1815 when they lost the battle, unaware that peace had been concluded weeks earlier.
3. *Virginia Argus* (Richmond), 21 Aug. 1814.
4. *Merrimack (Va.) Intelligencer*, 30 July 1814; *Petersburg (Va.) Intelligencer*, 26 July 1814; *Baltimore Sun*, 28 July 1814; *Boston Gazette*, 28 July 1814; *Salem (Mass.) Gazette*, 29 July 1814; R. Morriss, *Cockburn*, 100; *Niles' Weekly Register* (Baltimore), 16 July 1814.
5. *Montreal Herald*, 3 Sept. 1814; Tuckerman, *Life of John Pendleton Kennedy*, 70.
6. *New York Herald*, 27 Aug. 1814. As the city was not attacked during the war, it gets less attention than other areas where battles took place. But New Yorkers were ready in case of a British assault. "Forts, batteries and blockhouses were constructed on nearly every island and reef in New York's harbor and others along the coast." Matteo, "Fortification of New York Harbor."
7. *Connecticut Courant* (Hartford), 30 Aug. 1814; *Mercantile Advertiser* (New York), 20 Aug. 1814; *Connecticut Herald* (New Haven), 16 Aug. 1814; *New Hampshire Sentinel* (Keene), 16 Sept. 1814; Irving, *Life and Letters of Washington Irving*, 1:236; *Columbian* (New York), 19 Aug. 1814; *New York Gazette*, 29 Aug. 1814; *Shamrock* (New York), 3 Sept. 1814.
8. *Shamrock* (New York), 3, 24 Sept. 1814; *American and Commercial Daily Advertiser* (Baltimore), 27 Aug. 1814; A. Taylor, *Civil War of 1812*, 9; Monthly Return of the 1/21st Regiment, 25 Aug. 1814, WO 17/275.
9. Cobbett's remark was made in the context of praising the openness of the American press. See *Cobbett's Weekly Political Register* (London), 26 Nov. 1814.
10. Cochrane to Bathurst, 2 Sept. 1814, WO 1/141; "Capture of the City of Washington," 541; George, *Terror on the Chesapeake*, 78.
11. Lord, *Dawn's Early Light*, 23.

12. Skeen, "Madison's Secretary of War," 351; J. Williams, *Invasion and the Capture of Washington*, 357; *Boston Gazette*, 12 Sept. 1814; Ketcham, *Madison*, 573–74; Stagg, *Mr. Madison's War*, 407.
13. Lord, *Dawn's Early Light*, 25, 26; George, *Terror on the Chesapeake*, 78.
14. Ingersoll, *Sketch*, 16–18.
15. George, *Terror on the Chesapeake*, chaps. 4–5; *Niles' Weekly Register* (Baltimore), 12 Mar. 1814.
16. George, *Terror on the Chesapeake*, 72; Shomette, *Flotilla*, chap. 9.
17. George, *Terror on the Chesapeake*, 79; *Niles' Weekly Register* (Baltimore), 30 July 1814; Eshelman, Sheads, and Hickey, *War in the Chesapeake*, 143–44; Ewell, *Medical Companion*, 629–30.
18. Sir George Cockburn, "Memoir of Services," NMM, COC/11, fol. 132; Dudley and Crawford, *Naval War of 1812*, 3:220–23; J. Scott, *Recollections*, 239, 272.
19. North American Station, Letters from Codrington, 29 July, 15 Aug. 1814, NMM, COD/7/1.
20. George, *Terror on the Chesapeake*, 81; Chamier, *Life of a Sailor*, 1:200; Malcolm to Mrs. Malcolm, 14 Aug. 1814, MP; R. Morriss, *Cockburn*, 2.
21. Lord, *Dawn's Early Light*, 54. Oral tradition passed down through Ross's family suggests that the general could not believe how easy it was to raid on land in the region and that this persuaded him to go for Washington. John McCavitt, conversations with Stephen Campbell, a descendant of Major General Ross, n.d. According to a British officer involved, "that our little army had been allowed to penetrate so far into the land without any opposition worth mentioning, was a source of astonishment to us all." "Old Sub," 450.
22. Codrington, *Memoir*, 314.
23. "Old Sub," 449; Evans, *Facts Relating to the Capture of Washington*, 4.
24. Memorial to the Prince Regent on Behalf of the Navy and Army Employed in the Operations against Washington in the United States of America, Aug. 1814, LC, Cochrane Papers, MS 2328, reel 2; Evans Memorandum, fol. 14; North American Station, Letters from Codrington, 21 Aug. 1814, NMM, COD/7/1.
25. Return of the General and Staff Officers, 25 Aug. 1814, WO 17/1218. "Reconnaissance in force" is a term coined in this respect by Ross researcher Kevin Chambers.
26. George, *Terror on the Chesapeake*, 81., 83; Evans Memorandum, fol. 3.
27. MacDougall letter, *Times* (London), 25 May 1861.
28. Codrington, *Memoir*, 315; Gleig, "Diary," in C. Barrett, *85th King's Light Infantry*, 133; George, *Terror on the Chesapeake*, 83. For more on the artillery, see chapter 8.
29. Coss, *All for the King's Shilling*, 17, 20, 153; George, *Terror on the Chesapeake*, 83; Evans Memorandum, fol. 26; Burnett, *Regency Dandy*, 224.
30. *Dedham (Mass.) Gazette*, 26 Aug. 1814; *American and Commercial Daily Advertiser* (Baltimore), 22 Aug. 1814; *Quebec Gazette*, 15 Sept. 1814; U.S. Congress, *House Journal*, 708.

31. Jones to Rodgers, 19 Aug. 1814, NARA, M119, roll 11; Jones to Porter, 19 Aug. 1814, ibid.; Dudley and Crawford, *Naval War of 1812*, 3:200–201.
32. *American and Commercial Daily Advertiser* (Baltimore), 23 Aug. 1814; Elbridge Gerry to Mrs. Gerry, 21 Oct. 1814, facsimile copy in possession of the Office of the Curator of the White House. See also *National Intelligencer* (Washington, D.C.), 2 Sept. 1814; and *Concord (N.H.) Gazette*, 13 Sept. 1814.
33. Allgor, *A Perfect Union*, 281. Ross commended Major Jones for his conduct at the Battle of Bladensburg but made no reference to this supposed reconnaissance mission. See Ross to Bathurst, 30 Aug. 1814, in Dudley and Crawford, *Naval War of 1812*, 3:223–26. According to Charles Jared Ingersoll, when Ross arrived in Washington on August 24 at 9:00 P.M., he tried to make arrangements for supper with Mrs. Suter. She replied that she had nothing to eat and recommended McLeod's Tavern nearby. Not to be put off, the general insisted that he "preferred her house because he had some acquaintance with her, mentioning several familiar circumstances." See Ingersoll, *Sketch*, 186. This is a clear link to the story of a British spy visiting the American capital in the days prior to its capture.
34. "Capture of the City of Washington," 581; George, *Terror on the Chesapeake*, 87.
35. Monroe, *Writings*, 5:289; "Capture of the City of Washington," 536; Stagg, *Mr. Madison's War*, 416; Shomette, *Flotilla*, 253; *National Intelligencer* (Washington, D.C.), 7 Sept. 1814.
36. O'Neill, "To Annoy or Destroy the Enemy," 67–95; *Niles' Weekly Register* (Baltimore), 20 Aug. 1814; Dudley and Crawford, *Naval War of 1812*, 3:181–84.
37. McLane, "Col. McLane's Visit to Washington," 18.

Chapter 6

1. Gleig, *Subaltern*, 23; Gleig, *Narrative of the Campaigns*, 99–100.
2. Burnett, *Regency Dandy*, 223; Evans, *Facts Relating to the Capture of Washington*, 9–10; Evans Memorandum, fols. 4, 5; J. Scott, *Recollections*, 275–76; North American Station, Letters from Codrington, 21 Aug. 1814, NMM, COD/7/1.
3. Lord, *Dawn's Early Light*, 66; Burnett, *Regency Dandy*, 223–24.
4. Evans Memorandum, fol. 5.
5. Gleig, *Narrative of the Campaigns*, 109; J. Scott, *Recollections*, 277, 279; Pack, *Man Who Burned the White House*, 186; Burnett, *Regency Dandy*, 224; George, *Terror on the Chesapeake*, 89–91.
6. George, *Terror on the Chesapeake*, 89–91; Gleig, *Narrative of the Campaigns*, 107; Evans Memorandum, fol. 5; North American Station, Letters from Codrington, 21 Aug. 1814, NMM, COD/7/1; Dudley and Crawford, *Naval War of 1812*, 3:223–26.
7. Vogel, *Perilous Fight*, 96; Eshelman, Sheads, and Hickey, *War in the Chesapeake*, 76; Evans Memorandum, fols. 5, 6; Mason to Skinner and Key, 2 Sept. 1814, NARA, Area File of the Naval Collection, 1775–1910,

M625; Gleig, "Diary," in C. Barrett, *85th King's Light Infantry*, 137, 154.
8. Evans Memorandum, fol. 5; Gleig, *Narrative of the Campaigns*, 109; Marine, *British Invasion of Maryland*, 74.
9. J. Williams, *Invasion and the Capture of Washington*, 359; Evans, *Facts Relating to the Capture of Washington*, 11. In this respect it is worth bearing in mind that Sir George Prevost ended up requesting a court-martial to "clear his name" when a huge controversy erupted following the failure of British operations against Lake Champlain and Plattsburgh, New York, in September 1814. See D. E. Graves, *Where Right and Glory Lead*, 233.
10. Ross to Mrs. Ross, 1 Sept. 1814, PRONI, D2004/1A/3/8.
11. Corbett, "Campaigns"; *Delaware Gazette* (Wilmington), 27 Oct. 1814.
12. In both of his major operations, at Washington and against Baltimore, Ross's "little army" was bolstered by marines and seamen.
13. Captain Rowley remarked upon the supply difficulties. See Rowley, "Captain Rowley Helps to Burn Washington," 248.
14. Ingersoll, *Sketch*, 191.
15. H. G. Smith, *Autobiography*, 1:206; Evans, *Facts Relating to the Capture of Washington*, 11; J. Scott, *Recollections*, 279–80. According to another British account, from the "period that Nottingham and Pig Point had been captured we were continually employed on board clearing the numerous launches and barges which arrived at all hours laden with vast hogsheads of tobacco." R. Barrett, "Naval Recollections," 460. The British were also reported to be taking tobacco at Upper Marlboro. See Stahl, *Invasion of the City of Washington*, 129.
16. Evans to Torrens, 5 May 1815, WO 31/418. The authors wish to thank Kevin Chambers for this reference and for highlighting the crucial importance of Evans at this juncture. Ross asked Bathurst to secure Evans a virtually unprecedented double promotion—to major. Ross to Bathurst, 31 Aug. 1814, WO 31/412.
17. Dudley and Crawford, *Naval War of 1812*, 3:220. Deemed as necessary reinforcements for the expedition to Washington, that no marines or drilled seamen accompanied Cockburn indicates that the admiral was not orchestrating operations.
18. Dudley and Crawford, *Naval War of 1812*, 3:220–23; Evans Memorandum, fol. 7. This is the gist of a conversation between Cockburn and Dr. William Thornton in Washington as reported in J. Armstrong, *Notices*, 2:126. A Royal Marine recruitment poster from the period holds out the enticement of "pay and prize" to potential recruits. See Hitsman and Graves, *Incredible War of 1812*, 197.
19. Dudley and Crawford, *Naval War of 1812*, 3:220. To some extent, therefore, a "letter from one of the Captors of Washington to a friend in Edinburgh" was correct in revealing that the delay in proceeding to the capital had been occasioned "for the purpose of being joined by 400 seamen, to assist in dragging our guns when we marched for Washington." *Caledonian Mercury* (Edinburgh), 6 Oct. 1814.

20. Cockburn to Cochrane, 23 Aug. 1814, LC, Cochrane Papers, MS 2328, reel 2; *National Intelligencer* (Washington, D.C.), 4 June 1849; Evans Memorandum, fol. 2; Evans, *Facts Relating to the Capture of Washington*, 8.
21. Cockburn to Cochrane, 23 Aug. 1814, LC, Cochrane Papers, MS 2328, reel 2; J. Scott, *Recollections*, 280. The task of bringing up bread and rum was given to HMS *Surprize*. Codrington to Thomas Cochrane, 24 Aug. 1814, NLS, Cochrane Papers, MS 2448.
22. Evans Memorandum, fols. 7, 8; Robyns to Melville, 21 Nov. 1815, ADM 1/3459; McLane, "Col. McLane's Visit to Washington," 20; Lord, *Dawn's Early Light*, 28. In similar circumstances during the French advance on Moscow, there were "plenty of instances" when Russians supplied "forage and victuals to the French." Zamoyski, *1812*, 320.
23. George, *Terror on the Chesapeake*, 91; J. Madison, *Writings*, 293, 294.
24. *National Intelligencer* (Washington, D.C.), 1 Sept. 1814; U.S. Congress, *House Journal*, 873. The secretary of the navy had given orders to prepare for the removal on August 20. See ibid., 876.
25. Pitch, *Burning of Washington*, 45; *Portland (Maine) Gazette*, 5 Sept. 1814; D. Madison, *Memoirs and Letters*, 109; *Farmer's Cabinet* (Amherst, N.H.), 5 Sept. 1814; *Richmond (Va.) Enquirer*, 31 Aug. 1814; *Burlington (Vt.) Gazette*, 9 Sept. 1814.
26. J. Armstrong, *Notices*, 2:235; Barker, *Incidents*, 121. "Cassius," a correspondent to U.S. newspapers at the time, could not understand why a "mine" had not been planted at the Capitol. Had Winder been "ordered to have piloted the enemy to the entrance of the city, and one of those square columns had been blown into the air, the capital of Washington it is believed would at this time have been in other hands, and the British would never again have attempted a similar expedition." *Burlington (Vt.) Gazette*, 9 Sept. 1814.
27. George, *Terror on the Chesapeake*, 92–93.
28. Evans Memorandum, fol. 7; Gleig, *Narrative of the Campaigns*, 110; J. Williams, *Invasion and the Capture of Washington*, 361.
29. Pitch, *Burning of Washington*, 57; Gleig, "Diary," in C. Barrett, *85th King's Light Infantry*, 137; J. Williams, *Invasion and the Capture of Washington*, 361, 362; Lord, *Dawn's Early Light*, 85; Tucker, *Poltroons and Patriots*, 522; Dudley and Crawford, *Naval War of 1812*, 3:194–95.
30. George, *Terror on the Chesapeake*, 92; McKenney, *Memoirs*, 45. According to John Kincaid, who served in the Peninsular War, if camp was made "early in the day, the first thing to be done is to make some tea, the most sovereign restorative for jaded spirits." Kincaid, *Rifle Brigade*, 22. The location of the British camp is from Dr. Ralph Eshelman to Christopher T. George, 22 Oct. 2014, in author's possession.
31. Ingersoll, *Sketch*, 191; Evans Memorandum, fol. 6; McKenney, "Narrative," 360; Dudley and Crawford, *Naval War of 1812*, 3:220.
32. J. Williams, *Invasion and the Capture of Washington*, 360; McLane, "Col. McLane's Visit to Washington," 19; Eshelman, Sheads, and Hickey, *War in the Chesapeake*, 147–48; *Poulson's American Daily Advertiser* (Philadelphia), 5 Sept. 1814.

33. George, *Terror on the Chesapeake*, 93.
34. North American Station, Letters from Codrington, 22 Aug. 1814, 5 Mar. 1815, NMM, COD/7/1. Cockburn was considered a "braggart" by Americans at the time. See Lord, *Dawn's Early Light*, 27.
35. North American Station, Letters from Codrington, 23 Aug. 1814, NMM, COD/7/1.
36. Evans, *Facts Relating to the Capture of Washington*, 2–3; J. Scott, *Recollections*, 282–84.
37. Sir George Cockburn, "Memoir of Services," NMM, COC/11, fol. 134; J. Scott, *Recollections*, 280; Evans Memorandum, fols. 8, 25; Gleig, "Diary," in C. Barrett, *85th King's Light Infantry*, 138.
38. Malcolm to Mrs. Malcolm, 9 Oct. 1814, MP; Arthur, *How Britain Won the War of 1812*, 107.
39. Gleig, *Subaltern*, 61; Evans Memorandum, fols. 8–9.

Chapter 7

1. P. Jennings, *Colored Man's Reminiscences*, 17; Dudley and Crawford, *Naval War of 1812*, 3:205; Lord, *Dawn's Early Light*, 105, 110; Vogel, *Perilous Fight*, 123.
2. Casualties of Captain Samuel Miller at Battle of Bladensburgh, LMC, Samuel Miller Collection, COLL/3590; George, *Terror on the Chesapeake*, 93; P. Jennings, *Colored Man's Reminiscences*, 9–10; Dudley and Crawford, *Naval War of 1812*, 3:206.
3. Pitch, *Burning of Washington*, 64; Hadel, "Battle of Bladensburg," 207; O'Neill, "To Annoy or Destroy the Enemy," 68; Stahl, *Invasion of the City of Washington*, 109, 122; "Capture of the City of Washington," 526. Even if it had reached Pennsylvania authorities in time, the state would not have been able to comply with the request. See Ingraham, *Sketch of the Events*, 10.
4. George, *Terror on the Chesapeake*, 94; Brooke Diary; *Baltimore Sun*, 26 Aug. 1851; Costello, *Rifleman Costello*, 31–32; Zamoyski, *1812*, 187–88; J. Scott, *Recollections*, 284; *Daily Graphic* (New York), 12 July 1876.
5. George, *Terror on the Chesapeake*, 94; George Hoffman to John Hoffman, 9 Sept. 1814, MHSL, War of 1812 Collection; Pitch, *Burning of Washington*, 60.
6. George, *Terror on the Chesapeake*, 95; J. Armstrong, *Notices*, 2:148. As Carl Skeen has pointed out, Monroe's "action vividly demonstrates the lack of command at this critical time." Skeen, *Citizen Soldiers*, 136.
7. Lord, *Dawn's Early Light*, 115–16; "Capture of the City of Washington," 570.
8. George, *Terror on the Chesapeake*, 94. See also McKenney, "Narrative," 360.
9. *Connecticut Herald* (New Haven), 5 Sept. 1814; Stagg, *Mr. Madison's War*, 417; *Niles' Weekly Register* (Baltimore), 27 Aug. 1814; *Long Island (N.Y.) Star*, 31 Aug. 1814; "Capture of the City of Washington," 572–73, 586; *National Intelligencer* (Washington, D.C.), 31 Aug. 1814.
10. When he returned to the President's House after the battle, Madison took off his pistols. See Pitch, *Burning of Washington*, 96.

11. George, *Terror on the Chesapeake*, 95; "Capture of the City of Washington," 596; *Federal Republican* (Washington, D.C.), 10 Jan. 1815.
12. George, *Terror on the Chesapeake*, 95–96; "Capture of the City of Washington," 586; Skeen, *Citizen Soldiers*, 137.
13. *American Watchman* (Wilmington, Del.), 9 Sept. 1814; Wilkinson, *Memoirs*, 781; *Boston Gazette*, 12 Sept. 1814; Lovell, *Personal Narrative*, 160.
14. "Capture of the City of Washington," 557, 584; J. Williams, *Invasion and the Capture of Washington*, 363; McKenney, "Narrative," 360; Cooling, *Day Lincoln Was almost Shot*; *New Jersey Journal* (Elizabeth Town), 30 Aug. 1814; *Palladium of Liberty* (Morristown, N.J.), 1 Sept. 1814; *Chronicle* (Harrisburg, Pa.), 4 Sept. 1814; *Belfast Newsletter*, 11 Oct. 1814; Allgor, *A Perfect Union*, 281.
15. "Capture of the City of Washington," 529, 584; Evans Memorandum, fol. 10; H. G. Smith, *Autobiography*, 1:198; George, *Terror on the Chesapeake*, 94; Brooke Diary; Snow, *When Britain Burned the White House*, 79.
16. Wounded and taken prisoner at Bladensburg, Wood provided an oral account that was later published by U.S. congressman Charles Jared Ingersoll. See Ingersoll, *Sketch*, 178; and Lord, *Dawn's Early Light*, 358.
17. Ingersoll, *Sketch*, 192.
18. Dudley and Crawford, *Naval War of 1812*, 3:223–26. Colonel Wood and Lieutenant Evans also indicated there were two American lines. Ingersoll, *Sketch*, 193; Evans Memorandum, fol. 10.
19. Evans Memorandum, fol. 10; George, *Terror on the Chesapeake*, 97; Dudley and Crawford, *Naval War of 1812*, 3:223–26; Wallace to Jefferson, 29 Sept. 1814, Thomas Jefferson Papers, ser. 1, General Correspondence, 1651–1827, LC. Colonel Brooke might have considered the bridge too narrow when he remarked that it could accommodate only three men abreast. See Brooke Diary. Midshipman John Bluett described it as "barely broad enough to admit eight abreast." Bluett Diary. Capt. Robert Rowley, R.N., who was not an eyewitness to events at Bladensburg, wrote that only two men "abreast" could cross at a time. See Rowley, "Captain Rowley Helps to Burn Washington," 249.
20. Ingersoll, *Sketch*, 175, 191–92. Ingersoll visited Bladensburg three weeks after the battle. See ibid., 178.
21. J. Madison, *Writings*, 291; Malcolm to a friend, 1 Sept. 1814, MP.
22. Brooke Diary; Sheads, *Chesapeake Campaigns*, 26; H. G. Smith, *Autobiography*, 1:199.
23. Evans Memorandum, fol. 10; *Freeman's Journal* (Dublin), 4 Oct. 1814. Some reported that Colonial Marines, African American volunteers, "had the honour of being in the advance." Casualty records show that one colonial marine was killed and two wounded at Bladensburg. Whether they were part of the "advance" or the lead brigade is not clear. *Hampshire Telegraph and Sussex Chronicle* (England), 3 Oct.1814; Return of the Killed, Wounded, and Missing . . . in Action with the Enemy on the 24 August 1814, WO 1/141.

24. *Freeman's Journal* (Dublin), 4 Oct. 1814; J. Scott, *Recollections*, 286; Gleig, *Subaltern*, 69. See also Brooke Diary; and "Capture of the City of Washington," 529, 584, 597.
25. Gleig, *Narrative of the Campaigns*, 154; Snow, *When Britain Burned the White House*, 201; "Capture of the City of Washington," 29 Nov. 1814, 562; Drez, *War of 1812*, 140.
26. "Capture of the City of Washington," 574; Warner, *At Peace with All Their Neighbours*, 277; Lord, *Dawn's Early Light*, 62.
27. Lord, *Dawn's Early Light*, 125; Gleig, *Narrative of the Campaigns*, 121–22; "Capture of the City of Washington," 573.
28. *Political Intelligencer* (Annapolis), 3 Sept. 1814; J. Scott, *Recollections*, 286; Ingersoll, *Sketch*, 178; Stahl, *Invasion of the City of Washington*, 206–207; Spring, *With Zeal and Bayonets Only*, 252–55; Urban, *Rifles*, 17.
29. *Hampshire Telegraph and Sussex Chronicle* (England), 3 Oct. 1814; J. Scott, *Recollections*, 286; Corbett, "Campaigns."
30. "Capture of Washington," 562, 573; Sheads, *Rockets' Red Glare*, 12. One report suggests that it took the British five minutes to begin firing their rockets. See *Political Intelligencer* (Annapolis), 3 Sept. 1814. Ross once attended a dinner hosted by the weapon system's inventor, William Congreve. See Colburn, *Memoir*, 36.
31. George, *Terror on the Chesapeake*, 98; Gleig, *Narrative of the Campaigns*, 95. Donald Shomette notes a "discrepancy concerning the number of guns carried ashore and later used by the army." Shomette, *Flotilla*, 457n53. Apart from one 6-pounder gun, George Laval Chesterton of the Royal Artillery recorded that owing to the difficulties of the terrain, the rest were "sent afloat at Marlborough." Chesterton, *Peace, War, and Adventure*, 1:125–26. Evans also mentions one 6-pounder being used during the battle. Evans Memorandum, fol. 11. In his diary Brooke notes that Ross thanked Captain Mitchel for his "exertions in directing the six pounders." Brooke Diary.
32. *New Bedford (Mass.) Mercury*, 9 Sept. 1814; Capt. Henry Thompson to Brig. Gen. John Stricker, Aug. 24, 1814, MHSL, MS 1435; Perrett, *Real Hornblower*, 107; *Political Intelligencer* (Annapolis), 3 Sept. 1814; "Capture of the City of Washington," 562, 584. The Royal Marine Artillery lost a man killed and another wounded in the battle. Return of the Killed, Wounded, and Missing . . . in Action with the Enemy on the 24 August 1814, WO 1/141.
33. *Federal Republican* (Washington, D.C.), 2 Sept. 1814; *Rhode Island American* (Providence), 4 July 1815. The departure of the first couple from Washington was later characterized as "the flight of the Madisons." See Alden, *Flight of the Madisons*.
34. "The Bladensburg Races," *Connecticut Herald* (New Haven), 15 Mar. 1815.
35. "Capture of the City of Washington," 548, 558; Brant, *James Madison*, 301; Ingersoll, *Sketch*, 177; Lord, *Dawn's Early Light*, 128; *New York Herald*, 31 Aug. 1814; Sheads, *Rockets' Red Glare*, 12.

36. "Capture of the City of Washington," 558, 562, 573. "The enemy, finding on getting near the bridge he should have to pass a defile between the creek and marsh in front of our battery, instantly displayed a heavy column to the right and passed the ford higher up the creek."
37. Perrett, *Real Hornblower*, 113; McKenney, "Narrative," 360.
38. Hart and Penman, *1812*, plate 59; J. Scott, *Recollections*, 286; Gleig, "Diary," in C. Barrett, *85th King's Light Infantry*, 138; Gleig, *Narrative of the Campaigns*, 122; *Niles' Weekly Register* (Baltimore), 27 Aug. 1814; "Capture of the City of Washington," 562; Hart, *New Annual Army List* (1850), 22; Brooke Diary.

Chapter 8

1. *Charleston (S.C.) Mercury*, 18 Jan. 1858; George Hoffman to John Hoffman, 9 Sept. 1814, MHSL, War of 1812 Collection; Wallace to Jefferson, 29 Sept. 1814, LC, Thomas Jefferson Papers, ser. 1, General Correspondence, 1651–1827.
2. George Hoffman to John Hoffman, 9 Sept. 1814, MHSL, War of 1812 Collection. Many years later a workman's leg was broken when he reportedly dislodged a British cannonball at Bladensburg. Inside the projectile was a note written by Timson Howard, an American who had been press-ganged into British service, warning of the planned attack on Washington. See *Denver Post*, 5 Dec. 1902.
3. *Baltimore Patriot*, 5 Sept. 1814; Gleig, *Subaltern*, 71. The term "Bladensburg Races" was first used in the *Federal Republican* (Washington, D.C.), 7 Oct. 1814.
4. *Dedham (Mass.) Gazette*, 5 July 1816.
5. Buchan, *Royal Scots Fusiliers*, 170; *New York Herald*, 31 Aug. 1814; Wallace to Jefferson, 29 Sept. 1814; Return of the Killed, Wounded, and Missing . . . in Action with the Enemy on the 24 August 1814, WO 1/141; George, *Terror on the Chesapeake*, 98; *Delaware Gazette* (Wilmington), 5 Sept. 1814; *New York Spectator*, 3 Sept. 1814.
6. "Capture of the City of Washington," 558, 568; Tuckerman, *Life of John Pendleton Kennedy*, 89.
7. George, *Terror on the Chesapeake*, 99–100; "Capture of the City of Washington," 537. Several other reports emanating from the American side confirm that it was only after General Winder issued the order for his front line to retreat that President Madison withdrew from that part of the battlefield. See, for example, *Richmond (Va.) Enquirer*, 31 Sept. 1814; and *Federal Republican* (Washington, D.C.), 2 Sept. 1814.
8. Lovell, *Personal Narrative*, 161; Hitsman and Graves, *Incredible War of 1812*, 34; Marine, *British Invasion of Maryland*, 114; *Niles' Weekly Register* (Baltimore), supplement, 7:150; George, *Terror on the Chesapeake*, 97.
9. George, *Terror on the Chesapeake*, 97; Shomette, *Flotilla*, 298.
10. Shomette, *Flotilla*, 256. For the number of marines, see Casualties of Capt. Samuel Miller at Battle of Bladensburgh [sic], LMC, Samuel Miller Collection, COLL/3590.

11. "Capture of the City of Washington," 579; George, *Terror on the Chesapeake*, 97; J. Williams, *Invasion and the Capture of Washington*, 363. Thomas McKenney, another aide to Smith, believed that Peter was mistaken in this assumption. See McKenney, "Narrative," 366.
12. George, *Terror on the Chesapeake*, 100; Ingersoll, *Sketch*, 193; Barney, *Biographical Memoir*, 265; Gleig, *Narrative of the Campaigns*, 122. Harry Smith used the term "isolated" in relation to Thornton's attack on the bridge at Bladensburg followed by his advance on the American second line. H. G. Smith, *Autobiography*, 1:198–99, 201.
13. George, *Terror on the Chesapeake*, 100.
14. Barney, *Biographical Memoir*, 315–16; Ingersoll, *Sketch*, 193.
15. Barker, *Incidents*, 121; Ingraham, *Sketch of the Events*, 61–62.
16. Ingersoll, *Sketch*, 193; Weller, "Commodore Joshua Barney," 152; Gleig, "Diary," in C. Barrett, *85th King's Light Infantry*, 138; Barney, *Biographical Memoir*, 321; "Capture of the City of Washington," 579; McKenney, "Narrative," 362; George, *Terror on the Chesapeake*, 100; J. Scott, *Recollections*, 287; *Belfast Newsletter*, 12 Aug. 1870.
17. C. Barrett, *85th King's Light Infantry*, 153; R. Barrett, "Naval Recollections," 459; Gleig, "Diary," in C. Barrett, *85th King's Light Infantry*, 138; H. S. Smith, *Eighty-Fifth, Bucks Volunteers*, vi; Monthly Return of the 85th Regiment, 25 Aug. 1814, WO 17/281.
18. Barney, *Biographical Memoir*, 265, 321; Gleig, "Diary," in C. Barrett, *85th King's Light Infantry*, 138–39.
19. H. G. Smith, *Autobiography*, 1:199. Too often relied upon by historians without question, Smith's one-and-a-half-page account of Bladensburg is riddled with inaccuracies. While Major Brown was severely wounded, he did not die, despite Smith's claim to the contrary. Brown not only lived to send an engraved gold snuffbox to a Dr. Worthington from Georgetown for tending to his wounds but also later commanded the Light Division during the Crimean War (1853–56) some four decades later. In years past George Washington had been a frequent visitor to Dr. Worthington's home. Abbott, *Trolley Trips*, 71.
20. Gleig, *Subaltern*, 75; Gleig, "Diary," in C. Barrett, *85th King's Light Infantry*, 138–39; J. Scott, *Recollections*, 288.
21. J. Scott, *Recollections*, 288–89.
22. "Capture of Washington," 564; Ingersoll, *Sketch*, 194; McKenney, "Narrative," 363–65; J. Williams, *Invasion and the Capture of Washington*, 236.
23. King, *Turning on the Light*, 341–42. The flag was to hang in the chapel at Chelsea Hospital in London, where Gleig served as chaplain general to the British army at a later stage in his career. On a cautionary note, as Ed Seufert has emphasized to the authors, it is odd that Gleig never mentioned capturing the flag in either of his two books or that Ross did not make any comment about it in his dispatch.
24. Ball, *Slavery in the United States*, 404; J. Williams, *Invasion and the Capture of Washington*, 235; Marine, *British Invasion of Maryland*, 97; Ingersoll, *Sketch*, 178; Weller, "Commodore Joshua Barney," 152.

25. "Capture of the City of Washington," 558, 565; George, *Terror on the Chesapeake*, 100; McKenney, "Narrative," 362; J. Williams, *Invasion and the Capture of Washington*, 238.
26. George, *Terror on the Chesapeake*, 100; *Freeman's Journal* (Philadelphia), 4 Oct. 1814; *Gleaner* (Wilkes-Barre, Pa.), 5 Sept. 1814.
27. "Capture of Washington," 580; *New Jersey Journal* (Elizabeth Town), 6 Sept. 1814; George, *Terror on the Chesapeake*, 100.
28. George, *Terror on the Chesapeake*, 100; *Long Island (N.Y.) Star*, 31 Aug. 1814; *Palladium of Liberty* (Morristown, N.J.), 1 Sept. 1814; Bluett Diary; *Star* (Raleigh, N.C.), 9 Sept. 1814; Gleig, *Narrative of the Campaigns*, 125–26; *Federal Republican* (Washington, D.C.), 2 Sept. 1814; Burnett, *Regency Dandy*, 224. Barney had not run of ammunition completely. The British afterward reported recovering a "quantity of ammunition" for the commodore's guns. Return of Ordnance, Ammunition, and Ordnance Stores, Taken from the Enemy by the Army under the Command of Maj. Gen. Robert Ross, between the 19th and 25th August 1814, WO 1/141.
29. Tuckerman, *Life of John Pendleton Kennedy*, 79; Weller, "Commodore Joshua Barney," 164. The commodore was presented with a sword by the City of Washington for his valor in the battle. The musket ball lodged in his thigh was never removed, and Barney would die, possibly of lead poisoning, in Pittsburgh in December 1818. Norton, *Joshua Barney*, 191–92.
30. *Federal Republican* (Washington, D.C.), 20 Jan. 1815; *Portsmouth (N.H.) Oracle*, 18 Feb. 1815; Ingersoll, *Sketch*, 186; Codrington, *Memoir*, 328. See also *Harper's New Monthly Magazine*, 28:441. Capt. Robert Rowley recorded too that the president "fled on Barney's being wounded." Rowley, "Captain Rowley Helps to Burn Washington," 249.
31. *Baltimore Sun*, 12 Dec. 1855.
32. J. Scott, *Recollections*, 290. Dr. Ewell also detailed an account of this incident that Barney related to him. "You are a noble fellow!" said the commodore, "and I am sorry I have not a purse for you. But here's my gold watch: you are welcome to it." "No, sir," replied the Englishman, "I can assist a brave man without being paid for it." Ewell, *Medical Companion*, 655.
33. *Belfast Newsletter*, 11 Oct. 1814. Lieutenant Scott claims that the soldier was never found. J. Scott, *Recollections*, 290.
34. Barney, *Biographical Memoir*, 267. Lieutenant Scott claims that Cockburn paroled Barney. J. Scott, *Recollections*, 285–90. John Binns reported a conversation with Barney in which the commodore mentioned that the admiral paroled him. Binns, *Recollections*, 231.
35. Bathurst, *We'll All Die as Marines*, 236; *Niles' Weekly Register* (Baltimore), 1 Oct. 1814. Barney drew criticism at the time for failing to mention the marines, with George W. Wilson accusing him of craving "public applause." See Footner, *Sailor of Fortune*, 289.
36. J. Williams, *Invasion and the Capture of Washington*, 358; *Federal Republican* (Washington, D.C.), 2 Sept. 1814. John Stahl rejects the

notion "that the only good fighting done at Bladensburg was done by the men of the navy under Commodore Barney! And that shameful lie and libel is taught in our schools and is supposed to be the truth by many of our people to this day." Stahl, *Invasion of the City of Washington*, 218.

37. Return of the Killed, Wounded, and Missing . . . in Action with the Enemy on the 24th August 1814, WO 1/141; Dudley and Crawford, *Naval War of 1812*, 3:223–26; Brooke Diary; Return of the Wounded Left at Bladensburg and Washington, 5 Sept. 1814, WO 1/141. Faunce was promoted to the rank of lieutenant colonel on Ross's recommendation. See "Fourth (or the King's Own) Regiment of Foot," 566. Officers of the 1/4th Battalion agreed that the 1/4th and 85th "alone routed the whole Yankee army." See Cowper, *King's Own*, 8.

38. Return of the Killed, Wounded, and Missing . . . in Action with the Enemy on the 24 August 1814, WO 1/141; Faunce obituary, *Examiner* (London), 9 Mar. 1850; Brown obituary, *Belfast Newsletter*, 29 Aug. 1865; Gascoyne obituary, *Hampshire Telegraph and Sussex Chronicle* (England), 29 July 1876; Williams obituary, *Bell's Life in London and Sporting Chronicle*, 23 Dec. 1860; Wood obituary, *Belfast Newsletter*, 12 Aug. 1870; French obituary, *Pall Mall Gazette* (London), 29 Jan. 1874; Nolan, *Illustrated History of the War against Russia*, 1:386.

39. Ball, *Slavery in the United States*, 404; *Niles' Weekly Register* (Baltimore), 14 June 1817; H. G. Smith, *Autobiography*, 1:199–200; *Niles' Weekly Register* (Baltimore), supplement, 7:150; Burnett, *Regency Dandy*, 225. General officers had a number of horses. Wellington usually had fifteen chargers, for example. See Longford, *Wellington*, 221. Thanks to British army records, it can be ascertained that four horses belonging to the "General Staff" were killed in the battle. Return of the Killed, Wounded, and Missing . . . in Action with the Enemy on the 24 August 1814, WO 1/141. Perhaps two of these belonged to Lieutenant Evans. Nolan, *Illustrated History of the War against Russia*, 1:386.

40. Torrens to Vansittart, 11 Nov. 1814, WO 3/608; *Dedham (Mass.) Gazette*, 23 Sept. 1814; *Hampshire Telegraph and Sussex Chronicle* (England), 3 Oct. 1814.

Chapter 9

1. Gleig, *Narrative of the Campaigns*, 128; "The Capture of Washington City," in W. Elliott, *Washington Guide*, 154; *American Watchman* (Wilmington, Del.), 10 Sept. 1814; "Capture of Washington," 571; J. Armstrong, *Notices*, 2:231; Lord, *Dawn's Early Light*, 148–49. On the confused American retreat, see also McKenney, "Narrative," 364–65.

2. Dudley and Crawford, *Naval War of 1812*, 3:208–13. According to Mary Ingle, a young girl at the time, the "fathers and brothers" of Washington residents "all" remained with the militia. See Clark, "Abraham Young Mansion," 67.

3. Dudley and Crawford, *Naval War of 1812*, 3:208–13; Shomette, *Flotilla*, 143–54; George, *Terror on the Chesapeake*, 76; Lord, *Dawn's Early Light*, 161. Captain Bacon confirmed that he had assumed command

of the small marine contingent following the wounding of more-senior officers at Bladensburg. See Ockerbloom, "U.S. Marine Officer's Account," 258–62.
4. "Old Sub," 455; Dudley and Crawford, *Naval War of 1812*, 3:220–23; Gleig, *Narrative of the Campaigns*, 124; Eshelman, *Travel Guide*, 52; Brooke Diary; Evans Memorandum, fol. 12; J. Scott, *Recollections*, 297; Gleig, *Subaltern*, 78; *Long Island (N.Y.) Star*, 31 Aug. 1814.
5. Ross to Mrs. Ross, 1 Sept. 1814, PRONI, D2004/1A/3/8; Lord, *Dawn's Early Light*, 158; *Delaware Gazette* (Wilmington), 5 Sept. 1814.
6. McKenney, "Narrative," 368–69; Ewell, *Medical Companion*, 633. See also D. E. Graves, "Worthless Is the Laurel," 4–23; and D. E. Graves, "Every Horror Was Committed with Impunity."
7. Stuart, *Refutation of Aspersions*, 88–89.
8. H. G. Smith, *Autobiography*, 1:198; Petition of Joseph Gray, a Native of Washington, 28 July 1815, WO 1/661. Gray ended up traveling to London in an effort to secure payment of $260 he believed was owed to him. Evans later testified that while he could not remember that the agreed sum was $40 per day, he had been authorized to give Gray $120. Evans to Torrens, 26 July 1815, WO 1/661. The authors are grateful to Kevin Chambers for highlighting the role of Joseph Gray.
9. Memorial of Joseph Gray, 4 July 1815, WO 1/661; Muster, HMS *Royal Oak*, 1 July–31 Dec. 1814, ADM 37/5135; Muster, HMS *Tonnant*, 1 June–31 Oct. 1814, ibid., 37/5166.
10. "August 2012 Calendar," http://www.calendar-365.com/calendar/2012/August.html; Shiner, "Diary," 6; Evans Memorandum, fol. 12. Scott recalled that "ere we arrived at the immediate suburbs of Washington it was dark." J. Scott, *Recollections*, 297.
11. D. E. Graves, "Why the British Burned Washington," 1096; Zamoyski, *1812*, 297; J. Scott, *Recollections*, 298; Burnett, *Regency Dandy*, 223–25.
12. Zamoyski, *1812*, 297; *National Intelligencer* (Washington, D.C.), 9 Sept. 1814; *Federal Republican* (Washington, D.C.), 17 Sept. 1814; *Virginia Patriot* (Richmond), 21 Sept. 1814; Broussard, *Southern Federalists*, 352. See also Clark, "James Heighe Blake."
13. Bryan, "Diary of Mrs. William Thornton," 178.
14. Kevin Chambers used the term "profit and patriotism" in his unpublished paper, "Ross's Record." See also Eshelman and Kummerow, *In Full Glory Reflected*, 96. The cruise of the *Rossie* under Commodore Barney in 1812 exemplified the large sums of "prize and ransom" that could be accrued, in this case up to $1.5 million. See Lambert, *Challenge*; and Eshelman and Kummerow, *In Full Glory Reflected*, 18.
15. Prize Money for General Staff, including Commissariat and Medical Department for Captures in the River Patuxent at Fort Washington and Alexandria between 22nd and 29th August 1814, WO 164/563; Proposition for Granting Royal Bounties to the Widow and Family of the Late Maj. Gen. Robert Ross, 20 Jan. 1815, WO 43/359.
16. J. Scott, *Recollections*, 298; Stocqueler, *British Soldier*, 137. Scott reported that this "noble animal had carried his master during the whole of the Peninsular War." J. Scott, *Recollections*, 298.

17. Brooke Diary; Gleig, *Narrative of the Campaigns*, 129.
18. Timpson Memoir; Burnett, *Regency Dandy*, 223–25; D. Brown, "Diary of a Soldier," 77. Another account mistakenly indicates that the corporals were from the 1/4th. This battalion was not part of the Third Brigade, which accompanied Ross on his arrival at Washington. See Chartrand, *"Account of the Capture of Washington,"* 182.
19. Return of Noncommissioned Officers, Drummers, Fifers, and Private Men of the 1st Battalion, 21st Fusiliers, Who Have Died, Been Made Prisoner, or Transferred from 25 July to 24 August 1814, WO 25/1633; Burnett, *Regency Dandy*, 223–25; J. Scott, *Recollections*, 298. Anderson and Donaldson were the only two rank-and-file members of the 1/21st killed on 24 August.
20. J. Scott, *Recollections*, 298; Dudley and Crawford, *Naval War of 1812*, 3:220–23; MacDougall letter, *Times* (London), 25 May 1861; "Old Sub," 456; Coté, *Strength and Honor*, 303. Forty years later Evans gave the impression that the Americans were based in the Capitol. "Led 100 light infantry in the night attack upon Washington, dislodging the enemy and gaining possession of the Congress Houses, before entrance of any other portion of our troops." Lt. Gen. De Lacy Evans, Memorandum to be Submitted to His Grace the Duke of Newcastle, Secretary of State for the War Department, 12 Apr. 1854, British Library, Aberdeen MSS, 43,252.
21. M. Hunter, "Burning of Washington," 80–83; Lord, *Dawn's Early Light*, 149.
22. M. Smith, *First Forty Years of Washington Society*, 109; *Connecticut Journal*, 5 Sept. 1814; *New Jersey Journal* (Elizabeth Town), 6 Sept. 1814; Shiner, "Diary," 7; Eshelman, *Travel Guide*, 229.
23. Ingersoll, *Sketch*, 182; *New Bedford (Mass.) Mercury*, 9 Sept. 1814. Washington's "twin houses" were on Capitol Hill. G. Brown, *Incidental Architect*, 78.
24. Ingersoll, *Sketch*, 171; M. Smith, *First Forty Years of Washington Society*, 109; *New Jersey Journal* (Elizabeth Town), Sept. 1814; *Federal Republican* (Washington, D.C.), 30 Aug. 1814; *Virginia Patriot* (Richmond), 21 Sept. 1814; Broussar, *Southern Federalists*, 352.
25. *Poulson's American Daily Advertiser* (Philadelphia), 29 Aug. 1814; Pitch, *Burning of Washington*, 100; *Evening Star* (Washington, D.C.), 26 Oct. 1904; *Delaware Gazette* (Wilmington), 29 Aug. 1814; Ingersoll, *Sketch*, 182.
26. Lord, *Dawn's Early Light*, 161; "Sketches of the Private Life and Character of Wm H. Crawford," 264; *National Intelligencer* (Washington, D.C.), 10 May 1837; *American Watchman* (Wilmington, Del.), 10 Sept. 1814; *Montreal Herald*, 17 Sept. 1814; Pitch, *Burning of Washington*, 100. On the barber's reported escape, see *National Intelligencer* (Washington, D.C.), 10 May 1837.
27. Tucker, *Poltroons and Patriots*, 553; Lord, *Dawn's Early Light*, 161. See also Vogel, *Perilous Fight*, 168. Captain Bacon makes no mention of U.S. Marines attacking the British again. See Ockerbloom, "U.S. Marine Officer's Account," 258–62.

28. Eshelman, Sheads, and Hickey, *War in the Chesapeake*, 286; National Park Service, "Sewall-Belmont House," 8.
29. Tucker, *Poltroons and Patriots*, 553; Dudley and Crawford, *Naval War of 1812*, 3:208–13; Pitch, *Burning of Washington*, 106.
30. Hickey, *Don't Give Up the Ship*, 80; J. Armstrong, *Notices*, 2:131; *National Intelligencer* (Washington, D.C.), 7 Sept. 1814; Ingersoll, *Sketch*, 184; Pitch, *Burning of Washington*, 125; P. Jennings, *Colored Man's Reminiscences*, 12.
31. Muller, *Darkest Day*, 137; *Alexandria (Va.) Gazette*, 3 May 1814; Eshelman and Sheads, *Chesapeake Legends and Lore*, 146; *Southern Illustrated News* (Richmond, Va.), 30 May 1863; Dudley and Crawford, *Naval War of 1812*, 3:215–20.
32. Ewell, *Medical Companion*, 634; Hansard, *Parliamentary Debates*, 30:606–607. There is some doubt who ordered the house to be burnt, Ross or Cockburn. See *Columbian Patriot* (Middlebury, Vt.), 7 Sept. 1814; and Burnett, *Regency Dandy*, 223–25.
33. MacDougall letter, *Times* (London), 25 May 1861; H. G. Smith, *Autobiography*, 1:200; R. Morriss, *Cockburn*, 109; Ingersoll, *Sketch*, 171; Lord, *Dawn's Early Light*, 223; Best, *Humanity in Warfare*, 112.
34. There is some equine symbolism on the two monuments to General Ross in Rostrevor, County Down, N. Ireland.
35. Stocqueler, *British Soldier*, 137; *Baltimore Sun*, 14 Sept. 1858. A newspaper report stated that the horse "was lying" where it was shot "four days after the battle." Ross is likely to have ensured that his mount was buried. The animal referred to here may well have been the one that the British trumpeter was riding at the time of the shooting. *Federal Republican* (Washington, D.C.), 2 Sept. 1814.
36. Ewell, *Medical Companion*, 641; Ingersoll, *Sketch*, 190.

Chapter 10
1. Ross to Maria Ross, 2 Sept. 1814, PRONI, D2004/1A/3/9.
2. Clemmer, *Ten Years in Washington*, 134; *National Register* (Washington, D.C.), 3 Aug. 1816; *Virginia Argus* (Richmond), 7 Sept. 1814; Pitch, *Burning of Washington*, 112; Snow, *When Britain Burned the White House*, 133; M. Hunter, "Burning of Washington," 80–83; Fearon, *Sketches of America*, 325–26.
3. Allen, *United States Capitol*, 98; Ewell, *Medical Companion*, 642, 644; *National Register* (Washington, D.C.), 3 Aug. 1816.
4. J. Scott, *Recollections*, 302. Published accounts list six private houses that were set on fire as belonging to Messrs. Sewell, Ball, Frost, Philips, and Tomlinson and a Mrs. Hamilton. See *Virginia Argus* (Richmond), 7 Sept. 1814; and *Niles' Weekly Register* (Baltimore), 10 Sept. 1814. These premises were, it seems, known by different names. A Virginia newspaper noted that "Mrs. Hamilton's House, Jenkin's House, Tomlinson's Hotel [also known as Carroll's Hotel], and Brent's House, are destroyed." *Merrimack (Va.) Intelligencer*, 3 Sept. 1814. A young British midshipman mentioned that the "Josephine hotel" was burnt.

"From a Letter of a Young Midshipman of His Majesty's Brig, *Espoir*," *Niles' Weekly Register* (Baltimore), supplement, 7:150.
5. Ewell, *Medical Companion*, 638–39. Another of his American prisoners, a Dr. Martin, described Ross as "the perfect model of the Irish gentleman, of easy and beautiful manners, humane and brave, and dignified in his deportment to all." Arnold, "Battle of Bladensburg," 150–51.
6. Ewell, *Medical Companion*, 642. At the "banquet" at the President's House, Ross reportedly raised a toast, "Peace with America—war with Madison." Vogel, *Perilous Fight*, 178.
7. Elbridge Gerry to Mrs. Gerry, 21 Oct. 1814, facsimile copy in possession of the Office of the Curator of the White House.
8. Eshelman, *Travel Guide*, 231. According to one newspaper report, "if the despatches from France and the news from the Chesapeake and Virginia, don't drive the poor little Viceroy, in the White House crazy, he must be as tough as a pine knot." *Federal Republican* (Washington, D.C.), 10 Feb. 1813. Reference courtesy of Scott Sheads.
9. *Federal Republican* (Washington, D.C.), 16 Sept. 1814; *National Intelligencer* (Washington, D.C.), 6 Dec. 1813.
10. "Old Sub," 25; J. Scott, *Recollections*, 303; "Capture of the City of Washington," 597; Ingersoll, *Sketch*, 206; Pitch, *Burning of Washington*, 50.
11. Dudley and Crawford, *Naval War of 1812*, 3:208–13; P. Jennings, *Colored Man's Reminiscences*, 11–12; *Federal Republican* (Washington, D.C.), 2 Sept. 1814; V. Moore, "Reminiscences of Washington," 102. See also Pitch, *Burning of Washington*, 134.
12. "Attack of Washington from a Private Letter," *Belfast Newsletter*, 11 Oct. 1814; P. Jennings, *Colored Man's Reminiscences*, 11. See also E. Taylor, *Slave in the White House*.
13. Thomas, "Long Lost Washington Drawing," 120; P. Jennings, *Colored Man's Reminiscences*, 11; Howard, *Mr. and Mrs. Madison's War*, 192–93.
14. Ewell, *Medical Companion*, 642. Elbridge Gerry to Mrs. Gerry, 21 Oct. 1814, facsimile copy in possession of the Office of the Curator of the White House.
15. *Courier* (London), 27 Sept. 1814; *Gentleman's Magazine* (London) (1814): 385; Stuart, *Refutation of Aspersions*, 89; *Hampshire Telegraph and Sussex Chronicle* (England), 3 Oct. 1814; H. G. Smith, *Autobiography*, 1:200; *Derby Mercury* (England), 6 Oct. 1814; J. Scott, *Recollections*, 304; Chesterton, *Peace, War, and Adventure*, 1:132; "Memoir of Major General Robert Ross," 414–15.
16. Ingersoll, *Sketch*, 187; Tucker, *Poltroons and Patriots*, 564; McCormick, "First Master of Ceremonies," 183–84; Tuckerman, *Life of John Pendleton Kennedy*, 74–75; Lovell, *Personal Narrative*, 160.
17. Standiford, *Washington Burning*, 278; J. Scott, *Recollections*, 304; *Belfast Newsletter*, 11 Oct. 1814; Chesterton, *Peace, War, and Adventure*, 1:132.
18. Lord, *Dawn's Early Light*, 170. There are no letters written by President Madison among the Ross Family Papers in the Public Record Office of Northern Ireland.

19. *Quebec Gazette*, 22 Sept. 1814; John McCavitt, conversations with Niall Quinn, present owner of the sword and cane in Ireland, July 2013. The sword in question may be the one that Urquhart took from the White House.
20. Monkman, "White House Collection," 224. Information courtesy of William G. Allman, White House curator.
21. Vogel, *Perilous Fight*, 180; Serurier to Talleyrand, 27 Aug. 1814, LC, Foreign Affairs, Political Correspondence; Howard, *Mr. and Mrs. Madison's War*, 162. Mrs. Ross's will includes a reference to a "violin and case," perhaps one that was owned by her husband. Will of Elizabeth Catherine Ross, Widow, of Carraigh Bhan, Rosstrevor, 4 Aug. 1845, PROB 11/2023/109.
22. Elbridge Gerry to Mrs. Gerry, 21 Oct. 1814, facsimile copy in possession of the Office of the Curator of the White House.
23. Pitch, *Burning of Washington*, 122; Ingersoll, *Sketch*, 186; George, *Terror on the Chesapeake*, 113–15; Snow, *When Britain Burned the White House*, 152. See also Dallas, *Exposition*, 103.
24. Ingersoll, *Sketch*, 186. Cockburn indicates in his official dispatch that the War Office was burnt on the night of August 24, whereas Lieutenant Scott recorded that it was burnt the following morning. Dudley and Crawford, *Naval War of 1812*, 3:220–23; J. Scott, *Recollections*, 310.
25. Elbridge Gerry to Mrs. Gerry, 21 Oct. 1814, facsimile copy in possession of the Office of the Curator of the White House; Eshelman, Sheads, and Hickey, *War in the Chesapeake*, 287.
26. J. Scott, *Recollections*, 305–306; Snow, *When Britain Burned the White House*, 132; M. Morriss, "Life and Times of Pontius D. Stelle," 63.
27. Ingersoll, *Sketch*, 188. Aware that Cockburn was spending time with a "certain lady," local boys, it was later recorded, plotted to capture him. *Evening Star* (Washington, D.C.), 24 Aug. 1882.
28. Brooke Diary. It is not clear at what time of day Ross made this statement.
29. Gleig, *Subaltern*, 81–82; Clemner, *Ten Years in Washington*, 133–34; Return of Ordnance, Ammunition, and Ordnance Stores, Taken from the Enemy by the Army under the Command of Maj. Gen. Robert Ross, between the 19th and 25th August 1814, WO 1/141; *Newburyport (Mass.) Herald and Country Gazette*, 5 Sept. 1814.
30. Stuart, *Refutation of Aspersions*, 90. An American officer, Capt. George Stewart of the 5th Maryland Regiment, who had served at the Battle of Bladensburg and later the defense of Baltimore, corroborated Pringle's claim that he had successfully performed his duty in protecting private property in the capital to the satisfaction of both local citizens and General Ross. See Seaton, *William Winston Seaton*, 117–18.
31. Lord, *Dawn's Early Light*, 194–95; P. Jennings, *Colored Man's Reminiscences*, 11; *National Intelligencer* (Washington, D.C.), 31 Aug., 7 Sept. 1814; *Virginia Argus* (Richmond), 7 Sept. 1814. According to a newspaper account, Commodore Tingey's home was reputedly "pillaged" by the British. *Republican Star* (Easton, Md.), 13 Sept. 1814. Anthony Pitch blames "local mobs." Pitch, *Burning of Washington*, 135.

32. Stuart, *Three Years in North America*, 2:86.
33. MacDougall letter, *Times* (London), 25 May 1861; *Federal Republican* (Washington, D.C.), 9, 16 Sept. 1814; *American Watchman* (Wilmington, Del.), 10 Sept. 1814; *Poulson's American Daily Advertiser* (Philadelphia), 5 Sept. 1814; *National Register* (Washington, D.C.), 3 Aug. 1816.
34. General Orders, 16 May 1814, HL, WP1/439.
35. *Federal Republican* (Washington, D.C.), 9 Sept. 1814; *National Intelligencer* (Washington, D.C.), 1 Sept. 1814; Eshelman, *Travel Guide*, 52.
36. Pitch, *Burning of Washington*, 131. For the State Department occupying the same building as the War Department, see Office of the Historian, "Buildings of the Department of State: Public Buildings West of the White House, May 1801–August 1814," U.S. Department of State, http://history.state.gov/departmenthistory/buildings/section22.
37. Pitch, *Burning of Washington*, 131–32; *Times* (London), 4 Oct. 1814. A fanciful rumor was current for some time that General Ross hid $25,000 in the official residence of the commandant of the Marines Corps. Not surprisingly, the money has never been found. See *New Orleans Times-Picayune*, 7 Oct. 1934.
38. George, *Terror on the Chesapeake*, 110; Evans Memorandum, fol. 16.
39. J. Scott, *Recollections*, 313. One newspaper account called it a "dreadful hurricane." See *Federal Republican* (Washington, D.C.), 2 Sept. 1814.
40. Gleig, *Subaltern*, 85; J. Scott, *Recollections*, 313; Clark, "Abraham Young Mansion," 66. See also Lord, *Dawn's Early Light*, 182.
41. Ewell, *Medical Companion*, 649; Memorial of Capt. Nathaniel Cole, Royal Marines, 4 June 1815, ADM 1/3328; Clark, "Abraham Young Mansion," 67; *Connecticut Journal*, 5 Sept. 1814; J. Scott, *Recollections*, 312–13; Timpson Memoir.
42. Ewell, *Medical Companion*, 648, 649; Timpson Memoir; Return of the Wounded Left at Bladensburg and Washington, 5 Sept. 1814, WO 1/141. Capt. Nathaniel Cole recalled that he lost twenty of his men, killed or wounded, in the explosion. See Memorial of Capt. Nathaniel Cole, Royal Marines, 4 June 1815, ADM 1/3328.
43. *Niles' Weekly Register* (Baltimore), 10 Sept. 1814; Pitch, *Burning of Washington*, 115; Ewell, *Medical Companion*, 649, 650; Mahon, *War of 1812*, 128.
44. *National Intelligencer* (Washington, D.C.), 7 Sept. 1814; *Freeman's Journal* (Dublin), 4 Oct. 1814; Evans Memorandum, fol. 13.
45. Ewell, *Medical Companion*, 645; M. Smith, *First Forty Years of Washington Society*, 109.
46. *Poulson's American Daily Advertiser* (Philadelphia), 5 Sept. 1814.
47. Eshelman, Sheads, and Hickey, *War in the Chesapeake*, 220; Pitch, *Burning of Washington*, 142. To one newspaper in New York City, Lewis "was literally murdered by the British scoundrels." See *Shamrock* (New York), 24 Sept. 1814.
48. Ewell, *Medical Companion*, 646; Eshelman, Sheads, and Hickey, *War in the Chesapeake*, 21.

49. Stahl, *Invasion of the City of Washington*, 244; Evans Memorandum, fols. 13–14.
50. Cochrane to Hanchett, 26 Aug. 1814, NLS, Cochrane Papers, MS 2450, fol. 94. In the end a smaller vessel, HMS *Fairy*, was tasked with linking up with Gordon. See O'Neill, *To Annoy or Destroy the Enemy*, 114.
51. George, *Terror on the Chesapeake*, 113.
52. H. G. Smith, *Autobiography*, 1:203–204; *Freeman's Journal* (Dublin), 4 Oct. 1814; Dallas, *Exposition*, 103.
53. Eshelman and Sheads, *Chesapeake Legends and Lore*, 145, 146; Eshelman, "Washington City Myths during the War of 1812," n12.
54. Fabel, "Laws of War," 210–11; *United States Telegraph* (Washington, D.C.), 20 Oct. 1827.

Chapter 11

1. Cochrane later made an unsuccessful attempt to secure a "bounty" from the Prince Regent in compensation for the "booty" destroyed at Washington. See Memorial to the Prince Regent on Behalf of the Navy and Army Employed in the Operations against Washington in the United States of America, Aug. 1814, LC, Cochrane Papers, MS 2328, reel 2.
2. Dudley and Crawford, *Naval War of 1812*, 3:137–39; Vogel, *Perilous Fight*, 204.
3. H. G. Smith, *Autobiography*, 1:201; Dudley and Crawford, *Naval War of 1812*, 3:220–23; Gleig, *Narrative of the Campaigns*, 145–46; *National Intelligencer* (Washington, D.C.), 7 Sept. 1814.
4. Ewell, *Medical Companion*, 652; *Times* (London), 28 Sept. 1814. In part, this may have resulted from a mistaken belief that Barney was an Irishman. See J. Scott, *Recollections*, 329; and Weller, "Commodore Joshua Barney," 69, 93.
5. A native of Cork, the seventy-five-year-old Rodgers claimed that he was banished from his native land for wearing a "green-coloured coat" and sighing about "his dear native land." See Warden, *Chorographical and Statistical Description of the District of Columbia*, 27–28.
6. Ewell, *Medical Companion*, 652–54; V. Moore, "Reminiscences of Washington," 104.
7. H. G. Smith, *Autobiography*, 1:201; Gleig, *Narrative of the Campaigns*, 145–47.
8. Gleig, *Narrative of the Campaigns*, 148; Memorial of Assistant Surgeon Vallange, 8 Nov. 1814, WO 31/412; Callcott, *Mistress of Riversdale*, 17, 272, 282; *Examiner* (London), 5 Apr. 1840. The authors wish to thank Dr. Charles Brodine for this latter reference.
9. Gleig, *Narrative of the Campaigns*, 148; *Repertory* (Boston), 1 Sept. 1814; King, *Turning on the Light*, 341. Weller maintains that Ross "requested" Barney to take charge of the British prisoners, whereas Gleig, describing the commodore as an "officer of much gallantry and high sense of honour . . . , became without solicitation, the friend of his fellow-sufferers"—the British wounded at Bladensburg. Weller, "Commodore Joshua Barney," 148; Gleig, *Narrative of the Campaigns*, 144.

10. *Federal Republican* (Washington, D.C.), 2 Sept. 1814; *New York Evening Post*, 29 Aug. 1814. See similar sentiments in *New Hampshire Gazette* (Portsmouth), 30 Aug.1814.
11. Gleig, *Narrative of the Campaigns*,148; J. Scott, *Recollections*, 314, 325; Evans Memorandum, fol. 14; "Old Sub," 27; H. G. Smith, *Autobiography*, 1:202; Gleig, *Subaltern*, 92.
12. J. Scott, *Recollections*, 325; Gleig, *Narrative of the Campaigns*, 148–49; Ross to Bathurst, 1 Sept. 1814, WO 1/141. For 1/21st details, see Return of Noncommissioned Officers, Drummers, Fifers, and Private Men of the 1st Battalion, 21st Fusiliers, Who Have Died, Been Made Prisoner, or Transferred from 25 August to 24 September 1814, WO 25/1633. The 85th Regiment lists the men as taken prisoner on August 26. See Return of Noncommissioned Officers, Drummers, Fifers, and Private Men of the 85th Regiment of Light Infantry Who Have Died, Deserted, etc., from 25 August to 24 September 1814, WO 25/2078.
13. Return of Noncommissioned Officers, Drummers, Fifers, and Privates of the 1st Battalion, 44th Regiment of Foot, Whose Death, Desertion, etc., Has Been Ascertained from 25 August to 24 September 1814, WO 25/1788; Return of Noncommissioned Officers, Drummers, Fifers, and Privates of the 4th Regiment of Foot, 1st Battalion, Whose Death, Desertion, etc., Has Been Ascertained . . . from 25 July to 24 September 1814, WO 25/1522. Another army record indicates that 111 men "fell out on the march and have not since joined." These included 11 members of the 1/4th, 17 men from the 85th, 24 members of the 1/44th, and 50 men from the 1/21st. See Return of the Wounded Left at Bladensburg and Washington Whose Wounds Prevented Removal, also of the Men Who Fell Out on the March and Have Not Since Joined, 5 Sept. 1814, WO 1/141.
14. H. G. Smith, *Autobiography*, 1:206; Dudley and Crawford, *Naval War of 1812*, 3:220–23; *Morning Chronicle* (London), 1 Oct. 1814; J. Scott, *Recollections*, 325; Torrens to Cochrane, 30 Sept. 1814, WO 3/608; *Poulson's American Daily Advertiser* (Philadelphia), 26 Aug. 1814; *Repertory* (Boston), 1 Sept. 1814; *Albany (N.Y.) Register*, 29 Aug. 1814. See also *Centinel of Freedom* (Newark, N.J.), 30 Aug. 1814.
15. Evans Memorandum, fol. 14; Gleig, *Narrative of the Campaigns*, 149; "Old Sub," 27; Cochrane to Bathurst, 2 Sept. 1814, WO 1/141; Memorial of Joseph Gray, 4 July 1815, WO 1/661; Evans to Torrens, 26 July 1815, WO 1/661.
16. Chesterton, *Peace, War, and Adventure*, 1:131; Shomette, *Flotilla*, 333.
17. George, *Terror on the Chesapeake*, 112; E. Taylor, *Slave in the White House*, 50; *New Bedford (Mass.) Mercury*, 9 Sept. 1814; Eshelman and Kummerow, *In Full Glory Reflected*, 205; Monroe, *Writings*, 5:304; Gordon to Lord Commissioners of the Admiralty, n.d., LC, Cochrane Papers, MS 2326, reel 1.
18. Shomette, *Flotilla*, 332.
19. Ibid., 331–35; Evans Memorandum, fol. 14; Gleig, *Narrative of the Campaigns*, 115–16.

20. Marine, *British Invasion of Maryland*, 190; Vogel, *Perilous Fight*, 263.
21. Vogel, *Perilous Fight*, 22; Marine, *British Invasion of Maryland*, 190; Mason to Skinner and Key, 2 Sept. 1814, NARA, Area File of the Naval Collection, 1775–1910, M625; Eshelman and Kummerow, *In Full Glory Reflected*, 91; *Baltimore Sun*, 25 July 1890 (the authors are grateful to Donald G. Shomette for this reference); Ross to Mason, 7 Sept. 1814, NARA, Area File of the Naval Collection, 1775–1910, M625.
22. *National Advocate* (New York), 5 Sept. 1814; *Federal Republican* (Washington, D.C.), 28 Sept. 1814.
23. Gleig, *Subaltern*, 94–95; Evans Memorandum, fol. 14; Gleig, *Narrative of the Campaigns*, 151; Rowley, "Captain Rowley Helps to Burn Washington," 249.
24. *Middlesex Gazette* (Middletown, Conn.), 28 Aug. 1814; Clay, *Papers*, 1:988–89. See also Freymann, "View of the War," 503.
25. Shomette, *Flotilla*, 337. See also M. Smith, *First Forty Years of Washington Society*, 114.
26. *Belfast Newsletter*, 11 Oct. 1814; *Virginia Argus* (Richmond), 10 Sept. 1814.
27. Evans Memorandum, fol. 14; Ross to Mrs. Ross, 1 Sept. 1814, PRONI, D2004/1A/3/8; North American Station, Letters from Codrington, 31 Aug., 20 Sept. 1814, NMM, COD/7/1.
28. Ross to Mrs. Ross, 1 Sept. 1814, PRONI, D2004/1A/3/8.
29. Ibid.
30. Ross to Maria Ross, 2 Sept. 1814, ibid., D2004/1A/3/9.
31. Malcolm to a friend, 1 Sept. 1814, MP; Gubbins to Stannix, 31 Aug. 1814, WO 31/407; *National Intelligencer* (Washington, D.C.), 4 June 1849; Torrens to Ross, 30 Sept. 1814, WO 3/608.
32. Gubbins to Stannix, 31 Aug. 1814, WO 31/407; Lingel, "Manuscript Autobiography of Gordon Gallie Macdonald"; Evans Memorandum, fol. 18; Cochrane to Bathurst, 2 Sept. 1814, WO 1/141; *Niles' Weekly Register* (Baltimore), 14 Jan. 1815. In this same edition Niles also noted, "Admiral Cochrane, disappointed of dining in Baltimore, is reported to have said he would eat his Christmas dinner at New Orleans."
33. Ross himself had already targeted Baltimore before he left the American capital and before he received his wife's letters. The British commander would have empathized with the maxim governing American military operations: "the hotter the war the quicker the peace." See Eshelman and Kummerow, *In Full Glory Reflected*, 20.
34. Eshelman, Sheads, and Hickey, *War in the Chesapeake*, 54; Torrens to Sherbrooke, 1 Oct. 1814, WO 3/608.
35. Rowley, "Captain Rowley Helps to Burn Washington," 249.
36. Dudley and Crawford, *Naval War of 1812*, 3:271; Cochrane to Cockburn, 5 Sept. 1814, NLS, Cochrane Papers, MS 2450; J. Scott, *Recollections*, 331; North American Station, Letters from Codrington, 5 Mar. 1815, NMM, COD/7/1.
37. Evans Memorandum, fol. 19. Citing this document, Mahon averred some time ago that "General Ross seems to have originated the move

upon Baltimore." He did not explore this assertion. Mahon, "British Command Decisions," 56n8.
38. Codrington, *Memoir*, 320; Shomette, *Flotilla*, 336; Evans Memorandum, fol. 19; O'Neill, "To Annoy or Destroy the Enemy," 233–46; North American Station, Letters from Codrington, 10 Sept. 1814, NMM, COD/7/1. The *Royal Oak* on 8 September 1814 was "working into the Potomac." Log Book, HMS *Royal Oak*, 8 Sept. 1814, MP.
39. Dudley and Crawford, *Naval War of 1812*, 3:269–70, 289–91.
40. *Connecticut Journal*, 29 Aug. 1814; *Repertory* (Boston), 30 Aug. 1814; *Portsmouth (N.H.) Oracle*, 3 Sept. 1814.
41. *New York Evening Post*, 29 Aug. 1814; Porter to Jones, two letters dated 27 Aug. 1814, NARA, Area File of the Naval Collection, 1775–1910, M625; *National Intelligencer* (Washington, D.C.), 1 Oct. 1839; Balch, "Reminiscences of the War of 1812," 283–84; Extract from *Baltimore Patriot* in *Palladium of Liberty* (Morristown, N.J.), 1 Sept. 1814.
42. Piper, "Defence of Baltimore," 375–84.

Chapter 12

1. George, *Terror on the Chesapeake*, 137; Vogel, *Perilous Fight*, 287; Gleig, *Subaltern*, 113–14. For an American account that includes similar details, see *Baltimore Sun*, 8 Sept. 1907.
2. Cassell, "Baltimore in 1813," 359.
3. Brooke Diary; Gleig, *Narrative of the Campaigns*, 174; George, *Terror on the Chesapeake*, 137–38.
4. Gleig, *Subaltern*, 115–16; D. Brown, *Diary of a Soldier*, 78; Humble Petition of Francis Fitzgerald MacNamara to the Privy Council, [1 July 1820], PC 1/4185.
5. *National Intelligencer* (Washington, D.C.), 1 Oct. 1839; George, *Terror on the Chesapeake*, 135–37; Lossing, *Pictorial Field Book*, 950–54; *Niles' Weekly Register* (Baltimore), supplement, 7:158.
6. *Niles' Weekly Register* (Baltimore), supplement, 7:136; Stevenson to the Committee of Vigilance and Safety, 12 Sept. 1814, Baltimore City Archives, Record Group 22, War of 1812 Records, MSA-SC5458-45-20-0720; George, *Terror on the Chesapeake*, 136, 192 n35.
7. Evans Memorandum, fol. 20; Marine, *British Invasion of Maryland*, 162; George, *Terror on the Chesapeake*, 137.
8. Brooke Diary; Evans Memorandum, fol. 20.
9. Gleig, *Subaltern*, 119–20; Whitehorne, *Battle for Baltimore*, 179; *Baltimore Sun*, 8 Sept. 1907.
10. Hickey, *Don't Give Up the Ship*, 84–85; *Niles' Weekly Register* (Baltimore), 24 Sept. 1814. Captain Howard of the Mechanical Volunteers repeated the statement on the occasion of the erection of the monument to Aquila Randall in 1817. See *Niles' Weekly Register* (Baltimore), 2 Aug. 1817.
11. Rees, *Wanderer*, 27, 99n7; Scharf, *History of Baltimore City and County*, 311. Mary Bagot, wife of Charles Bagot, who was appointed British minister plenipotentiary and envoy extraordinaire to the United

States in July 1815, recalled staying at Gadsby's in Baltimore. See Hosford, "Exile in Yankee Land," 39.

12. Hickey, *Don't Give Up the Ship*, 85. Other uncomplimentary comments about the American militia attributed to Ross include calling them "ragamuffins" and that he considered a contest with them "like playing Guineas against half pence." *Arkansas Weekly Gazette* (Little Rock), 29 May 1847. To Maj. Gen. Samuel Smith is credited a remark that American militia fighting against British regulars was like "staking dollars against cents." See Hickey, *War of 1812*, 211.

13. *Courier* (London), 28 Sept. 1814; *Federal Republican* (Washington, D.C.), 28 July 1815; *National Intelligencer* (Washington, D.C.), 26 July 1815; U.S. Congress, *Senate Journal*, 204.

14. Gleig, *Narrative of the Campaigns*, 176; Marine, *British Invasion of Maryland*, 162–63; *Baltimore Patriot*, 2 Dec. 1821; George, *Terror on the Chesapeake*, 137.

15. Hitsman and Graves, *Incredible War of 1812*, 96–99.

16. Sir George Cockburn, "Memoir of Services," NMM, COC/11, fols. 141–42; J. Scott, *Recollections*, 333–34; Evans, *Facts Relating to the Capture of Washington*, 12–13; *American Turf Register and Sporting Magazine* (Baltimore), June 1833, 528–31; *National Intelligencer* (Washington, D.C.), 1 Oct. 1839; Hawkins, *Life of John H. W. Hawkins*, 8–9; *Caledonian Mercury* (Edinburgh), 29 Oct. 1814; *Bristol Mirror* (England), 22 Oct. 1814; *Morning Post* (London), 18 Oct. 1814. In a letter that he sent to Ross's mother-in-law, Crofton included a "piece of hair cut from the honored head" of the departed general. Crofton to Mrs. Glascock, 7 Aug. 1815, PRONI, D2004/1/4/16.

17. Sir George Cockburn, "Memoir of Services," NMM, COC/11, fols. 141–42.

18. Evans, *Facts Relating to the Capture of Washington*, 16–17; "Old Sub," 31; Gleig, *Subaltern*, 116–20; D. Brown, "Diary of a Soldier," 78; Humble Petition of Francis Fitzgerald MacNamara to the Privy Council, [1 July 1820], PC 1/4185; Timpson Memoir; *American Turf Register and Sporting Magazine* (Baltimore), June 1833, 528–31; *National Intelligencer* (Washington, D.C.), 1 Oct. 1839; Hawkins, *Life of John H. W. Hawkins*, 8–9; Dudley and Crawford, *Naval War of 1812*, 3:289. Colonel Brooke remarked that Ross's "only fault, if it may be deemed so, was an excess of gallantry, enterprise and devotion to the service." *London Gazette*, 17 Nov. 1814.

19. In the middle of April, during a sortie near Toulouse, Sir John Hope was wounded and taken prisoner by the French—fulfilling Wellington's "prediction" of three months earlier that if he "persisted in managing the front skirmishing line he would get shot." Oman, *Peninsular War*, 7:510.

20. *Cobbett's Weekly Political Register* (London), 29 Oct. 1814; *North Wales Chronicle*, 3 Nov. 1840; *Niles' Weekly Register* (Baltimore), 27 Oct. 1814; *National Intelligencer* (Washington, D.C.), 1 Oct. 1839. According to a British newspaper report some years later, Ross "fell

by the hand of a boy of eleven years of age." See *Northern Liberator* (Newcastle-Upon-Tyne), 8 June 1838.
21. *National Intelligencer* (Washington, D.C.), 1 Oct. 1839; Vogel, *Perilous Fight*, 304.
22. George, "Who Killed Robert Ross"; *American and Commercial Daily Advertiser* (Baltimore), 13 Sept. 1851; *New York Herald Tribune*, 4 Sept. 1889. William Marine lists a Corporal Hulse in Aisquith's Rifle Company. Marine, *British Invasion of Maryland*, 331.
23. Scott S. Sheads, "Death of Ross File"; "Old Sub," 31.; [Surgeon Alexander Baxter], "Account of the death of General Ross, killed in the Action near Baltimore on the 12th of September, 1814," 17 Sept. 1814. MHSL, MS 1846, Vertical File. Oral tradition in his native Rostrevor reckons that the father of the man who killed General Ross is buried in a local graveyard, i.e., McComas. A family of that name was reported to be from Water Street in the village. Meantime, a correspondent writing from Rostrevor at the time reported that "it is asserted here, that the rifleman, who ejected the ball, that stuck in the General's spine, is no other than Paddy Cassidy," a former United Irishman rebel. Farrell O'Shea to Mr. Cox, 30 Oct. 1814, *Irish Magazine*, Nov. 1814, 516–17.
24. [Baxter], "Account of the death of General Ross"; George, "Family Papers of Maj. Gen. Robert Ross, Diary of Col. Brooke," 313; Chartrand, "Account of the Capture of Washington," 182; Brooke Diary; *Times* (London), 18 Oct. 1814; *Morning Post* (London), 18 Oct. 1814; *Freeman's Journal* (Dublin), 21 Oct. 1814; *Bristol Mirror* (England), 22 Oct. 1814. Another account indicates that Ross struggled to communicate with Colonel Brooke and Rear Admiral Cockburn. See *Caledonian Mercury* (Edinburgh), 29 Oct. 1814.
25. Brooke "Diary"; Dudley and Crawford, *Naval War of 1812*, 3:282–85; George, "Family Papers of Maj. Gen. Robert Ross, Diary of Col. Brooke," 313; *Baltimore Patriot*, 29 May 1849. Vice Pres. Elbridge Gerry wrote at the time that Ross "delivered his watch and some jewels to a brother officer, and charged him to deliver them with his own hands to Mrs. Ross." Austin, "Letters of Elbridge Gerry," 511. According to Crofton, Ross's "last words were Oh! my beloved wife and family." Crofton to Mrs. Glascock, 7 Aug. 1815, PRONI, D2004/1/4/16.
26. *Examiner* (London), 9 Dec. 1832; Dudley and Crawford, *Naval War of 1812*, 3:277; Memoir of Capt. Peter Bowlby, 4th (or The King's Own) Regiment of Foot, NAM, 2002-02-729; Spiers, *Radical General*, 146.
27. *Rhode Island American* (Providence), 14 Feb. 1815; Freymann, "View of the War," 509; De Bathe to Torrens, 16 Sept. 1814, WO 31/407. Captain De Bathe was wounded at the Battle of North Point. *Belfast Monthly Magazine*, 38:374.
28. Dudley and Crawford, *Naval War of 1812*, 3:287; Evans Memorandum, fol. 21; *Caledonian Mercury* (Edinburgh), 29 Oct. 1814; Gleig, *Narrative of the Campaigns*, 178. See also Gleig, "Diary," in C. Barrett, *85th King's Light Infantry*, 168–69; and Corbett, "Campaigns."
29. Lingel, "Autobiography of Gordon Gallie Macdonald."

30. Lossing, *Pictorial Field Book*, 963–64; Lord, *Dawn's Early Light*, 263; *Baltimore Sun*, 8 Sept. 1907. Other evidence indicates that the cart belonged to the Trotten family. See Eshelman and Sheads, *Chesapeake Legends and Lore*, 91–92.
31. *Baltimore Patriot*, 29 May 1849.
32. *Baltimore Sun*, 8 Sept. 1907; Lambert to Cochrane, *18 Feb. 1815*, ADM 1/509; Brooke to Cochrane, *1 Dec. 1815*, LC, Cochrane Papers, MS 2329; Log Book, HMS *Royal Oak*, 13 Sept. 1814, ADM 51/2760. The authors are grateful to Scott S. Sheads for the log-book reference.
33. J. Scott, *Recollections*, 340; George, *Terror on the Chesapeake*, 145.
34. Freymann, "View of the War," 510; *Eastport (Mass.) Sentinel*, 13 Oct. 1827; Evans Memorandum, fol. 24.
35. Evans Memorandum, fols. 24–25; Eshelman and Kummerow, *In Full Glory Reflected*, 146; Capt. Henry Thompson journal, Sept.–Oct. 1814, MHSL, MS 820; Thompson to the Baltimore Committee of Vigilance and Safety, 4 Oct. 1814, Baltimore City Archives, Record Group 22, War of 1812 Records, MSA-SC5458-45-20-0787.
36. Pitch, *Burning of Washington*, 194, 203; J. Scott, *Recollections*, 344–45; Lord, *Dawn's Early Light*, 271; Evans Memorandum, fol. 25.
37. Evans Memorandum, fol. 25; Malcolm to Mrs. Malcolm, 9 Oct. 1814, MP.
38. Malcolm to Mrs. Malcolm, 2 Oct. 1814, MP. See chap. 13.
39. R. Barrett, "Naval Recollections," 465.
40. Codrington, *Memoir*, 320.
41. Malcolm to Mrs. Malcolm, 9 Oct. 1814, MP; R. Barrett, "Naval Recollections," 464; Chesterton, *Peace, War, and Adventure*, 1:158.
42. *National Intelligencer* (Washington, D.C.), 1 Oct. 1839; Chesterton, *Peace, War, and Adventure*, 1:145. Ross researcher Kevin Chambers argues that Ross would have been aware that the landing at North Point occurred fifty-five years to the very day when Maj. Gen. James Wolfe, like Ross a former commander of the 20th Regiment, launched his successful assault on Quebec, which began with a nighttime operation on 12 September 1759. Wolfe was killed the following day. Conlin, *American Past*, 110.
43. Lovell, *Personal Narrative*, 164; Evans Memorandum, fol. 28; "Old Sub," 32–33.
44. Freymann, "View of the War," 511; Senator Goldsborough to his wife, 21 Sept. 1814, Goldsborough, "Contemporary Report of the Battle of Baltimore," 230–32; Balch, "Reminiscences of the War of 1812," 283–84; Duncan, *Travels*, 1:228; Gleig, *Narrative of the Campaigns*, 190; *Bristol Mirror* (England), 22 Oct. 1814.
45. Ross's body was transferred from the *Royal Oak* to the *Tonnant* on 19 September. See Log Book, HMS *Royal Oak*, 19 Sept. 1814, MP.
46. Codrington, *Memoir*, 321. In contrast, the bodies of Generals Pakenham and Gibbs, who were both killed at New Orleans, were repatriated. See Pakenham, *Soldier, Sailor*, 133.

47. Senn, *Haligonians*, 115. Rum is sometimes referred to as "Nelson's blood," owing to the fact that sailors drank from that admiral's funeral cask.
48. *Baltimore Sun*, 23 Oct. 2011; Erik Zygmont, " A Battle Worth Re-Fighting at Least Three Times," 4 Sept. 2013, Baltimore Guide, http://baltimoreguide.com/a-battle-worth-re-fighting-at-least-three-times/; North American Station, Letters from Codrington, 28 Sept. 1814, NMM, COD/7/1.
49. D. L. Graves, *Midst of Alarms*, 360; Jason Ridler, "Sir John Coape Sherbrooke," 28 Feb. 2011 (edited 4 Mar. 2015), Canadian Encyclopedia, http://www.thecanadianencyclopedia.com/articles/sir-john-coape-sherbrooke; Parker, *Fortress Halifax*, 150. Conveying the grim news of Ross's death to Governor General Prevost, Sherbrooke noted that the expenses of the funeral were to be borne by the public purse. Sherbrooke to Prevost, 1 Oct. 1814, Library and Archives Canada, RG-8, C-231, fols. 165–66, microform c.2844 (viewed online).

Chapter 13

1. *Federal Republican* (Washington, D.C.), 30 Aug. 1814; *Newburyport (Mass.) Herald and Country Gazette*, 5 Sept. 1814. *Cobbett's Weekly Political Register* (London), 10 Sept. 1814.
2. H. G. Smith, *Autobiography*, 1:209–11; *Times* (London), 27, 28 Sept. 1814.
3. H. G. Smith, *Autobiography*, 1:213; *Niles' Weekly Register* (Baltimore), 31 Dec. 1814. See also Brooks and Hohwald, *How America Fought Its Wars*, 198.
4. Bickham, *Weight of Vengeance*, 167; *Courier* quotation cited in Lord, *Dawn's Early Light*, 302. This sentiment was repeated in *Trewman's Exeter Flying Post or Plymouth and Cornish Advertiser* (England), 29 Sept. 1814.
5. Lord, *Dawn's Early Light*, 307; Perkins, *Castlereagh and Adams*, 94, 135.
6. Lord, *Dawn's Early Light*, 302–303; *Morning Chronicle* (London), 28 Sept. 1814; *Times* (London), 28 Sept. 1814.
7. *Caledonian Mercury* (Edinburgh), 1, 31 Oct. 1814; *Niles' Weekly Register* (Baltimore), 3 Dec. 1814; *Cobbett's Weekly Political Register* (London), 12 Nov. 1814.
8. *Montreal Herald*, 3 Sept. 1814; McEvansoneya, "Racism/Ethnography," 26.
9. Clippings, GWU, Gelman Library, Special Collections, Ross Papers, Box 1:14; Farrell O'Shea to Mr. Cox, 30 Oct. 1814, *Irish Magazine*, Nov. 1814, 516–17; *Northern Post* (Salem, N.Y.), 12 Jan. 1815; *Morning Chronicle* (London), 3 Oct. 1814; *Belfast Newsletter*, 15 Nov. 1814.
10. *Leeds Mercury*, 1 Oct. 1814; *Liverpool Mercury*, 7 Oct. 1814. Bickham, *Weight of Vengeance*, 204; "Mr. Vansittart's Speech on the Burning of Washington," *Irish Magazine*, Dec. 1814, 536–37. The *Belfast Monthly Magazine* was no less sparing. See *Belfast Monthly Magazine*, Oct. 1814.

11. Wellington, *Supplementary Dispatches*, 9:290–91, 292; *Examiner* (London), 16 Oct. 1814; *Bury and Norwich Post; Or, Suffolk, Norfolk, Essex, Cambridge, and Ely Advertiser* (England), 19 Oct. 1814; *Baltimore Patriot*, 9 Feb. 1815. On the day Wellington received news of the capture of Washington in Paris, a crowd gathered at his hotel and hissed. See *Morning Chronicle* (London), 7 Nov. 1814.
12. A. L. Latour, *Historical Memoir of the War in West Florida and Louisiana in 1814–15* (Philadelphia: John Conrad, 1816), xvi; Perkins, *Castlereagh and Adams*, 95; Dangerfield, *Era of Good Feelings*, 72.
13. Liverpool to Cochrane, 28 Sept. 1814, NLS, Cochrane Papers, MS 2574, fols. 175–76. The Duke of York, commander in chief, passed on his congratulations too. See Torrens to Cochrane, 30 Sept. 1814, WO 3/608.
14. Bathurst to Ross, 10 Aug. 1814, WO 6/2; Bunbury to Torrens, 26 Aug. 1814, WO 6/136; Bathurst to Ross, 10, 13 Sept. 1814, WO 6/2. For the deployment of the 1/40th, see Expedition to the Southern Coast of the United States, Miscellaneous, 6 Sept. 1814, WO 1/142.
15. Expedition to the Southern Coast of the United States, Miscellaneous, 6 Sept. 1814, WO 1/142; Bathurst to Lambert, 5 Oct. 1814, WO 6/2; Bathurst to Ross, 29 Sept. 1814, ibid.; Torrens to Duke of York, 27 Sept. 1814, WO 3/608; Torrens to Bathurst, 28 Nov. 1814, ibid.
16. Torrens to Ross, 30 Sept. 1814, WO 3/608; [Miss Ross-of-Bladensburg], *Newry Reporter*, 25 Feb. 1936; Will of Elizabeth Catherine Ross, Widow, of Carraigh Bhan, Rosstrevor, 4 Aug. 1845, PROB 11/2023/109. Cockburn's knighthood was made public in January 1815. R. Morriss, *Cockburn*, 120; *European Magazine and London Review*, 67:164–65.
17. Elbridge Gerry to his wife, 19 Oct. 1814, in Austin, "Letters of Elbridge Gerry," 511; "Attack on Baltimore, Maryland," *Irish Magazine*, Nov. 1814, 523.
18. H. G. Smith, *Autobiography*, 1:217; *Lancaster Gazette*, 22 Oct. 1814; Dangerfield, *Era of Good Feelings*, 76; A. Taylor, *Civil War of 1812*, 401; Jason Ridler, "Sir Gordon Drummond," 28 Feb. 2011 (updated 4 Mar. 2015), Canadian Encyclopedia, http://www.thecanadianencyclopedia.com/articles/sir-gordon-drummond.
19. Clippings, GWU, Gelman Library, Special Collections, Ross Papers, Box 1:14. In the nearby town of Newry, which Ross's ancestors represented in the Irish parliament, the local journal "sincerely regretted and deplored" his death. "Description of Rosstrevor," *Newry Magazine* (1815): 108.
20. *Hampshire Telegraph and Sussex Chronicle* (England), 31 Oct. 1814; *Times* (London), 18 Oct. 1814. See also *Bristol Mirror* (England), 22 Oct. 1814.
21. *London Gazette Extraordinary*, 17 Oct. 1814; *Quebec Gazette*, 27 Oct. 1814; Bathurst to Brooke, 3 Nov. 1813, WO 6/2; Wellington, *Supplementary Despatches*, 9:367; Zuehlke, *For Honour's Sake*, 350. For a modern account of Prevost's campaign in New York, see Fitz-Enz, *Final Invasion*.

22. Perkins, *Castlereagh and Adams*, 102; Torrens to the Duke of York, 17 Oct. 1814, WO 3/608; *London Gazette Extraordinary*, 17 Oct. 1814. After proceeding to the Gulf of Mexico, plans were for Pakenham to go to the Chesapeake the following April. See Historical Manuscripts, Commission, *Report on the Manuscripts of Earl Bathurst*, 300.
23. Wellington, *Supplementary Despatches*, 9:367.
24. Torrens to the Duke of York, 17 Oct. 1814, WO 3/608; *Morning Post* (London), 18 Nov. 1814; Wellington, *Supplementary Despatches*, 9:403–404; Melville to Cochrane, 25 Oct. 1814, NLS, Cochrane Papers, MS 2574, fols. 203–204; Latimer, *1812*, 360; *Morning Post* (London), 18 Nov. 1814; Hickey, *Don't Give Up the Ship*, 140; D. E. Graves, *Where Right and Glory Lead*, 233; D. E. Graves, foreword to Grodzinski, *Defender of Canada*, x.
25. Perkins, *Castlereagh and Adams*, 108–109; Dangerfield, *Era of Good Feelings*, 77, 79; Jenkins, *Henry Goulburn*, 87.
26. *Times* (London), 4 Nov. 1814. A "council" was held at the Foreign Office "when the subject of the speech for the opening of Parliament was taken into consideration." For a detailed account of the proceedings in Parliament, see D. E. Graves, "Why the White House Was Burned."
27. Dangerfield, *Era of Good Feelings*, 73. The prime minister informed Parliament that he sent instructions to Vice Admiral Cochrane with a view to preventing further acts of British retaliation. The chancellor of the exchequer clarified this statement by explaining that Cochrane was "to abstain from further inflictions, unless rendered necessary by fresh enormities." See Hansard, *Parliamentary Debates*, 29:24, 180–83.
28. Dangerfield, *Era of Good Feelings*, 73; Hansard, *Parliamentary Debates*, 29:1–4; *Cobbett's Weekly Political Register* (London) 12 Nov. 1814; Lord, *Dawn's Early Light*, 302–303.
29. Hansard, *Parliamentary Debates*, 29:16, 46–47. Bickham notes that "Members of Parliament regularly cited extracts from American newspapers in debates." Bickham, *Weight of Vengeance*, 15.
30. Perkins, *Castlereagh and Adams*, 99. After decades of conflict, war weariness—not least with the financial cost—had set in. See D. E. Graves, "Why the White House Was Burned," 1119.
31. Hansard, *Parliamentary Debates*, 29:183–84, 186; I. Jennings, *Party Politics*, 78; Whitshed Keene obituary, *Gentleman's Magazine* (London), 92, pt. 1 (1822): 278. William Cobbett, the pro-American radical newspaper editor, later accused the editor of the *Morning Chronicle*, the leading Whig opposition newspaper, of being influenced by the fact that Ross was "his countryman" when describing the raid on Washington as the "most brilliant dash of the whole war." *Cobbett's Weekly Political Register* (London), 2 Sept. 1815.
32. Wellington, *Supplementary Despatches*, 9:513–14; Hansard, *Parliamentary Debates*, 29:24.
33. Perkins, *Castlereagh and Adams*, 95; Jenkins, *Henry Goulburn*, 86–87. Dangerfield argues that the acceptance of this ultimatum was qualified. The British also "made some menacing comments upon the illegality

of the Louisiana Purchase and the avarice and oppression of the United States in its acquisition of territory in Florida." Dangerfield, *Era of Good Feelings*, 74–75.

34. *National Advocate* (New York), 5 Sept. 1814; Wellington, *Supplementary Despatches*, 9:366.
35. Jenkins, *Henry Goulburn*, 87.
36. D. E. Graves, *Where Right and Glory Lead*, 225; Dangerfield, *Era of Good Feelings*, 82–83; Eshelman and Kummerow, *In Full Glory Reflected*, xi. On how the war endangered the existence of the United States, see Buel, *America on the Brink*.
37. Dangerfield, *Era of Good Feelings*, 76; H. Adams, *History*, 2:212, 221–22; U.S. Congress, *House Journal*, 311–22, 341–92.
38. Pasley, *"Tyranny of Printers"*; Lord, *Dawn's Early Light*, 315; *Baltimore Patriot*, 26 Aug. 1814. For similar remarks, see *Shamrock* (New York), 10 Sept. 1814.
39. *New Hampshire Patriot* (Concord), 6 Sept. 1814; *National Advocate* (New York), 5, 10 Sept. 1814.
40. *Richmond (Va.) Enquirer*, 31 Aug. 1814; Lord, *Dawn's Early Light*, 219; Stagg, *Mr. Madison's War*, 436. See also Bickham, *Weight of Vengeance*, 167.
41. *Delaware Gazette* (Wilmington), 1 Sept. 1814; *Connecticut Journal*, 5 Sept. 1814; *Federal Republican* (Washington, D.C.), 2 Sept. 1814; *Washingtonian* (Washington, D.C.), 5 Sept. 1814.
42. *Delaware Gazette* (Wilmington), 29 Aug. 1814; *Vermont Mirror* (Middlebury), 31 Aug. 1814; *Repertory* (Boston), 3 Sept. 1814; *Portsmouth (N.H.) Oracle*, 3 Sept. 1814. As far as one Pennsylvania paper was concerned, "the *nation* is not yet at war:—it is only a *party* which is at war." *Gleaner* (Wilkes-Barre, Pa.), 5 Sept. 1814.
43. *Boston Spectator*, 3, 10 Sept. 1814; *Federal Republican* (Washington, D.C.), 2 Sept. 1814.
44. Stagg, *Mr. Madison's War*, 432, 436; *Engine of Liberty and Union Town (Md.) Advertiser*, 8 Dec. 1814.
45. Don Hickey notes the failure of "bipartisanship" in response to the "crisis." See Hickey, *War of 1812*, 244–45.
46. U.S. Congress, *House Journal*, 710, 720–32, 743, 790, 797, 798, 904; U.S. Congress, *Senate Journal*, 58, 78, 205.
47. H. Adams, *History*, 2:280, 289, 307; Bickham, *Weight of Vengeance*, 167.
48. C. P. Stacey, "An American Plan for a Canadian Campaign: Secretary James Monroe to Major-General Jacob Brown, Feb. 1815," *American Historical Review* 46 (1940–41): 348–58; Austin, "Letters of Elbridge Gerry," 521; Perry to Benjamin Homans, acting secretary of the navy, 25 Dec. 1814, NARA, Captains Letters, 1805–61, M125.
49. Freneau, *Collection of Poems*, 68–72. The authors are grateful to Dr. Donald Kennon of the U.S. Capitol Historical Society for this reference.
50. Porter, *Memoir*, 261; *Niles' Weekly Register* (Baltimore), 29 Oct., 5 Nov. 1814. The *True Blooded Yankee* "took an island on the coast of Ireland, and held it for six days." Ibid., 26 Mar. 1814.

51. Bailey, *Records of Patriotism*, 194; Stuart, *Three Years in North America*, 2:86–87. The house reportedly being targeted in Rostrevor was one that Ross grew up in, though by this stage it belonged to his brother.
52. *Belfast Newsletter*, 18 Oct. 1814. In 1776 an American privateer anchored in the "harbour of Newry [Warrenpoint—within sight of Rostrevor] and demanded provisions, for which payment was offered." It was also noted that the American privateer that "put into Newry . . . shipped a number of hands there, and that the Irish are generally in favour of the Americans, except a few placemen." O'Brien, *Hidden Phase of American History*, 67.
53. Arthur, *How Britain Won the War of 1812*; Lambert, *Challenge*; Perry to Benjamin Homans, acting secretary of the navy, 25 Dec. 1814, NARA, Captains Letters, 1805–61, M125.

Epilogue

1. Gleig, *Narrative of the Campaigns*, 152.
2. *Morning Post* (London), 20 Oct. 1814; *Derby Mercury* (England), 27 Oct. 1814; *Lancaster Gazette*, 29 Oct. 1814. See also "On the Death of General Ross, at the Battle of Baltimore," *European Magazine, and London Review*, 66:339–40; *Morning Post* (London), 28 Oct. 1814 (also published in *Belfast Newsletter*, 29 Oct. 1814); Steele, *Eva*, 89–93; and Clippings, GWU, Gelman Library, Special Collections, Ross Papers, Box 1:18.
3. Steele, *Eva*, 89–93. See also *Morning Post* (London), 21 Oct. 1814; and *Hampshire Telegraph and Sussex Chronicle* (England), 31 Oct. 1814.
4. *Morning Post* (London), 21 Oct. 1814; *Derby Mercury* (England), 8 Dec. 1814; Allston, *Correspondence*, 84.
5. Maguire, "Major General Ross," 128. When Ross died, his assets were valued at £7,500. Ross family correspondence, 13 Feb. 1871, PRONI, D2004/6/144.
6. D. L. Graves, *Midst of Alarms*, 407; Maguire, "Major General Ross," 128. John Stagg describes Ross as "Sir Robert." Stagg, *War of 1812*, 128.
7. Extract from *London Gazette* in *Morning Chronicle* (London), 18 Sept. 1815.
8. Turner, *Astonishing General*, 9–10, 29–30. For Brock's heroic reputation in Britain at the time, see also Bickham, *Weight of Vengeance*, 137.
9. Forester, *Naval War of 1812*, 201; Hitsman and Graves, *Incredible War of 1812*, 262–63, 267. For the battle experience of these officers, see Grodzinski, *Defender of Canada*, 161–62; and Turner, *British Generals of the War of 1812*, 115.
10. H. G. Smith, *Autobiography*, 1:207–208.
11. Brooke to Bathurst, 12 July 1816, WO 1/144; Brooke to Bathurst, 17 Sept. 1816, WO 1/676. In 1848 a bar added to a naval medal was granted to 107 survivors of Captain Gordon's expedition up the Potomac. O'Neill, *To Annoy or Destroy the Enemy*, 307.
12. Brooke to Bathurst, 17 Sept. 1816, WO 1/676; Hitsman and Graves, *Incredible War of 1812*, 312; *John Bull* (London), 28 Jan. 1854; *Lady's*

Newspaper (London), 4 Nov. 1854. Bladensburg was to feature on the regimental color of the 1/44th. Carter, *Historical Record of the Forty-Fourth*, 56.
13. W. Scott, *Memoirs*, 162–63, 164–67.
14. *Morning Chronicle* (London), 20, 21 Nov. 1821; G. Smyth, *Worthies of England*, 6; Holger Hoock, *Empires of the Imagination: Politics, War, and the Arts in the British World, 1750–1850* (London: Profile Books, 2010), 151, 182; Officers of the 20th Regiment to Christopher Moore, 13 Oct. 1814, PRONI, D2004/1A/4/11; B. Smyth, *Lancashire Fusiliers*, 1:274; *American Beacon* (Norfolk, Va.), 31 Oct. 1815; Meeting of the Inhabitants of Newry, [post-12 Sept. 1814], PRONI, D61/c12/141; Clippings, GWU, Gelman Library, Special Collections, Ross Papers, Box 1:17; "General Ross's Monument," 400; List of Subscribers to General Ross's Monument, n.d., GWU, Gelman Library, Special Collections, Ross Papers, Manuscripts, Box 1:5.
15. Unknown to Christopher Moore, Newry, n.d., PRONI, D2004/1/14/3; David Ross of Bladensburg to MacDougall, n.d. [1826], ibid., D2004/1A/4/25. Robert Ross's objections on this score were revealed when his son responded in 1826 to a letter from his father's former aide-de-camp, then Lieutenant Colonel MacDougall, who informed him that the general's grave in Halifax, Nova Scotia, was in a dilapidated state. MacDougall wanted to erect a monument there more suitable to his fallen commander's memory. See MacDougall to David Ross of Bladensburg, 11 Apr. 1826, ibid., D2004/1A/4/24. For an article on the interesting career of David Ross, see Whitehead, "David Ross of Bladensburg."
16. Mrs. Ross letter, n.d., PRONI, D2004/1/14/12; Mrs. Ross to Roger Hall, n.d., ibid., D/2004/1/14/5; Mrs. Ross letter, n.d., ibid., D2004/1/14/12; Mrs. Ross to Roger Hall, n.d., ibid., D/2004/1/14/5; Cannon, *Historical Record of the Twentieth*, 76. No residence was ever erected on the originally proposed site, but there is reason to believe that the trees planted by General Ross remain to this day.
17. *Baltimore Patriot*, 21 Sept. 1814; *National Intelligencer* (Washington, D.C.), 4 June 1849.
18. Balch, "Reminiscences of the War of 1812," 284. During this recorded conversation, Key noted that "while a prisoner he experienced from the enemy much kindness and courtesy."
19. Emmons, *Defense of Baltimore and the Death of General Ross*; Oaks, *American Writers*, 130; Freneau, *Collection of Poems*, 2:68–72, 78–81, 90–91, 112–13.
20. W. Hunter, "Battle of Baltimore Illustrated," 236. Cpl. Andrew Duluc was a member of Capt. Philip B. Sadtler's Baltimore Yagers, who were in the main battle at North Point and apparently not engaged in the skirmish in which Ross was shot. Thus, Duluc's claim to have witnessed the general's mortal wounding seems unlikely. See Hickman, *Citizen Soldiers*, 27.
21. Filby and Howard, *Star Spangled Banner Books*, 165; Pitch, *Burning of Washington*, 98.

22. *Boston Commercial Gazette*, 29 Dec. 1814.
23. *American and Commercial Daily Advertiser* (Baltimore), 13 July 1815; *Poulson's American Daily Advertiser* (Philadelphia), 18 Mar. 1815.
24. *New York Evening Post*, 3 Oct. 1821; *Baltimore Patriot*, 12 Sept. 1823. The transparency was also displayed the following year. See ibid., 25 Sept. 1824.
25. *Baltimore Patriot*, 12 Sept. 1829; *Baltimore Gazette*, 9 Jan. 1832; *Philadelphia Inquirer*, 5 Feb. 1833.
26. E. Williams, *Addresses and Messages of the Presidents of the United States*, 1:394–95; Lambert, *Challenge*, 6. Among the lasting legacies of this initiative is Fort Monroe, Old Point Comfort, Virginia. It was erected to "protect the nation's capital" and is the "largest stone fort ever built in America." Copeland, *Historic North American Forts*, 41.
27. William Thornton to Benjamin Russell, 30 Apr. 1817, American Antiquarian Society Records, Correspondence, 1812–19, Box 2, available online at "Fellow Finds Horse's Head," Past Is Present (blog), American Antiquarian Society, 2 Oct. 2009, http://pastispresent.org/2009/fellowsfinds/fellow-finds-horses-head/; Waldo, *Tour of James Monroe*, 52. See also *New York Daily Advertiser*, 5 June 1817; *National Advocate* (New York), 5 June 1817; and *Watch-Tower* (Cooperstown, N.Y.), 19 June 1817.
28. Stagg, *Mr. Madison's War*, 423n15; K. Armstrong, *Review of T. L. McKenney's Narrative*, 4.
29. J. Adams, *Memoirs*, 337, 523, 538; "Ebony and Topaz," John Hopkins University, Special Collections, John Quincy Adams Collection, MS 218; Swint, *Mudslingers*, 213; *New Hampshire Sentinel* (Keene), 2 Nov. 1827; Parsons, *Birth of Modern Politics*, 167; Turner, *Astonishing General*, 9. The Committee of Correspondence for Philadelphia appointed by the Republican convention considered Adams's toast highly offensive for the manner in which it gloried in the death of a brave enemy. See *Richmond (Va.) Enquirer*, 25 Oct. 1828.
30. *United States Telegraph* (Washington, D.C.), 20 Oct., 15, 20 Nov. 1827, 20 June 1828; *Ariel* (Natchez, Miss.), 16 Feb. 1828; *American Mercury* (Hartford, Conn.), 6 Nov. 1827. William B. Giles, governor of Virginia, also criticized the president. See *Eastern Argus* (Portland, Maine), 22 Apr. 1828.
31. *New Brunswick (N.J.) Fredonian*, 28 Nov. 1827; *United States Telegraph* (Washington, D.C.), 15 Nov. 1827; Bennett, *America*, 222. A carved hickory cane cut from near the spot where Ross was mortally wounded was presented to Pres. James Polk in 1845. James K. Polk, *Correspondence of James K. Polk, July–December 1845*, ed. W. Cutler and J. L. Rogers (Knoxville: University of Tennessee Press, 1969), 281.
32. Marine, *British Invasion of Maryland*, 170; G. H. Stewart to David Ross of Bladensburg, 12 Mar. 1853, accompanying a presentation copy of Ingraham, *Sketch of the Events*, in possession of Stephen Campbell, descendant of Major General Ross, Rostrevor, County Down, N. Ireland.

33. Bailey, *Records of Patriotism*, 194; *Baltimore Gazette*, 23 Nov. 1827; *Niles' Weekly Register* (Baltimore), 14 June 1817; *National Advocate* commentary cited in *Times* (London), 24 June 1817.
34. *Baltimore Sun*, 1 Aug. 1909, 5 July 1914.
35. The authors are grateful for this anecdote to Gerard McGivern, whose family were the last occupants of the caretaker's cottage at the Ross monument, Rostrevor, before it was demolished.
36. Lt. Gen. Sir Robin Ross to Francis De Courcy Hamilton, 13 Nov. 2009, in possession of Francis De Courcy Hamilton, Melrose, Scotland.
37. Hart and Penman, *1812*, 153.
38. Sentiment expressed by Rachael Penman in an e-mail to John McCavitt, 24 Jan. 2013.

Bibliography

Manuscript Sources and Legislative Records

American Antiquarian Society Records, Worcester, Mass.
    Correspondence, 1812–19, Box 2. Available online at "Fellow Finds Horse's Head," Past Is Present (blog), American Antiquarian Society, 2 Oct. 2009, http://pastispresent.org/2009/fellowsfinds/fellow-finds-horses-head/.

Baltimore City Archives, Baltimore, Md.
    Record Group 22

British Library, London, England
    Aberdeen MSS, 43,252

Clements Library, University of Michigan, Ann Arbor
    Malcolm Papers (consulted on microfilm at the Naval Heritage Command Library, Washington, D.C.)

Fort McHenry, Baltimore, Md.
    War of 1812 Collection

Georgetown University, Washington, D.C.
    Father McElroy's Diary

Special Collections Research Center, Estelle and Melvin Gelman Library, George Washington University, Washington, D.C.
    Robert Ross Papers

Hartley Library, University of Southampton, Southampton, England
    WP1, WP9

John Hopkins University, Special Collections, Baltimore, Md.
    MS 218

Kilbroney Parish Church, Rostrevor, N. Ireland
    Vestry Records (handwritten notes by Robert Linden)

Library and Archives Canada, Ottawa, Canada
    RG-8, C-series. Available online at http://www.collectionscanada.gc.ca/

Library of Congress, Washington, D.C.
    Cochrane Papers (microfilm)
    Cockburn Papers (microfilm)
    Foreign Affairs, Political Correspondence, Paris to United States, 1814
    Thomas Jefferson Papers, ser. 1, General Correspondence, 1651–1827. Available online at Library of Congress, American Memory, http://memory.loc.gov/ammem/collections/jefferson_papers/mtjser1.html
    Machen Papers
    Madison Papers (microfilm)
    Monroe Papers (microfilm)

Perry Papers
Rodgers Family Papers
Rush Papers
Thornton Papers
Library of the Marine Corps, Quantico, Va.
    Samuel Miller Collection, COLL/3590
Maryland Historical Society Library, Manuscripts Department, Baltimore
    MS 794, MS 820, MS 1435, MS 1846 Vertical File
    War of 1812 Collection
Miscellaneous Ross Family Papers in the Possession of Francis De Courcy Hamilton, Melrose, Scotland
Miscellaneous Ross Family Papers and Artifacts in the Possession of Stephen Campbell, Rostrevor, N. Ireland
Mullan, Robert A., and Son, Solicitors
    Ross Family Legal Correspondence in the Possession of Lord and Lady Ballyedmond, Newry, N. Ireland
National Archives and Records Administration, Washington, D.C.
    M119, M125, M625, RG 45
National Archives and Records Administration II, College Park, Md.
    RG59, RG 107
National Archives, Kew, London, England
    Admiralty Papers, 1, 2, 36, 37, 51
    Audit Office, 1
    Colonial Office, 5, 43
    Foreign Office, 1, 557
    Privy Council, 1
    Probate, 11
    Public Record Office, 30, 43
    War Office, 1, 3, 4, 6, 17, 25, 27, 30, 31, 43, 71, 100, 164
National Army Museum, London, England
    1973-02-8, 1992-06-184, 2002-02-729
National Library of Ireland, Dublin
    MS 2223
National Library of Scotland, Edinburgh
    Cochrane Papers, MS 1574, MS 2265, MS 2333, MS 2448, MS 2450, MS 2574, MS 3022
    Lt. George De Lacy Evans, Memorandum of Operations on the Shores of the Chesapeake in 1814, Adv. MS., 46.6.6
    Murray Papers, Acc. 13175, Adv. 46.1.22, Adv. 46.3.5, Adv. 46.5.5, Adv. 46.3.19, Adv. 46.8.9
National Maritime Museum, London, England
    COC/11, COD/6, COD/7
Public Record Office of Northern Ireland, Belfast
    D607, D671, D2004/1, D2004/1A, D2004/6
Royal Marine Museum, Portsmouth, England
    Capt. Mortimer Timpson Memoir
Royal Navy Museum, Portsmouth, England
    Diary of Midshipman J. C. Bluett

Trinity College, Dublin
  MUN/V/5/5; MUN/V/23/4; MUN/V/27/3; TCD, MUN/SOC/HIST/5 and 6.
Ulster American Folk Park, Omagh, Northern Ireland
  Arthur Brooke Diary
White House, Office of the Curator, Washington, D.C.
  Miscellaneous Papers

Published Primary Sources

Adams, John Quincy. *Memoirs of John Quincy Adams, Comprising Portions of His Diary from 1795 to 1848.* Edited by Charles F. Adams. Vol. 3. Philadelphia: J. B. Lippincott, 1874–77.
Allston, Washington. *The Correspondence of Washington Allston.* Edited by Nathalia Wright. Lexington: University Press of Kentucky, 1993.
Amyot, Thomas, and William Windham, eds. *Speeches in Parliament of . . . William Windham.* 3 vols. London: Longman, Hurst, Rees, Orme, and Brown, 1812.
Andrews, Charles. *The Prisoners' Memoirs; Or, Dartmoor Prison: Containing a Complete and Impartial History of the Entire Captivity of the Americans in England, from the Commencement of the Last War between the United States and Great Britain, until All Prisoners Were Released by the Treaty of Ghent: Also a Particular Detail of All Occurrences Relative to the Horrid Massacre at Dartmoor, on the Fatal Evening of the 6th of April, 1815:* New York: Printed for the author, 1815.
Annual Register, 1815. London, 1816.
Anonymous. "Narrative of Naval Operations in the Potomac." *United Services Magazine* 53 (1833): 469–81.
Anonymous ("Old Sub"). "Recollections of the Expedition to the Chesapeake and against New Orleans in the Years 1814–1815." *United Services Journal* (April 1840): 443–56; (May 1840): 25–36; (June 1840): 192–95; (July 1840): 337–52.
Armstrong, John. *Notices of the War of 1812.* 2 vols. New York: Wiley and Putnam, 1840.
Armstrong, Kosiuscko. *A Review of T. L. McKenney's Narrative of the Causes which, in 1814, Led to General Armstrong's Resignation of the War of Office.* New York: R. Craighead, 1846.
The Army List, 1790. 38th Ed. London: War Office, 1 February 1790.
The Army List, 1792. 40th Ed. London: War Office, 1 January 1792.
The Army List, 1799. 47th Ed. London: War Office, 1 March 1799.
Austin, Catherine, ed. "Letters of Elbridge Gerry, 1797–1814." *Proceedings of the Massachusetts Historical Society* 47 (1914): 480–523.
Bailey, William. *Records of Patriotism and Love of Country.* Washington, D.C.: N.p., 1826.
Balch, L. P. W. "Reminiscences of the War of 1812." *Historical Magazine* 7 (September 1863): 283–84.

Ball, Charles. *Slavery in the United States: A Narrative of the Life and Adventures of Charles Ball*. New York: John S. Taylor, 1837.
"Baptisms Performed by Reverend D. P. Cosserrat." Malta Family History. http://website.lineone.net/~stephaniebidmead/baptism.htm.
Barker, Jacob. *Incidents in the Life of Jacob Barker of New Orleans, Louisiana*. Washington, D.C.: N.p., 1855.
[Barrett, Robert J.]. "Naval Recollections of the Late American War. I." *United Service Journal* 149 (April 1841): 455–67.
Bayard, James Asheton. *Papers of James A. Bayard, 1796–1815*. Edited by Robert Goodloe Harper and Elizabeth Donnan. 1915. Reprint, Charleston, S.C.: BiblioBazaar, 2010.
Bell, George. *Rough Notes by an Old Soldier during Fifty Years' Service*. London: Day and Son, 1867.
Binns, John. *Recollections of the Life of John Binns*. Philadelphia: Parry and McMillan, 1854.
Blakeney, Robert. *A Boy in the Peninsular War: The Services, Adventures, and Experiences of Robert Blakeney, Subaltern in the Twenty-Eighth Regiment*. Edited by Julian Sturgis. London: John Murray, 1899.
Brown, David. "Diary of a Soldier, 1805–1827." *Journal of the Royal Highland Fusiliers* 8 (June 1973): 75–84.
Bryan, W. B. ed. "Diary of Mrs. William Thornton." *Records of the Columbia Historical Society, Washington, D.C.* 19 (1916): 172–82.
Bunbury, Henry E. *Narratives of Some Passages in the Great War with France, from 1799 to 1810*. London: Richard Bentley, 1854.
"Capture of the City of Washington." 29 November 1814. *American State Papers*, House of Representatives, 13th Cong., 3rd sess., *Military Affairs*, 1:524–99.
Carr, William. *Rosstrevor, a Moral and Descriptive Poem, with Other Miscellaneous Pieces*. Newry, N. Ireland: King Murray, 1810.
[Castlereagh, Viscount]. *Correspondence, Despatches, and other Papers, of Viscount Castlereagh*. Edited by Charles W. Vane. Military and Diplomatic, 3rd ser., 4 vols. London: John Murray, 1853.
Chamier, Frederick. *The Life of a Sailor by a Captain in the Navy*. 2 vols. New York: J. and J. Harper, 1833.
Chartrand, René. "An Account of the Capture of Washington, 1814." *Military Collector and Historian* 37 (Winter 1985): 182.
Chesterton, George Laval. *Peace, War, and Adventure: An Autobiographical Memoir of George Laval Chesterton*. 2 vols. London: Longman, Brown, Green, and Longmans, 1853.
Clark, Allen C. "The Abraham Young Mansion." *Records of the Columbia Historical Society, Washington, D.C.* 12 (1909): 53–70.
———. "Margaret Eaton, (Peggy O'Neal)." *Records of the Columbia Historical Society* 44–45 (1942–43): 1–33.
Clay, Henry. *The Papers of Henry Clay*. Edited by James F. Hopkins and Mary W. M. Hargreaves. 11 vols. Lexington: University Press of Kentucky, 1959.

Clemmer Ames, Mary. *Ten Years in Washington: Life and Scenes in the National Capital as a Woman Sees Them*. Hartford, Conn.: A. D. Worthington, 1879.
[Codrington, Edward]. *Memoir of the Life of Admiral Sir Edward Codrington*. Edited by his daughter, Lady Bourchier. London: Longmans, Green, 1873.
Colburn, Zerah. *A Memoir of Zerah Colburn*. Springfield, Mass.: G. and C. Merriam, 1833.
Cooke, John Henry. *A Narrative of Events in the South of France, and of the Attack on New Orleans, in 1814 and 1815*. London: T. and W. Boone, 1835.
Cooper, John S. *Fusilier Cooper: Experiences in the 7th (Royal) Fusiliers during the Peninsular Campaign of the Napoleonic Wars and the American Campaign to New Orleans*. Leonaur Books, 2007. First published as *Rough Notes of Seven Campaigns, 1809–1815*.
Corbett, John C. "The Campaigns of John Corbett, a Peninsular Veteran." Transcribed by Elias Vaughan. In *Pontypool Free Press*, 10 February 1872.
Costello, Edward. *Rifleman Costello: The Adventures of a Soldier of the 95th (Rifles) in the Peninsular & Waterloo Campaigns of the Napoleonic Wars*. Leonaur Books, 2005.
Dallas, Alexander J. *An Exposition of the Causes and Character of the War between the United States and Great Britain*. Concord, Mass.: Isaac and Walter R. Hill, 1815.
Dalrymple, Hew. *Memoir Written by General Sir Hew Dalrymple, Bart. of His Proceedings as Connected with the Affairs of Spain, and the Commencement of the Peninsular War*. London: Thomas and William Boone, 1830.
Daniel, John E. *Journal of an Officer in the Commissariat Department of the Army*. London: Porter and King, 1820.
De Jomini, Antoine Henry. *The Art of War*. Philadelphia: J. B. Lippincot, 1862.
Dixon, William L., ed. *Lady Morgan's Memoirs: Autobiography, Diaries, and Correspondence*. 2nd ed., Vol. 2. London: William H. Allen, 1863.
Downing, James. *A Narrative of the Life of James Downing*. 5th ed. London: N.p., 1817.
Dudley, William S., and Michael J. Crawford, ed. *The Naval War of 1812: A Documentary History*. 3 vols. Washington, D.C.: U.S. Department of Defense, 2002.
Duncan, John M. *Travels through Part of the United States and Canada in 1818 and 1819*. 2 vols. Glasgow: Hurst, Robinson, 1823.
Elliott, William. *The Washington Guide*. Washington, D.C.: Franck Taylor, 1837.
Emmons, Richard. *Defense of Baltimore and the Death of General Ross*. 3rd ed. Washington, D.C.: William Emmons, 1831.
Evans, Sir George De Lacy. *Facts Relating to the Capture of Washington, in Reply to Some Statements Contained in the Memoirs of Admiral Sir George Cockburn, G. C. B.* London: Henry Colborn, 1829.

Ewell, James. *The Medical Companion*. Philadelphia: Anderson and Meehan, 1816.
Fearon, Henry B. *Sketches of America*. London: Longman, Hurst, Rees, Orme, and Brown, 1818.
Freneau, Philip. *A Collection of Poems, on American Affairs and a Variety of Other Subjects*. Vol. 2. New York: David Longworth, 1815.
"General Ross's Monument." *United Services Journal* (1831, pt. 1): 400.
Goldsborough, Robert H. "Contemporary Report of the Battle of Baltimore." *Maryland Historical Magazine* 40 (September 1945): 230–32.
[Gleig, G. R.]. *A Narrative of the Campaigns of the British Army at Washington, Baltimore, and New Orleans*. 1821. 2nd ed., 1826. 3rd ed., corrected and revised. London: John Murray, 1827.
———. *A Subaltern in America*. Philadelphia: E. L. Carey and A. Hart, 1833.
Hansard. T. C. *The Parliamentary Debates from the Year 1803 to the Present Time*. Vols. 9, 27, 29, 30. London: T. C. Hansard, 1806–50.
Hart, L. G. *New Annual Army List, 1840*. London: John Murray, 1840.
———. *New Annual Army List, 1840*. London: John Murray, 1850.
Hawkins, William G. *Life of John H. W. Hawkins*. Boston: John P. Jewett, 1859.
Historical Manuscripts Commission. *Report on the Manuscripts of Earl Bathurst Preserved at Cirencester Park*. London: His Majesty's Stationery Office, 1923.
Hunter, Mary. "The Burning of Washington, D.C." *New York Historical Society Quarterly Bulletin* (1924): 80–83.
Ingersoll, Charles J. *Historical Sketch of the Second War between the United States of America and Great Britain*. Vol. 2. Philadelphia: Lea and Blanchard, 1849.
Jennings, Paul. *A Colored Man's Reminiscences of James Madison*. New York: George C. Beadle, 1865.
Kennedy, John Pendleton. *Memoirs of the Life of William Wirt, Attorney General of the United States*. Vol. 1. Philadelphia: J. B. Lippincott, 1860.
Key, F. S. *Poems of the Late Francis S. Key, Esq*. New York: Robert Carter and Brothers, 1857.
Kincaid, John. *The Rifle Brigade, including Adventures in the Rifle Brigade and Random Shots from a Rifle Man*. Barnsley, England: Pen and Sword Military, 2005.
Latrobe, Benjamin Henry. *The Correspondence and Miscellaneous Papers of Benjamin Henry Latrobe*. Edited by John C. Van Horne. Vol. 3. New Haven, Conn.: Yale University Press, 1988.
Lingel, Robert, ed. "The Manuscript Autobiography of Gordon Gallie Macdonald." *New York Public Library Bulletin* (March 1930): 139–47.
A List of the Officers of the Army and of the Corps of Royal Marines on Full and Half-Pay. London: War Office, 1821.
Lovell, William Stanhope. *Personal Narrative of Events, from 1799 to 1815, with Anecdotes*. 2nd ed. London: William Allen, 1879.

Lowry, T. K., ed. *The Hamilton Manuscripts*. Belfast: Archer and Sons, 1867.
Luddy, Maria, ed. *Drennan-McTier Letters, 1794–1801*. Dublin: Irish Manuscripts Commission, 1998.
Madison, Dolley. *Memoirs and Letters of Dolly Madison: Wife of James Madison, President of the United States*. Edited by Lucia B. Cutts. Boston: Houghton, Mifflin, 1887.
Madison, James. *The Papers of James Madison*. Edited by William T. Hutchinson, William M. E. Rachal, Charles F. Hobson, and Robert A. Rutland. 17 vols. to date. Chicago and Charlottesville: University of Chicago and University of Virginia Presses, 1962.
———. *The Writings of James Madison*. Edited by Gaillard Hunt. 9 vols. New York: G. P. Putnam's Sons, 1900–1910.
Mason, Jeremiah. *Memoir, Autobiography, and Correspondence of Jeremiah Mason*. 1873. Reprint, Kansas City, Mo.: Lawyers' International, 1917.
McClane, Col. Allen. "Journal of the Campaign." In *Notices of the War of 1812*, by John Armstrong, 2:232–36. New York: Wiley and Putnam, 1840.
McKenney, Thomas L. *Memoirs, Official and Personal; with Sketches of Travels among the Northern and Southern Indians: Embracing a War Excursion and Embracing a Description of Scenes along the Western Borders*. 2 vols. New York: Paine and Burgess, 1846.
———. "A Narrative of the Battle of Bladensburg in a Letter to Henry Banning, Esq., by an Officer of General Smith's Staff." *Portico* 5 (January–February 1818): 359–70.
———. *Reply to Kosciusko Armstrong's Assault upon Col. McKenney's Narrative of the Causes That Led to General Armstrong's Resignation of the Office of Secretary of War in 1814*. New York: William H. Graham, 1847.
McLane, Allen. "Col. McLane's Visit to Washington, 1814." *Bulletin of the Historical Society of Pennsylvania* 1 (June 1845): 16–22.
"Memoir of Major General Robert Ross." *United Services Journal* (1829, pt. 1): 412–16.
Monroe, James. *The Papers of James Monroe: A Documentary History of the Presidential Tours of James Monroe, 1817, 1818, 1819*. Vol. 2. Edited by Daniel Preston and Marlena C. DeLong. Westport, Conn.: Greenwood, 2003.
———. *The Papers of James Monroe: Selected Correspondence and Papers, 1776–1794*. Vol. 1. Edited by Daniel Preston and Marlena C. DeLong. Westport, Conn.: Greenwood, 2006.
———. *The Writings of James Monroe*. Edited by Stanislaus Murray Hamilton. 7 vols. New York: G. P. Putnam's Sons, 1898–1903.
Moore, Sir John. *The Diary of Sir John Moore*. Edited by J. F. Maurice. 2 vols. London: Arnold, 1904.
Moore, Virginia C. "Reminiscences of Washington as Recalled by a Descendant of the Ingle Family." *Records of the Columbia Historical Society, Washington, D.C.* 3 (1900): 96–114.

Napier, Lt. Gen. Sir William. *Life and Opinions of General Sir James Napier, G.C.B.* 4 vols. London: John Murray, 1857.
"Narrative of the Naval Operations in the Potomac." *United Services Journal* (1833, pt. 1): 469–81.
Palmer, T. H., ed. *The Historical Register of the United States, Part II for 1814.* Washington, D.C.: T. H. Palmer, 1816.
Piper, James. "Defence of Baltimore, 1814." *Maryland Historical Magazine* 7 (December 1912): 375–84.
Porter, David D. *Memoir of Commodore David Porter: Of the United States Navy.* Albany, N.Y.: J. Munsell, 1875.
Rees, James. *The Wanderer: A Rambling Poem.* Philadelphia: Grigg and Elliot, 1836.
Rowley, Peter, ed. "Captain Rowley Helps to Burn Washington, D.C., Part 1." *Maryland Historical Magazine* 82 (Fall 1987): 240–50.
Scott, James. *Recollections of a Naval Life.* Vol. 3. London: Bentley, 1834.
Scott, Winfield. *Memoirs of Lieut. General Winfield Scott, L.L.D.* New York: Sheldon, 1864.
Sessional Papers of the House of Lords: Session 1840. London: Her Majesty's Stationery Office, 1840.
Sheads, Scott S. "Death of Ross File." Unpublished.
Shiner, Michael. "The Diary of Michael Shiner Relating to the History of the Washington Navy Yard, 1813–1869." http://www.history.navy.mil/research/library/online-reading-room/title-list-alphabetically/d/diary-of-michael-shiner.html.
Smith, Harry George Wakelyn. *The Autobiography of Lieutenant-General Sir Harry Smith Baronet of Aliwal on the Sutlej G.C.B.* Edited by G. C. Moore Smith. 2 vols. New York: E. P. Dutton, 1902.
Smith, Margaret B. *The First Forty Years of Washington Society.* Edited by Gaillard Hunt. New York: Charles Scribner's Sons, 1906.
The Spirit of the Public Journals for 1814. London, 1815.
Steele, Sarah. *Eva, an Historical Poem, with Notes, Accompanied by Some Lyric Poems.* Dublin: John Jones, 1816.
Steevens, Nathanial. *Reminiscences of My Military Life from 1795 to 1818.* Edited by Charles Steevens. Winchester, Va.: Warren and Son, 1878.
Stuart, James. *Refutation of Aspersions on "Stuart's Three Years in North America."* London: Whittaker, 1834.
———. *Three Years in North America.* 2 vols. Edinburgh: Robert Caddell, 1833.
Timbs, John, ed. *Wellingtonia: Anecdotes, Maxims, and Characteristics of the Duke of Wellington.* London: Ingram, Cooke, 1852.
U.S. Congress. *House Journal.* 13th Cong., 3rd sess., 19 September 1814. Available online at Library of Congress, American Memory, http://memory.loc.gov/cgi-bin/query/r?ammem/hlaw:@field(DOCID+@lit(hj009195)):.
———. *Senate Journal.* 13th Cong., 3rd sess., 19 September 1814. Available online at Library of Congress, American Memory, http://memory.loc.gov/cgi-bin/query/r?ammem/hlaw:@field(DOCID+@lit(sj005501)).

Waldo, S. Putnam. *The Tour of James Monroe, President of the United States, in the Year 1817.* Hartford, Conn.: F. D. Bolles, 1818.
Warden, D. B. *A Chorographical and Statistical Description of the District of Columbia, the Seat of the General Government of the United States.* Paris: N.p. 1816.
[Wellington, Arthur Wellesley, Duke of]. *The Dispatches of Field Marshal the Duke of Wellington, K.G, during His Various Campaigns. . . .* Edited by J. Gurwood. Vols. 9–12. London: John Murray, 1837–39.
———. *Supplementary Despatches, Correspondence, and Memoranda of Field Marshal Arthur Duke of Wellington, K. G.* Edited by his son, the Duke of Wellington, G. G. Vols. 7–9. London: John Murray, 1861.
Wilkinson, James. *Memoirs of My Own Times.* Vol. 1. Philadelphia: Abraham Small, printers, 1816.
Williams, Edwin. *The Addresses and Messages of the Presidents of the United States, Inaugural, Annual, and Special, from 1789 to 1846, with a Memoir of Each of the Presidents, and a History of Their Administrations.* 2 vols. New York: Edward Walker, 1849.
Williams, John S. *History of the Invasion and the Capture of Washington and All the Events Which Preceded and Followed It.* New York: Harper and Brothers, 1857.
Wolfe Tone, W. T. *Life of Theobald Wolfe Tone.* Vol. 1. Washington, D.C.: Gales and Seaton, 1826.

Secondary Sources

Abbott, Katharine M. *Trolley Trips in and about Fascinating Washington.* Washington, D.C.: J. F. Jarvis, 1900.
Adams, Henry. *History of the United States of America during the Second Administration of James Madison.* 2 vols. London: G. P. Putnam's Sons, 1892.
Adkins, Lesley, and Roy Adkins. *The War for All the Oceans: From Nelson at the Nile to Napoleon at Waterloo.* London: Little, Brown, 2006.
Alden, Robert Ames. *The Flight of the Madisons.* Fairfax, Va.: Fairfax County Council of the Arts, 1974.
Allen, William C. *The United States Capitol: A Brief Architectural History.* Washington, D.C.: Government Printing Office, 1990.
Allgor, Catherine. *A Perfect Union: Dolley Madison and the Creation of the American Nation.* New York: Henry Holt, 2006.
Ammon, Harry. *James Monroe: The Quest for National Identity.* New York: McGraw-Hill, 1971.
Arnold, James Riehl. "Battle of Bladensburg." *Records of the Columbia Historical Society, Washington D.C.* 37–38 (1937): 145–68.
Arthur, Brian. *How Britain Won the War of 1812: The Royal Navy's Blockades of the United States, 1812–1815.* Woodbridge: Boydell, 2011.
Bardon, Jonathan. *A History of Ulster.* Belfast: Blackstaff, 1992.
Barney, Mary, ed. *A Biographical Memoir of the Late Joshua Barney from Autobiographical Notes and Journals in Possession of His Family and Other Authentic Sources.* Boston: Gray and Bowen, 1832.

Barrett, C. R .B., ed. *The 85th King's Light Infantry*. London: Spottiswood, 1913.
Bartlett, C. J. *Castlereagh*. London: Macmillan, 1966.
Bartlett, Thomas. *Ireland: A History*. Cambridge: Cambridge University Press, 2010.
Bartlett, Thomas, and Keith Jeffery, eds. *A Military History of Ireland*. Cambridge: Cambridge University Press, 1996.
Bathurst, Jim. *We'll All Die as Marines: One Marine's Journey from Private to Colonel*. Bloomington, Ind.: iUniverse, 2012.
Beatson, F. C. *Wellington and the Fall of France. The Gaves and the Battle of Orthez*. Vol. 3. Reprint, Leonaur Books, 2007.
Beatty, Michael A. *The English Royal Family of America, from Jamestown to the American Revolution*. Jefferson, N.C.: McFarland, 2003.
Beirne, Francis F. *The War of 1812*. New York: Dutton, 1949.
Bennett, William J. *America: The Last Best Hope*. Vol. 1, *From the Age of Discovery to a World at War, 1492–1914*. Nashville: Thomas Nelson, 2007.
Best, Geoffrey. *Humanity in Warfare: The Modern History of the International Law of Armed Conflicts*. London: Methuen, 1983.
Bickham, Troy. *The Weight of Vengeance: The United States, the British Empire, and the War of 1812*. Oxford: Oxford University Press, 2012.
Black, Jeremy. *The War of 1812 in the Age of Napoleon*. Norman: University of Oklahoma Press, 2009.
Blumberg, Arnold. *When Washington Burned: An Illustrated History of the War of 1812*. Philadelphia: Casemate, 2013.
Bolton, Nelson Mott, and Christopher T. George. "Captain Henry Thompson's First Baltimore Horse Artillery in the Defense of Baltimore in the War of 1812." *Maryland Historical Magazine* 92 (Winter 2013): 420–44.
Borneman, Walter R. *1812—The War That Forged a Nation*. New York: Harper Perennial, 2005.
Brant, Irving. *James Madison: Commander-in-Chief, 1812–1836*. New York: Bobbs-Merrill, 1961.
Brooks, Victor, and Robert Hohwald. *How America Fought Its Wars: Military Strategy from the American Revolution to the Civil War*. Conshohocken, Pa.: Combined, 1999.
Broussard, James H. *The Southern Federalists, 1800–1816*. Baton Rouge: Louisiana State University Press, 1978.
Brown, Gordon S. *Incidental Architect: William Thornton and the Cultural Life of Early Washington, D.C., 1794–1828*. Athens: Ohio University Press, 2009.
Brumwell, Stephen. *Paths of Glory: The Life and Death of General James Wolfe*. London: Hambledon Continuum, 2006.
Buchan, John. *The History of the Royal Scots Fusiliers (1678–1918)*. London: Thomas Newton and Sons, 1925.
Buel, Richard. *America on the Brink: How the Political Struggle over the War of 1812 almost Destroyed the Young Republic*. New York: Palgrave Macmillan, 2005.

Burtchaell, George D., and Thomas U. Sadleir. *Alumni Dublinenses: A Register of the Students, Graduates, Professors, and Provosts of Trinity College in the University of Dublin (1593–1860)*. Dublin: A. Thom, 1935.

Burnett, T. A. J. *The Rise and Fall of a Regency Dandy: The Life and Times of Scrope Berdmore Davies*. London: John Murray, 1981.

Callcott, Margaret L., ed. *Mistress of Riversdale: The Plantation Letters of Rosalie Stier Calvert, 1795–1821*. Baltimore: John Hopkins University Press, 1991.

Cannon, Richard. *Historical Record of the Twentieth, or the East Devonshire Regiment of Foot*. London: Parker, Furnivall, and Parker, 1848.

Carr, Peter. *Portavo: An Irish Townland and Its Peoples*. Pt. 1. Belfast: White Ross, 2003.

Carter, Thomas. *Historical Record of the Forty-Fourth or the East Essex Regiment of Foot*. London: W. O. Mitchel, 1864.

———. *Medals of the British Army and How They Were Won*. London: Groombridge and Sons, 1861.

Cassell, Frank A. "Baltimore in 1813: A Study of Urban Defense in the War of 1812." *Military Affairs* 33 (December 1969): 349–61.

———. *Merchant Congressman in the Young Republic: Samuel Smith of Maryland, 1752–1839*. Madison: University of Wisconsin Press, 1971.

———. "Response to Crisis: Baltimore in 1814." *Maryland Historical Magazine* 107 (Spring 2012): 83–101.

Chambers, Kevin. "Ross's Record." Unpublished paper read at the General Ross Conference, Rostrevor, County Down, Northern Ireland, October 2013.

Chandler, David G. *Napoleon*. London: Weidenfield and Nicolson, 1973.

Chapmen, John H. *The Register Book of Marriages Belonging to the Parish of St. George, Hanover Square, in the County of Middlesex*. Vol. 14, in 2 parts. London: Mitchell and Hughes, 1886.

Clark, Allen C. "James Heighe Blake, the Third Mayor of the Corporation of Washington [1813–17]." *Records of the Columbia Historical Society, Washington, D.C.* 24 (1922): 136–63.

———. *Life and Letters of Dolley Madison*. Washington, D.C.: W. F. Roberts, 1914.

Clifford, James. "The Battles That Saved America: North Point and Baltimore, September 1814." *On Point: Journal of Army History* 10 (2004): 9–15.

Cole, John W. *Memoirs of British Generals Distinguished during the Peninsular War*. 2 vols. London: Richard Bentley, 1856.

Colston, Frederick M. "The Battle of North Point." *Maryland Historical Magazine* 2 (1907): 111–25.

Conlin, Joseph R. *The American Past: A Survey of American History, Ninth Edition*. Boston: Cengage Books, 2009.

Conner, Eugene H. "William Beanes, M.D. (1749–1829), and the Star-Spangled Banner." *Journal of the History of Medicine and Allied Sciences* 34 (1979): 224–29.

Cooling, Benjamin Franklin, III. *The Day Lincoln Was almost Shot: The Fort Stephens Story.* Plymouth, UK: Scarecrow, 2013.
Copeland, Peter F. *Historic North American Forts.* Mineola, N.Y.: Dover, 2000.
Corrigan, Gordon. *Wellington: A Military Life.* London: Continnuum-3PL, 2006.
Coss, Edward J. *All for the King's Shilling: The British Soldier under Wellington, 1808–1814.* Norman: University of Oklahoma Press, 2010.
Coté, Richard N. *Strength and Honor: The Life of Dolley Madison.* Mount Pleasant, S.C.: Corinthian Books, 2005.
Cowper, L. I. *The King's Own: The Story of a Royal Regiment.* 2 vols. Oxford: Oxford University Press, 1939.
Crowe, W. H. *Village in Seven Hills.* Reprint, Dundalk: Dundalgan, 1991.
Dangerfield, George. *The Era of Good Feelings.* Chicago: Elephant, 1989.
Davies, D. W. *Sir John Moore's Peninsular Campaign, 1808 to 1809.* The Hague: Martinus Nijhoff, 1974.
Drez, Ronald J. *The War of 1812, Conflict and Deception: The British Attempt to Seize New Orleans and Nullify the Louisiana Purchase.* Baton Rouge: Louisiana State University Press, 2014.
Dudley, Wade G. *Splintering the Wooden Wall: The British Blockade of the United States, 1812–1815.* Annapolis: Naval Institute Press, 2003.
Eden, Steven. "Commodore Barney at the Bladensburg Races." *Naval History* 24 (October 2010): 46–52.
Elliott, Marianne. *The Catholics of Ulster: A History.* London: Penguin Books, 2001.
———. *Wolfe Tone.* New Haven, Conn.: Yale University Press, 1989.
Elting, John R. *Amateurs to Arms! A Military History of the War of 1812.* New York: Da Capo, 1995.
Engelman, Fred L. *The Peace of Christmas Eve.* New York: Harcourt, Brace, 1962.
Eshelman, Ralph E. *A Travel Guide to the War of 1812 in the Chesapeake.* Baltimore: John Hopkins University Press, 2011.
———. "Washington City Myths during the War of 1812." In *America under Fire: Mr. Madison's War and the Burning of Washington City,* 63–74. Washington, D.C.: White House Historical Association, 2014.
Eshelman, Ralph E., and Burton K. Kummerow. *In Full Glory Reflected: Discovering the War of 1812 in the Chesapeake.* Baltimore: Maryland Historical Society, 2012.
Eshelman, Ralph E., and Scott S. Sheads. *Chesapeake Legends and Lore from the War of 1812.* Charleston, S.C.: History Press, 2013.
Eshelman, Ralph E., Scott S. Sheads, and Donald R. Hickey. *The War of 1812 in the Chesapeake: A Reference Guide to Historic Sites in Maryland, Virginia, and the District of Columbia.* Baltimore: Johns Hopkins University Press, 2010.
Eustace, Nicole. *1812: War and the Passions of Patriotism.* Philadelphia: University of Pennsylvania, 2012.
Fabel, Robin F. A. "The Laws of War in the 1812 Conflict." *Journal of American Studies* 14 (August 1980): 199–218.

Fedorak, Charles J. "The Royal Navy and British Amphibious Operations during the Revolutionary and Napoleonic Wars." *Military Affairs* 52 (July 1988): 141–46.
Field, Charles. *Britain's Sea Soldiers: A History of the Royal Marines.* Vol. 1. Liverpool: Lyceum, 1924.
Filby, P. W., and Edward G. Howard. *Star Spangled Banner Books.* Baltimore: Maryland Historical Society, 1972.
Fitz-Enz, David G. *The Final Invasion: Plattsburgh, the War of 1812's Most Decisive Battle.* New York: Cooper Square, 2001.
Fletcher, Ian. *Wellington's Regiments The Men and Their Battles from Rolica to Waterloo, 1808–1815.* Stapelhurst, Kent: Spellmount, 1994.
Footner, Hulbert. *Sailor of Fortune: The Life and Adventures of Commodore Barney, U.S.N.* 1940. Reprint, Annapolis: Naval Institute Press, 1998.
Forester, C. S. *The Naval War of 1812.* London: Michael Joseph, 1957.
Fortescue, John W. *A History of the British Army.* Vol. 9. London: Macmillan, 1920.
"Fourth (or the King's Own) Regiment of Foot." *United Services Magazine* (1830, pt. 2): 558–67.
Freymann, John G. "A View of the War and the World from Baltimore, 1813–1815." *Maryland Historical Magazine* 107 (Winter 2012): 485–518.
Friend, Melinda K. "Defense of Baltimore Correspondence, 1814." *Maryland Historical Magazine* 86 (Winter 1991): 443–49.
Genet-Rouffiac, Nathalie, and David J.Murphy, eds. *Franco-Irish Military Connections, 1590–1945.* Dublin: Four Courts, 2009.
George, Christopher T. "The Family Papers of Maj. Gen. Robert Ross, the Diary of Col. Brooke, and the British Attacks on Washington and Baltimore of 1814." *Maryland Historical Magazine* 88 (Fall 1993): 300–316.
———. "Mirage of Freedom: African Americans in the War of 1812." *Maryland Historical Magazine* 107 (Spring 2012): 36–55.
———. *Scots in Maryland and a History of the St. Andrews's Society of Baltimore, 1806–2006.* Timonium: St Andrew's Society of Baltimore, 2007.
———. "Sunk to Save Baltimore: Compensating the Owners of Ships Sunk in Baltimore Harbor during the War of 1812." *Journal of the War of 1812* 14 (Summer 2011): 10–23.
———. *Terror on the Chesapeake: The War of 1812 on the Bay.* Shippensburg, Pa.: White Mane Books, 2000.
———. "Who Killed Robert Ross." Monumentally Speaking. http://www.baltimoremd.com/monuments/whokill.html.
Glover, George. *Wellington's Voice: The Candid Letters of Lieutenant Colonel John Fremantle, Coldstream Guards, 1808–1821.* Barnsley: Pen and Sword Books, 2012.
Graves, Dianne L. *In the Midst of Alarms: The Untold Story of Women and the War of 1812.* Montreal: Robin Brass Studio, 2007.

Graves, Donald E. *Dragon Rampant. The Royal Welch Fusiliers at War, 1793–1815.* Montreal: Robin Brass Studio, 2010.

———. "'Every Horror Was Committed with Impunity . . . and Not a Man Was Punished!': Reflections on British Military Law and the Atrocities at Hampton in 1813." *War of 1812 Magazine* 11 (June 2009). Available online at the Napoleon Series, http://www.napoleon-series.org/military/Warof1812/2009/Issue11/c_hampton.html.

———. "Field Artillery of the War of 1812: Equipment, Organization, Tactics, and Effectiveness." *War of 1812 Magazine* 12 (November 2009). Available online at the Napoleon Series, http://www.napoleon-series.org/military/Warof1812/2009/Issue12/c_Artillery.html.

———. "'The Finest Army Ever to Campaign on American Soil'? The Organization, Strength, Composition, and Losses of British Land Forces during the Plattsburgh Campaign, September, 1814." *Journal of the War of 1812* 7 (Fall–Winter 2003): 6–13.

———. *Fix Bayonets! A Royal Welch Fusilier at War, 1796–1815.* Toronto: Robin Brass Studio, 2006.

———. "The Redcoats Are Coming! British Troop Movements to North America in 1814." *Journal of the War of 1812* 6 (Summer 2001): 12–16.

———. *Where Right and Glory Lead: The Battle of Lundy's Lane, 1814.* Rev. paperback ed. Montreal: Robin Brass Studio, 1997.

———. "Why the White House Was Burned. An Investigation into the British Destruction of Public Buildings at Washington in August 1814." *Journal of Military History* 76 (October 2012): 1095–1127.

———. "'Worthless Is the Laurel Steeped in Female Tears': An Investigation into the Outrages Committed by British Troops at Hampton, Virginia, in 1813." *Journal of the War of 1812* 7 (Winter 2002): 4–23.

Grodzinski, John R. *Defender of Canada: Sir George Prevost and the War of 1812.* Norman: University of Oklahoma Press, 2013.

———. "Documents, Artifacts, and Imagery: Instructions to Major-General Sir Edward Pakenham for the New Orleans Campaign." *War of 1812 Magazine* 16 (September 2011). Available online at the Napoleon Series, http://www.napoleon-series.org/military/Warof1812/2011/Issue16/c_PakenhamOrders.html.

———. "The Duke of Wellington, the Peninsular War, and the War of 1812. Part II: Reinforcements, Views of the War, and Command in North America." *War of 1812 Magazine* 6 (April 2007). Available online at the Napoleon Series, http://www.napoleon-series.org/military/Warof1812/2007/Issue6/c_Wellington1.html.

———. "Much to Be Desired: The Campaign Experience of British General Officers of the War of 1812." *War of 1812 Magazine* 7 (September 2007). Available online at the Napoleon Series, http://www.napoleon-series.org/military/Warof1812/2007/Issue7/c_BritishGenerals.html.

Groves, John P. *Historical Records of the 7th or Royal Regiment of Fusiliers.* Guernsey: Frederick B. Guerin, 1903.

Hadel, Albert Kimberley. "The Battle of Bladensburg." *Maryland Historical Magazine* 1 (June 1906): 155–67; (September 1906): 197–210.

Hall, Christopher D. *British Strategy in the Napoleonic War, 1803–15.* Manchester: University Press, 1992.
Hart, Sidney, and Rachael L. Penman. *1812: A Nation Emerges.* Washington, D.C.: Smithsonian Institution Scholarly Press, 2012.
Haythornthwaite, Philip. *Corunna 1809: Sir John Moore's Fighting Retreat.* Botley: Osprey, 2001.
Heidler, David S., and Jeanne T. Heidler. *The War of 1812.* Westport, Conn.: Greenwood, 2002.
Heron, Denis C. *The Constitutional History of the University of Dublin.* Dublin: James McGlashan, 1847.
Herrick, Carole L. *August 24, 1814: Washington in Flames.* Falls Church, Va.: Higher Education Publications, 2005.
Hickey, Donald R. *Don't Give Up the Ship: Myths of the War of 1812.* Urbana: University of Illinois Press, 2006.
———. "1812: The Old History and the New." *Reviews in American History* 41 (September 2013): 436–44.
———. *187 Things You Should Know about the War of 1812.* Baltimore: Johns Hopkins University Press, 2012.
———. "'War Hawks': Using Newspapers to Trace a Phrase, 1792–1812." *Journal of Military History* 78 (April 2014): 725–40.
———. *The War of 1812: A Forgotten Conflict.* Urbana: University of Illinois Press, 2012.
Hickman, Nathaniel. *The Citizen Soldiers at North Point and Fort McHenry, September 12 & 13, 1814.* Baltimore: N. Hickman, 1858.
Hildt, John C. "Letters Relating to the Capture of Washington." *South Atlantic Quarterly* 6 (1907): 58–66.
Hitsman, J. Mackay, and Donald E. Graves. *The Incredible War of 1812: A Military History.* Toronto: Robin Brass Studio, 1999.
Holmes, Richard. *Wellington: The Iron Duke.* London: Harper Collins, 2003.
Hopton, Richard. *The Battle of Maida, 1806: Fifteen Minutes of Glory.* Barnsley: Leo Cooper, 2002.
Horsfield, Paul. "Recipients of the Army Gold Cross, 1813–1814." *Journal of the Orders and Medals Research Society* 45 (September 2006): 174–77.
Horsman, Reginald. *The War of 1812.* New York: Alfred A. Knopf, 1969.
Hosford, David. "Exile in Yankee Land: The Journal of Mary Bagot, 1816–1818." *Records of the Columbia Historical Society, Washington, D.C.* 51 (1984): 30–50.
Howard, Hugh. *Mr. and Mrs. Madison's War. America's First Couple and the Second War of Independence.* New York: Bloomsbury, 2012.
Hunter, Wilbur H., Jr. "The Battle of Baltimore Illustrated." *William and Mary Quarterly*, 3rd ser., 8 (April 1951): 235–37.
Ingraham, Edward D. *A Sketch of the Events Which Preceded the Capture of Washington by the British on the Twenty-Fourth of August, 1814.* Philadelphia: Carey and Hart, 1849.
Irving, Pierre M., ed. *The Life and Letters of Washington Irving.* 3 vols. London: Richard Bentley, 1862.

James, William. *A Full and Correct Account of the Chief Naval Occurrences of the Late War between Great Britain and the United States of America*. London: T. Egerton, 1817.

———. *The Naval History of Great Britain during the French Revolutionary and Napoleonic Wars*. 6 vols. 1847. Reprint, with new introduction by Andrew Lambert, London: Conway Maritime, 2002.

Jenkins, Brian. *Henry Goulburn, 1784–1856: A Political Biography*. Montreal: McGill-Queen's University Press, 1996.

Jennings, Ivor. *Party Politics*. Vol. 3, *The Stuff of Politics*. Cambridge: Cambridge University Press, 1962.

Johnston-Liik, E. M., ed. *History of the Irish Parliament, 1692–1800*. 6 vols. Belfast: Ulster Historical Foundation, 2002.

Ketcham, Ralph, *James Madison: A Biography*. Charlottesville: University Press of Virginia, 1971.

Kieran, Brian L. *Corunna 1809: Sir John Moore's Battle to Victory and Successful Evacuation*. Milton Keynes: AuthorHouse, 2011.

King, Horatio. *Turning on the Light: A Dispassionate Survey of President Buchanan's Administration*. Philadelphia: J. B. Lippincott, 1895.

Lambert, Andrew. *The Challenge: America, Britain, and the War of 1812*. London: Faber and Faber, 2012.

Lane-Poole, Stanley. "Sir Richard Church." *English Historical Review* 5 (January 1890): 7–30.

Latimer, Jon. *1812: War with America*. Cambridge, Mass.: Belknap, 2007.

Longford, Elizabeth. *Wellington*. Reprint, London: Abacus, 2004.

Lord, Walter. *The Dawn's Early Light*. New York: W. W. Norton, 1972.

Lossing, Benson J. *Pictorial Field Book of the War of 1812*. New York: Harper and Brothers, 1869.

Macksey, Piers. *British Victory in Egypt, 1801: The End of Napoleon's Conquest*. New York: Routledge, 1995.

Magruder, Caleb Clarke, Jr. "Dr. William Beanes: The Incidental Cause of the Authorship of the Star-Spangled Banner." *Records of the Columbia Historical Society, Washington, D.C.* 22 (1919): 207–25.

Maguire, W. A. "Major General Ross and the Burning of Washington." *Irish Sword: The Journal of the Military History Society of Ireland* 14 (Winter 1980): 117–28.

Mahan, Alfred Thayer. *The Influence of Sea Power upon History, 1660–1783*. 2 vols. Boston: Little, Brown, 1905.

Mahon, John K. "British Command Decisions in the Northern Campaigns of the War of 1812." *Canadian Historical Review* 46 (1965): 219–237.

———. "British Command Decisions Relative to the Battle of New Orleans." *Journal of the Louisiana Historical Association* 6 (Winter 1965): 53–76.

———. *The War of 1812*. Reprint, New York: Da Capo, 1972.

Malcomson, Robert. *Capital in Flames: The American Attack on York, 1813*. Montreal: Robin Brass Studio, 2007.

Mansfield, Kenneth. "Maida, 1806." *War Monthly* 12 (1975): 9–15.

Marine, William M. *The British Invasion of Maryland, 1812–1813.* Baltimore: Society of the War of 1812 in Maryland, 1913.

Matteo, Thomas W. "The Fortification of New York Harbor." WCNY, http://www.wcny.org/education/war-of-1812/the-fortification-of-new-york-harbor/.

McCormick, John H. "The First Master of Ceremonies at the White House." *Records of the Columbia Historical Society, Washington, D.C.* 7 (1904): 170–94.

McEvansoneya, Philip. "Racism/Ethnography: 'Hottentot Venus': The Exhibition of Sara Baartman in Dublin in 1812." *History Ireland* 21 (2013): 26–28.

Monkman, Betty C. "The White House Collection: Reminders of 1814." *White House History* 1 (Fall 1998): 223–27.

Moon, Joshua. *Wellington's Two-Front War: The Peninsular Campaigns, at Home and Abroad, 1808–1814.* Norman: University of Oklahoma Press, 2011.

Morriss, Maud B. "The Life and Times of Pontius D. Stelle." *Records of the Columbia Historical Society, Washington, D.C.* 7 (1904): 49–65.

Morriss, Roger. *Cockburn and the British Navy in Transition: Admiral Sir George Cockburn, 1772–1853.* Columbia: University of South Carolina Press, 1997.

Muir, Rory. *Britain and the Defeat of Napoleon, 1807–1815.* New Haven, Conn.: Yale University Press, 1996.

Muller, Charles G. *The Darkest Day: The Washington Baltimore Campaign during the War of 1812.* 1963. Reprint, Philadelphia: University of Pennsylvania Press, 2003.

Napier, William F. P. *English Battles and Sieges in the Peninsula.* London: Chapman and Hall, 1852.

———. *The Life and Opinions of General Sir Charles James Napier, G.C.B.* Vol. 1. London: John Murray, 1857.

National Park Service. "Sewall-Belmont House." http://lcweb2.loc.gov/pnp/habshaer/dc/dc0900/dc0963/data/dc0963data.pdf (URL no longer available).

Nolan, Edward H. *The Illustrated History of the War against Russia.* 2 vols. London: James S. Virtue, 1857.

Norton, L. A. *Joshua Barney: Hero of the Revolution and 1812.* Annapolis: Naval Institute Press, 2000.

Oaks, Elizabeth H. *American Writers.* New York: Infobase Publishing 2004.

O'Brien, Michael J. *A Hidden Phase of American History: Ireland's Part in America's Struggle for Liberty.* Bowie: Heritage Books, 1999.

Ockerbloom, John N. "The Discovery of a U.S. Marine Officer's Account of Life, Honor, and the Battle of Bladensburg, Washington and Maryland, 1814." *Military Collector and Historian* 61 (Winter 2009): 258–63.

Oman, Charles. *A History of the Peninsular War.* Vols. 6–7. Reprint, London: Greenhill Books, 2005.

———. *Wellington's Army*. London: E. Arnold, 1913.
Ó Muirí, Réamonn. "Newry and the French Revolution, 1792." *Seanchas Ardmhacha: Journal of the Armagh Diocesan Historical Society* 13 (1989): 102–20.
O'Neill, Patrick L. *"To Annoy or Destroy the Enemy": The Battle of the White House after the Burning of Washington*. Burke, Va., 2014.
Pack, James. *The Man Who Burned the White House: Admiral Sir George Cockburn, 1772–1853*. Annapolis: Naval Institute Press, 1987.
Pakenham, Eliza. *Soldier, Sailor: An Intimate Portrait of an Irish Family*. London: Weidenfeld and Nicolson, 2007.
Parker, Mike. *Fortress Halifax: Portrait of a Garrison Town*. Halifax: Nimbus, 2004.
Parsons, Lyn Hudson. *Birth of Modern Politics: Andrew Jackson, John Quincy Adams, and the Election of 1828*. Oxford: Oxford University Press, 2009.
Pasley, Jeffery L. *"The Tyranny of Printers": Newspaper Politics in the Early American Republic*. Charlottesville: University Press of Virginia, 2001.
Perkins, Bradley. *Castlereagh and Adams: England and the United States, 1812–1823*. Berkeley: University of California Press, 1964.
Perrett, Bryan, *The Real Hornblower: The Life of Rear Admiral Sir James Gordon G.C.B.* Annapolis: Naval Institute Press, 1997.
Pitch, Anthony S. *The Burning of Washington*. Annapolis: Naval Institute Press, 2000.
Ralfe, James. *The Naval Biography of Great Britain: Consisting of Those Officers of the British Navy Who Distinguished Themselves during the Reign of His Majesty George III*. Vol. 3. London: Whitmore and Fenn, 1828.
Ray, Cyril. *Regiment of the Line: The Story of the XX Lancashire Fusiliers*. London: B. T. Batsford, 1963.
Reilly, Robin. *The British at the Gates. The New Orleans Campaign in the War of 1812*. London: Cassell, 1974.
Riley, Jonathon. *A Matter of Honour: The Life, Campaigns, and Generalship of Sir Isaac Brock*. Montreal: Robin Brass Studio, 2011.
Rose, Hugh J. *A New General Biographical Dictionary*. Vol. 3. London: B. Fellowes, 1848.
Ross, John. "The Capture of Washington by the English, 1814." *Genealogical Magazine* 1 (1898): 229–36.
———. "Ross of Bladensburg." *National Review* 93 (May 1929): 443–50.
Scharf, J. Thomas. *Chronicles of Baltimore*. Baltimore: Turnbull Brothers, 1874.
———. *History of Baltimore City and County from the Earliest Period to the Present: Including Biographical Sketches of Their Representative Men*. 1881. Reprinted in 2 vols., Baltimore: Regional Publishing, 1971.
Seaton, Josephine. *William Winston Seaton of the "National Intelligencer."* Boston: James R. Osgood, 1871.

Seddall, Henry. *Malta: Past and Present.* London: Chapman and Hall, 1870.
Senn, Roma. *The Haligonians: 100 Fascinating Lives from the Halifax Region.* Halifax: Formac, 2005.
Sheads, Scott S. *The Chesapeake Campaigns, 1813–15: Middle Ground of the War of 1812.* London: Osprey, 2012.
———. *The Rockets' Red Glare: The Maritime Defense of Baltimore in 1814.* Centreville, Va.: Tidewater, 1986.
Shomette, Donald G. *Flotilla: The Patuxent Naval Campaign in the War of 1812.* Baltimore: The Johns Hopkins University Press, 2009.
Sidney, Edwin. *The Life of Lord Hill.* London: John Murray, 1845.
Skeen, Carl Edward. *Citizen Soldiers in the War of 1812.* Lexington: University Press of Kentucky, 1999.
———. "Mr. Madison's Secretary of War." *Pennsylvania Magazine of History and Biography* 100 (July 1976): 336–55.
"Sketches of the Private Life and Character of Wm H. Crawford." *Southern Literary Messenger* 3 (1837): 262–65.
Smith, G. C. Moore. *The Life of Colborne: Field Marshal Lord Seaton.* London: John Murray, 1903.
Smith, Henry Stooks. *An Alphabetical List of the Officers of the Eighty-Fifth, Bucks Volunteers, the King's Light Infantry Regiment, from 1800 to 1850.* London: Simkin, Marshall, 1851.
Smyth, Benjamin. *A History of the Lancashire Fusiliers, Formerly XX Regiment.* Vol. 1. Dublin: Sackville, 1903.
Smyth, George L. *Biographical Illustrations of St. Paul's Cathedral.* London: Whittaker, 1843.
———. *The Worthies of England.* London: John J. Griffin, 1850.
Snow, Peter. *To War with Wellington: From the Peninsula to Waterloo.* London: John Murray, 2010.
———. *When Britain Burned the White House: The 1814 Invasion of Washington.* London: John Murray, 2013.
Spiers, Edward M. *Radical General: Sir George de Lacy Evans, 1787–1870.* Manchester, UK: Manchester University Press, 1983.
Spring, Matthew H. *With Zeal and with Bayonets Only: The British Army on Campaign in North America, 1775–1783.* Norman: University of Oklahoma Press, 2010.
Stagg, John C. *Mr. Madison's War: Politics, Diplomacy, and Warfare in the Early American Republic, 1783–1830.* Princeton, N.J.: Princeton University Press, 1983.
———. "Soldiers in Peace and War: Comparative Perspectives on the Recruitment of the United States Army, 1802–1815." *William and Mary Quarterly*, 3rd ser., 57 (January 2000): 79–120.
———. *The War of 1812: Conflict for a Continent.* Cambridge: Cambridge University Press, 2012.
Stahl, John Meloy. *The Invasion of the City of Washington: A Disagreeable Study in and of Military Unpreparedness.* New York: Van Trump, 1918.

Standiford, Les. *Washington Burning*. New York: Crown, 2008.
Stocqueler, J. H. *The British Soldier: An Anecdotal History of the British Army, from Its Earliest Formation to the Present Time*. London: Wm S. Orr, 1857.
Stricker, John, Jr. "General John Stricker." *Maryland Historical Magazine* 107 (2012): 110–17.
Sutherland, Stuart. *His Majesty's Gentlemen: A Directory of British Regular Army Officers of the War of 1812*. Toronto: Iser, 2000.
Swanson, Neil H. *The Perilous Fight*. New York: Farrar and Rinehart, 1945.
Swint, Kerwin C. *Mudslingers: The Twenty-Five Dirtiest Political Campaigns of All Time*. Westport, Conn.: Praeger, 2006.
Taylor, Alan. *The Civil War of 1812: American Citizens, British Subjects, Irish Rebels, & Indian Allies*. New York: Alfred A. Knopf, 2010.
Taylor, Elizabeth D. *A Slave in the White House: Paul Jennings and the Madisons*. New York: Palgrave Macmillan, 2012.
Thomas, Katherine E. "The Long Lost Washington Drawing by Major L'Enfant and the Historic McKean House." *Records of the Columbia Historical Society, Washington, D.C.* 39 (1938): 105–26.
Thompson, Neville. *Earl Bathurst and the British Empire*. Barnsley, South Yorks.: Leo Cooper, 1999.
Tidridge, Nathan, *Prince Edward, Duke of Kent: Father of the Canadian Crown*. Toronto: Dundurn, 2013.
Tucker, Glenn. *Poltroons and Patriots: A Popular Account of the War of 1812*. 2 vols. Indianapolis: Bobbs-Merrill, 1954.
Tuckerman, Henry Theodore. *The Life of John Pendleton Kennedy*. New York: G. B. Putnam and Sons, 1871.
Turner, Wesley B. *The Astonishing General: The Life and Legacy of Sir Isaac Brock*. Toronto: Dundurn, 2001.
———. *British Generals of the War of 1812: High Command in the Canadas*. Kingston, Ont.: McGill-Queen's University Press, 1999.
Urban, Mark. *Rifles: Six Years with Wellington's Legendary Sharpshooters*. London: Faber and Faber, 2003.
Vogel, Steve. *Through the Perilous Fight: Six Weeks That Saved the Nation*. New York: Random House, 2013.
"War of 1812 Fortifications in New York City." Rootsweb. http://www.rootsweb.ancestry.com/~nyccusd/index_files/Page377.htm (URL no longer valid).
Warner, William W. *At Peace with All their Neighbours: Catholics and Catholicism in the National Capital, 1787–1860*. Washington, D.C.: Georgetown University Press, 1994.
Weber, William. *Neither Victor Nor Vanquished: America in the War of 1812*. Dulles, Md.: Potomac Books, 2013.
Weller, Michael I. "Commodore Joshua Barney, the Hero of the Battle of Bladensburg." *Records of the Columbia Historical Society, Washington, D.C.* 14 (1911): 67–183.
Whelan, Kevin, "The Green Atlantic: Radical Reciprocities between Ireland and America in the Long Eighteenth Century." In *A New*

Imperial History: Culture, Identity, and Modernity in Britain and the Empire, 1660–1840, edited by Kathleen Wilson, 216–38. Cambridge: Cambridge University Press, 2004.
Whitehead, David. "David Ross of Bladensburg: A Nineteenth-Century Ulsterman in the Mediterranean." *Hermathena* 164 (Summer 1998): 89–98.
Whitehorne, Joseph A. *The Battle for Baltimore, 1814.* Baltimore: Nautical and Aviation Publishing, 1997.
Williams, Glenn F. "The Bladensburg Races." *Military History Quarterly* 12 (1999): 58–65.
Wilson, David A. *United Irishmen, United States: Immigrant Radicals in the Early Republic.* Ithaca, N.Y.: Cornell University Press, 1998.
Zamoyski, Adam. *1812: Napoleon's Fatal March on Moscow.* London: Harper Collins, 2004.
Zuehlke, Mark. *For Honour's Sake: The War of 1812 and the Brokering of an Uneasy Peace.* Toronto: Alfred A. Knopf, 2006.

Newspapers and Journals

Aberdeen Journal (Scotland)
Albany (N.Y.) Register
Alexandria (Va.) Gazette
Alexandria (Va.) Herald
American and Commercial Daily Advertiser (Baltimore)
American Beacon (Norfolk, Va.)
American Mercury (Hartford, Conn.)
American Turf Register and Sporting Magazine (Baltimore)
American Watchman (Wilmington, Del.)
Ariel (Natchez, Miss.)
Arkansas Weekly Gazette (Little Rock)
Baltimore American
Baltimore Gazette
Baltimore Patriot
Baltimore Sun
Belfast Monthly Magazine
Belfast Newsletter
Bell's Life in London and Sporting Chronicle
Boston Commercial Gazette
Boston Gazette
Boston Spectator
Bristol Mirror (England)
Burlington (Vt.) Gazette
Bury and Norwich Post; Or, Suffolk, Norfolk, Essex, Cambridge, and Ely Advertiser (England)
Caledonian Mercury (Edinburgh)
Centinel of Freedom (Newark, N.J.)
Charleston (S.C.) Mercury
Chronicle (Harrisburg, Pa.)

City Gazette (Charleston, S.C.)
Cobbett's Weekly Political Register (London)
Columbian (New York)
Columbian Centinel (Boston)
Columbian Patriot (Middlebury, Vt.)
Concord (N.H.) Gazette
Connecticut Courant (Hartford)
Connecticut Herald (New Haven)
Courier (London)
Daily Graphic (New York)
Dedham (Mass.) Gazette
Delaware Gazette (Wilmington)
Denver Post
Derby Mercury (England)
Dublin Penny Journal
Dublin University Magazine
Eastern Argus (Portland, Maine)
Eastport (Maine) Sentinel
Edinburgh Review
Engine of Liberty and Union Town (Md.) Advertiser
European Magazine, and London Review
Evening Star (Washington, D.C.)
Examiner (London)
Farmer's Cabinet (Amherst, N.H.)
Federal Republican (Washington, D.C.)
Freeman's Journal (Dublin)
Freeman's Journal (Philadelphia)
The Gentleman's Magazine (London)
Gleaner (Wilkes-Barre, Pa.)
Hampshire Telegraph and Sussex Chronicle (England)
Hull Packet (England)
Irish Magazine
John Bull (London)
Lady's Newspaper (London)
Lancaster Gazette
Leeds Mercury
Liverpool Mercury
London Gazette
London Literary Gazette and Journal of Belles Lettres, Arts, Sciences, Etc. for the Year 1820.
Long Island (N.Y.) Star
Mercantile Advertiser (New York)
Merrimack (Va.) Intelligencer
Middlesex Gazette (Middletown, Conn.)
Montreal Herald
Morning Chronicle (London)
Morning Post (London)
Mourne Observer (Newcastle, N. Ireland)

National Advocate (New York)
National Intelligencer (Washington, D.C.)
National Register (Washington, D.C.)
New Bedford (Mass.) Mercury
New Brunswick (N.J.) Fredonian
Newburyport (Mass.) Herald and Country Gazette
New Hampshire Gazette (Portsmouth)
New Hampshire Patriot (Concord)
New Hampshire Sentinel (Keene)
New Jersey Journal (Elizabeth Town)
New Orleans Times-Picayune
Newry Magazine (Ireland)
Newry Reporter (N. Ireland)
New York Daily Advertiser
New York Evening Post
New York Gazette
New York Herald
New York Herald Tribune
New York Spectator
Niles' Weekly Register (Baltimore)
Northern Liberator (Newcastle-Upon-Tyne)
Northern Post (Salem, N.Y.)
Palladium of Liberty (Morristown, N.J.)
Pall Mall Gazette (London)
Petersburg (Va.) Intelligencer
Philadelphia Inquirer
Political Intelligencer (Annapolis)
Portland (Maine) Gazette
Portsmouth (N.H.) Oracle
Poulson's American Daily Advertiser (Philadelphia)
Quebec Gazette
Repertory (Boston)
Republican Star (Easton, Md.)
Rhode Island American (Providence)
Richmond (Va.) Enquirer
Salem (Mass.) Gazette
Shamrock (New York)
Southern Illustrated News (Richmond, Va.)
Star (Raleigh, N.C.)
The Times (London)
Trewman's Exeter Flying Post or Plymouth and Cornish Advertiser (England)
United States Telegraph (Washington, D.C.)
Vermont Mirror (Middlebury)
Virginia Argus (Richmond)
Virginia Patriot (Richmond)
Washingtonian (Washington, D.C.)
Watch-Tower (Cooperstown, N.Y.)

Index

Page numbers in *italics* refer to illustrations.

Adams, Henry, 202, 267n29
Adams, John Quincy, 4, 216–17
African Americans, 116, 170
Alexandria, Va., *109*, 157, 163
Armstrong, John (U.S. Secretary of War), 3, 69, 70, 71, 77, 86, 87, 116, 119, 127, 139, 140

Bacon, Samuel, 139
Baltimore, Md.: fear of British attack in, 181; Gladsby's Hotel, 182; reputation of Ross in, 181; as target of British, 65–66, 77
Barker, Jacob, 87, 154
Barney, Joshua (Commodore, U.S. Navy), 71, 73, 79, 97, 116, 130, 134, 135–37
Bathurst, Henry, 58–59
"Battle of Bladensburg" (poem), 135
Bayard, James, 42
Beanes, William, 82, 148, 171–72, 212
Benedict, Md., 71, 74, 75, 79, 80, 173
Belknap, William G., 117
Bermuda, 55, 60
Bladensburg, Battle of, 3, 116–38, *128*, 179
Bladensburg, Md., 79, 80, 82, 116, 163
"Bladensburg Races" (poem), 125, 203, 205
Blake, James H., 77, 87
Booth, Mordecai, 153
British Army: 4th Regiment, 54, 75, 122, 134, 135; 20th Regiment, 13, 17–20, 24, 28–29, 31–39, 51, 212; 21st Regiment, 48, 75, 122, 143, 211; 25th Regiment, 10; 44th Regiment, 48, 52, 54, 75, 122, 134; 85th Regiment, 52, 54, 122; 90th Regiment, 12; light infantry tactics, 123–24, 126
Brock, Isaac, 183–84, 209
Brooke, Arthur (Colonel, British Army), 50, 52, 75, 122, 134, 179, 187–88, 189
Brown, George, 122, 179

Campbell, George W., 204
Capture of the City of Washington, 107
Catlett, Hanson, 120
Chamier, Frederick, 72
Chesapeake Bay, 49, 69, 57, 63–64, 72
Chesapeake Bay Flotilla (U.S. Navy), 71, 73, 79, 80, 130, 135
City of Washington, capture of (engravings), *107–108*
Cobbett, William, 69, 193, 200
Cochrane, Sir Alexander (Vice Admiral, Royal Navy), 40, 41, 43, 44, 57, 65, 71–72, 75, 79, 81, 85, 89, 90, 91, 149, 150, 164, 169, 170, 175, 176, 177, 178, 184, 188, 189
Cockburn, George (Rear Admiral, Royal Navy), 5, 16, 57, 65, 70–73, 79, 84, *95*, 155–56, 158, 182–83, 184, 205
Codrington, Edward, 6, 58, 61, 75, 78, 79, 89, 176, 189, 190–91
Colborne, John, 13, 23, 24, 38, 53
Cole, Lowry, 10, 21, 31, 44
Colonial Marines, 75, 180
Congreve rockets, 125
Cork, Ireland, 29
Costello, Edward, 117

293

Crofton, Edward, 184
Culiver, Francis B., 217

Death of General Ross, near Baltimore,The (G. M. Brighty), 112
Death of General Ross at Baltimore (Alonzo Chappel), 111
Defense of Baltimore and the Death of General Ross (Richard Emmons), 214
De Peyster, Robert G. L., 154
District of Columbia militia, 89, 130, 134
Downing, James, 15, 16
Duluc, Andrew, 214
Dyson, Samuel T., 170

"Ebony and Topaz" (toast by John Quincy Adams), 216–17
Emmons, Richard, 213–14
Evans, George De Lacy, 6, 53, 64, 90, 94, 120, 122, 161, 164, 170, 211
Ewell, James, 71, 140, 147, 151, 162–63

Fall of Washington . . . or Maddy in Full Flight, 101
Falls, Thomas, 29, 36
Faunce, Alured, 138, 247nn37–38
Federal Republican (newspaper), 153, 160, 193, 203
Fort McHenry, Baltimore, Md., 180, 189, 190, 213
Fort Washington, Md., 80, 82, 170
French and Indian War, 8
Freneau, David, 206

Gallatin, Albert, 42, 143
George Washington (Gilbert Stuart), 100
Georgetown, Washington, D.C., 163
Georgetown Light Artillery, 130
Gerry, Elbridge, 77, 156–57, 204
Gleig, George R., 52, 54, 56, 62, 75, 79, 82, 123, 130, 133, 134, 180

Gordon, James (Captain, Royal Navy), 78, 109, 117, 142, 157, 170, 177
Gorsuch farm, 182, 183
Gosselin, Gerard (General, British Army), 61–62
Graves, Dianne, 30
Graves, Donald E., 16, 33, 44, 58, 183, 199
Gray, Joseph (British spy), 170

Halifax, N.S., 11, 191
Hayes, Thomas G., 217
Hickey, Donald, 6
Hill, Sir Rowland (General, British Army), 44, 46, 47, 48, 49, 56, 60, 67–68, 78
HMS *Dictator*, 164
HMS *Royal Oak*, 54, 56, 176, 187
HMS *Tonnant*, 60, 133, 172, 192, 212
Hoban, James, 123
Howard, Benjamin, 177, 185, 190, 257n10
Hulse, John, 185, 259n22

Irish, in the United States, 68–69

Jackson, Andrew, 204, 211
John Bull and the Baltimoreans (William Charles), 113
Johnny Bull and the Alexandrians (William Charles), 109
Jones, William, 76, 81, 204

Kennedy, John Pendleton, 129, 155
Key, Francis Scott, 53, 110, 130, 172, 188–89, 203, 212–13
King, Cyrus, 205

Lewis, John, 163–64
London Gazette (newspaper), 36
Lord, Walter, 80, 88, 156
Lovell, William Stanhope, 155
Lower Marlboro, Md., 79

MacDonald, Gordon G., 175, 187

MacDougall, Duncan, 74, 184
MacNamara, Francis Fitzgerald, 180
Madison, Dolley, 77, 86–87, 98, 100, 116, 153–55
Madison, James (President), 4, 41, 42, 57, 69–70, 77, 86–87, 96, 101, 116, 119–20, 124–25, 127, 129, 131, 135–36, 142, 146, 147, 153–57, 194, 202–205
Maida, Battle of, 20–23
Malcolm, Pulteney, 6, 55, 61, 189
Malta, 17–20, 171
Maryland militia: 5th Maryland Militia, 129, 217; organizational problems and, 78; Ross's views of, 182–83
Mason, John, 172
McClane, Allen, 78, 87
McComas, Henry Gough, 185
McGraw, Thomas, 154
Miller, Samuel (Captain, U.S. Marines), 130, 135, 137
Minor, George, 117
Monroe, James, 75, 77–78, 88, 204–205
Moore, Sir John, 24–27, 30

Napoleon Bonaparte, 212
National Intelligencer (newspaper), 158, 160, 204
New Orleans, La., 44, 60, 64, 188–89, 211
Niles, Hezekiah, 181, 217
Niles' Weekly Register (newspaper), 71, 182, 206
North Point, Battle of, 180, 186, 187–88
Nottingham, Md., 170, 172

"Ode on the Death of General Ross" (Samuel Taylor Coleridge), 208
Orthes, Battle of, 37–39, 209

Pakenham, Edward, 10, 45, 209
Patterson, William (Colonel, British Army), 75

Patuxent River, 65, 71, 73, 75, 79, 143, 164, 172
Perry, Oliver Hazard, 205, 207
Peter, George, 87–88, 130
Pinkney, William, 118
Porter, David, 177, 205
Potomac River, 71, 163
Poulson's American Daily Advertiser (newspaper), 3
Pratt, George, 156
President's House, The (George Munger), 103
Prevost, Sir George (General, British Army, and Governor General of Canada), 41, 43, 47, 49, 57–58, 74, 199
Prince Regent (later, George IV), 48, 193, 200
Pringle, Norman, 155, 158, 159, 206
Pyrenees, Battle of, 31–32

Quebec, Que., 11
Queenston Heights, Battle of, 183–84

Rhode Island, 175
Robb, Andrew, 212
Robyns, John, 86
Rodgers, John, 177
Ross, Elizabeth ("Ly"), 17, 24, 50–52, 54, 55, 61, 93, 174, 175, 206, 208–209, 211–12
Ross, Robert (General, British Army): ancestry of, 7–8; and American militia, view of, 183; appointment to command brigade, 31; Battle of Orthes, wounded in, 37–39; burns Executive Mansion and other public buildings, 156–57, 160; burns U.S. Capitol, 150–51; Canadian posting of, 11–12; character of, 9, 148, 161, 182–83; and Chesapeake expedition, 48, 50, 55, 58–59; and Cockburn, relationship with, 73, 182–83; and "contribution,"

Ross, Robert (*continued*)
  instead of burning public buildings of Washington, D.C., 142–43, 146; corpse of, 187; death of, *111–12*, 214–15; discipline and training of troops, 19–21, 24; distress, at killing of horse, 145; early life, 7–10; and Elizabeth Glascock, marriage to, 17; funeral of, in Halifax, N.S., 191–92, 214; and Gorsuch farm, remarks at, 182–83; and health of wife, concerns about, 55–56, 174, 175; Irishness of, 12, 56, 205; and light infantry tactics, 123–24, 126; military career, to February 1814, 10–39; and military etiquette, American breaches of, 148, 171–72; military reputation of, 121–22; monuments to, 211–12; mortal wounding of, and controversy about, 183–86, 259nn22–23; portrait of, 92; and private property, respect for, 75, 149–50, 155, 159, 161, 181; reputation of, 3–6, 12, 181, 189–90, 208–210, 217–18; and Washington, D.C., advances and attacks on, 3, 70, 116
Ross, Thomas (Reverend), 13, 29
"Ross of Bladensburg," *114*, 209
Rostrevor, Northern Ireland, 7–8, 12–13, 27–28, 29, 39, 195, 206, 217, 218; Kilbroney Parish (Church of Ireland), 29; monuments to Ross in, 4–5, *115*, 211–12, 218
Rowley, Robert, 172
Royal Marines, 49, 73, 75, 86, 162, 122, 180, 218
Rush, Richard, 204

Scott, James, 72, 85, 94, 136, 155–56, 158, 184
Scott, Winfield, 211

Shaw, Henry, 102, 156
Skinner, John S., 85, 212–13
Smith, Harry, 53, 74, 193
Smith, Martha Bayard, 145, 163
Smith, Samuel (General, Maryland militia), 177, 178, 179, 180–81, 258n12
Smith, Walter, 130, 134
Sioussat, "French John," 99, 153–55
Snow, Peter, 121
Stansbury, Tobias, 123
"Star-Spangled Banner," 53, 203, 213
Sterett, Joseph, 117, 129
Stewart, George, 217
St. Paul's Cathedral, London, 211
Stricker, John (General, Maryland militia), 180–81, 187–88
Stuart, James, 151, 206
Suter, Barbara, 77, 153, 157, 195

Taking of the City of Washington in America, The, 106
Taney, Roger Brooke Taney, 172
Tone, Wolfe, 11–12
Thornton, William (architect), 78, 105, 162, 215–16
Thornton, William (Colonel, British Army), 74, 75, 122, 179, 211
Torrens, Henry, 14, 42, 50

United Irishmen (revolt of), 11–12, 29
Upper Marlboro, Md., 81–82, 87, 170
U.S. Capitol, after the conflagration, *104*
U.S. Congress, 40
U.S. Marine Corps, 130, 135, 137

Vansittart, Nicholas, 14
Virginia militia, 78, 163
Vitoria, Battle of, 31–32

Wadsworth, Decius, 118, 128
Washington, A Representation of the Capture . . ., *108*

Washington, D.C.: American reaction to capture of, 202–206; British reaction to capture of, and Ross's death, 193–202; and Cockburn, as instigator of attack plan, 64–66, 84–85; Executive Mansion and other public buildings, 156–57, 160; Greenleaf Point, explosion at, 162–63; Sewall-Belmont House, 104, 107, 151; as target of British, 60, 64–66, 70–72, 77, 84–85; U.S. Capitol, 150–51; Washington Navy Yard, 105, 161

Washington Artillery Company, 123

Waterloo, Battle of, 212

Waterfront fire, watercolor by William Thornton, 105

Wellington, Arthur Wellesley, Duke of, 8–9, 25–26, 30–32, 48, 180, 199

Wells, Daniel, 185

Wilkinson, James, 119

Winder, Levin (Governor, Maryland), 69, 172

Winder, William H. (Brigadier General, U.S. Army), 70, 97, 119

Wood, William, 88

York, Ont., 74